Tales from the Front Line

The Middle East Hunter Squadrons

Tales from the Front Line

The Middle East Hunter Squadrons

Ray Deacon

Pen & Sword
AVIATION

First published in Great Britain in 2019 by
PEN AND SWORD AVIATION
an imprint of
Pen & Sword Books Limited
Yorkshire – Philadelphia

Copyright © Ray Deacon, 2019

ISBN 978 1 52672 146 4

Printed and bound in India by Replika Press

Typeset in Times New Roman 11/13.5 by
Aura Technology and Software Services, India

Pen & Sword Books Ltd incorporates the imprints of
Pen & Sword Aviation, Pen & Sword Maritime, Pen & Sword Military,
Wharncliffe Local History, Pen & Sword Select,
Pen & Sword Military Classics and Leo Cooper.

For a complete list of Pen and Sword titles please contact
PEN & SWORD BOOKS LTD
47 Church Street, Barnsley, South Yorkshire, S70 2AS, England
E-mail: enquiries@pen-and-sword.co.uk
Website: www.pen-and-sword.co.uk

Or

PEN & SWORD BOOKS
1950 Lawrence Rd, Havertown, PA 19083, USA
E-mail: Uspen-and-sword@casematepublishers.com
Website: www.penandswordbooks.com

Contents

CONTENTS

Preface

Tales from the Front Line is published by Pen & Sword Books Ltd as a companion volume to *Hunters over Arabia*, recently published by the same stable. It is produced by the same author and, although it is not the intention to replicate the material between books, a short résumé is included for the benefit of the reader.

Whereas *Hunters over Arabia* concentrates on the history of RAF Hunter operations in the Middle East during the 1960s, *Tales from the Front Line* comprises tales and anecdotes from the pilots who flew them and airmen who maintained them.

Background

Aden had been a well-known hotbed of dissident revolt for many years and the inter-tribal feuding that dated back to the Middle Ages had become a major problem in more recent times. Locally-recruited Arab armies were regularly called in to separate feuding tribesmen, backed by the British Army and an air force equipped with obsolescent fighters and bombers. By the late 1950s, driven on by his conquest at Suez, a jubilant General Abdel Nasser and his henchmen turned their attention to the British garrison in Aden. Every opportunity was taken to attack Army convoys, patrols and guard posts, a situation that had become untenable and could not be tolerated any longer

One of the main problems facing the British government during this period was the ability to supply its military forces with the equipment it needed to manage the deteriorating security situation in Aden State while, at the same time, maintaining law and order across a vast swathe of Southern Arabia. A bigger stick was needed to contain these rebellious tribesmen!

A crystal-clear photograph of the southern-most tip of Arabia with Khormaksar airfield prominent in the foreground. It was taken from a 1417 Flight FR.10 nose camera by Flight Lieutenant Richard Johns on 20 August 1965. The background is dominated by Mount Shamsan, an extinct volcano with the aptly named town of Crater within its core. The townships of Ma'alla and Steamer Point occupy much of the harbour coastline further to the right (*via Roger Wilkins*).

Enter the Hunter

The Hawker Hunter, reincarnated in the role of ground attack, was that stick, and it quickly established its credentials as the most potent truncheon in the Middle East armoury. As the Fighter Ground Attack (FGA) Mark 9, the new variant first entered service as a Venom replacement with 8 Squadron at RAF Khormaksar in January 1960. Six months later 208 Squadron became the second Middle East Venom unit to convert to type when it received the Mark 9 at RAF Eastleigh in Kenya. It did not stop there! In the summer of 1961 the Fighter Reconnaissance version of the Hunter, the Mark 10, displaced the Meteor FR.9s then in service with 8 Squadron. The ground-attack force reached peak strength in March 1963 following the redeployment of 43 Squadron and its FGA.9s from Cyprus to Khormaksar.

A high percentage of operations in the Middle East required close co-operation between the various other RAF squadrons and units of the

Army based in the area and Royal Navy when its carriers were close by. You will, therefore, find at relevant points throughout the narrative, reference to the squadrons which flew a diverse range of types from Middle East bases. These ranged from the RAF's Shackleton, Beverley, Argosy, Valetta, Twin Pioneer and Belvedere, to the Auster, Beaver and Scout of the Army Air Corps operating from isolated up-country airstrips, and Royal Navy Sea Vixens, Scimitars and Buccaneers flying off carriers in the waters around Arabia.

Whereas *Hunters over Arabia* consists of a factual account of operations carried out by Middle East Command Hunter squadrons and is based on squadron Operations Record Books (ORBs (Form 540)) held at the National Archives in Kew, *Tales From The Front Line* comprises anecdotes and stories, not only from the pilots who flew the Hunter, but also the airmen who serviced and maintained them. It is not all about Aden, as life at Bahrain, Sharjah and other route stations contribute to much of the story.

Acknowledgements

It is impossible to adequately thank all those whose generous co-operation has made this book possible. In sending my appreciation to everyone who submitted photographs and material for the project, I recognise that this book would have been far less comprehensive without your enthusiastic support.

In particular I would like to offer my special thanks to the following people who made time to write their stories, contribute their treasured photographs and were always ready to respond to my persistent questions: David Ainge, Chris Bain, David Baron, Ben Bennett, Mike Bennett, Roy Bowie, Rodney Carter, Ralph Chambers, Phil Champniss, Paul Constable, Vic Cozens, Chris Cureton, David Drake, Les Dunnett, Richard Grevatte-Ball, Mal Grosse, Tony Haig-Thomas, Mo Hawkins, Brian Hersee, Terry Kingsley, Ted Lambe, Peter Lewis, William Lonergan, Doug Marr, Anthony McLauchlan, Peter McLeland, Sandy McMillan, Mike Murden, Tim Notley, Bill Overy, Ken Parry, Alan Pollock, Roger Pyrah, Ken Rochester, Bill Romer-Ormiston, John Severne, Bill Sheppard, Ken Simpson, Peter Sturt, Tam Syme, Peter Taylor, Fred Trowern, Mike Veale, Nigel Walpole, Jock Watson, Roger Wilkins and Graham Williams, not forgetting the numerous photographic contributors whose names appear in their respective captions.

I am also indebted to Richard Doherty for the enthusiastic and professional manner in which he proof edited the draft manuscript and in particular, identifying a number of inaccuracies regarding the other two services.

Without the enthusiastic encouragement and co-operation of staff at Pen & Sword Books this work would certainly have been a much slimmer volume.

While every endeavour has been made by the author to acknowledge the correct ownership of the photographs reproduced in this book, sincere

Finally, a special thank you to my dear wife Rose for her encouragement and understanding during the long periods when I was glued to my PC.

Ray Deacon
December 2018.

A perfectly framed aerial view of the Tactical Wing flight line, office accommodation and hangar as it was in 1962. Several 208 Squadron Hunter FGA.9s and a T.7 occupy the nearest end of the dispersal leaving the 8 Squadron complement of FGA.9s, FR.10s and a T.7 parked on the remainder.

The Shackletons of 37 Squadron and a Sycamore of the SAR Flight can be seen in the middle distance with Transport Wing aircraft parked on their various dispersals at the far end of the airfield.

The photograph was taken by Valetta pilot Flight Lieutenant Keith Webster during a 'round-the-island' photo jolly in a SAR Flight Sycamore helicopter (*Keith Webster*).

Chapter 1

British Forces, Arabian Peninsula

Following the nationalisation of the Suez Canal in 1956, Middle East Air Force Command (MEAF) was effectively divided into northern and southern sectors. As communications between the two became increasing disjointed, the decision was taken to create a separate southern command and British Forces, Arabian Peninsula (BFAP) was established at RAF Steamer Point later that year. Thereafter British forces based in South Arabia, the Persian Gulf and East Africa reported to the new Command, although the three service elements, RAF, Army and RN, maintained separate organisational structures with headquarters in different locations. The Middle East Air Force (MEAF) formed the RAF element with an HQ at RAF Steamer Point.

Middle East Command

On 1 March 1961 the three service elements became fully integrated and the name changed to Middle East Command (MEC). Staff officers from the three services were brought under the same roof in a new headquarters at Steamer Point, in close proximity to the Commander-in-Chief (C-in-C). As control of British forces in South Arabia had been headed by an RAF officer since 1928, the trend continued, Air Chief Marshal Sir Hubert Patch KBE CBE taking over as the first C-in-C of the new Command. The RAF element was renamed Air Forces, Middle East (AFME) with Air Vice-Marshal D.J.P. Lee CB CBE as its first AOC.

The Middle East Command territory encompassed a vast area of the Arabian continent, from Bahrain Island in the north, through the Trucial States and Muscat and Oman on the east coast, to Aden Colony and the Protectorates in the south. Four RAF route stations, namely Sharjah, Masirah, Salalah and Riyan, were positioned at strategic locations in between to provide refuelling facilities for aircraft in transit and others on short duration detachments. The majority of operations were carried out from the main airfield at RAF Khormaksar, located on the neck of the Aden peninsula. Across the Horn of Africa to the south lay Ethiopia, Somalia and the lush green hills of Kenya. At the latter, close to the capital, Nairobi, RAF Eastleigh provided airfield facilities for the Command's East Africa sector.

A brief outline of the eight MEC stations is included here, beginning with Bahrain in the north and working down through the eastern side of Arabia to the southern tip in Kenya.

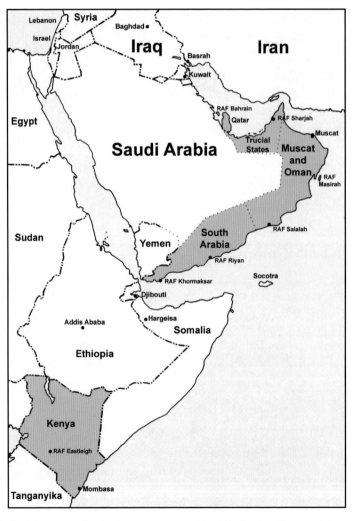

The dark shaded areas depict the huge area covered by Middle East Command through much of the 1960s. The distance from RAF Bahrain in the north to RAF Eastleigh in the south was approximately 2,500 miles (4,000 kilometres).

Captured in this overcrowded scene at RAF Muharraq in 1964 are four Beverleys of 30 and 84 Squadrons, a Britannia of 511 Squadron, one Pembroke of 152 Squadron and a pair of 8 Squadron Hunters (*Gordon Macadie*).

RAF Bahrain

The Kingdom of Bahrain consists of a group of thirty-three small islands covering an area of 300 square miles (770 sq km) in the Persian Gulf off the north-east coast of Saudi Arabia. The kingdom takes its name from the largest island, Bahrain, and is linked by causeway to Muharraq Island, the current home of the international airport and one-time operational base for the RAF.

Until 1960 RAF Bahrain functioned mainly as a sleepy civil airport and staging post between the UK and the Far East. It was also home for the Twin Pioneer and Pembroke aircraft of 152 Communications Squadron. Then, in the summer of 1961 and within the space of a few days, the airfield was transformed into one of strategic importance. To deter Iraq from invading the tiny oil-rich protectorate of Kuwait, a considerable number of RAF fighter and transport aircraft were flown in, the latter carrying a large force of ground troops and their weaponry. Once the crisis was over, Bahrain never returned to the idyllic peace of earlier times, the airfield playing permanent host to rotating detachments of Hunters from Khormaksar, Canberras from Akrotiri

3

and Beverleys from Khormaksar and Eastleigh. On 1 December 1963 the name of the military section of the airport was changed to RAF Muharraq.

The status quo prevailed until 1964 when 208 Squadron relocated its Hunters to Muharraq on a permanent basis and further expansion occurred in 1967 with the arrival of aircraft evacuated from Aden in line with the closure of Khormaksar. Muharraq remained an operational airfield until British forces pulled out in December 1971.

RAF Sharjah

Located in the Trucial States (now part of the United Arab Emirates), some 200 miles (320 km) east of Bahrain and twelve miles east of Doha, RAF Sharjah played an increasingly important role during the final decade of the RAF's tenure in the Persian Gulf.

In addition to performing a primary role as a major routing station for MEC and other RAF aircraft transiting to and from the Far East, the close proximity of the Jeb-a-Jib range offered the Hunter squadrons an ideal base from which to hold regular Armament Practice Camps. With its closure in December 1971, transiting aircraft were re-routed via Masirah.

A view looking across the 8 Squadron Hunter line towards the control tower and Visitors pan at Sharjah in November 1963. FGA.9 XF376 had recently returned from refurbishment in the UK, hence its smart-looking condition (*Ray Deacon*).

4

A mixed line-up of Hunters at Masirah in October 1966, comprising 8/43 Squadron FGA.9s and at least one 1417 Flight FR.10 (*Ross Bennett*).

RAF Masirah

Located in the Indian Ocean, some twelve miles off the coast of Oman, RAF Masirah was an important refuelling station for aircraft flying between Khormaksar and Bahrain throughout the fifties and sixties. Until then, most of the fuel and food provisions were delivered by sea and transported via a unique RAF narrow-gauge railway from the quay to the airfield between the months of November and February; it was too difficult for ships to dock during the south-west monsoon (March to October).

Following the construction of a concrete runway in 1963/4, however, stores were delivered by air. Having a close proximity to Oman, and being better suited for training exercises, Masirah took over as the regular destination for MEC Hunter detachments. After the closure of Muharraq and Sharjah, Masirah also became the sole route station for aircraft flying between Cyprus and Gan. When the RAF withdrew from the airfield in March 1977 Masirah was developed for use by Omani Air Force Hunters and Strikemasters.

RAF Salalah

RAF Salalah was a route station located in the fertile coastal plain of Dhofar in the Sultanate of Muscat and Oman, some 650 miles (1,050 km) north

A 105 Squadron Argosy captured during a refuelling stop at Salalah in late 1962, shortly after the type's introduction to service in the Middle East (*Alan Lowe*).

of Aden. The airfield dated back to 1928, having been built as a military and civilian staging post.

Throughout the 1960s Salalah provided refuelling and replenishment facilities for Valetta, Beverley, Argosy, Dakota and other transport aircraft operating on the Aden-Masirah-Sharjah-Bahrain route, and accommodation for a limited number of personnel should an overnight stop be necessary.

The climate could cause problems, more especially between May and September when the normally arid Arabian Waste is subjected to the south-west monsoon. The broad strip of land 100 miles (160 km) either side of Salalah endures lengthy periods of continuous light rain and low cloud for much of that period, requiring pilots to ensure they have adequate reserves of fuel should they need to divert.

RAF Riyan

Situated in the Quaiti State, within the Eastern Aden Protectorate, some 273 miles (440 km) along the coast to the north-east of Aden, RAF Riyan was the smallest of the route stations. It consisted of a collection of white, flat-topped buildings, with a compacted sand airstrip laid in the centre of shallow scrub-covered desert, surrounded on three sides by high mountains. The station was built in 1945 and most of the buildings were those erected at the time. They were, however, in good condition, providing an airy and cool home for the two officers and thirty airmen who were based there.

As a route station, Riyan was primarily concerned with the refuelling of short-range RAF and AAC aircraft operating in the South Arabian area, although much of the traffic was civilian. Aden Airways operated a scheduled service almost every day and was popular with those travelling between Aden and the Hadhramaut. The local population consisted of a mix of Bedouins, Somalis, Malays and Arabs. Deemed to be friendly and honest, a number of them were employed on ancillary tasks on the station.

RAF Khormaksar

The primary role of the RAF in Aden was to support British and Arabian Army units in the defence of the Colony and Protectorates from external attack, and maintaining law and order within its territory.

Approximately 75 per cent of Middle East Command aircraft were allocated to the main operational base at RAF Khormaksar, a joint-user airfield straddling the neck of a peninsula at the southernmost tip of Arabia. In addition to providing facilities for a wide range of aircraft types, the RAF was responsible for providing airfield, navigation, meteorological and communications facilities for military and civil aircraft transiting through Aden.

A huge building programme instituted in the early 1960s saw Khormaksar expand into the largest staging-post between the UK and the Far East. In providing a home for nine squadrons and three flights it became the busiest airfield in the RAF. As such it was equipped to handle the multiplicity of tasks unique to the Middle East theatre. Most of the flying units were maintained on semi-permanent alert in readiness for redeployment at a moment's notice to locations anywhere within the Command's territory.

In January 1960 No. 8 Squadron replaced its venerable Venom FB.4s with the Hunter FGA.9, the first squadron in the RAF to receive the latest mark, followed six months later by 208 Squadron which re-equipped with the aircraft at its Eastleigh base. In co-operation with Shackleton MR.2s

An overhead view of Khormaksar airfield as seen from Hunter T.7 XL613 on 14 February 1964. Working up from the lower centre of the photograph are the Civil Airport followed by the Hunter, Shackleton/SAR, Twin Pioneer, Visitors, and Transport Wing dispersals (*Ray Deacon*).

of 37 Squadron, the two ground-attack squadrons were soon using their Hunters to great effect when operating up-country. The strike capability was expanded in 1963 when 43 Squadron moved its FGA.9s from Cyprus to Khormaksar and a reformed 1417 Flight, equipped with Hunter FR.10s, undertook the fighter-reconnaissance role. The Khormaksar Hunter allocation now numbered forty-six aircraft, a formidable force with which to defend and police this vast area.

RAF Steamer Point

The second of two stations located in Aden Colony, RAF Steamer Point was built on the hillside site of the original garrison and, many years later, became the Headquarters of Middle East Command and an RAF hospital. Overlooking Aden Harbour, Steamer Point had no airfield facilities apart from a helicopter pad and was financially independent of its neighbour, Khormaksar.

RAF Steamer Point provided administrative services for most of the units in the base's area which roughly consisted of the 'boot' of Aden

8

Peninsula. It was responsible for a diverse group of units that included the RAF Aden Communications Centre, No. 114 Maintenance Unit, the Aden Supplies Depot, 50 Movement Unit, the HQ Provost and Security Services (responsible for enforcing service discipline and keeping down crime throughout the Colony), the staff at Command HQ, RAF Hospital, Aden Protectorate Levies Hospital, No. 7 Anti-Malarial Unit and a single Army unit, No. 222 Signals Squadron, which manned the telephone exchange and had responsibility for maintaining up-country land lines.

Perhaps one of its most challenging and thankless tasks was the management of all RAF and Army hirings, comprising houses and flats rented by the Air Ministry to supplement married quarters.

RAF Eastleigh

RAF Eastleigh was located on the eastern fringe of Nairobi and was the principal RAF station in East Africa. Eastleigh also provided civil airport facilities for airlines such as BOAC, EAA and SAA before a new airport opened at Embakasi in 1958.

At an altitude of 5,300 feet, however, and with short, red murram-surfaced runways, Eastleigh was not a suitable airfield from which to operate fully-armed and fuelled Hawker Hunters, requiring 208 Squadron to operate its aircraft from Embakasi Airport. Second-line servicing continued to be undertaken at Eastleigh, the aircraft being flown to and from with light fuel loads.

Other squadrons deployed at Eastleigh in the early sixties were, 21 Squadron equipped with Twin Pioneers, 30 Squadron with Beverleys and the East African Communications Flight, operating Pembrokes.

Chapter 2

Everywhere unbounded – 8 Squadron

Dave Ainge (Flight Lieutenant)

Dave Ainge was the 8 Squadron Pilot Attack Instructor (PAI) at RAF Muharraq, Bahrain, from November 1970 to September 1971, and then RAF Sharjah until December 1971. This followed tours on 1 (F) Squadron at RAF West Raynham and 234 (R) Squadron at RAF Chivenor. This is his account of his time there.

'For me my posting to 8 Squadron as the squadron PAI fulfilled the aspiration of so many former AFME (Air Forces Middle East) Hunter pilots. In the lament of the old AFME song:

> I wanted to be a PAI bold,
> Never to do as I was told,
> But now I'm just an AFME Hunter pilot

Number 8 Squadron was commanded by Squadron Leader Bill Stoker who had recently been through the refresher course on 79 Squadron after a ground tour; he was an old Hunter squadron hand with several Hunter tours including FR. The flight commanders were Frank Hoare, OC A Flight, and Al Cleaver, OC B Flight. A Flight was ground attack (GA) while B Flight was the region's specialist fighter reconnaissance (FR) unit. There were a number of old friends, including Pete Griffiths, and other pilots I had known as they had passed through Chivenor on the various courses. Amongst these were Ron Elder, the first FR pilot to be trained straight out of flying training and Bob Iveson, a first tourist. Both, like me, were on officially unaccompanied tours and so we all lived in private accommodation in Kanoo Gardens with our wives.

As with most squadrons, I was welcomed in the mess at lunch time on my first day with plenty of beer after which it was suggested we went into the adjoining garden for a squadron photo. Only then did I discover the real reason when I was handed a large squadron trophy full to the brim with ice cold Tiger beer which I was required to down in one. The trophy held well over four cans of Tiger which had been in the freezer for several hours until ice crystals were starting to form. For many this often proved a major challenge, especially after moving from the air conditioned bar to the 40-degrees C and high humidity outside, and a number of cameras were on hand in the event of the stomach refusing to accept the challenge. I`m afraid that I disappointed all the budding Lord Lichfields and, after downing it as required, returned to the bar to carry on.

David Ainge pictured outside the 8 Squadron office at Sharjah in 1971 (*David Ainge*).

No. 8 Squadron and its sister squadron, 208, were the ground attack element of AFME with headquarters in Bahrain. At the time the UK had treaties with several Gulf states including Kuwait, Sharjah and Ras Al Kaima as well as Bahrain itself, and the squadrons were there to support ground forces in the event of any hostilities. We were free to train and fly over most of the Gulf States including Oman, Dubai, Abu Dhabi, Sharjah, Ras Al Kaima and Qatar, although the latter was for overflight only. We had the use of an air-ground weapons range in Dubai and so for weapons training we usually deployed to Sharjah for an APC (armaments practice camp). Unfortunately there was no facility for air-air weapons training so we had to be content with gunsight cine film taken on practice combat sorties to assess our capability in that respect. As the squadron PAI, I was responsible not only for all the weapons training but also ensuring that the gunsights were regularly calibrated, so I was kept busy, particularly on the APCs.

Armament Practice Camps

My first APC started two days after I arrived on the squadron and my first flight was a guns and skip-bombing cine sortie on Rashid Range in Dubai before landing at RAF Sharjah. I was straight into my main job, that of improving the overall weapons capability of the squadron and coaching all the pilots in the finer points of weaponry, both with dual sorties and in the briefing and cine rooms. Frank Hoare was also a PAI and helped out, but it was still my domain. There were some first tourists but, from the newest FNG (flippin' new guy) right up to the "Boss", we all needed the continuation training the three weeks gave us. We practised all the air-ground deliveries and occasionally had the chance to fire a live load of either guns or rockets in a simulated operational attack against a derelict truck and all revelled in the competition for Top Dog.

Rashid Range was only five minutes flying time down the coast just to the south west of Dubai town and a duty pilot would drive there by road each day to act as the Range Safety Officer (RSO). This was an interesting drive as it went past the airport at Dubai before going round Dubai town and the creek and continuing along the coast past where the Sheik`s new palace and a few houses belonging to local dignitaries were situated. This provided the only bit of green as the lawns were well watered. The range itself was on the coast with the targets being arranged in the dunes and attacks were made from inland towards the sea.

The Hunter was well armed with a gunpack of four 30mm Aden cannon holding 540 rounds of HE ammunition and two pods of nineteen SNEB anti-armour rockets. There was also the capability of carrying two 1000lb bombs or two 100-gallon Napalm tanks but, although we practised the delivery of the latter, we never used either of them.

The guns targets were 15-feet squares of hessian supported on metal frames and the rocket target consisted of a circle around a central marker. The guns attack was made in a 10-degree dive with a minimum firing range of 550 yards. A half second burst covered 100 yards so the aim was to start at 650 yards from the target and then recover in a 6-g pull-out to avoid ricochets and flying into the ground! Scoring guns was merely a matter of counting the new holes, the old ones having been marked with paint.

The SNEB rockets were also fired in a 10-degree dive firing at 900 yards which allowed for recovery from 750 yards if firing a full pod. The impact was plotted on a chart from angles taken from two sighting towers set at right angles to each other from the target, the score being passed to the pilots as a distance and bearing from the centre.

The bombs target consisted of two guns targets side by side with a court marked out front and rear rather like an elongated tennis court. The attack was in level flight fifty feet above ground level at 420 knots to simulate a Napalm attack and was all done using the "Mark One Eyeball", the Hunter having no radio altimeter. The bomb had to land within the court to count as a hit, front court was a 'skip hit' and rear court a "hit on the fly". This was assessed by the RSO alone who was sometimes open to bribery in the bar the night before, but woe betide anyone if I overheard.

As well as passing the scores, the RSO had to assess the minimum firing range and altitude of the various attacks and any infringement led to a warning, two of which resulted in being sent home. Indeed if an attack was considered sufficiently dangerous it led to instant dismissal. The assessment continued in the cine room where scores could be halved or even deleted by the PAI when proof of infringement appeared on the silver screen. It was not unknown to alter the distance of the projector from the screen as a jape, further away producing a larger image and therefore an assessment of being too close. This was usually restricted to anyone who had previously argued with the PAI!

After work we would go back to the mess for lunch and continue the debrief in the bar before retiring for a siesta through the heat of the afternoon. We also had the opportunity to explore the local area. Sharjah town was little more than a small village with a souk, fort and a branch of the British Bank of the Middle East, as well as a few shops, hardly worth the visit. Dubai was larger, although still only a small town straddling either side of Dubai creek where a multitude of dhows could be found loading and unloading cargoes from all parts of the Gulf as well as India, Pakistan and Oman, and even the African coast. There was the old fort, the Sheik's palace and various government buildings and shops but most interesting were the souks, particularly the gold souk which had the reputation for being the best in the Gulf, and still has. It was truly a glittering display and we were soon tempted into buying something for a birthday or anniversary, but only after hard haggling. This was essential and fully expected by the traders who always started by asking around three times the value, finally happily settling for well under half the initial price. Nowadays the souk is still there but it has become a tourist trap and it is far harder to arrive at a sensible price, the traders knowing that a sucker will soon come along and happily pay up.

The weather in the Gulf was a major factor. Whilst the winter months were pleasant with temperatures in the mid-20s, in summer it was not unusual to reach the mid-40s with humidity over 90 per cent, not only very unpleasant but liable to lead very quickly to dehydration if exposed to it for too long. For this reason we normally flew early, from 06:30 through to 13:30, before the real heat of the afternoon set in and we also had a limit of ten minutes taxi time before take off when we could get the air-conditioning going.

Here I should give praise to the work carried out by our ground crew without whose support we would have had no serviceable aircraft to fly. They were not limited by the hours and restrictions we enjoyed and, indeed, most of the maintenance, other than turning aircraft round between sorties, was carried out after we had finished flying, very hot and difficult work with the aircraft being parked outside all the time, only going into the hangar for major overhaul. It is true that you could fry an egg on the wing of an aircraft in that heat. That they did it so cheerfully and without complaint, other than the normal banter typical of all servicemen, is a tribute to their professionalism and commitment to the squadron and to the RAF.

Harmonising the guns

I soon found out how hot it was in the afternoons myself when my duties of calibrating, or harmonising, the gunsights had to be carried out. Harmonisation involved the armourers jacking the aircraft off the ground so that it could not settle on the undercarriage as we worked and then aligning a sighting board, set up about thirty metres in front of the aircraft, to the gun barrels. Once this had been done and I had checked that the alignment was accurate, it was my job to align the gunsight to the appropriate markings on the board and make sure all the differing settings for guns, bombs and rockets were correct. Even with an umbrella over the cockpit this was very hot work using tiny spanners and screw drivers, always slippery from sweat, to make the adjustments and I soon realised how difficult the working conditions of the ground crew were on a daily basis; they deserve all the plaudits possible. If later an aircraft was found to be out of harmonisation by analysing the cine film against the scores, it was my neck that was on the block especially if it was the Boss who was missing the target!

Most of our training on A Flight consisted of flying either as a pair or as a four-aircraft formation to Abu Dhabi, overflying Qatar on the way, to carry out practice strikes against targets found and photographed by the FR pilots. These sorties were sometimes bounced (attacked) by a fifth aircraft and then the results thoroughly debriefed, with me assessing the

Above: The Office, as pilots liked to refer to their Hunter cockpits. Dominating the layout on that of XF442-H is the centrally-mounted gunsight, with a loaded film magazine clipped to the top (*David Ainge*).

Below: 8 Squadron FGA.9 XF442-H is seen parked on the ramp during an APC at Sharjah in 1971 (*David Ainge*).

attacks, including that of the bounce, in the cine room. Sometimes these sorties were flown to Sharjah and Oman as a hi-lo-hi sortie, flying out and back at high level and only descending in the area to achieve longer range. We also flew solo to practise our low-level navigation, something which required a completely different approach to that in the UK or Europe, the desert lacking roads, railways, rivers and built-up areas, and resembling a seemingly identical rocky lunar landscape with only small variations in colour and topography. The maps we used were the normal 1:500,000 scale, the 'half mill' which, at first glance, appeared to have been produced by an art student told to paint an abstract with just variations of brown and with only the coast line as a definite feature. In reality they were a true reproduction derived from high-level photographs taken by the Canberra photo-reconnaissance squadrons and were completely accurate; it was just a case of getting used to interpreting and trusting them. Combat and cine air-air training rounded off our work out of Bahrain and these were usually flown out over the sea.

We also exercised with the Royal Navy and the US Navy, practising ship strikes as well as gunnery against the "splash" target, a float towed behind the ship which produced a wave at which we aimed. Obviously it could not be scored other than by observation from the ship – hit, short or long, and the only advantage was that it was a moving target. Other training included practice interceptions using Bahrain radar, practice combat, mainly one-versus-one or two-versus-two, and "low-level cine weave", a canned exercise which tested tracking and ranging skills, all of which were assessed at length in the cine room afterwards.

Ferry to Kemble

From time to time we flew ferry flights back to UK to rotate aircraft through the maintenance unit at RAF Kemble and I was programmed to lead a pair back in January 1971. For a ferry, the outer pylons were fitted with 100-gallon drop tanks which gave us about three-and-three-quarter-hours' endurance, around 1,600 miles range, so we flew back in stages. We first had to carry out high-level "cold soak" checks to make sure we would not develop any fuel or hydraulic leaks due to contraction of the pipes and joints with the very low temperatures, minus-60-degrees C not being unusual at 40,000 feet. The first leg was north to Tehran in Persia, now Iran, for refuelling before carrying on to RAF Akrotiri in Cyprus for our night stop. Navigation up to Tehran was fairly straightforward with air traffic coverage most of the way and normally clear conditions, so we could see the ground. The leg from Tehran carried on north-west and then west over Turkey before turning south-west to Cyprus. There were far larger gaps in air traffic coverage and no reliable radio beacons to use our radio compass and we were only allowed to continue from Tehran if the cloud below was forecast to be less than half cover so that we could navigate on ground features alone. The other reason for not using the radio compass was that the Soviet Union was known to broadcast using very strong signals on the same frequencies as the Turkish radio beacons and the needle was more likely to be pointing north than towards the beacon selected. That leg was also towards the upper limit of our range and so we could not proceed if the headwinds were forecast to be above a certain figure but, come the day, all was fine and we finally arrived, tired but pleased with ourselves, at Akrotiri.

After a pleasant evening with a few beers and a *mezze* in the local town we set off the next day for RAF Luqa in Malta for a fuel stop before continuing to Istres near Marseille, a French Air Force station, for our last stop before UK. The Istres stop was interesting as, not only did we have to refuel but we had to refill the Avpin fuel for the starter motor (although why we didn't do it at Luqa I don't know). This we collected in a five-gallon drum from the fuel depot and, after refilling both the aircraft, we left the drum by the side of the apron while we finished the turn-round checks. At some point we became aware of a Frenchman, Gauloise stuck in his mouth, puffing away and heading for the drum. Now Avpin is akin to liquid explosive and highly volatile. In a voice perhaps a couple of octaves higher than normal I screamed, in my impeccable French, 'Fumez pas, fumez pas!' only to see him give a Gallic shrug, walk casually up to the drum and, after taking a couple of last good puffs, proceed to stub it out on the drum. I saw all this over my shoulder as I put distance between us that would surely have stood as an Olympic record! Nothing happened and, with another Gallic shrug, he continued on his way, all his preconceptions of the English now fully confirmed. A little shaken, we continued on our way arriving into RAF Kemble in the late afternoon and, after a brief night stop, we travelled on to Lyneham to catch the VC10, the Moon Rocket, back to Bahrein.

APCs and Other Activities

My second APC came up in February/March and our third and final APC was in May. All the normal academic weaponry was practised on Rashid Range but we also had the opportunity for live weapons training with

17

FACs (Forward Air Controllers) on Jeb-a-Jib Range, a bit further along the coast. Frank Hoare received his posting and I took over as acting OC A Flight while continuing as the squadron PAI. This involved supervising the squadron flying programme with Al Cleaver and writing assessments on pilots as well as checking logbooks and so on.

For the May detachment we found a new avenue for a bit of R and R (rest and recuperation). The Boss, Bill Stoker, had made friends with an Englishman who was the Dubai State chief engineer. He lived on his own in one of the villas beyond Dubai which we could see on the way to the range and I have already described how they provided the only bits of green to be seen in those parts. He very kindly invited us to use his swimming pool and make ourselves at home even if he wasn't there and we passed several pleasant afternoons relaxing there.

The Dubai airport was being developed with a new terminal building having just been completed and the opening ceremony due in a few days. The State engineer had been tasked with finding some way of marking the occasion and Bill offered to provide a formation flypast. The proposal was put to Sheik Rashid bin Said al Muktar, Sheik of Dubai, who agreed and so we started practising for a diamond-nine close-formation flypast, which I was to lead, followed by a four-ship formation led by Bill breaking away to fly a limited aerobatic display on their own.

The rundown begins

By this time, with the withdrawal of military forces in Bahrain planned for the end of the year, the two squadrons had slowly been reducing numbers of both aircraft and pilots, as well as ground crew. This was rather depressing as we were losing two or three colleagues every three or four weeks and it was impossible to dine them out in the normal fashion. Rather than continue as two squadrons each reducing together it was decided that 208 would disband, the remaining pilots transferring to us, and 208's final dining-out was scheduled while we were at Sharjah. Bill received a signal from the station commander saying that we all were required to return to Bahrain for our sister squadron's dining-out on the Friday night before the planned flypast!

Now Bill hadn't actually told anyone in authority back at Bahrain about the flypast. After a rather one-sided telephone call with the Muharraq station commander he was told that, come what may, we were all to be present and we would not leave the celebrations until 02:00 at the earliest on Saturday morning, the day of the flypast due at 11:00.

Above: Dressed in typical flying gear of the era, Pete Griffiths and Rocky Goodalls make their way out to the line at Sharjah appearing to be in deep discussion about their next session on the range (*David Ainge*).

Below: 8 Squadron FR.10 XF460-X skims across the sea off the coast near Sharjah in September 1971 (*David Ainge*).

Having passed on the news, Bill then set about trying to arrange suitable transport, having been forbidden to fly back in the Hunters. There were two resident squadrons at Sharjah, 84, an Andover transport squadron, and 201, a Shackleton maritime squadron. We had struck up a good relationship with the Shack crews but the same could not be said of 84 who regarded us as an infernal nuisance, disturbing the peace and quiet of 'their' mess, so it was not totally unexpected when they flatly refused. As Bill was talking to them on the phone, getting rather heated, a Shack captain happened to be passing and asked if there was a problem. Bill gave a quick outline to which the response was, "What time do you want to go and what time do you want picking up to come back?" Now that's what I call service camaraderie!

The dining-out went well although Bill did keep an uncharacteristically low profile, and next morning we were all out on the Muharraq apron in our flying suits waiting for the Shack to arrive. The Shackleton was really a descendant of the Lancaster bomber of the Second World War and, although it had updated engines and modifications to the airframe, was essentially very similar. As it taxied in we noticed that they had shut down one of the starboard engines and we thought that it was just for our comfort getting on board; how considerate. We positioned ourselves around as best we could, there being no spare seats as it wasn't designed to carry passengers, and off we set, the engine being restarted as we taxied out. However, to our surprise, after take off the engine was again shut down and, inquiring why, were told they had an oil leak and it was the only way they could have picked us up. The crew provided us with copious quantities of black coffee and toast to act as blotting paper and we were duly delivered right outside our squadron building, the engine having been restarted for the landing, just in time for a quick, last-minute brief before we launched our nine. Needless to say, we plied our Shack mates with large quantities of beer that night. It was therefore fitting that many present were to be posted to 8 Squadron when it reformed as a Shackleton maritime squadron at RAF Kinloss in Scotland on 1 January 1972.

The flypast went as planned and, after Bill had split off for his separate display, we all joined up again before landing back at Sharjah. The Sheik invited us to lunch at his palace that afternoon so, after a quick change out of our smelly flying suits into something more appropriate, we set off trying to remember which hand to eat with and hoping we wouldn't be the one to pick the sheep's eye out of the stew. All went off very well, the Sheik was delighted with the flypast and display, we were all presented with a watch with his name on the face in Arabic and no one disgraced themselves. We then all retired to the engineer's villa and swam and drank beer, thoroughly content, even the Boss who had been told that the matter hadn't been forgotten and he had better have a pretty good reason for committing us to the flypast for a State with which we didn't even have a treaty.

That was our last APC and our last planned detachment to Sharjah. By way of thanks for how much we had contributed to the mess profits over the years, the mess manager laid on a special breakfast, the full Monty with Black Velvet (champagne and Guinness) to wash it down. Needless to say it was a non-flying day and we then continued to add to the profits in the bar afterwards. We flew back to Muharraq on 22 May, sorry to say goodbye to a station for which we all had such fond memories and not realising that some of us would be returning.

Before 208 finally disbanded we arranged some inter-squadron training in the form of large formation combat, something we rarely had the opportunity to do. Four and even six aircraft from one squadron would go up against two or four from the other and this resulted in the nearest we would ever get to the mass combats seen during the Second World War. Trying to maintain a mental plot and control of what was going on whilst at the same time trying to get into a firing position without being "shot" down yourself was one of the most difficult forms of leadership I ever encountered and some stood out especially. Both Rod Dean and Rog Wholey of 208 were outstanding, having benefited from a squadron visit to Pakistan where they had flown practice combat against the Pakistani MiGs, but the likes of Griff, Al and I gave them a good run for their money. The resulting debriefs were often hotly contested with claims on both sides of what had happened and who had managed a 'kill' and which was only concluded in the cine room or even after in the bar. It was altogether a memorable experience.

No. 208 Squadron held their disbandment parade on 22 August and we provided a diamond-nine formation flypast for the occasion. The remaining personnel transferred over to 8 and, as the squadron had already been dined out, 208 just ceased to exist.

Cross training

By September the squadron training was fairly limited, so Al and I discussed doing some cross-training between the 'mud movers' on A Flight and the "happy snappers" on B Flight. While we gave some of the fighter-recce specialists training in rockets and bombs delivery and flying four-aircraft air-ground strikes, Al organised a mini-FR course for Pete Griffiths and me.

FR is flown with one aircraft and calls for very accurate navigation to find and take photographs of targets whilst at the same time noting down all the salient features. So it was back to ground school first of all, finding out that bridges, for example, come in half a dozen forms made of several types of materials and designed for different types of use. All had to be noted down with the precise location and with a photo taken in the few seconds the target was in view before then giving an in-flight report by radio back to the RAF specialist located with the army. Back on the ground the film would be immediately taken away for processing while the pilot gave a detailed report from his notes and what he could remember before then going over the developed photos with the PI, the photographic interpreter, whose eagle eyes would often pick out details that we had missed.

To put all this into practice we flew as a pair, the 'student', Pete or me, with either Al or the Boss as wingman assessing everything we did.

The retro look of 8 Squadron pilots at the culmination of a moustache-growing competition at Sharjah in 1970 with, standing, Ken Miles, Ken Parry, Dave Ainge, Frank Hoare, Steve Glencorse, Al Cleaver, and seated, Rocky Goodall, Pat Kiggell and Mick Herberts (*David Ainge*).

Planning was incredibly detailed using the smallest scale maps available, the 1:50,000 or "fifty thou", to plot the final approach to the target area. This sometimes resulted in several feet of map concertinaed so that we could thumb our way along in the cockpit whilst flying at 100 feet and 420 knots. This took careful cockpit management and sometimes didn't go as planned, resulting in the cockpit rapidly resembling the inside of a dustbin with us searching around for the bit of the map we should be looking at!

The flight itself was assessed throughout with particular emphasis on accuracy of navigation and the in-flight report. Some of the targets were in the Awali Hollows, a huge range of sand dunes, some over 500-feet high and stretching for over 200 miles, on the Dubai border with Saudi Arabia. Others were in the northern mountains of Oman, stretching south from the Straits of Hormuz, and most called for flying high level there and back because of the range. The joint exercise led to a much greater understanding of the different facets of flying the same aircraft and also respect for our different trades. Although never officially qualified as FR pilots, Pete and I were honoured to be mentioned in Nigel Walpole's excellent account *Best of Breed – The Hunter in Fighter Reconnaissance*.

It was then that the station commander dropped the bombshell that our presence was no longer welcome at Bahrain and that we had less than three weeks to pack up before leaving. We initially thought it was good news, back to UK early without dragging it out to the end, reducing numbers gradually as we had been doing. He quickly put that thought aside when he told us that the squadron, to be reduced immediately to eight aircraft and twelve pilots, was going to Sharjah to see out the treaty until just before Christmas when it would fly back from there. I was among those selected to stay and we were told that under no circumstances would we be allowed to commute back and forth and that all families would in any case be repatriated to the UK over the next month. Knowing that space on flights home would soon be at a premium I managed to get my wife, Mo, and two children away that very same night on the VC10 back to Brize Norton. Flexibility has always been a requirement of service life, for families as well as serving personnel!

RAF Sharjah, September to December 1971
Having packed everything at the squadron we were dined out from the station and then, on 29 September 1971, all eight aircraft took off for

the final three months in the Gulf. We already knew Sharjah well, so we settled quickly into a routine. The treaty included three islands, Abu Musa and the Greater and Lesser Tumbs, which lay to the north of Sharjah halfway towards Persia and which were under the administration of Sharjah and Ras al Khaima. No. 201 Squadron, the Shackleton squadron, was still there but due to leave shortly and we took over its role of checking that the treaty had not been violated. This involved flying past the islands and checking that the Sharjah flag was flying and waving to the few soldiers who had drawn the short straw to sit on these tiny and otherwise deserted islands.

The weapons range had already been closed so we were unable to carry out any live weapons training but we were close to the northern mountains of Oman which provided an exhilarating opportunity for "wadi bashing", flying low level through the many wadis that exist there. We discovered some army engineers repairing a bridge in a particularly remote area so we loaded some cans of beer attached to a withdrawal drogue from a drag chute in the air brake and dropped them at the site. A message to the "wadi-bashing pongos" from "wadi-bashing 8" was attached and we received a thank you note in similar vein some weeks later.

Practice four-ship strikes with a bounce aircraft were the main form of training as well as practice combat, so we had plenty of excellent flying available to us. I also tried out Rog Wholey's 'last ditch manoeuvre' which he had employed against me in combat back at Bahrain just as I was getting into a good firing position and which consisted of pulling a 6-g turn and then applying full bottom rudder. I can only say that the result was astonishing as it produced an incipient spin or "flick", manoeuvre ending up going completely the other way; no wonder he had disappeared! I decided that it was definitely something to have in reserve, but only to be used under extreme circumstances, the thought of the stresses on the fin and rudder being enough to deter everyday use.

I had taken my Honda and hi-fi which I had bought in Bahrain and so I had wheels to get around the station and visit Sharjah town and Dubai. There was little to do at Sharjah, so once a week we entertained ourselves sitting around a bonfire in the evening with a few beers listening to my tapes and yarning. It helped to pass the time.

We were all waiting for our posting notices to tell us where we were going next and I had been expecting either a return to Hunters in UK or Jaguars as I was well qualified for both. My actual posting, as Wing PAI at RAF Honington, a Buccaneer station, therefore came somewhat as a

Above: The date is 29 September 1971 and, having left Muharraq for the final time, 8 Squadron's eight remaining aircraft arrive at Sharjah, their home base for the next two months (*David Ainge*).

Below: And what better greeting could anyone wish for! Dave Ainge receives an ice-cold beer from the Station Commander (*David Ainge*).

surprise, having never flown the Buccaneer or gone through the BAI course, the Buccaneer equivalent of our PAI qualification. I have to say I was at a bit of a loss as to how I could actually do the job, entailing as it did the supervision of all weapons training on the station, but at least I saw that conversion to the Buccaneer was to be arranged by 1 Group, part of Strike Command to which Honington belonged.

As we approached December we again started to pack up, my motorbike and hi-fi with my few other possessions being crated ready for shipment back by Royal Fleet Auxiliary. The aircraft were being fitted with outboard drop tanks for our transit back and planning for the trip, which was to be flown as an eight-aircraft formation, was completed.

Our departure date was planned for 22 December but, on 30 November, having finished work, I called by my room before going to lunch. As usual I switched on the BBC World Service to get the headlines to hear that the Persians (now Iran) had invaded the three islands, Abu Musa and the two Tumbs, which were still part of the treaty! Bill Stoker, who hadn't heard, rushed off to phone the station commander with instructions to me to get everyone together. He soon returned only to inform us that the British response was to do nothing; we were to stay in the bar! On hindsight, there was probably little we could have done; the aircraft were all in transit fit and the Persian air force, apart from vastly outnumbering us, operated the Phantom air defence fighter which was, in the right hands, far superior to the Hunter as a combat aircraft. We were confined to base and there followed a couple of days of tension and demonstrations in Sharjah and Ras al Khaima in which the British Bank of the Middle East was set alight but it quickly died down as everyone accepted it as a *fait accompli*. Our planned departure was brought forward and, after flying final air tests and cold-soak checks at high level for fuel and hydraulic leaks, we were ready to go. My last training flight had been on a reconnaissance and simulated strike in area B, to the north of Oman on 29 November.

Farewell to the Middle East

On 7 December we set off with our eight aircraft on our first leg to Tehran, the capital of Persia, as if nothing had happened, but without the customary final flypast which would have only added insult to injury to the local population. Bill was leading with me as deputy lead and we were spread out in wide battle formation. Bill didn`t bother himself with calling any of the air traffic services, leaving such mundane work to me, and I spent much of the leg off the formation frequency clearing us through. Approaching Tehran we received clearance to descend and follow the instrument approach pattern but Bill decided that he would lead his squadron in in style with a straight-in approach from high level followed by a high-speed break into the circuit, all this being done on the formation frequency with me switching to air traffic to tell them what was actually happening.

The break and landing went uneventfully but after we had parked we found ourselves surrounded by armoured vehicles, their guns all pointing at us, to be followed by a fleet of staff cars. We then watched the Boss receive a right, royal b*******ing whilst it was explained to him that we had nearly been shot down by their anti-aircraft weapons, the country being on full alert as a result of the Indian/Pakistani crisis. Apparently the sight of eight fighter aircraft diving towards the airfield at high speed had led to some very itchy trigger fingers!

We were told that we were to be confined to our hotel where we were to stay until it had been decided whether we would be allowed to continue. An uneasy night followed, particularly I suspect for Bill who was probably wondering how he could explain this one away to his superiors. The night was further interrupted by a continuous flow of tanks, armoured vehicles and troops going along the street outside and we realised that the Persians were, indeed, a bit jumpy.

The following day we were given our clearance, with dire warnings of what would happen if we deviated from our cleared route, and off we set on our leg to RAF Akrotiri in Cyprus and a few beers in the mess. After a two-day delay due to an unserviceable aircraft and subsequent air test, the rest of our return to UK via Luqa in Malta and Istres in southern France went uneventfully. We finally arrived at RAF Kemble on the evening of 11 December in dreadful weather to be met by our families and then we all went our separate ways.

The Squadron Standard was handed over to 8 Squadron (Maritime) at RAF Kinloss on, I believe, 21 December 1971. The Boss, Bill Stoker, and about six of the final number travelled up with our wives in a Hastings from Colerne and, after circling around for about forty-five minutes trying to confirm the undercarriage was locked down, we finally landed uneventfully. (The wives were not impressed and we returned by train; whether the two events were connected I don't know.) Rocky Goodall was our Standard bearer and we felt it was left in good hands, not least because we already knew a fair number of the aircrew from Sharjah. It was truly the end of an historic era, not only for 8 Squadron but for the RAF.'

Chris Bain (Flight Lieutenant)

The author is indebted to Chris Bain for allowing him to include extracts from his excellent book *Cold War, Hot Wings*, another from the Pen & Sword stable.

Flying Officer Chris Bain became an experienced fighter and recce pilot but was only twenty-years-old when his operational career began, flying Hunters with 8 Squadron at Khormaksar in 1964. His extended tour in Aden lasted until the summer of 1967 when he left the colony, flying one of three redundant Hunters to Amman for presentation to the Royal Jordanian Air Force.

Khormaksar Operations

'My first squadron, 8 Squadron, was famous throughout the Middle East, having often been the ONLY squadron in theatre. Known as "Aden's Own", the squadron finally left the colony in 1967 after forty years of continuous service there, but not before it had left its mark on the place. Formed in 1915 at Brooklands as part of the RFC, 8 Squadron saw service in France where one pilot won a VC. During the Second World War, it played a valuable part in the East African campaign, flying over 800 sorties. During 1943-44, it also sank two German submarines. Italian planes bombed Aden and Perim Island at the mouth of the Red Sea, but otherwise it was an oasis of peace, remote from the main battle areas, continuing its prime role as a refuelling and re-supply port. However, up-country the usual inter-tribal rivalries continued. It took part in the ill-fated Suez campaign in 1956, and participated in the operations against the Mau-Mau in Kenya. It was one of the two Hunter squadrons that had gone into Kuwait with 42 and 45 Commandos during the first crisis in 1961 and stopped the problem dead in its tracks; if we'd been there in 1991 and 2003, we'd have stopped two more wars, and the Middle East would be a better place today. So much for pulling out of "East-of-Suez".

During the emergency operations from 1964 to 1967, we fought two distinct and separate campaigns: security operations against terrorism in the Aden State, and guerrilla warfare in the mountains of the Federation. As we were based in the Aden State, the former affected our daily lives, but it was the latter with which we, the RAF fighter force there, were intimately involved. Air surveillance with its threat of punitive bombing, the flying gunboats of the overlapping colonial and air ages, was a swift, easy answer to control of the up-country tribes.

Squadron operational reports from the 1940s all said much the same thing and the *modus operandi* had not changed by the mid-60s: "The Quatari tribe of the village of Al-Qradi owed HMG £200.14s.9d. in unpaid taxes. They had been warned twice to no avail. Therefore, leaflets will be dropped warning them that their village is going to be bombed on the following day." The report would then go on to dictate a full bombing operation, the rules of engagement, and the results including a political officer's report.

On the following day when, surprise, surprise, the tax had remained unpaid, the squadron would simply attack the village while the villagers looked on from the hillsides around. They would then rebuild their village and carry on life as if nothing had happened - but I don't think it endeared us to them. Any blood spilt instantly produced a blood feud. Hence, we were often cleared to fire but told not to hit! Typically British – fighting with one hand tied! Nevertheless, the South Arabian Arabs only took note of excessive power; it was the only thing they really understood. We never did succeed in subduing the Radfani hill-tribes, and we finally pulled out in 1967 with our tails between our legs.

Strike Wing structure 1964 -1967

RAF Khormaksar's Strike Wing was not only tasked with army support work, but was responsible for the air defence of the whole region. It also had the best working shift system ever devised, and all because we had so many aircraft and personnel available by today's standards.

Despite two large fighter squadrons, 8 and 43, both needed their rest periods, and one squadron alone was usually adequate to maintain the operational task and complete our necessary training flying. Hence, uniquely to my knowledge in the RAF up to that time, all the wing aircraft had both squadron markings on them and were shared by both squadrons. On the forward side of the fuselage roundel were the three yellow-red-and-blue horizontal stripes of 8 Squadron, while at the back were the black-and-white chequers of 43. It was oft quoted that the three 8 Squadron colours were those of Aden: yellow for the sand, blue for the sky and red for blood! Well the squadron had been on almost continuous operations there for some four decades, so there's probably some truth in it. To complete the picture, besides our two Hunter squadrons, a separate Flight of FR.10 fighter recce and T.7 Hunters called 1417 Flight was also part of the wing. This was the flight I was to command later in my career.

The squadrons were organised very simply: twenty-four aircrew; one squadron leader 'Boss', four flight lieutenants, two of whom were flight commanders plus a squadron QFI and a squadron Pilot Attack Instructor (PAI). The other nineteen were first-tour flying officer bachelors, average age twenty-two, and I was the youngest. What a recipe for some high jinks! Never a moment went by when somebody wasn't up to something, and I'm glad I wasn't the Boss during this period. I was still only twenty when I started here on my first operational tour, and my twenty-first was a few drinks in the mess bar soon after I arrived. Well, a few more than a few!

In operational terms, every pilot had a rating that decided how many aircraft in combat you were qualified to lead. You started as a non-operational pilot usually taking six months training to arrive at full operational status, allowing you to man the standby pair as the wingman and fly on operations up-country. You then progressed to Op2 (leader of a pair), Op4 (leader of four aircraft) and so on. Everyone made Op2 on his first tour, and the good ones made Op4. Only the flight commanders could lead eight, and notionally the Boss had all sixteen, if there was ever that number serviceable! But the standard battle routine was pairs, and four-ships, and that's how we trained.

We only had one squadron on duty at any one time and we worked a twenty-four-hours-on/twenty-four-hours-off shift, from lunchtime to lunchtime, handing over to the oncoming squadron at midday. A pair of aircraft, and pilots, was always kept on fifteen-minute stand-by; sometimes this became four if the alert state increased. This system continued seven days per week, though with minimum manning at weekends. This meant that every twenty-four hours you finished work at lunchtime, went down to the beach for the afternoon, got pissed in the evening, slept it off the following morning and at lunchtime stumbled back to work again! And they paid you to do it!

Hunter Armament

We were equipped only with Second World War 3-inch calibre HE anti-tank rockets, and the four internal 30mm Aden cannon; no napalm or bombs, (traditionally, the four-engined Lincoln aircraft had done the bombing role, subsequently taken over by the Shackletons), our usual fit being twelve 60lb rockets under the outer wings, and 120 rounds of 30mm HE ammo in each gun. So armed, the stand-by pair, on fifteen minutes readiness dawn till dusk, was manned by two pilots, the leader of whom had to be a qualified Op4, with an Op2/Op as a wingman. This quick reaction alert was not only for army support up-country, but also for air defence if required. Our main

A posed photograph of an 8 Squadron Hunter FGA.9 at Muharraq and the wide range of armaments available for operations in the Middle East in 1967. They comprise 30mm cannon, 3in underwing rockets, SNEB rocket pods, napalm and 500lb bombs (*via David Ainge*).

task was army support but, few and far between as they were, we used to enjoy the air defence scrambles.

There were two reasons for this taste, the first being that with both ends of the runway ending in the sea, whichever way you took off, and as soon as the wheels were up, it was standard operating procedure to jettison everything under the wings into the ocean on air defence scrambles. This was thought crucial to lighten the aircraft load for the fastest possible climb to height. It didn't happen often! But two full 230-gallon fuel tanks and twelve rockets going off together into the sea was a sight worth watching. The second was that an air defence mission usually meant climbing to high level which, in turn, meant you found the only cool part of South Arabia for once. As 90 per cent of our flying was low-level army support and ground attack, we spent most of our flying drenched in sweat, since it was desperately hot in the cockpit at low level throughout the year.

The job in hand
The task, both then and today, of bringing fugitives, dissidents or terrorists to justice, was complicated by a daunting combination of factors from

31

the country's complicated social and tribal composition, to the sheer in-hospitality of the geography of the place, which is both huge and unforgiving. The inhabitants are some of the poorest in the world, with no natural resources and little water. Three-quarters of a million of them in a country the size of France. Of course, it didn't help matters that, with the exception of the tarmac Aden-Dhala Road being built by our Royal Engineers, there wasn't a single metalled road in the whole of South Arabia outside Aden Colony. From the 7,000-feet sheer escarpments of black granite rising above the Lawdar Plain, to the unending vastness of the Empty Quarter, with only a few sand-graded airstrips able to accept a Dakota size aircraft, it's an impossible world for all but the toughest.

It is hard to conceive in the modern world of the communications problems prevalent throughout the Arabian Peninsula; lack of landlines between RAF bases, no satellites, inefficient, short-range, radio-telephones and dependence upon time-consuming teleprinters, morse code and tardy air-mail. Communications throughout the Arabian Peninsula were totally inadequate and would have been severely tested if ever any major operation had had to be carried out. We fell foul of this problem during a fighter transit of Turkey on the way home in late 1967.

The variety of airfields and landing grounds that had to be used by the force was almost unlimited, though only the international standard of Khormaksar could take fighters. For the rest, every conceivable kind of surface, length and gradient could be found, down to rough, short and precipitous landing grounds like Dhala in the Western Aden Protectorate. Hard, natural surfaces were usually stony with a great danger to tail-planes, main-planes and undercarriages from large flying stones. The wear and tear on tyres and on nose and tail wheels from these conditions was excessive, and a significant number of unservicabilities could always be attributed to the landing and take-off conditions to which all aircraft were subjected. We were constantly being asked to operate from airfields which had been adequate for the old Vampires and Venoms but which were no more than marginal for Hunters, such as Beihan, Riyan and Salalah. It is understandable that our overall accident rate tended to be higher than the RAF average, not because of any lack of skill, but because of the greater hazards up-country with which pilots had to contend.

Hazards

Occasionally while flying low-level, we had to contend with the massive, black four-foot wingspan kites, or 'shitehawks' as we colloquially called them, which, being the largest birds in the region and the fore queen of the local skies, didn't give way to anything. The usual strikes on the leading edges of our main-planes and engine intake areas usually meant the loss of the aircraft for many months for major repairs, though, thank goodness, the Avon engine withstood enormous damage without coughing and aircraft were rarely lost for this reason. The Hunter was so sturdy that even after ingesting a kite with enormous intake damage, it generally flew, sometimes long distances, home safely.

In 1966 we had a remarkable Hunter incident which totally vindicated our problems with corrosion in the eyes of the powers back home. Dick Wharmby was trying to land his Hunter one day after experiencing a hydraulic failure. The Hunter's back-up system was a compressed-air accumulator used to blow the undercarriage down after any loss of hydraulic pressure. A simple mechanical pull lever in the cockpit controlled the accumulator and, having lost his hydraulics, Dick pulled the lever. It just came off in his hand, the heavy steel cable attached to the lever having corroded right through since its replacement less than three months earlier. Dick finally landed the aircraft wheels up on its empty underwing 230-gallon drop tanks and, keeping the runway clear for other aircraft, skidded down the taxiway in a shower of sparks, damaging nothing but the drop tanks. A measure of how robust an aircraft was the Hunter is also proven in this incident, in that the aircraft was jacked up, drop-tanks changed, a hydraulic valve substituted, the handle replaced, and was flying again the following day!

Operating continuously in this environment posed us many problems which, at times, demanded the highest standards of airmanship. Not least of the problems was that of combating intense heat, glare and sandblasting. The perspex cockpit canopy tended to focus the rays of the sun onto the head of the pilot, and prolonged exposure to this concentration could induce headaches and sunstroke. In this type of aircraft, however, we normally wore protective helmets, or "bone-domes", for safety in ejection but, astonishing as it may seem today, just ordinary desert shoes on our feet! Cockpit windscreens suffered most. Constant sandblasting etched a six-month life into a screen which lasted years in a European environment, and progressively aggravated the sun's glare. Squinting into the small quarterlight on each side, the only recourse, did little to facilitate landing on a runway ill-defined in full sun.

Spending over fifteen minutes on the ground in the cockpit where temperatures often exceeded 150 degrees F (65.5 C) was precluded by an air-conditioning system unusable prior to engine start, and certainly not designed with Aden in mind; it couldn't cope with normal low-level flying which was always a hot, sweaty affair. The inviolable fifteen-minute rule then was to cancel the mission to avoid heat exhaustion; the subsequent recovery seated in air-conditioning included much "jungle juice" (powdered orange-juice) consumption provided by the ground crew. Only in Aden were two plates of pills kept permanently on all mess dining tables: one of vitamins and, by far the more important, one of salt pills which we all took religiously to avoid the vertiginous effects of sodium deficiency. Although a tubular-framed, mobile canopy reduced cockpit ground temperatures, it was insufficient to prevent spending the ensuing hour or so at high level, strapped into a refrigerated cockpit, soaked to the skin in our own sweat. Notwithstanding some acclimatisation, avoiding pneumonia was miraculous!

Back on the ground, if the technical problems were trying, the conditions under which our airmen had to solve them were even more demanding. Conditions for servicing aircraft could hardly be worse than they were at Khormaksar. Salt and sand posed alarming problems for the maintenance of metal-skinned aircraft, engines, vehicles, equipment and buildings, often necessitating complicated and difficult repairs. Almost all work had to be

Armourers undertake the daunting task of sorting 30mm ammunition under a blazing hot sun at Bahrain in 1962 (*Alan Lowe*).

carried out in the open exposed to incessant heat, sand and dust. It was oft said that the humid, dust-filled, salt-laden atmosphere of Aden produced the finest grinding compound in the world, with immense patience needed to re-assemble components with bearing surfaces free from these harmful agents. In Fighter Command our Aden gunpacks were serviced and stored in special air-conditioned armouries. Not so in the Middle East. If a suitable building was available, it was fortuitous. Often a square patch of sand denoted the armoury, and Aden guns were destined to swallow their allotted portion of sand like everything and everybody else.

The extraordinary thing was that, though the rate of wear was fairly high, the guns worked extremely well with stoppages happening but rarely. This caused many an eyebrow to be raised at the luxurious accommodation being provided in the UK, but at Khormaksar the choice between stifling heat but reasonably clean conditions inside a hangar, and salt-laden, blowing sand but cooler air in the open was often a difficult one to make. After an incident occurred in which an NCO died of heat exhaustion while working behind one of the engines inside the main wing of a Beverley, some change to working practices had to be made. He collapsed and was not found in time to revive him, which immediately caused a standing order stating that they had to work in pairs, causing some bemusement in new arrivals.

The Alert standby
As pilots we each had to do our stint as part of the standby pair on the fifteen-minute readiness. This meant all the pre-flight checks had been completed on the aircraft, which included two 230-gallon underwing tanks inboard, the twelve rockets and the four integral cannon in the nose, with one's cockpit set up to personal requirements when taking over the duty. As usual we then lolled around the crewroom in air-conditioning, hoping that something might happen, having been ready either half an hour before dawn for duty until lunchtime, or lunchtime until half an hour after dusk.

Khormaksar was the largest and busiest RAF station anywhere, housing not less than three wings of nine squadrons and three flights. Security was a constant cause of concern as Aden was at that time being subjected to a mounting wave of terrorist attacks, some 286 in 1965 and almost double that number a year later. Although most fighter patrols were flown at low level to ensure the dissidents on the ground heard us and knew we were there, occasionally, high-level patrols were flown in the fond hope that their air force would know we were around and make them think twice about coming across the border. In any case there were many transit flights to and from the Gulf, and ferry flights to and from UK, all of course flown at high level. It is difficult to describe sensations during high-level, long-distance transit flights or border patrols in that part of the world. As the patrol pair, we were usually up at 36,000 feet in wide battle formation, some two miles line abreast, flying slowly at Mach 0.75 along the border for endurance. The cloudless sky was so vast, and limpid with patches of dissolving fleeciness and usually no horizon. One felt stunned by this cavernous airspace we, alone, inhabited, while below, the ground was barely discernible, hidden by the dreaded 'Goldfish Bowl' conditions. This yellow haze made orientation difficult, made possible only by frequent recourse to instrumentation!

You knew that the hostile, granite South Arabian mountains were somewhere below and, despite the minus-40 degrees C of cold outside the canopy, you could still feel the sun's rays burning through, blinding your vision, and impairing even further your capacity to make visual sweeps of the sky. Instead of breathing the usual air/oxygen mix, the system was often turned to pure oxygen, especially if you'd had a few pints too many the night before! Breathing pure oxygen always gave you a lift and put you on a "high". It increased the curious but satisfying sensation of being isolated and totally detached from reality. You couldn't hear any engine noise at that height, just a slight swish of the airflow across the outer skin, and the constant minor static from the radio. There is little relative movement to show speed, only what's on the dial. Time appears to go so slowly that everything seems unreal and remote. The cockpit environment gradually becomes a sort of low, noisy growl in your earphones, blocking out everything else and forming a neutral background that ends up by merging into a profound, vague, and dreamy silence, threatening to break the ingrained discipline of constant scanning.

At the other extreme of our ops were the many frantic, frenzied scrambles that found you airborne within minutes, still trying to strap into the ejection seat whilst already halfway to the target area. On occasion the target area came into view before my seat safety pins came out! Such was the hurry to help the army guys, especially the 10 Field Squadron Royal Engineers who were being sniped at on the Dahla Road. It was a matter of pride and professionalism that you got airborne as fast as possible; after all, "health and safety" hadn't been invented in those days, thank goodness. If it helped to save lives up-country, you risked leaving the strapping-in and safety checks until you were on the way at full throttle, and to hell with the consequences if something went wrong on take off!

The Yemenis were always encroaching upon the border in the Beihan area, which was round the corner of an S-bend in the border some 150 miles north-east of Aden. It was right on the edge of the Rub-al-Khali (the Empty Quarter), probably the most far-flung, desolate outpost of any British forces. We had traditionally provided exorbitantly expensive, standing airborne patrols in the area three times per day. Beihan stood some 2,500 feet above sea level in a natural, narrow rock and sand wadi running north-east-to-south-west, and surrounded by escarpments along its forty-mile length. A main natural surface road ran along the centre of the wadi and through Beihan town. About half a mile south-west of the town, that road had been turned into a short concrete airstrip, but with a large hill at the south-western end. Back in 1957 a mixed force of 500 Yemeni irregulars and their regular army had crossed the Beihan border and ambushed a dawn patrol of RAF armoured cars, forcing them to fight the first pitched battle of the frontier troubles. Indeed, an attack by two MiG fighters in June 1965 on the village of Najd Marqad and a nearby Frontier Guard post near Beihan caused the death of two Arab women and injury to three other villagers. This incident necessitated the re-introduction of our Beihan Air Defence Patrol, a wasteful and time-consuming commitment. By 1966 the problems in the area had become insurmountable without air support, but Beihan runway, only 1,440 yards in length, was too short for Hunters. Consequently, after one Yemeni incursion in July, in which MiG 17s shot up the nearby village of Nuqub, it was decided to lengthen the runway to 1,800 yards for Hunters, much to the delight of the Sharif of Beihan, the local Marib Sheik.

Having to transit each way round the corner to and from Beihan created a 360-mile round trip, instead of the direct line across Yemeni territory of only 300 miles, which further decreased the short time we could stay on patrol there. Maintaining diversion fuel for Djibouti on the African coast, a further 135 miles in the opposite direction from Khormaksar, didn't help. As a result, many were the occasions when we ran short of fuel and had to return across Yemeni territory as the crow flies. Fortuitously, the artificial, vaguely-defined and unpatrolled borders on the edge of the Empty Quarter were pretty meaningless.

The rough and the smooth
To land on the newly lengthened Beihan runway, a very tight left turn had to be flown around a tall, narrow spit of rock jutting vertically upwards to a pointed top that was positioned almost in the middle of the desired

approach to the runway. This circular Jebel called Jash Sha'bah was a phallic symbol shape on short base leg, requiring a tight S-bend to be flown on short finals. If your speed was exactly right, a landing attempt could then be made north-eastwards towards the village. Of course, in order to stop safely on such a short, 'hot and high' runway, you had to have no more than the exact minimum fuel state with empty drop tanks on board with which to fly back home to base. There, at 2,000 feet above mean sea level, you were committed to stay until the temperature reduced sufficiently around dusk for a safe take off, otherwise you'd have still been on the ground rolling down the main village street. Committed for take off, the aircraft was launched in the same direction regardless of wind conditions, and an operation "hairy" to say the least. I was reminded of this commitment by a saying of General Schwarzkopf after the First Gulf War. On being interviewed by a UK reporter about his troops' involvement and commitment, he answered by saying, "It's like your Limey breakfasts ... you know, your eggs and bacon!" He went on, "The chicken's involved but the pig's committed!" At Beihan, we were the pigs.

The more senior pilots flew a pair into Beihan at dawn each day and maintained a ground standby until dusk when they took off, did a very short patrol, and returned to Khormaksar for the night. With the new part of Beihan runway being at the southern end, the further down the take-off run, the bumpier was the ride, until at about 20 knots below flying speed, a particularly bad bump could throw you into the air. The next few seconds were spent, nose high in the air, half stalled and desperately clambering for speed and height, mushing down the main street of the village. Happily, the wadi and the road were dead straight, although I wouldn't like to have been walking down the main street minding my own business at the time.

It is long enough ago to now admit it! Although I wasn't one of those chosen to land at Beihan, I certainly used to do touch-and-go approaches there, just to relieve the boredom of desert patrols, and I know I wasn't the only one. The Wing flew an enormous number of these Beihan missions: 186 in August, 98 in September, and 151 in October 1966. I alone flew seven Beihan patrols in the month of August 1966, having flown none in the previous eighteen months, but this patrol level was not to last. Beihan was too difficult logistically and, in any case, how were we going to obtain an alert to get airborne anyway, even if the heat had allowed it? It appeared to be nothing more than a show of force to keep up the locals' confidence.

Practice makes perfect!

We were kept busy operationally during 1967 and ACM Sir David Lee is quoted as writing:

> The accuracy of 8 Squadron's rocket attacks proved excellent, and the Squadron became one of the most accurate and experienced rocket firing squadrons in the RAF, with average errors measured in feet where others were measured in yards!

I was always proud of my rocket average, which for the whole three years was less than twenty feet, and during one four-month period, came down to less than fourteen feet. This may not sound too accurate to the uninitiated, until it is realised that this was accomplished with very inaccurate, Second World War rockets employed by Typhoons. But 960lb of explosive in a full load of sixteen rockets detonating five or six yards away was more than enough to make you blink!

On the other hand, our use of this rocket was one of many weapon-to-target mismatches, for which the Air Force is infamous. The shaped-charge warhead was designed to put a small-diameter hole into Second World War armour-plate; single rocket use against soft targets such as Radfan mud forts, at low attack angles, produced a small hole in the side of the fort, another small hole on the other side of the fort as it exited, little change in between, and the rocket disappearing stage right! A full salvo solved that problem, but by far the most effective were the four 30mm cannon.

Each gun fired 1,200 rounds per minute of 30mm high explosive shells, putting down 4,800 rounds per minute, an enormous amount of firepower with all four guns firing, and as good as any Gatling gun. Indeed, at the time it was the heaviest gun-armed fighter in the world. When practising on the range, short half-second bursts from a single gun opening at 500 yards down to 350 yards, were the best for greater accuracy, producing less time of bullet flight and a small bullet spread. However, operationally it was usual to fire one- to two-second bursts using two or all four guns, thus putting between 80 and 160 rounds on target on every attack pass. For the uninitiated, a low-angle, 10-degree attack dive at 420 knots meant you moved 1,400 feet (466 yards) across the ground during a two-second burst. Having to pull out of the dive at 350 yards to clear the target safely meant opening fire at about 800 to 900 yards. At that range the bullet spread was too large for accuracy, so a one- to one-point-five-second burst was about all that was operationally possible as a reasonable compromise.

Above and below: Running in low at around 420kts, an 8 Squadron FGA.9 (above) unleashes a short burst of cannon fire on the Jeb-a-Jib range in October 1963. Later the same day, another FGA.9 fires a salvo of rockets at the canvas targets (*both, Ray Deacon*).

Despite the heavy armament, the use of all four guns together, which only ever occurred on operations, produced some dramatic consequences, and not just for the enemy. The first time I used all four, it felt as if the aircraft had hit a brick wall – the recoil was so great. The vibration set up throughout the airframe usually popped numerous circuit-breakers, and the radio would go off-line as would most of the electrical services. Not a nice position to be in, pulling out of a dive 100 feet above a target who was firing back at you!

Surprisingly, one aspect of the Aden cannon was used as currency. The two under-fuselage Sabrinas were a later addition to collect the ammo belt-links which otherwise would have damaged the fuselage's underside on ejection. However, the 30mm brass cartridge-cases were ejected. The locals whom we used on our air-firing range as a maintenance party were not paid, except that they were allowed to pick up the spent cases which fetched a premium downtown. Moreover, 41 Commando personnel told me that after firing in their support up-country in the Dhala region, the guns' brass cases were so valuable that the dissidents would down arms and break cover to collect them. Once collected, they then recommenced firing at the marines. Indeed, it is thought that they only fired on our troops to get us called in to provide them with brass currency. In effect we were paying them to fight us.

However, Heath-Robinson had nothing on our drainpipe rockets. They were propelled by long sticks of cordite, some of which would inevitably be ejected unburnt out of the rear-end during the rocket's flight, producing peculiar flight patterns and most uncertain impact points. Indeed, when acting as Range Safety Officer on our training range at Khormaksar Beach, I would walk the range and pick up the cordite strips after a mission had finished. When ignited together in a pile, these would boil a billycan of water for our tea exceptionally rapidly.

Together with the lack of a proper rocket sight in the aircraft, the subsequent inaccuracy of the rockets, sometimes with twirling flight paths, could only be overcome by considerable skill. It is said that a fighter pilot is an infinitely adaptable machine that can make allowances for the most impossible equipment designs to make them work regardless, but there is a limit. By and large, when we did hit the target, all the errors had likely cancelled each other out. Even so, when we came back from missions with empty rocket rails and soot round the gun ports, both armourers and our groundcrew were happy; they knew then that their efforts had been rewarded.

Scrambled

In order that our operations can be better understood, and the way we trained for them, and bearing in mind that there were forty-odd operational Hunter pilots on the wing, if you take my sixty-six as an average, and multiply by the number of pilots, there were somewhere around 2,600 to 2,700 operational Hunter missions flown during the last two years of occupation, at a rate of roughly four per day. Compared with the 642 missions flown during the two-month Radfan campaign in 1964, our 2,600 were flown at a more leisurely pace, but were sustained over a longer period with the enemy becoming stronger throughout.

To take just one of my missions, the strike in the Radfan area of Wadi Tiban on 4 May 1966, the Boss (Squadron Leader Des Melaniphy) and I were scrambled from standby after a party of approximately twenty armed dissidents had infiltrated from Yemen into the Federation. On the previous night, using explosive bullets, they attacked a British Army patrol operating in the area twenty miles west of Habilayn (forty-five miles north of Aden and five miles from the Yemen border), under the command of the FRA. At first light, the Boss and I did an armed recce flagwave over the area, but that didn't deter them. So, later that morning, we were scrambled with full firing permission. I say that because we needed GOC's or AOC's express permission before being allowed to fire, and many was the time we were overhead obvious firefights, and couldn't find either of them because they were otherwise engaged with matters clearly more important than the up-country lives, and no delegation of responsibility was ever given.

This was to be my first live-firing mission, and I was initially very nervous. I was curious and anxious at the same time to know how I would react, not to the danger, because I never once doubted our invincibility, but to firing weapons at live human targets for the first time. On this occasion, with full firing permission, we went on to direct all our rockets and ammunition at the dissidents, whom we found patrolling down the boulder-strewn, palm-tree-lined Wadi Tiban. On my first, steep, rocket attack I caught glimpses of the dissidents running away down the wadi through the trees and boulders but, despite repeated attacks thereafter, there were no further sightings. We were told later that thirteen of them had been killed, and five wounded, out of a party of twenty, whilst no British soldiers or locals had been injured at all. We considered that one of the few successes after all the flagwaves and armed recces we'd flown while not being allowed to fire.

On the ground afterwards, we were quietly excited, not quite grasping what we had done. I had completed my first real mission, not made a hash of it, and a great weight had fallen from me after years of training. It was the first time I'd experienced that strange exultation that often accompanies hard fighting, and I had come of age that day. This was the first time I had knowingly killed anyone, and I have to say that, whereas it has preyed on my mind over many years since, I have no conscience about it. I was doing my job, the job I had been trained for, without which it would have been British soldiers' lives, and I'd certainly do it again in the same circumstances. That's all there is to it.

Finally, the posting home came through the mail, but life is never simple, and neither was this. In short, this was to one of the only two elite fighter-recce squadrons of 2 TAF in Northern Germany, flying the Hunter FR.10 on low-level tactical army reconnaissance. Agreeably, this was my first choice, and providentially to be my next home. Specifically, "Tatty Two", or 2 (Army Co-operation) Squadron at RAF Gütersloh, but my withdrawal from Aden, and how I got to 2 Squadron became another saga.

Initially unplanned, I would take the scenic route home, spending five weeks en route. The journey commenced as a result of the Arab-Israeli Six Day War. During those six days in June 1967, Jordan lost most of its operational air force. They only had fifteen fighter aircraft, all Hunters, at the beginning, and lost fourteen of them. Within weeks the British government had decided to replace them, and three of the 'new' aircraft came from our wing. Owing to our departure from Aden with several disbandments and amalgamations, aircraft surplus to our future requirements were now available.

Hence, on 9 September 1967, twenty-four hours after the disbandment of 1417 Flight and its amalgamation into 8 Squadron, I finally departed from the cauldron of Aden for Amman in my own aircraft, XG255, as part of a flight of three Strike Wing aircraft. All were Hunter FGA.9s, repainted beforehand in Royal Jordanian Air Force colours, which Wing Commander "Pancho" Ramirez (the Strike Wing Commander), Wally Willman from 43 Squadron and I flew to Jordan via Jeddah on their delivery flights, and that take off from Khormaksar in a Jordanian Hunter was my last, never to return.

While planning this two-stage ferry flight, we signalled the air attaché (AA) in Jordan, to ask which airfields we could use for diversion

Above: Wally Willman, Chris Bain and 'Pancho' Ramirez about to depart Khormaksar on 9 September 1967 with three Hunter FGA.9s destined for the Royal Jordanian Air Force (*Chris Bain*).

Below: Repainted in Jordanian markings, the three Hunters (XG298, XE645 and XG255) fly low over Aden Harbour before turning north and heading for Amman (*David Griffin*).

purposes, if needed, and suggesting, tongue in cheek, that Jerusalem International would suit. The reply contained one of those, "NOT, repeat NOT . . . s" in its text – no way would we be allowed anywhere near Jerusalem. But he did give us Dawson's Field, a large 25,000 by 4,000-yard strip of desert which, exactly three years later, came to fame as the rough airstrip where the PFLP, a Palestinian terrorist organisation, blew up three airliners, a Swissair DC-8, a TWA Boeing 707, and a BOAC VC10. Perhaps the AA was right; as we passed over Aqaba at 40,000 feet, only a few miles from the Israeli border town and airfield of Eilat, an Israeli Air Force aircraft shadowed us north all the way to abeam Amman. Nevertheless, we landed safely at the old combined Amman military/civil airport at Marqa, albeit on a heavily bomb-damaged runway, and handed the aircraft over to the RJAF.

We were lauded in Amman. After all, we had quadrupled the size of their air force. Tea at the palace, party at the embassy, five-star Intercontinental Hotel accommodation, once-in-a-lifetime trips to the Living City of Petra, the colonnaded ruins of Jerash, probably the best preserved city of the Roman Empire, and a free day's water skiing – they couldn't do enough for us.

We were there for nearly a week waiting for the repairs to the main runway, one side of which was still unuseable after the Israeli bombings of the recent war. Eventually, our RJAF hosts asked about our sporting activities and we cynically suggested water skiing only because 8 Squadron had had its own boat in Aden, we all skied, and there was no water in Jordan. What we didn't tell the Jordanians was that our boat was a tiny aluminium one with only a 35hp Johnson outboard that couldn't pull two up. Imagine our surprise, then, when the next day we were ushered into an RJAF Dakota, and flown down to Aqaba just to go water skiing at the Royal Jordanian Water Skiing Club. Incredibly, the captain of the Dakota, Hassan, had trained with me in the UK on Hunters some four years earlier, and a good reunion was had in the cockpit all the way there, especially as, having flown Daks with the Communication Flight in Aden, I was allowed to fly it into and out of Aqaba. A great treat for me, but not without some concern and trepidation on the part of Pancho and Wally.

On the beach at Aqaba we found a water hangar, out of which they drove a twin-diesel, twin-screw 215hp inboard polished limousine of a speedboat. You've heard the phrase, "pride comes before a fall"? Well, it does when you are drenched in front of all those Jordanian pilots. I don't think any of us stayed up on the skis for more than a minute at a time, but we did have a lot of laughs, mainly at our own expense.

Arriving back in Amman, we found a different mood afoot. By this time the RJAF groundcrew had started pulling our Hunters apart to service them. One of the first things to attend to on a Hunter's major servicing is the dismantling of the rear fuselage for access to the engine. The whole rear comes away in one piece, exposing the jet pipe. Our wonderful squadron groundcrew in Aden who had repainted the fuselages and wings in Jordanian colours had also, it appeared, painted Stars of David on the outside of the jet-pipes, which were now exposed to the Arab groundcrew. The Jordanians were not amused.

This was bad news for us, and almost caused an international incident. We were quickly out of the hotel, into the embassy, and onto the next plane out of the country; they couldn't get rid of us fast enough. Thus, after Aden, this was the second country out of which I'd been kicked.

We flew out to Beirut where, after a good night out (Beirut was the Monte Carlo of the Middle East in those days), Pancho and Wally flew back "civvyair" to Aden, but I journeyed on by myself on the Lebanese airline, Middle East Airways, direct to Bahrain to rejoin 8 Squadron. That last flight out of the Lebanon was my first-hand experience of Arab cooking on primus stoves in the alleyway between the aircraft seats. The smells would make you sick on the ground, never mind while airborne.'

David Baron (Flying Officer)

Having completed flying training on the Provost T.1 and Vampire T.11, David reported to 229 OCU at RAF Chivenor in early August 1962 to join No. 88 Day Fighter/Ground Attack Course on the Hunter. On completion of the course, he was posted to 8 Squadron and arrived at RAF Khormaksar as a pilot officer, on 2 January 1963. His first operational sortie (although still officially 'non-op') took place just two days after his promotion to Flying Officer on 24 February.

'Shortly after my arrival, as occurred from time to time, the squadron was involved in patrols along the disputed border between the Aden Protectorate and the Yemen in the Beihan district, some 140 miles north-east of Aden. The requirement was to have two Hunters on station from dawn to dusk (some thirteen hours per day) in order to "show the flag" and counter interdiction by Yemeni aircraft. High-level transit to and from the area took twenty minutes each way, allowing each pair one hour on task. As time went by, the squadron became increasingly short of serviceable aircraft but, more importantly, the operational-qualified pilots were hard-pressed to keep up with demand and it was therefore decided that Pilot Officer Baron should fill in as a No. 2 for occasional sorties.

My first such op was flown without incident on 26 February, followed by one per day from 2 to 7 March shortly after which, if I remember correctly, the requirement came to an end – at least temporarily. It was on 7 March that I was tasked to fly as No. 2 to my deputy flight commander, Nick Adamson. We took off from Khormaksar only to find that Nick couldn't raise his undercarriage. Given that he had to abort his own sortie, he asked if I felt sufficiently confident to go it alone. I answered in the affirmative and, on being given his approval, settled into a climb to the transit altitude. Some three to four minutes later, I felt a marked deceleration and immediately scanned the instruments to see the RPM, which for some reason had wound down, now increasing back to the maximum setting. The throttle had not been moved so I deduced that something was amiss either with engine or fuel system and that I should return to Khormaksar with all speed. And yet! All now seemed well! And I had an important job to do – indeed, the security and well being of not only Beihan, but the entire Aden Protectorate was in my hands. So I decided to carry on and, fifteen minutes later, was on patrol at 250 feet over territory we considered to be ours and the Yemenis insisted was theirs. Some time later, on reaching the minimum fuel state for recovery, I set the appropriate heading and applied full power for the climb. The RPM wound up only slightly and my stomach turned over – if I couldn't get full power I couldn't climb, and if I couldn't climb then I couldn't get home. I recycled the throttle very slowly and, to my intense relief, the engine accelerated as it should. I returned to Khormaksar in a rather subdued state and reported my experience in full. Well, almost in full!'

Keeping them flying

Respect for the way in which the ground crews went about their onerous task of ensuring there were adequate serviceable aircraft for operations has been referred to on several occasions by the pilots. As the Hunter was intended for service in the relatively cool and clear climate of the European theatre, maintaining the aircraft in the hot and hostile environment of the Middle East required a high degree of skills and dedication from the engineering teams. Ben Bennett has the privilege of making the first contribution on behalf of his fellow ground crew members.

Ben Bennett (Senior Aircraftsman)

Ben Bennett was an instrument mechanic (Mech) and his two-year tour on 8 Squadron began in May 1960, having travelled out to Aden on one of a dwindling number of troopships, the HMT *Dilwara*. Having previously experienced trips in Meteor T.7 and Vampire T.11 aircraft at Cranwell, the piece de resistance for Ben occurred in February 1962.

(**Author's note**: The designation HMT (Hired Military Transport) was used for merchant ships employed as troopships. Although many believe HMT to denote 'His/Her Majesty's Troopship', such vessels were never part of the Royal Navy. In Naval terms, HMT meant 'His Majesty's Trawler' during the Second World War and was used for convoy escort vessels usually manned by the Royal Naval Reserve.)

An adrenalin-charged adventure!

'With Flying Officer Brian Voller in the port seat telling me to lightly grip the top of the control column stick top, brakes on – flaps set for take off – throttle forward – engine rpm winding up – nose-leg oleo shortening like a compressed spring. Sitting there adrenalin pumping in a vibrating, tethered noise. Brakes off. WHAM! Rammed back into my ejection seat as the nose sprang up and we shot forward and upward the aircraft taking itself off without any human intervention pulling back on the stick – what amazing aerodynamics! There followed a bit of general handling, including loops and rolls, which I seemed to manage OK followed by some very boring mountains and sand. Then we got to the good bit, a bit of simulated rocket-firing practice on some rocks out at sea. On the pull-out I was sure I was as heavy as Jabba the Hutt. To finish off we completed a GCA approach which was a bit "monkey see, monkey do" but most useful in bad weather. Overall, an exhilarating experience and clearly one which has stayed with me. Although I was on the cusp of "chucking up" towards the end because of the sweet smell of oxygen on rubber, I managed to keep it down. This might just be because I feared the wrath of the armourers having to clear up the mess plus the obligatory donation of a case of "Slops".

Keeping clean and tidy!

The *dhobi wallahs* were not very efficient at their task. Leave soiled kit wrapped in a towel at the foot of the bed before leaving for the squadron in the morning and, hey presto, it would magically return that same afternoon – all starched, cleaned and pressed. Of course, each item had to be indelibly marked with one's own hieroglyph – I can still remember mine. As if their task was not onerous enough (many of the poor little blighters were bandy-legged from the great weights they had to carry from an early age), I don't think we helped their situation any by paying the grinning *wallahs* fourteen shillings every fortnight in the customary way, East African halfpennies strung in necklace fashion, each coin having a hole through the middle. Never had a complaint.

Antics at the Astra

There occasioned a bizarre event one evening outside the Astra cinema. It was published in Khormaksar routine orders that airmen were to wear KD trousers to the cinema lest they offend members of the opposite sex who might very well catch a glimpse of male genitalia. Naturally the lads did not take very kindly to this order as wearing long trousers made their nether regions even hotter and so they ignored the order. When the dogs were brought out to quell the ensuing 'riot', a jolly time was had by all. It should be remembered that any behaviour was fair game to break the monotony.

As a prelude to the evening's big film, cartoons would be shown. Mickey Mouse featured every night. As the credits rolled and Fred Quimby's name appeared, up would go a roar from the audience, 'GOOD OLD FRED!' – quite scary upon first experience. Another example of intuitive audience participation was in the form of a postscript to an advert for Alsops lager where, in championing the lager's attributes, the final voiceover would say "cools your blood", the response to which was "AND ROTS YOUR GUTS." Oh, what joy to be in the anonymity of the crowd.

Into Kuwait

With General Kassim poised to enter Kuwait, 8 Squadron was ordered up to Bahrain and from there on to the tiny oil-rich state. Having just touched down at Kuwait New Airport, which was still under construction, in an 84 Squadron Beverley, we deplaned and prepared to unload our equipment and gear. I was convinced I was standing in the exhaust of a Houchin petrol/electric power-generating set as the heat was so intense when compared to Aden. As the newly-laid tarmac had not fully set, the aircraft slowly began to sink into it and we actually cracked an egg on the wing of a Hunter and it fried quite quickly. With regards to our accommodation, it can be described as skeletal at best; no fans or air-conditioning, and we had to sleep on spring-wire camp-beds sharing each other's warm, secondhand body odours – not very nice. I seem to recall that most of our time was spent in assembling HE rockets.

Brotherly Love.

It was in mid-1961 that my brother Mick was posted to Khormaksar. In an attempt to get him on to the squadron, I paid a visit to the general office and completed a form to 'claim' him. Much to my surprise, my efforts were rewarded and Mick was duly posted to 8 Squadron. Imagine his chagrin, however, when he discovered that he could have spent two blissful years in the instrument bay – *air-conditioned.* He hasn't forgiven me to this day!

On our first detachment to Bahrein (that was the original spelling) at the end of a busy day's operations with the aircraft on the line "chocked and locked", I decided to show my "Mooney" brother one of the tricks of the

Due to their lily-white skin, new arrivals in Aden were easy to spot and were known by the derogatory term 'Moonies!'. Just in case it is not apparent, in this photograph Ben Bennett is pointing out the latest influx of airmen on the 8 Squadron line in early 1962, Vic Cozens to his right and an airman who prefers to remain anonymous. To the left, Roy Porter and Pete Hall maintain a degree of restraint (*Ben Bennett*).

trade, such as how to gain entry into the cockpit when there was no access ladder available.

> Grab hold of the port wing extension, leg up onto the 230-gallon drop tank, onto the wing, then the spine, slide back the hood and "hey presto" you're in.
>
> Take a running jump, stick your left foot into the spring-loaded ladder flap whilst simultaneously sliding back the hood and "hey presto" you should be in. Didn't quite make it, bounced off the fuselage, a bit winded and thought no more of it. Next morning, on attempting to rise from my bed, no way – result, three cracked ribs. Moral – don't show off when you're tired.

Common ailments that could make you "crook" in Aden were sunburn, heatstroke, Montezuma's revenge, camel-spider bites (very often in the nether regions) and Aden ear. Now this last agony was caused by seawater entering the ear canal and not finding its way out – hence severe pain. The cure, however, was far worse than the ailment itself, viz., a long thin bandage duly soaked in ascetic acid (vinegar) and threaded into the raw ear canal – excruciating.

And finally

Some memories are unique to that place and time. As a fresh-faced 19-year-old, they were mostly good ones, accepted in the true spirit of adventure and the fact that we were all in the same level of discomfort. The reader should bear in mind that political correctness had not raised its inane head at this time. As the locally-employed labour was want to steal water from the water coolers in our hangar, one wag hit upon a surefire way to stop this dastardly habit – a rasher of bacon around the tap outlet. Another quirky habit of several airmen was to place each of their bed legs in an upturned, empty shoe polish tin filled with various liquid concoctions to stop the crawlies, bities and stingies from getting at them whilst asleep. Bearing in mind that up until 1962 there was no air-conditioning, we were sleeping under ceiling fans and when there was a power cut, we all (thousands) woke as one. It was common for numerous fires to be lit in protest in the airmen's three-storey blocks, only to be rapidly extinguished just before the fire engine arrived. A jolly time was had by all and anything (once again) to break the boredom. Drinking beer naturally played a large part in our off-duty

Brothers Ben (left) and Mick Bennett in Conquest Bay with Mick, the younger of the two, pulling Ben's leg about the size of his knife sheath (*Ben Bennett*).

time (we worked 07:00 to 13:00) and games involving this thirstquenching activity were very popular, especially "Cardinal Puff". This involved telling a story accompanied by a particular sequence of actions performed at a fast rate. When, as most did, the chosen victim failed, he had to buy the next round of beer. An amusing spectator sport.'

Mike Bennett (Senior Aircraftsman)

Ben's elder brother, Mike, was also an aircraft Instrument mechanic and began his two-year tour with 8 Squadron in June 1961.

The unconnected MASB
'One incident in particular that remains very vivid in my memory occurred just two weeks before I became tour-ex on 2 June 1963. A pilot, whose name escapes me (slim, tall dark hair with a parting), offered me a trip in a T.7 as a treat but I turned it down being so near to going home. So off he flew in an FGA.9 instead, unaware that the master armament safety break (plug) had not been connected properly. He very soon, however, became aware of the fact when he discovered that he could not raise the undercarriage and would have to fly around at low level and at 150 knots

for an hour-and-a-half to burn off his full fuel load. Needless to say he was steaming when he eventually taxied in and all airmen were assembled in the prefabricated line hut to witness the sparks flying. On examining the F700 and discovering that a short, blond-haired armourer had carried out the Before Flight inspection, the poor soul was duly admonished in no uncertain terms in front of us all. Not a pretty sight.'

Rod Carter (Corporal)

Posted to 8 Squadron as an airframe fitter, Rod Carter was flown out to Khormaksar by RAF Britannia in September 1965.

'For single personnel, a posting to Aden was usually of two years duration, and for married personnel one year. The latter was considered as an unaccompanied tour unless a person was considered important for the continuity of a task in hand. This was known as a 'Key Post', and they were afforded the privilege of an unaccompanied tour of two years. I was lucky enough to qualify for the latter and embarked on two years of what transpired to be the beginning of the decline of British rule in South Arabia.

Hello 8 Squadron!
When I arrived, 8 Squadron shared its Mark 9 Hunters with 43 Squadron (Fighting Cocks), with 1417 Flight operating the Mark 10s. Each squadron acquired ownership of the aircraft for twenty-four-hour periods starting at 12:00 every day. For the groundcrews, this meant that we had the responsibility of recovering aircraft from each day's flying and preparing them for the first operation on the next day. Dawn strikes often necessitated late nights and very early mornings. I recall that we had to have a minimum number of serviceable aircraft before being allowed to stand down for the night. Improved aircraft availability was, if I recall correctly, the reason for sharing aircraft and both 8 and 43 Squadron markings were applied on either side of the fuselage roundels.

Our regular routine was to take the handover from 43 Squadron between 12:00 and 12:30, with normal stack around about 19:00. This got progressively later as the time approached for the withdrawal in November 1967. Morning starts could be anytime from 04:00, depending upon whether we were operational or range-flying. Operational flying required the aircraft to be armed with 60lb HE rockets and HE rounds in the Aden gunpack whilst range practice needed 60lb concrete-headed rockets and ball ammunition. The highest number of gunpacks I spotted being towed behind a tractor was eighteen, all clearly marked as to their contents.

Safety last!

The pressure of work, on at least one occasion, resulted in an aircraft being on the range inadvertently fitted with an HE gunpack. Over enthusiastic use of the cannon, firing all four guns at once, could result in nose undercarriage door locks vibrating loose and a red light in the cockpit. When this occurred, the aircraft had to be disarmed and moved to the hangar for rectification and retraction tests. I recall one occurrence when "there but for the grace of God go I" springs to mind. An aircraft returned with a nosewheel red light plus an elevator run-away tail-trim defect. As the NCO detailed to carryout the rectification, I had the aircraft made safe and positioned it in the hangar, on jacks, and carried out the necessary work. This included work by the electricians combined with independent checks on both systems, carried out by six personnel. On completion of the work the aircraft was returned to the flight line and made ready for flight. This included replacing the safe ballast-laden gunpack with one loaded with HE. The armourers were puzzled to find the gunpack electrically connected but were mortified to find it already fully loaded with HE. Investigation revealed that, although the F700 clearly certified that the aircraft was safe, an armourer had made the wrong aircraft safe. The significance of this is that in order to retract the undercarriage in the hangar the aircraft Master Armament Safety Break (MASB) plug needed to be connected, thus arming the gun circuit. And to check the elevator trim, the stick-top trim button was used and this was next to the gun firing switch. The aircraft was not, therefore, safe and any accidental discharge could have proved disastrous to my team and me. The old adage, "don't just assume, check", has lived with me from that day on.

Given that pressure and intensity of work, it is not surprising that other incidents occurred, both minor and more serious, in which both aircrew and groundcrew contravened one order or another. It was the norm, wherever possible, to keep justice informal and within the squadron, resulting in the offender being fined a number of beers depending on the severity of the occurrence, and it made for great monthly parties. Working on the flight line under the control of a chief tech and supported by one other junior NCO, we had the responsibility of all flight servicing and aircraft handling, with the exception of the aircraft armament. Our days were extremely busy and, apart from the occasional sandstorm, we never enjoyed weather-induced respites.

The temperature and humidity were regularly around the 100-degrees F at 100 per cent humidity mark at the height of summer, although winter was a little cooler. Always shirtless with the infamous KD shorts rolled down at the waist and up at the legs, the bottom of the pockets dangled below while the 'shreddies' protruded from the top.

The dreaded guard duty

In addition to our normal work pattern we also had guard duty to contend with. In 1965 this came round approximately every two weeks but, by 1967, it had reduced to every four days. Armed with the trusty Lee Enfield .303 and five rounds of ammunition, we either performed a twenty-four-hour guard, comprising of two hours on and four off followed by a day's rest, or a twelve-hour guard of two hours on and two off with no rest day. As the pressure of work on the Hunter squadrons increased towards the end of 1967, we were detailed for the twelve-hour duty only. Being assigned a duty at the 8 Squadron/Civil Airport picquet point was always appreciated as the lads would ensure you received a quota of Stims (a soft drink) to keep you going. Other picquet points of note were the power house adjacent to the Causeway, a lonely spot at night, or the bomb dump over by the Sheikh Othman road at the far side of the airfield, a twenty-minute drive round the perimeter track. When one of our senior corporals was asked by the guard commander one night what he would do if the bomb dump came under attack, he quickly retorted by pointing in the direction of the darkened runway and stating that he would run that way as fast as possible, Sir. Taken aback, the guard commander questioned the wisdom of deserting his post when his orders clearly stated that he must attempt to defend it while his unarmed *chowkidar* called for re-enforcements, and noting that this action would make him liable to court martial. My friend responded by explaining that given the length of time it would take for back-up to reach him, five rounds were hardly sufficient and that his family would be better off with him under court martial than dead. As a result, the number of rounds was increased to ten for guards assigned to the bomb dump at night. Hardly a solution. In addition to guarding the station infrastructure, every vehicle being driven by someone not possessing a service ID card had to be searched, including the refuse truck as it entered the station.

Author's note: By contrast, during the period 1960-64, a time of relatively little local hostility, guard duty came round once every two months and we were issued with a bandolier containing fifty rounds of ammunition.

Off duty

When off duty life was quite pleasant with two cinemas, one at Khormaksar and another at Steamer Point, an excellent amateur dramatic society that put on frequent productions and, of course, the beaches at Steamer Point. Elephant Bay had a good restaurant and Conquest Bay was also worth a visit. When allocated to the afternoon shift, we would make the trip to Elephant Bay in time for breakfast and have a couple of hours in the sunshine before going to work. Snorkelling was a favourite sport but sharks were a known hazard in the area. Shopping was always available with Steamer Point providing a mecca for tax-free purchases. Hi-Fi systems, Japanese cameras and watches were all the vogue. Cheap bargain watches were subject to the Tiger test: dropped in a glass of Tiger beer as a quality check before being accepted as good value. My new and original Omega Seamaster succumbed to Hunter hydraulic oil within two weeks of purchase. I recall buying a demonstration stereo record to play on my new valve-driven audio system and we had a record club with each member having a monthly choice of record. It was then passed on to other members for them to record on reel-to-reel systems. A visit to Steamer Point to see the large cruise ships was always worthwhile, many being en route to Australia with cargos of emigrants and anchored in the harbour decked out in bright lights and flags. We often sat drinking freshly-squeezed orange juice in a cafe on the Crescent looking over the gardens towards Queen Victoria's statue (her head was a magnet for the seagulls), watching them bartering with shopkeepers for duty-free goods. Passenger ships ceased to visit Aden as the situation became more dangerous, preferring the French port at Djibouti across the Red Sea instead.

Keep your head down!

For those of us lucky enough to live off-base in Ma'alla Straight, we also had the additional duty of married quarters (MQ) guard from 16:00 to 22:00 once the curfew started. It was not unknown for terrorists to throw grenades from moving vehicles and I recall an exchange of gunfire late one afternoon when one of the wives was superficially wounded by friendly fire from a would-be John Wayne. The rippling sound of a

Above: Looking north across Aden Harbour towards RAF Khormaksar in 1960. Being a free port, it was nearly always full of tankers, freighters and cruise ships plying their trade. It was also home to RAF MCU and RN Minesweeper units (*Bob Hambly*).

Below: Looking down on Ma'alla Straight from SAR Flight Sycamore XG518 in 1962. Many of the flats on south side of this mile-long dual-carriageway had been built on reclaimed land during the previous eighteen months or so and used as hirings for service personnel (*Keith Webster*).

Lee Enfield being cocked, coming down the road, as a suspicious vehicle approached is as vivid today as it was then. When I did guard duty on consecutive days and was on shift, my weapon was safely stored in the standard RAF issue wooden wardrobe in the bedroom. My wife, of course, had the rudimentary skills as to how to use it if necessary. I remember watching the King's Own Yorkshire Light Infantry (KOYLI), or the Cameron Highlanders, from my MQ balcony, enter a mosque opposite to flush out terrorists or chase them through the back streets of Ma'alla, with a deadly conclusion on a number of occasions. As the situation continued to deteriorate, stop and search went unnoticed and we gradually grew to accept it. In order to prevent terrorists from escaping through passageways leading from the Ma'alla Straight to the shanty town area behind it, the alleys were bricked up. This proved extremely successful until the heavy rains of April 1967 when, acting as dams, they backed the deep water into the surrounding buildings.

Lucky escape!
Just how serious the trouble was became personal when, at 22:00 on 20 March, 1967, my wife and I were woken by a loud explosion in our bedroom: it had been hit by an armour-piercing rocket fired from a drainpipe from across the road. Fortunately our flesh wounds were superficial and we were thankful for our luck. It was the second time No. 22 Felixstowe had been hit by a rocket and my wife and I had been the first tenants after re-build. My wife was offered the opportunity of catching the first available "trooper" home but declined. Next day we moved into Walleed House (forget the number) round the corner on the back street next to the Medical Centre and behind the NAAFI shop. No big deal but on signing the inventory I discovered that the previous occupier had also occupied 22 Felixstowe when it was bombed before (how spooky was that). Then the rains came, everything turned green, the next block of flats had to be evacuated because the water affected their foundations. On camp the Camel Club, mess and accommodation (Hunter, Beverley and Valetta blocks) all lost power. Cold showers weren't a problem; the water was hot anyway. Cold food was mildly irritating as was the lack of lights and air-conditioning, but warm beer did not go down well. The situation lasted a few days and was made worse when the officers' mess held a formal dinner complete with all the bells and whistles. To ease their situation and pass the time, many airmen took to occupying their respective balconies. This, fuelled by drink, led to a great deal of inter-squadron barracking

which encouraged some fool to set his mattress on fire while another felt his locker produced a better fire. As the bonfire spread and the situation escalated, armed RAF Police eventually moved in to quieten things down. It was never referred to as a mutiny but folk law and those involved could probably tell a different story.'

Paul Constable (Flight Lieutenant)

Having been originally posted to 8 Squadron when it operated Venoms in 1957, Paul's posting was cancelled whilst he was on embarkation leave as a result of the Duncan Sandys' defence cuts. After a tour on Hastings, partly in Transport Command but mainly in Coastal, he "escaped" and returned to flying fighters, this time with 54 Squadron at Stradishall following his conversion to the Hunter. At the completion of his tour, the deserts of Aden beckoned once again and he joined 8 Squadron in August 1962.

Paul Constable (left) and Bill Stoker ponder the spectacular scenery from a ridge overlooking the Wadi Bana, deep in the Radfan mountains (*Paul Constable*).

Radfan incident

'The photograph was taken up country in the Radfan. I went up there as a stand-in Brigade Air Support Officer (BASO) at the headquarters in Thumeir. In fact, the Hunter squadrons had to provide a suitably experienced replacement when the permanent BASO went back to the UK for a couple of weeks. Number 43 Squadron pilot Bill Stoker was there when I arrived and I then replaced him. Things had quietened down by then; hence we had time to do an area recce – interesting.

It was June 1964 and we were just coming up to the end of our first week of real operations. I say 'real' because these were sorties where we were actually firing our guns and using the historic 3-inch drain in anger, unlike the hours we had spent on Beihan patrol or the more enjoyable and interesting Operation RANGI. Operation RADFAN was using us as we had been trained and, when I say us, I definitely mean all the squadron, aircrew and ground crew alike.

Actually this is where the term 'limited war' took on a new meaning. The Tactical Wing squadrons were working from dawn, well actually well before dawn when you think about aircraft preparation and aircrew briefing, to well after last light. And this was for seven days a week. The rest of the base and most of the Hill (Command Headquarters at Steamer Point) continued with its normal routine of five days a week, 07:00 to 13:00, then off to the beach. Well so it seemed to us at the sharp end.

It was Saturday and we had been on operations from midday. The two Hunter squadrons did twenty-four hours on operational standby with the changeover occurring at midday. Normal training flying was squashed in between, depending upon operational demands. The ground crew were really doing an amazing job of turning the aircraft round and re-arming them, not to mention the odd repair as well. It was my second trip and last sortie of the day and I was leading a pair (Martin Johnson, I seem to remember, was my number two) and we were tasked to provide close support to our ground forces, getting target details and contact information through our Brigade Air Support Officer (BASO) on the ground in Thumeir. Armament 3-inch HE rockets and 30mm HE guns.

The sun was certainly getting a little low in the sky as we made contact with the ground troops and started to get our target information. The correct wadi was identified and our voice on the ground confirmed that he had us visual. Detailed target descriptions followed and soon I was happy that we were talking about the same hillside, rocks and caves. I went in for my first pass using a short burst from my guns as a marker. Great, came the voice from the ground, spot on, more there please.

The two of us then proceeded to put our rockets into the target area. We then changed to guns, selecting a pair first in order to allow us more firing passes (in case the target changed) and also to avoid the various problems that occurred when you fired all four guns at once on a low-level pass. The radio would fail, the fuel-booster pump circuit-breakers trip and the gyro gun-sight recording camera would vibrate off its mount, drop down and dangle alarmingly between the control column and the instrument panel. All problems that could be resolved, once you recovered from the dive and had regained straight and level flight at a safe altitude.

The nature of the wadi was such that we were constrained in our attack heading and things quickly developed into something like a normal range training pattern, one aircraft on the attack and the other in a downwind position, monitoring what was happening – highly untactical. I continued with what was going to be my last pass, just a little ammunition left. Speed good, pipper on target, slight correction for wind, steady. Suddenly I became aware of lines of liquid light emanating from the hillside and moving towards me. Fascinating but then realisation dawned that it was tracer and someone was firing at ME. I continued my attack, which seemed to take an eternity and then pulled up high, turning hard left. I called the guys on the ground – "Fortune, Red lead, I think that someone on the ground is firing at us. Roger, Red lead, that's affirmative. They have been shooting at you all the time", came the calm response.

Martin caught up with me and settled into battle formation as we set off back to Khormaksar, somewhat chastened – there are two sides in a war.

However, the day was not yet over. Dusk was rapidly setting in, soon it would be dark and Hunter pilots have a natural aversion to night flying. We had plenty of fuel so we transited at well over 500 knots, just to beat the onset of darkness. Once visual with the airfield I suddenly thought of all the hard work the guys had put in over the week and particularly that day so what they deserved was a bit of recognition and colour. On the blue note (about 540 knots) and at about 100 feet we flew over the squadron line and broke, climbing and decreasing speed to downwind. What a great finish to a very rewarding day. "Red section Downwind", I called, "Roger Red Lead, you are cleared to finals. Report to Station Commander on landing." Just what a chap needs as he is negotiating his finals turn.

Above and below: During their short period together in the mountains, Paul and Bill were able to visit the Cap Badge and Gin Sling hill-top picket posts, courtesy of AAC Scout helicopter XR629. Many similar posts had been taken by British forces following night-time assaults. The pair then moved on to the Wadi Taym and finally to the Wadi Bana, a main rebel supply route between Yemen and Aden. It proved to be a very enlightening experience (*Paul Constable*).

We landed, taxied in and shut down, A quick thank you to the ground crew and off into Tac Ops for a debrief. My personal debrief lasted a little longer as it transpired that the station commander had also recognised the amazing effort that the squadron had put in over the last week and had chosen the moment of my arrival to draw up at Tac Ops in his car to come and pass on those comments. "Who the hell is that? I want to see him as soon as he lands." he was heard to exclaim.

For my breach of flying discipline I was grounded for two weeks and given the task of completing a Board of Enquiry into a marine craft accident. I learnt from that, not only about flying and tactics but also about the Marine Craft Branch, who proved to be a great bunch of guys.

You might think that that was the end of the story but not so. These things have a habit of resurfacing when you least expect them.

After I left Aden in September 1964 my next tour was as an instructor on the Hunter Operational Conversion Unit at Chivenor in North Devon. One of my responsibilities there was the running of the Forward Air Controllers' course. This was a course we ran, in conjunction with the Joint Warfare Establishment at Old Sarum, designed to train army officers (and others) to control or direct supporting attack aircraft onto specific ground targets. The first part of the course was all lectures at Old Sarum and then the practical bit, the actual controlling, was done at Chivenor and in the local low-flying area. To assist in continuity, I would attend the lecture week. On this particular occasion I had arrived in time to sit at the back of the room as the introductory lecture about what Forward Air Controlling was, and what it could achieve, was in progress. The lecturer finished and called for questions and comments. A hand went up towards the front of the class. "I have seen this in operation," said the voice. "Great," said the lecturer, "what happened?" "Well, it was in Aden about a year ago," said the storyteller. "We were involved in the Radfan operation and had been trying to clear the hills of troublesome tribesmen that dominated our main routes of access. We had great air support from the Hunters at Khormaksar." I started to take more interest, this was my sort of chap. "Yes," he said, "they supported us nearly all day and it was fantastic. Funny thing though, almost at the end of the day one of them called us on the radio and said that someone was firing at him from the hillside as he conducted his attack." The audience dissolved into much laughter. I sank lower into my seat.

I did speak to the gentleman concerned later in the bar and confessed to all that I had been the guilty party. We all laughed, had more beer and became more purple (joint service) in our outlook.'

Vic Cozens (Senior Aircraftsman)

Vic Cozens joined the RAF in June 1958 as a "Boy Entrant Airframes, 34th entry". His initial training took place at RAF Cosford, due to the Empire Games being held at Cardiff and their entry's intended accommodation at RAF St Athan being used by athletes. After eleven weeks they moved to St Athan.

'I passed out in December 1959 and was posted to RAF Honington on V-bombers; Valiants and Victors. Being quite small I spent most of my time there in the tank bay as a 'tank rat'. After two years I received the dreaded news that I was being posted to Aden, a location that didn't have a good reputation in those days. So, in March 1962, off I went to RAF Innsworth for a couple of days to get fitted out with KD. It was bitterly cold then and, as there was not enough fuel for the pot-bellied stove, the only form of heating in the room, several bits of furniture, etc., found their way into it (pity the poor inventory holder). I was luckier than those who travelled out by troopship as, after a few hours by coach to Stansted, we flew in a Britannia ("Whispering Giant") to Aden, stopping at Khartoum en route to refuel.

Vic Cozens expends minimal energy while assisting a photographer with the removal of a nose cone from an FR.10 (*Vic Cozens*).

Aden

I arrived at RAF Khormaksar on 6 March 1962 and was allocated to 8 Squadron; known as 'hate eight' I was informed. But I found it to be anything but. It was a great squadron. Good bunch of lads, always something going on, never time to get bored, lots of detachments to exotic places such as Bahrain, Sharjah, Masirah. Alright, maybe they were not so exotic but we enjoyed life to the full when there and we did get to Embakasi in July 1963: what a fantastic detachment that was.

I was billeted in Hunter block, one of the new more luxurious blocks when compared to the older ones. There were four men to a room and each room had air-conditioning. There was also a ceiling fan, which had its down side when someone got bored. They would throw a flip-flop or something into the blades, causing everyone to duck or get dinged by a flying object. The other good thing about Hunter block was that it was right next door to the Camel Club, so not too far to stagger back after a night on the "pop".

Time on the flight line passed very quickly as it was always busy. I can vividly remember one day, three weeks after I arrived, the station held an open day. After launching three Hunters we sat outside the line hut to watch the flying display when one of the three, XE607/Echo, failed to pull out of its dive and crashed on the opposite side of the airfield, killing the pilot instantly. What made things worse was that the pilot's girlfriend had been watching the display from outside the aircrew hut and saw it happen.

At the end of the day on the line, blanks and control locks were fitted to the aircraft. Our unofficial method of fitting the elevator and rudder locks was to stand on the seat of our old trusty Davy Brown tractor and slide them in place, instead of dragging steps out. I did not have a driving licence then but had had a few lessons. One day I was driving the tractor, locks at the ready, when someone yelled "look out, here comes Chiefy!" I slammed the tractor in gear and took off at top speed around the end of the line of aircraft and headed for the line tent and safety. However, the dispersal pan was a bit higher than the bondu where the line tent was located and the tractor dropped into the soft sand, making it extremely difficult to control. I found myself heading straight for the tent at what felt like 100mph but was probably only 15mph. The lads in the tent saw me coming and, with smoke and sand flying everywhere, made a rapid evacuation via all available openings. Luckily I stopped with inches to spare and legged it away from the steaming tractor. Phew, a close escape!

To the beach!

Although we worked hard in hot difficult conditions we did have time for rest and relaxation. Often a bunch of us would go to Conquest Bay to swim, as the NAAFI Club beach at Steamer Point was usually crowded. The taxi ride to Conquest Bay was not for the fainthearted as the road ran along the edge of a cliff at one point with a drop into the sea on the other. However, the beach was great, a major downside being the lack of shark

The view from a taxi crossing the bridge on the cliff-side road that led from Steamer Point to Conquest and Elephant Bays (*Ray Deacon*).

netting and one kept constant vigilance for 'snappers' (anything that could bite). One day we were swimming and messing about when the shout went up, 'Stingray', to which everyone performed their walking-on-water act. Once safely on the beach one of our group grabbed a spear-gun, intent on bagging this denizen of the deep. Inching into the water he fired and hit it, to great aplomb, but as he lifted the spear out of the water the stingray turned out to be a pair of coloured underpants! Never did find out whose they were.

On another day at the beach, we were throwing a ball around and some Lebanese guys joined in. As we packed up to return to base, they invited us over to Little Aden where they worked in the oil terminal. They had an excellent social club there which we visited several times and we invited them to the Camel Club in return. At times it was hard to understand each other's language but "cheers" is much the same the world over.

After I had been on the squadron a few months, Chalky "Belcher" White arrived. Having been my sergeant at Honington; he and his lovely wife Vi more or less "adopted" me. So once they settled in I received lots of invites

The beaches were popular leisure attractions for service personnel and their families. Elephant Bay is the location for this family snap portraying Vic, Chalky White, his wife Vi and her friend one afternoon in 1963 (*Vic Cozens*).

to visit them in their married quarter at Ma'alla Straight and enjoy family life. I recall lots of parties which involved filling the bath with beer and ice and having a good time. Our noisy goings-on were often drowned out by the din of car horns, marking a wedding when everyone drove up and down the straight hooting like mad.

There was one guy on the squadron who I will call "Fred" to protect his identity. Now Fred had a habit of taking pictures of well-endowed donkeys wherever we went. One day Chalky came into the crew room and bellowed out, "Fred there's a donkey outside with a camera: it wants to take your picture." The crewroom erupted with laughter. Sadly Chalky passed away a few years ago but all those who knew him will remember his immortal words, "Rot me Yogger!"

Bahrain

After a few months at Khormaksar I went on my first squadron detachment to Bahrain. On exiting the aircraft, a Britannia, I thought the heat that hit me was the exhaust from the turbo-props, but oh no,

Every Christmas, units across the Middle East took great delight in building their Christmas bars. The aptly named Wet Start Inn was 8 Squadron's artistic rendering for the December 1963 festive season while at Muharraq. The mural behind an amply stocked bar depicts the Squadron Gambia beheading the 208 Squadron Sphinx and 43 Squadron Cockerel (*Ray Deacon*).

this was the norm there and quite different to that in Aden. So as well as acclimatising once again, we had to get used to the everyday smell that hung in the Bahraini air.

A popular trip when up at Bahrain was to take a taxi to the oil refinery, followed by refreshments in the bar. They were very generous with their beer. I also remember as we passed through the workers' housing area, seeing a large open square with a huge TV set in the corner, still quite a rarity in those days. The workers would bring chairs out at night to watch the programmes.

On my last trip to Bahrain at the end of 1963 we should have returned to Aden for Christmas but had to extend the detachment and spend Christmas up there. In those days every section built a billet bar for the festive season, so we set to work and produced "The Wet Start Inn" which wasn't bad considering the short notice we'd been given. The mural behind the bar depicted the squadron emblem, a "Gambia" beheading the 208 Squadron Sphinx and the 43 Squadron Cockerel (The Fighting Cocks). Some of the other billet bars were real works of art and a prize was given for the best one. It was a great shame when they had to be dismantled. Whilst the bar was being built, the T.7 was despatched to get more drinks as there was not enough locally and, on its return, the crew (bless 'em) unloaded an RAF hold-all filled with bottles of gin. Now I know why I don't like the stuff. The ritual was to go from bar to bar and, once you had drunk enough, collapse on the nearest bed. On waking up, you'd start all over again.

On Christmas day a group of us went into Manama town, woke up a restaurant owner and asked if he would he knock up Christmas lunch for us. Well, he produced a curry so hot that it sobered us up. I don't think I have ever had a hotter dish.

Sharjah

During the Bahrain detachment we would move down to Sharjah for a couple of weeks for weapons' practice on the local range. There was nothing to keep us entertained at Sharjah apart from a few section clubs and the NAAFI. As each had a bar we used to have some great times there. On my first visit we drank all of the clubs out of beer. One of the squadron pastimes when on detachments was to collect objects as trophies and on this trip signs were the in thing and every sign that could be removed was removed. The station, however, took exception to this, especially on finding the station headquarters sign missing, so we were called together and told to put them back or else. We did escape with a special brick at the airfield entrance with the number of miles to England and Aden embossed on it. Someone had leaned out over the cab of the 3-tonner whilst the guard's attention was diverted and snaffled it.

On one trip to Sharjah I was carrying out an after flight inspection (A/F) on one of the Hunters. The drill was that once you had climbed into the cockpit the aircraft steps would be removed and taken to the next kite in line, leaving you to exit the cockpit by straddling the canopy and shutting it as you slid back onto the fuselage. Access to the ground from there was via the wing and the drop tank. I had just completed this manoeuvre and was opening the Sabrina panels underneath to check the nitrogen pressures when there was an almighty bang followed by the sound of breaking Perspex. On looking up I noticed the ejection seat drogue-chute swinging in the breeze. It had inadvertently fired off and pierced the canopy. I broke the 100-metres record as I dashed to the Engineering Officer, Owen Truelove, to report this, but I couldn't speak, only stammer and point, for the thought of how lucky I had been. A minute earlier I had been sitting astride that canopy. Phew, another lucky escape!

Dave Barnes, Ray Byatt and Taff Price are among the throng watching colleagues as they dig for liquid gold; the 'Slops' cans they buried earlier – somewhere. The photograph was taken during an APC at Sharjah in December 1963 (*Vic Cozens*).

On another trip to Sharjah a group of us volunteered to be taken several miles by truck into the desert, the objective being to test our map and compass reading skills by hiking back to base. Needless to say we had food and drink (Tennent's lager) aplenty. By luck or good judgement, we found our way to the coast and started on the trip back along the shore line. After a few miles a stop for lunch was made and some cans opened. Someone suggested burying the beer at the water's edge would keep it cool and although the sea looked mighty tempting, the sight of dorsal fins bobbing up deterred everyone from jumping in. Everything was going great until we decided to dig up some cans of beer and, to our horror, discovered that the whole cache was sinking in the soft sand. A vision of panic stations springs to mind as everyone fell down on their knees in an attempt to rescue the golden liquid. Fortunately, a number of Arabs were digging sand nearby so we borrowed their shovels and managed to rescue most of the beer. We lost a few cans, but as we left we spotted the Arabs digging a huge hole in the spot we had vacated, in the hope of finding a beer mine perhaps. A few miles further on we reached Sharjah Creek but we had to get across. A couple of the lads attempted to wade it but it was too deep so we talked one of the locals into sending a boat across for us. Great fun!

Embakasi

One of best detachments I ever went on was to Kenya in August 1963. Our Hunters operated from Nairobi Airport at Embakasi but we were billeted some ten miles away at RAF Eastleigh. A new experience was sleeping under mosquito nets, something which we didn't need to do in Aden. Pinewood was the main fuel for heating our billets and I still think of Eastleigh whenever I smell pinewood smoke. Naturally, there were lots of parties and late nights and we would often not get back to camp until the early hours, just enough time to get changed and catch the transport to Embakasi. Once the aircraft were prepped and airborne, it was time to grab a nap before their return.

SAC Merv Patterson had a contact there (he had contacts everywhere) who lent him a car, a huge Humber Hawk. This was put to good use touring round the area, although it was a tight squeeze with eight or nine of us in it.

Who can forget sitting outside the "Thorn Tree" sidewalk cafe at the New Stanley Hotel, supping a Tusker beer, watching the world go by and wannabe big-game hunters arriving. All life passed by there. On the subject of game, a couple of lads brought their chameleon mascots back to Aden and would walk around with them on their shoulders, great for zapping flies.

Transit

On trips to and from Aden and Bahrain we flew in either Britannia, Beverley (joy of joys) or Argosy transports. On one occasion our groundcrew departed Bahrain in a Beverley just as 43 Squadron's groundcrew were leaving Aden in an Argosy, both aircraft destined for Masirah where each unit's Hunters were scheduled to land for refuelling. However, as the Beverley was required for another tasking back at Bahrain as quickly as possible, the forty-three guys jumped into the Bev and flew off, leaving us to refuel and turn round two squadrons of Hunters and load up the Argosy. I often thought of the lads based at Masirah, a normally sleepy route station, when suddenly two heavy transport aircraft and two squadrons of Hunters arrive, men and machines everywhere. Station resources were stretched to the limit that day and I'm sure that once we had departed and the dust had settled, they collapsed in a heap.

Other memories

About once every two months each airman would have to do overnight guard duty, both in Aden and at Bahrain. It was quite spooky being out on the airfield sometimes on your own on a pitch-black night, walking around

When visiting RN carriers dropped anchor in Aden Harbour, RAF personnel were invited for group tours of these magnificent ships. This photograph of Sea Vixen FAW.1 XN705 was taken during a visit to HMS *Victorious* in January 1964 (*Vic Cozens*).

parked aircraft with only a .303 rifle as company. As the aircraft cooled down they would emit weird creaking and clicking sounds and you'd imagine all sorts of things. With your rifle came a belt containing fifty rounds (five rounds only in Bahrain) of ammo. You were very relieved when the second of your two-hour stints was up.

No sooner had our new Boss, Squadron Leader Tammy Syme, arrived than the number of beer calls/parties seemed to increase. I think it was Tam who introduced a party game called "Everybody Rumble" which involved making lots of noise, making signs and drinking lots of beer if you got it wrong. At one do it was suggested to him that we rename his aircraft; quick as a flash he replied that you are not calling my aircraft (coded B) Bol****s and that's that.

The long and the short! Merv Patterson demonstrates his opposition to the 3" above the knee rule as Taff Price reveals what he believes the rule should be (*Ray Deacon*).

In those days, when we still had a Navy, we were invited to visit aircraft carriers moored in Aden harbour and I recall making trips to HMS *Centaur* and HMS *Victorious*. I thought some of our aircraft showed signs of wear and tear, but they were in pristine condition when compared to the Fleet Air Arm aircraft, especially the Scimitars which had multiple metal repairs, skin patches and cracks that had been stopped and drilled. The Buccaneers and Sea Vixens were little better. Working and living conditions onboard a carrier were certainly hard; our line seemed positively luxurious by comparison, which of course it wasn't. Whilst the carriers were in harbour, some of their aircraft operated from Khormaksar and would often beat up the airfield before landing, very impressive.

Looking at the picture of Merv Patterson, wearing extra-long shorts, it looks as though he has lost his front teeth. Not so, he placed Mars-bar wrapping paper over his teeth as one of his party tricks which he used to raise a few laughs at dances. He loved to watch the reactions of girls when he asked them to dance and gave them a big cheesy grin.

We often used to go to the pictures and apart from the Astra on camp there was the Shenaz cinema at Ma'alla. The evening would be rounded off with a meal of shark or barracuda and chips at the kiosk outside – delicious.

It may sound like we drank a lot, but isn't that what is advised when in a hot climate? Finally, if the legend is to believed, I should at sometime get a recall to Aden as I never did climb Shamsan.'

Chris Cureton (Flight Lieutenant)

A pilot on 8 Squadron from 1962 to 1964, Chris recalls a landing incident he was involved in while on detachment at RAF Muharraq.

Who needs a nosewheel!

'On 23 May 1963 I flew FGA.9 XG255 on a simulated strike training flight somewhere over the Gulf. On return to the circuit with the rest of the formation I noticed that I had only two greens, the nosewheel indicating red. I tried the usual positive 'g' to help the hydraulics thrust it down but, when that did not work, I tried the emergency air bottle in case there was a problem with the hydraulics. That did not work either. By then my fuel was a bit low, but with an MEA Comet on long finals, I held off for him to land first. The landing was uneventful and I managed to lower the nose gently onto the runway. After shutting down I left the aircraft, nearly crushing a few fingers. As the electrics were off, I de-clutched the hood and pulled it back, forgetting the now very nosedown attitude, which caused the hood to very rapidly close again. I just managed to get my fingers off the front screen frame in time. Amusingly, when I climbed out, the Comet's captain was standing at the side of the runway with a thumb up.

The aircraft had only flown in from Khormaksar a couple of days before after major servicing. As it was now blocking the only runway, a team of airmen set about getting it clear, fitting ground locks to the main undercarriage and placing heavy lifting straps over the rear fuselage. Several of them then pulled down on the straps, raising the nose sufficiently for the line chiefy to lie on the tarmac and kick the nosewheel door free. It came down quite easily and, after a ground lock was fitted, the aircraft was towed from the runway. On inspection, no trace of lubricant on the nosewheel doors could be found. Little damage was sustained by the airframe and with a new nosecone and nosewheel door, XG255 was cleared to rejoin the flight line three days later.

Above and below: Two views of Chris Cureton's copybook two-wheeled landing at Bahrain on 23 May 1963. As the captain of the MEA Comet is being driven back to his aircraft (above), the 8 Squadron groundcrew (below) set about retrieving FGA.9 XG255 from the airport's single runway. Only minor damage was sustained to the forward fuselage and the aircraft was back on the line three days later (*Ray Deacon and Chris Cureton*).

A close shave

On 3 October 1964 I took part in a four-ship simulated strike with two other aircraft briefed to act as 'enemy' aircraft and to intercept us along the way. At the briefing we were told that the target was at 3,000 feet amsl and we would, therefore, have to carry out a non-standard simulated rocket (RP) attack by putting on full power on the pull up so that our speed at the top of the RP dive would be sufficient. Normally we left the power alone during the complete RP attack.

The flight to the target was uneventful, but on my pull-up I spotted the 'enemy' aircraft and reported their position to the rest of the formation. Then it was time to start my RP dive. I noticed that I seemed a bit steeper than the normal 25 degrees, so thankfully I decided to fire early, and start my normal 6.5g pull-out. However, almost immediately the control column seized and I had nowhere near 6.5g. I thought that the hydraulics had failed and I must be in manual flight controls. But the power control dolls' eyes were black and the hydraulic gauge showed normal pressure. However, the adjacent gauge was the mach meter, which read 0.94 increasing to 0.96 mach. Too fast! I throttled back and selected airbrakes and the speed dropped quickly and the aircraft started to pull out of the dive. The normal 6.5g pull-out got you out of the dive some 600 to 700 feet above ground, but I had a much closer view of the ground than that, probably about 200 feet maximum. Thank goodness I fired early. Still, not knowing why the aircraft had not pulled out properly despite the high speed, I flew back to base very sedately.

During our debrief we were told that the elevator jacks could only pull high 'g' below 0.84 mach, but why had I been so fast? Then one of the pilots asked if I had remembered to throttle back a bit at the top of the dive. There was the answer, I had been distracted during a non-standard attack by the two 'enemy' aircraft and dived with full power on. I think we all learned something from that trip.'

Ray Deacon (Senior Aircraftsman)

After passing out as a Boy Entrant "brat" from Cosford in December 1959, Ray Deacon's first two-and-a-half years were spent working on Vampire T.11s with the Central Flying School at RAF Little Rissington.

No, not the desert!

'In January 1962 the fast jet squadrons at CFS – Vampire, Meteor and Canberra – moved on a six-month detachment to nearby RAF Kemble while heavy maintenance work was carried out on the Little Rissington main runway. Shortly after the move, and while watching a pair of CFS Hunter F.4s taking off, I was called into 'Chiefy's' office and, having been on PWRs for several months, had an inkling of what I was about to hear.

He informed me that my overseas posting had come through and, yes, it was the dreaded Aden! My heart sank; how could they? Having entered 'Germany' three times when filling in my preferences and listened to countless horror stories from airmen who had experienced the place, the prospect of two years on a desert posting filled me with dread. Being a redhead who could not

The C-in-C Middle East Command, General Sir Charles Harington, enquires about life on a Hunter squadron with Ray Deacon during an inspection of Tactical Wing (*Ray Deacon*).

endure fifteen minutes under a British summer sun without burning, how on earth would I survive the heat of Aden. No point in dwelling on it, I thought; make the most of my final few months at 'god's little aerodrome'.

Cruise to Aden

To add insult to injury I would not be enjoying the luxury of a BUA Brit but would join an 'elite' group of thirty or so airmen aboard the HMT *Nevasa* on her last round-trip to the Far East. On around 10 April 1962, we slipped away from Southampton Docks at the beginning of our 'cruise', routing via Malta and Port Said. The voyage lasted ten days and, as this was deducted from the 730-day tour duration, going by sea did have one blessing. Having by-passed Gibraltar we docked in Valetta around mid-afternoon and were given an eight-hour pass, long enough to savour some of the the delights of the island's capital. Needless to say, most of the time after dark was spent in The Gut. All too soon it seemed, we were on our way and heading for the next stop, Port Said. Security difficulties prevented us leaving the ship but the locals, never wanting to miss an opportunity, came alongside in an armada of 'bum-boats' selling their merchandise. Once a deal had been

Local traders besiege the HMT *Nevasa* in their 'Bum' boats (above) during the ship's brief stop in Port Said, April 1962 (*Ray Deacon*).

struck, the goods were hauled up on ropes thrown up to occupants as they leaned out of the portholes. Their technique was to use a doubled piece of rope with a bag at the top end and the goods at the bottom; once a sum of money had been agreed and the cash placed in the bag, the goods were attached to the bottom – as the money went down the goods came up.

The following morning found us in the still waters of the Bitter Lakes, partway down the Suez Canal, together with a flotilla of merchant vessels spread at anchor while waiting for the passing of a northbound convoy. Egyptian Air Force MiG fighters took great pleasure in buzzing us, flying low and at high speed across the mirror-like surface. Some seventeen boring hours passed before the engines were restarted, the anchor raised, and we resumed our southward crawl down the narrow waterway.

Over on the east bank Arab labourers, working on widening of the canal, shouted and waved their arms in gestures of an obscene nature. A concerted deluge of foul language blasted back across the water from the ship and the exchange continued for a while until, bored by the proceedings, a number of Arabs lifted their clothing, exposing themselves to the audience watching from the ship. Throughout the voyage we were entertained by

The HMT *Oxfordshire*, sister-ship to the *Nevasa*, at anchor in Aden Harbour during the final voyage of a British troopship to the UK in September 1962 (*Ray Deacon*).

a continual stream of incoherent messages and instructions bellowing from the ship's tannoy in true regimental fashion, by a sergeant major. On seeing what was going on, he blasted out the command 'all officers, their wives and families move to the starboard side of the ship immediately and remain there until further notice', leaving the lower ranks to continue their exchange of unpleasantries with the locals. Apart from the accompaniment of a shoal of porpoises heading us down through a clear blue Red Sea and passing *Nevasa*'s sister-ship, the HMT *Oxfordshire*, heading in the opposite direction, the remainder of the journey was uneventful although noticeably warmer.

Sun, sand, heat and flies!

On disembarkation at Steamer Point, those destined for Khormaksar were taken by RAF transport to the airfield and assigned transit accommodation while awaiting their unit postings. Assigned to No. 8 Squadron, I moved into the aptly named Hunter block, one of three recently constructed and comprising twenty-one four-man, air-conditioned rooms on each of the three floors. With hindsight I need not have worried about the sun or the heat as, after an initial month or so of discomfort and 'moonie' image, I got used to it. "Don't forget to take your salt tablets", was the regular advice but, having disgorged my lunch over the bondu outside the mess after the first couple of pills, I gave them up as a bad job. Perhaps the most difficult aspects of

An early morning view of the 8 Squadron Hunter line photographed from a SAR Flight Sycamore in 1962 (*Keith Webster*).

getting used to life in Southern Arabia were the flies and being in a constant sweat, continually mopping one's face, arms and hands with a sweat-towel.

My tour in Aden was spent solely on 8 Squadron, a Hunter ground-attack unit based at RAF Khormaksar. Located at the eastern extremity of the airfield next to the civil airport, the squadron operated fourteen Mark 9 Hunters for fighter/ground attack, four Mark 10s for fighter/photo-reconnaissance and a couple of two-seat Mark 7 trainers. The other end of the pan was allocated to a second Hunter squadron, No. 208, equipped with twelve Mark 9s and a solitary trainer. Tasked with supporting a large number of diverse British and Arab army units in their pursuit of policing, not only in the Aden Protectorate, but the whole Middle East Command area, from Kenya, 1,000 miles to the south, to Bahrain Island, some 1,300 miles to the north, a heavy responsibility was shared by the two Hunter units.

Gulf crisis

Tranquillity was a rare phenomenon in Southern Arabia. At the time of my arrival, in April 1962, there was relative calm in much of the command area, most of the flying activities being devoted to training and familiarisation of new pilots in the operational arenas. Back in the previous July, however, things could hardly have been different. When General Kassim of Iraq aligned his forces along the border with Kuwait in readiness for invasion and capture of the lucrative oilfields, the British government ordered 8 Squadron to fly up to Bahrain, some 250 miles east of Kuwait, and prepare to defend the tiny kingdom in the event of an Iraqi attack. No. 208 Squadron, which at that time was based at Embakasi Airport in Kenya, was ordered to Bahrain to reinforce the British air defence and strike capability should the need arise. Several Canberra units were despatched from European bases to airfields on Cyprus and RAF Sharjah while a third Hunter ground-attack squadron, No. 43, moved from Leuchars to Cyprus, leaving the errant general in no doubt as to Britain's intent should he foolishly decide to cross the border. In addition, troop numbers in the Gulf region were rapidly reinforced with deployments from Europe and other Middle East Command bases. In the event, Kassim backed down and the situation gradually returned to normal – well as normal as can be expected.

Operation LONGSTOP

Concerned that a total withdrawal of British forces from the Gulf area would tempt Iraqi into making a surprise assault, the decision was taken to maintain a squadron of Hunters at Bahrain on permanent standby together with a pair of photo-reconnaissance Canberra PR.9s from 13 Squadron, Cyprus. In what became known as Operation LONGSTOP, aircraft and personnel from 8 and 208 Squadrons were rotated from Khormaksar to Bahrain on a bi-monthly basis and this had become the regular routine by the time I arrived. Every other month Hunters from one of the squadrons would depart Khormaksar for a two-month stint at Bahrain, the ground crews following on in a Beverley, Argosy, or a Britannia, if one happened to be in theatre. Although blessed with permanent sunny skies, the climate in the Gulf was noticeably different to that in Aden, being much hotter and humid in the summer, yet cool enough to warrant a change into working blue (uniform) in winter. During these eight-week detachments, the opportunity was taken for the squadrons to spend two weeks at Sharjah to make use of the air-to-ground range at Jeb-a-Jib.

Life on the line

Due to the intensity of the heat in the afternoon, the normal working day at Khormaksar was from 07:00 to 13:00, followed by lunch and a two-hour siesta. The routine could change at any moment, and often did when Hunter support was called for by Army units operating up-country. Assigned to the aircraft line as one of a handful of wireless mechs, my job was to ensure that the radio equipment on each Hunter was in good working order before and after each sortie. Inspecting the aerials on top of the fuselage required early mastery of a challenging technique when clambering onto the wing, if blistering of the knees on a baking-hot drop tank was to be avoided. The knack was to stand some ten paces back from the front of the wing, run at it and bounce one knee on the drop tank while hauling oneself up and onto the wing, using the saw-tooth leading edge as a handgrip. Everyone developed their own style and a mistimed leap made for good spectator sport as the unfortunate's body ended up in a crumpled, painful heap on the concrete pan. In a Bahraini summer, the metal surfaces were so hot that it was possible to fry an egg on a Hunter wing, one intrepid pilot taking twenty minutes to prove the point.

One of the hardest jobs as a radio mechanic was working out on the Hunter pan inside a cramped radio bay in temperatures which could reach 140 degrees F. The bay was so small that you could not turn or twist your body once inside. Changing one of the two 30lb VHF sets was not so much of a problem as they could be lowered on your shoulder as you lowered yourself down and out of the bay, but it was a different story once these 'lightweights' were superseded by a single, much larger, 56lb Collins ARC52 UHF unit. Changing one of those could be a real struggle, the sweat literally pouring down the legs, a contributing factor, no doubt, to our overall fitness.

The radio/radar guys may have had it somewhat easier than some trades, the armourers, engines and airframes guys in particular, as their jobs demanded spending much longer in physical contact with the aircraft. The energy and enthusiasm of the armourers in particular deserves a special mention, for it was their job to change gunpacks and load rockets with great gusto under operational conditions and during air-to-ground range sessions. Working in teams, each would try to beat the 'record' for changing the gunpack which, if I recall correctly, was a little over eight minutes. I thought I would try and help out once. Lowering the empty pack onto the trolley was quite easy but winching a fully-armed pack back up to the locking points was a totally different ball game. Nearing the top, arms aching, I ran out of energy and received some well-deserved stick for stopping, forcing the two armourers to await my recovery.

Flight safety

From the first day of training, the importance of flight safety is drummed into every airman. On front-line squadrons, where aircraft were regularly armed with live weapons, additional safeguards were imposed. The start-up procedure on a Hunter was straightforward enough, but an alert mind and an awareness of what was going on around you was important for one's self preservation. One airman was assigned to each Hunter and it was his job to check the area round the aircraft for clearance of ground equipment and that a ladder was attached to the aircraft as the pilot proceeded with his pre-flight checks. With the pilot seated in the cockpit, the parachute and ejector-seat straps were aligned over the pilot's shoulders and, when requested, his helmet and bone-dome were handed to him, before plugging the radio connector in to its socket. Finally, and again upon request, the ejector-seat safety pin was removed, shown to the pilot, and stowed in a pocket in the side of the seat. On climbing down, the ladder was removed and positioned in a safe place on the pan. A short wait then ensued as the pilot carried out his pre-start checks.

Once ready, the pilot gave a quick twirl of his forefinger and, having checked that everything was clear behind, the airman reciprocated the forefinger gesture. On the press of the start button the automated engine-start sequence began. When the highly volatile AVPIN fuel used to start the RR Avon 207 engines on the FGA.9 and FR.10 ignited, an acrid gas and flame was exhausted from a duct under the fuselage and, as this had been the cause of several starter-bay fires, the door was left open until the starting cycle finished. An asbestos glove was used by the airman to pat out any flames issuing from the duct. The door was then closed and the airman stood ready to remove the nosewheel chock before marshalling the aircraft out.

A 'phantom' on the trigger!

Folklore had it that sometime during the early period of Hunter operations in Aden, the cannon on an armed Hunter parked on the pan fired off several rounds across the Khormaksar runway, hitting the wall of the FRA barracks on the opposite side of the airfield. Fortunately, there were no aircraft taking off or landing at the time and no one was hurt in the barracks, but the outcome could have been quite serious. Reality soon dawned that no one was working on or near the aircraft at the time. A hasty investigation discovered that the excessive heat had induced a short in the gun-firing circuit. Under normal conditions, a microswitch, in the port undercarriage bay, broke the circuit between the invertors supplying power to the gun-firing circuit when the undercarriage was down, so the guns should not have been able to fire. As secondary protection, a modification was introduced whereby a safety plug was inserted into the same gun-firing circuit; the Master Armament Safety Break (MASB). Access to the plug was via a small panel under the port wing, directly behind the engine air intake. It became the responsibility of an assigned armourer to stand by the peri-track and disconnect the MASB on each aircraft as it taxied in and connect

To keep everyone on their toes, fire drills were carried out on the aircraft pans. In the view above, airmen rush to move the Hunters out of the way to allow firemen to spray foam at the source of the pretend fire as a SAR Sycamore hovers close by.

(below) When a pair of former Fleet Air Arm Seahawks passed through Sharjah while on their way to join the Indian Navy in November 1963, 8 Squadron personnel gave a helping hand to see them safely on their way. Here we see the aircraft (IN181 and IN184) starting up for the next leg of their ferry (*both, Ray Deacon*).

Armourers gather round a trolley laden with 3in concrete-headed practice rockets (above) prior to loading them onto the designated aircraft. In the background, an airman helps a pilot strap himself into FR.10 XE614-W.

(below) Chirpy chappies! Fred Rawson and Larry Forster enjoy their last day on the Khormaksar line before returning home at the end of their tours. The inscription on the drainpipe reads 'From Fred and Larry: goodbye Eight'. Fred never went anywhere without his mug of tea (*both, Ray Deacon*).

them when taxiing out. An order was also issued that armed Hunters must be identified by the placing of a red-painted ammunition box in front of the nose, attached via a short piece of rope to the top of the nosewheel door. Personnel were also instructed not to walk in front of armed aircraft.

Despite all the precautions, accidents still occurred and on one occasion a sergeant armourer, deep in thought, was walking behind the line of Hunters when he stepped directly into the jet blast of an aircraft about to taxi out. The force flung him across the pan, which in itself did not cause injury, but the side of his face quickly reddened and blistered. He was rushed to sick quarters for treatment and, on return to work a few days later, the 'toasted' half of his face was jet black, earning him the nickname 'black and white' minstrel, after the popular TV show of the time.

Time to relax …

After an afternoon's kip and with the heat of the day relenting, it was off to Steamer Point to haggle with shopkeepers in The Crescent, take a dip in the pool or make for one of the shark-protected beaches, or a game of tennis, football or rugby for the energetically inclined, before winding down with a can or more of 'Slops' (Allsops lager) in the Camel Club.

… but not for long!

The routine was forcibly changed in September 1962 when, following repeated strafing attacks by Yemeni Air Force MiG-15s on villages close to the Yemen border, the decision was taken for TacWing Hunters to fly dawn-to-dusk patrols along the border as a deterrent. With the quieter times confined to the past, and with one of the two Hunter squadrons on the Kuwait standby in Bahrain, it was left to the squadron at Khormaksar to maintain the border vigil. Pilots and groundcrews were split into shifts, one shift starting at 06:00 and finishing at 13:00 with the second overlapping from 12:00 to 19:00. As part the new routine, a pair of Hunters would take off at dawn and fly in a north-easterly direction along the coast, then inland until reaching the border before turning west to start their lengthy patrol along the mountainous, indistinct border before returning to Khormaksar from the north-west. Further pairs would take off at hourly intervals, thus ensuring that there was at least one pair in the vicinity of the border at all times. Fully-armed and equipped with long-range, 230-gallon underwing fuel tanks, a round trip took approximately an hour and a half. Additional Hunters were maintained on armed standby, ready for despatch at a moment's notice to support Army units operating up-country.

Pressure on both air and groundcrews during this period was intense, the high workload taking its toll on both man and machine. Aircraft unserviceability levels became critical for a while and with only half the number of pilots and airmen available for each half of the working day, temporary relief appeared with the arrival of eight Hunter FGA.9s on detachment from the UK, No. 1 Squadron arriving at Khormaksar in late October 1962. A new work pattern evolved whereby 8 Squadron started work at midday, continuing through to dusk on day 1, and from 06:00 the following morning until 13:00 on day 2. No. 1 Squadron started work at midday on day 2 and became the operational squadron for the next twenty-four hours. The system worked very well. After a month in the desert, its crews' tans suitably honed, 1 Squadron departed for home leaving 8 Squadron to revert to the split-shift system. In February 1963, 54 Squadron brought its Hunters out to Aden for a month's detachment, bringing short-term relief for 208 Squadron, 8 Squadron having moved up to Bahrain on Operation LONGSTOP. With the permanent transfer of 43 Squadron and its Hunters from Cyprus to Khormaksar in March 1963, Operation LONGSTOP was rescheduled with the squadrons required to move to Bahrain at four-monthly intervals.

Head for heights
Up in Bahrain the NAAFI was the hub of an airman's social life and many an evening was spent 'sipping' Tiger beer. On one particular detachment in December 1963, the 8 and 13 Squadron groundcrews merged for a Christmas Eve party at the end of which everyone was two-sheets-to-the-wind. Having staggered our way from billet to billet, offering our rendition of raunchy songs and doctored carols, which were not well received, we found ourselves at the foot of the station's 50-foot-high water tower. A challenge not to be rejected, we climbed to the top of the ladder and continued with the serenade. Within a few minutes a couple of 'Snowdrops' (service police) appeared demanding that we come down or face the consequences. A few choice words had the desired effect and they disappeared out of sight. On walking by the tower a day or so later, it dawned on us how lucky we were that none of us had fallen off the three-foot wide ledge encircling it; and there were no safety rails.

Dream come true!
Since my arrival in Aden, not a single airman had been offered a flight in a T.7. So, partway through a squadron bash, held at Bahrain in December 1963, SAC 'Taff' John and I took advantage of a the alcoholic cloud to ask Squadron Leader Tam Syme, our squadron commander, if it would be

All kitted up and ready to go, Ray Deacon gives XL613 a friendly pat on the nose before taking to the skies with Sid Bottom at the controls (*Ray Deacon*).

possible for airmen to experience a trip in a T.7. He said he saw no reason why not and that he would bear it in mind; he did not forget. Shortly after our return to Khormaksar, a policy of offering airmen a flight in the right-hand seat a few months before they became tour-ex, was implemented for which we were truly grateful.

In January 1964 'Taff' became the first 8 Squadron airman to savour the delights of a trip in a Hunter. On 14 February 1964, it was my turn and I achieved my dream of flying in the T.7. With Flying Officer Sid Bottom at the controls, XL613/Z took to the clear blue skies in the late afternoon. Keeping low, we flew north-east along the sandy coast line for a while, passing a customs post and village, before climbing to 10,000 feet or so for some aerobatics. Sid showed me how to loop and barrel roll before letting me loose. I'd been taught how to do both on Vampire T.11s by Pete Broughton, a QFI at CFS, so I had some idea of what was required. My efforts were not so successful this time but, nevertheless, it was fun and I enjoyed having a go.

Sid then suggested we try some 'wadi-bashing' which sounded exciting and so off we headed for the mountainous region towards the north of the Protectorate where the peaks rise up to more than 7,000 feet. My 'driver' knew the rocky escarpment like the back of his hand and we hugged the sandy valley floors, flying at around 500 knots, the steeply sloping cliff-like mountains rising high either side. I suspect the roar of the Avon would have echoed long after we had gone. I had been quietly hoping for a more sedate ride so as to take photographs and, on enquiring as to why we were flying so fast, exciting as it was, Sid calmly elucidated that it was to avoid being shot at. A plausible riposte and I settled back to watch in awe as we weaved in and out of the high-sided wadis. One vivid sight that appeared through the windscreen comprised a narrow, U-shaped rock formation jutting out

Above: The view looking over the nose of XL613 towards the forbidding mountains in the distance (*Ray Deacon*).

Below: Flying low and fast over up-country plantations, a hilltop fort suddenly appeared and quickly disappeared below the nose of the speeding jet (*Ray Deacon*).

from the walled sides, the narrow gap at the base allowing plenty of room through which to pass. Safely through, the valley floor dropped away some thousand feet or more. Down we went to continue our thrilling high-speed ride. In a blink of an eye we were out into the open, flying low and fast over a flat landscape endowed with a generous covering of green vegetation, as we continued south and homeward-bound towards Khormaksar. I asked Sid if we could climb up and fly round Shamsan in order to take some photographs of Aden and its extinct volcano and he kindly obliged. And so, at the conclusion of one of the most exhilarating experiences of my life, we touched down and I flopped forward into my harness as the brake parachute deployed and the brakes were applied. Thank you Sid!

The strike on Fort Harib – my tiny role

In one of several raids by Egyptian MiGs, a frontier guard-post and a village near Beihan were attacked with rockets and bombs by an armed helicopter and a pair of MiGs. Immediate retaliation was ordered by the British government and the Yemeni fort at Harib, some three miles north of the border, was selected for destruction. At 03:30 on the morning of 28 March 1964, we were rudely awoken by the dulcet tones of the duty sergeant, ordering us to report to squadron HQ immediately: no shaving, no washing, just get dressed and board the transport waiting outside. Fortunately, the rare sobriety of the previous evening meant that hangovers were few and, apart from lack of sleep, most of us had clear heads. As we were driven away, the realisation dawned that we had never been called out in the middle of the night before and that something special was about to happen.

On arrival at the pan, small groups of pilots could be seen talking to each other as they darted from one office to another. We were given no reason for the early call but 'Chiefy' called us together and told us to prepare seven FGA.9s (two as reserves) and two 1417 Flight FR.10s (one as reserve), as 43 Squadron personnel prepared five FGA.9s (one in reserve) for a joint TacWing operation. With pre-flight checks completed, those of us who were free assisted the riggers and armourers with the removal of the outer drop tanks and their pylons and fitting of additional rocket rails, a lengthy and fiddly task on the poorly lit pan. An hour or so later, rocket trolleys were towed along the back of the line and, while some helped with the mounting and connection of these high-explosive projectiles, others stuffed warning leaflets in the wing-flaps of the Mark 10s and two Mark 9s.

As dawn broke, the first two pilots walked out to the line hut and signed the F700s for their particular aircraft, Flight Lieutenant Peter Lewis for an

FR.10 and Flying Officer Sid Bottom, an FGA.9; both were fitted with HE gunpacks but no rockets were carried. Once strapped-in, they started up and taxied out for take off. I was assigned to start one of the eight main-force FGA.9s, this particular aircraft being flown by a youthful-looking Flight Lieutenant Martin Johnson. He was very excited and eager to complete his pre-flight checks, almost running up the ladder and jumping into the cockpit. I handed him his parachute and seat straps, waited until he was safely belted in, removed the ejection-seat safety pin and stowed it away before removing the ladder. At a given signal from Wing Commander John Jennings in the lead aircraft, eight pilots hit their starter buttons and seven Avpin starters burst into life, their Avons lighting up within a few seconds. Why seven? Sod's Law; if something can go wrong it will and it did. The starter on Martin's aircraft failed. Having applied a couple of hefty thumps on the starter-relay boxes with the handle of my screwdriver in the vane hope it might fire at the second attempt, I gave the signal to try once more, but again the starter failed.

In an instant, the straps were flying over Martin's shoulders and he was standing on the seat, helmet still in place, ready for the ladder to be re-attached. He clambered out and sped to a spare aircraft, with me in hot pursuit. As he clambered in, the other Hunters began to taxi and, between the two of us, he was belted-up in record time. Safety pin out, ladder away, a twirl of the forefinger and a welcoming blast from the Avpin starter, closely followed by the healthy roar of the Avon. It could hardly have reached idling speed before he throttled up and raced out onto the taxiway. By this time the others were accelerating down the runway on their take-off runs, while he must have reached a similar speed on his way to the threshold. Round the corner and on to the runway with Avon seemingly at full power throughout, then off he went in hot pursuit of the rest who were disappearing into the distant haze.

Did he catch them? Of course he did, and the attack was executed precisely as planned. Meanwhile, as Sid Bottom in the 'solo' FGA.9 flew fast and low over the target, he lowered the flaps to release the warning leaflets as the FR.10 took photographs as proof of the warning. By the time the fort's inhabitants realised what was about to happen, they would have had minutes to vacate the area or face the consequences. On arrival the main force went straight into the attack using both 30mm HE cannon and rocket fire, while the leaflet-carrying aircraft and the FR.10 maintained top cover. Once the attack was over and the smoke had cleared, the FR.10 made a final sweep to photograph the damage inflicted on the target.

Photographs revealed that the stone-built fort was virtually destroyed, as were a number of anti-aircraft guns and vehicles. So good were they that warning leaflets could be clearly seen lying in and around the fort. The attack had the desired effect; incursions by Yemeni aircraft ceased, at least for the time being.

The Shamsan myth

When asked, the vast majority of servicemen who experienced a tour in Aden said they never wanted to see the place again and over the years the myth that by climbing to the top of Mount Shamsan (1,800 feet) that wish would be granted had become engrained in the military psyche. A trek to the peak, therefore, became a must for many of those nearing the end of their tour. One quiet Sunday I was among a small group of 8 Squadron airmen to undertake the pilgrimage. There were various routes up the craggy escarpment but we decided to take the easiest and caught a taxi to Elephant Bay. After a short walk along a valley floor we found the well-worn track and climbed to the top without too much difficulty, pausing for a drink around halfway. As expected, the view across Khormaksar and the flat desert land towards the Yemen was adequate reward for our efforts. After a short break we made our way down the other side into Crater and caught a taxi back for a beer or three in a Steamer Point bar.

Made it! Jebel Shamsan, at 1,808 feet, the highest point in Aden State has just been conquered by 8 Squadron airmen Terry McNally, Taff Price, Ray Byatt, Taff John and Ray Deacon (*Ray Deacon*).

Recreation

For many people, one of their first thoughts on hearing that they had been posted to the Middle East was what on earth am I going to do to keep my sanity. They very soon found out that there was plenty on offer to keep them entertained, with activities ranging from swimming at one of the plentiful beaches, horse-riding, go-karting and gliding, to a wide variety of organised sports, including football, rugby, hockey, basketball, swimming and tennis. There was even a golf course to the north of Khormaksar airfield. Like many, photography was a keen hobby for me, the local environment and fascinating array of aircraft types offering a plentiful supply of subjects.

The privilege of wearing the 8 Squadron football team colours was really special for me and we were a successfull side. I cannot recall the team being beaten but well remember a hard-fought contest with the Parachute Regiment team while on detachment to Bahrain. Owen Truelove and Brian Watling were responsible for the design of our rather striking kit. The Khormaksar league consisted of teams from various sections on the airfield and, due to the squadron rotation system when each Hunter squadron was away on detachment for two months, there was a single team called Hunter Wing.

The all-conquering 8 Squadron football team pictured before a match at Bahrain in 1963. Back row, l to r; Jock Harman, Bill Sheppard, Chris Cureton, Geordie Hall, A.N. Other and A.N. Other. Front row, l to r; Tom Banks, Brian Watling, Owen Truelove, Ray Deacon and Taff Evans (*Ray Deacon*).

Having left Khormaksar for Bahrain with Hunter Wing placed firmly near the top of the league, it was somewhat disconcerting to find that, on our return, the team was languishing near the bottom. By the time the next detachment came round, we were back near the top.

Tour-ex!

All-in-all, with ten months in Bahrain, three weeks in Kenya to cover a rebellion by the country's army and a month home on leave, my two-year tour flew by and by April 1964 my time was up. The camaraderie and family spirit on 8 Squadron had made it a much more bearable experience than anticipated and, having survived the sun, heat, sand and flies, I could look forward to the sanctity of life back in the UK. Or so I thought. After two years in a faraway land where the locals spoke foreign, the beer was tolerable and the climate unbearable, my posting came through – RAF Valley on Anglesey – where the locals spoke foreign, there was no beer on Sundays and the climate was iffy. What had I done wrong?'

Mal Grosse (Flying Officer)

Mal Grosse, a pilot on 8 Squadron from July 1964 to May 1966, recalls his relief at walking away unscathed from a serious incident along with his

Mal Grosse pictured beside his Hunter at Khormaksar in 1965 (*Mal Grosse*).

recommendations for recuperating after such an episode.

Who needs wheels?!!

'On 5 August 1965, I was No. 2 of a four-ship simulated strike being led by Iain Porteous in the Wadi Meifa area. In a starboard turn at low level, I had a hydraulic failure warning, quickly followed by the controls going into manual. Accompanied by Iain, I climbed to high level for the return to Khormaksar and during the subsequent recovery to base I started my landing checks, which included blowing down the undercarriage with emergency air. The procedure involved a push 'n pull

94

Bearing the dual markings of 8/43 Squadron, ill-fated FGA.9 XE530 sits on the foam-drenched runway at Khormaksar following a wheels-up landing on 5 August 1965. As the groundcrew attach a lifting cradle, senior officers ascertain the position of the flying controls (*Mal Grosse*).

on the emergency undercarriage selector, which was fastened by a length of cable to a bicycle-type brake connector on top of the air bottle. Sadly, on the previous major servicing, the aforesaid connector had been left unconnected, and I found myself grasping the selector which was attached to a dangling piece of unattached cable. Fortunately the emergency flap lever was connected, and the inevitable wheels-up arrival on the 100-gallon drop tanks was relatively uneventful. I seem to recall that XE530 was repaired and back on the line during the following month.

The incident took place around lunchtime, and by mid-afternoon I was in the Tarshyne bar downing a quantity of freely provided Amstel, revelling in the adoration of the lovely BOAC ladies who had arrived from the UK that morning. The rest is for me to remember and others to guess.

Duuuuuck!!

In another incident, I landed with a 3-inch RP hang-up from a range sortie. I forgot to get the thing unplugged at the end of the runway, and taxied back to the pan with the firing lead still attached. Having shut down I casually walked back towards the line-hut where I heard this tremendous WHOOSH. One of the linies was unaware that the rocket was still electrically armed, and began his turnround checks. Putting on the cockpit battery master switch, the thing fired – and proceeded to cross the main runway at a fast pace, with a long plume of smoke – just in front of a Shackleton which was about to lift off. The armourer was fined a fortnight's pay by the Boss (Des Melaniphy, I think), and I was interviewed and reprimanded by the then Marshal of the RAF, Sir Michael Beetham – who, with an uncustomary wry smile, added that I would also pay the armourer's fine! This I did, but I can't remember his name.'

Tony Haig-Thomas (Pilot Officer)

The author is indebted to Tony Haig-Thomas and his publisher (Old Forge Publishing) for allowing him to use extracts from his riveting, tongue-in-cheek, book *Fall out Roman Catholics and Jews*.

As a young 21-year old pilot officer, Tony Haig-Thomas was posted to Aden in 1959, arriving at Khormaksar on a Comet C.2 on 6 May at the start of his two-year tour. Having 'marched' himself in at the relevant station sections, he reported for duty with 8 Squadron on the following day. Already an experienced pilot with several types under his belt, Tony was one of those rare pilots who experienced the transition from Venom to Hunter while on an active front-line squadron.

Day one and shot at – welcome to Aden

'On the morning of 7 May I awoke early, breakfasted and hastened on foot and in the heat to 8 Squadron. There I met Andy Devine, my flight commander, who had flown F-86 Sabres in Korea with the USAF and he took me up to see my boss, Squadron Leader Rex Knight, also a Korean War Sabre pilot. The squadron was equipped with eighteen Venoms and a pair of Vampire T.11s and shared a hangar with the Arabian Peninsular Reconnaissance Flight (APRF), which was equipped with four Meteor FR.9s and a T.7.

The squadron adjutant, Barry Wylam, brought some papers into the office and, being a curious type, when he and the boss went out for a moment, I had a look at some other papers on the boss's desk. The signal on top of the pile was to inform the squadron of my posting; on it the boss had written "who is this chap; do we want him?" Probably not was the answer, but dear me, I certainly needed them. My interview over, it was down to the crewroom to see if I could get someone to put me on the flying programme. "No," was the answer, so I went next door to the Meteor Flight to let them know that another Meteor-qualified, current, and instrument-rated pilot of exceptional ability had arrived. Their T.7 was serviceable, and not being flown, so Sam Small was authorised to show me the operational area. Soon we were airborne and heading north at low level down the winding road through the mountains that led to Dhala, an army camp on the Yemen border beyond and home to the baddies trying to destabilise loyal tribes in the Aden Protectorate on behalf of their communist paymasters. I found the low-level operational flying very exciting. Soon Sam pulled up and flew over some mountains further east to show me Al Qara, a pretty medieval town built on a pinnacle of rock. I had no idea that, later on, however pretty it might have been I would have to knock down one of the houses. We flew round it twice and then suddenly Sammie Small said, "Look at that bastard shooting at us from the roof of that house." In the back seat, and under a sudden and violent increase in 'g' loading, I was not sure that to do an aggressive low pass was a particularly good idea with someone actively shooting at us. Perhaps the baddie would run out of ammo before we got too close.

Venom debut

Two days later, and after another Meteor recce, Andy Devine put me down for an acceptance check in the Vampire T.11 and then he said I could fly the Venom. I flew the Vampire, passed a quiz on the Venom and was scheduled for a solo the next morning. The Venom was a pilot's dream. On my first solo I was the only one flying from the squadron as the other aircraft were being prepared for ops the next day. I completed my general handling including a compressibility run up to the Mach 0.88 limit, where it was just as twitchy as the little Vampire FB.5 on which I had trained, and then returned to the Khormaksar overhead for a practice flame-out landing. The sky was blue and the visibility unlimited, unusual for that time of year, as I set up my flame-out pattern at 12,000 feet. Suddenly I heard a pair of Venoms call for taxi; they were being flown by two ferry pilots from England to 208 Squadron, our sister unit in Nairobi. The pair got airborne and then, suddenly, I heard "Red Leader turning down wind for immediate landing." "Roger Lead do you have a problem?" replied the tower. "Negative, my ammo door has come open. I will land and have it closed." They were the last words he spoke; the aircraft flicked and spun in from around 600 feet; a huge pillar of black smoke rose up to me. I flew round it a couple of times at 10,000 feet and then, remembering that 8 Squadron had lost seven Venoms and six pilots in the previous six months, decided to do a nice wide, gentle circuit before landing.

That was not quite the end of the story as Andy Devine came out of our crewroom and, not aware that there were any Venoms in transit, saw one turning crosswind after take off then crash and burn. He knew that I was the only aircraft airborne so he ran up to the boss's office to tell him that the new pilot had crashed and was definitely dead. The boss rang the wing commander flying who told the group captain, at which point I taxied into the squadron's apron to everyone's relief – mine too. Perversely, one of the recent run of 8 Squadron 'fatals' had been caused by the same problem with the ammunition door. These two small panels just behind the cockpit

Impenetrable from ground level it may have been but Al Qara's lofty position on top of a mountain left it exposed to accurate bombardment from the air as can be judged from this photograph taken from an FR.10. The pilot, Roger Pyrah, wrote the words 'Dissident HQ and Arsenal' on the print (*Roger Pyrah*).

covered the ammunition tanks and were the only place for a pilot to put any belongings or clothes. I do not think, even today, that anyone knows whether the pilot stalled in the turn at nearly maximum all-up weight, or if the open door caused a breakdown of the airflow over the tail plane. If I had to guess, it would be the former as both Vampire and Venom, although fitted with wings of different sections, were very prone to violent departures at low speed.

Smile please!

One day we were briefed that some heavy machine guns had arrived at Al Qara and we were not to fly near the place. Unfortunately, Al Qara was a very picturesque town on top of a pinnacle of rock in the upper Yaffa district north-east of Aden and Manx Kelly, one of the APRF Meteor pilots, having just acquired a new Japanese cine camera, thought Al Qara would make a nice shot for the film he was making of flying in Aden. He throttled back, dropped one third flap and flew slowly past the town, cine camera in hand; his filming was rudely interrupted, however, and on landing it was found that he had thirty-eight bullet holes in his aircraft. The squadron engineering

A plume of smoke signals the beginning of the start-up sequence for this 8 Squadron Venom FB.4. The concrete-headed rockets were intended for use on the Khormaksar range but were sometimes pressed into used on live targets (*Aviation Bookshop*).

A rare colour photograph of an 8 Squadron Venom FB.4 flying high above the Arabian hinterland (*Peter Goodwin*).

officer said that the aircraft was to be written off but the group captain overruled him as it was his favourite Meteor and, in spite of the 400 man hours required to repair it, repair it they must. Eventually, three months later it was done and Manx took off for an air test which, naturally, included a lot of low flying, that is until he collided with an Egyptian vulture, which finally did for the aircraft what the thirty-eight bullets had failed to do and the aircraft was scrapped.

Dodging the flak

There were many variations to our day-to-day operational flying. We used methodology transposed direct from the NW Frontier of India, a very similar wild terrain, and with an equal amount of misplaced hope that dissident tribes could easily be brought to heel with a demonstration of airpower. Most of both protectorates were peaceful but the wild men in the hills were more or less untouchable. Anyone who was operational in Aden knows that the contemporary hunt for Osama bin Laden was doomed to failure unless he was betrayed, the Afghan-Pakistan border being a carbon copy of the Upper Yaffa district in Aden. I have mentioned flag waves but we also dropped leaflets to tell residents of a village that so and so's house would be knocked down the next day. This triggered a standard response with the doors being taken off the house, as wood in South Arabia is scarce and valuable. The appointed hour would see most of the village guns ready for the first drive of the day – the arrival of the Venoms. Hundreds of rounds would be fired at each aircraft as it made its precision attack on the designated house and holes were frequent in our aircraft. At one stage our squadron had twenty-two Venoms and in two days eighteen of them had small-arms damage; if I hadn't seen it for real I wouldn't have believed that a jet aircraft could take as much punishment as they did without any effective damage.

One day they got lucky. Andy Devine and John Morris were knocking down a house at good old Al Qara when Andy heard "Red 2 I have been hit." Andy enquired as to whether John could finish the job with one more pass, assuming it was just the usual bullet hole, and was surprised to hear "Negative Lead, I have lost control of my engine and am bleeding quite a lot." A lucky round had come through the cockpit, severing the throttle and high-pressure cock control runs, and then passed through the top of his shoulder before stopping in his parachute. Luckily, John had 9,000rpm set and this was sufficient to clear the mountains and return to Khormaksar where he flew round and round until his fuel was exhausted. He was then able to carry out a flame-out landing, as with no HP cock control, he was unable to shut down the engine; the LP cock was unusable by him as it was on the floor of the left-hand side of the cockpit and his bullet wound was in his left shoulder.'

The Hunter arrives
Following a six-month stint as station adjutant at RAF Salalah, some 600 miles north of Khormaksar, Tony returned to Aden and a squadron fully re-equipped with Hunter FGA.9s but mourning the loss of two pilots.

T.7 fatality
'On 1 June 1960 Andy Devine, who was due to go home shortly, and had been posted to a ground job in the UK (as flight commander at a recruit school which must have pleased him), kindly asked John Morris and me if we would join him and his wife April for dinner. I had had a good day and at last flown two sorties in our twin-seat Hunter with John, so we much looked forward to a social evening with April and Andy. John and I arrived at 19:30 but Andy had not turned up as the squadron had been night flying, so April gave us a couple of drinks and we waited. Suddenly there was a knock on the door and the Station Commander appeared; he said nothing

to us, but John and I, realising that this was not a social call, left at once. Andy was dead.

One of the new pilots, Mike Walley, had been having a dual night check and both he and Andy were used to flying the much higher performance Hunter FGA.9. They had climbed to what would have been 20,000 feet, by time, in the Mark 9 single-seat aircraft but was, in reality, only 10,000 feet in the T.7. Aden nights are dark and altitude can in any case only be determined by reference to an altimeter. Misreading of altimeters by 10,000 feet was very common indeed in the Hunter era and came about due to the mismatch of power between the single-seaters, which were flown all the time, and the trainer version with the smaller 100-series Avon, flown very seldom. The standard let-down in those days was to home overhead at 20,000 feet, be given an out-bound heading which was then followed by a steep descent to half the start height plus 2,000 feet. Hunter T.7 XL615 started its descent and called "Turning left in-bound at 12,000 feet." A few seconds later there was a big flash in the desert as the aircraft buried itself in the sand and exploded. It had actually been at 2,000 feet when it started its turn, and not 12,000 feet.

Rhodesian detachment

The squadron was being sent to Rhodesia on a deployment, via Nairobi, to Gwelo, a Royal Rhodesian Air Force station some 300 miles south of Salisbury. Paralysis had set in as a great deal of work is involved in deploying an entire fighter squadron, including of course spares and engineers, some 2,000 miles and so no-one was particularly interested in getting me airborne, except myself. "Starry" Knight, the squadron CO, had decided that I needed a dual check before I could fly a Hunter again and that, as I was out of practice, I should fly down to Rhodesia in a Beverley of 30 Squadron with the ground crew. I was elated as can be imagined.

A most memorable flight

Back in Aden, I was briefed to take two Hunters up to Bahrain and bring two very tired aircraft back to Aden, refuelling at Sharjah each way. It was one of my more memorable flights. Tim Seabrook flew as my No. 2 and we arrived at Bahrain and night-stopped. The next day, fully fuelled, we left for Sharjah and, having more fuel than we needed, flew low-level to burn it off. All RAF low sorties are flown at 420, 480 or 540 knots representing 6, 7 or 8 nautical miles a minute. I went for 480 in crystal-clear conditions at 4,000 feet. Qatar appeared, looking exactly like the map, and we passed across its northern tip. Whenever I see a map of the Persian Gulf today I remember that sortie. We landed at Sharjah, refuelled, and departed high level for the nearly 1,000-mile flight to Aden via overhead Salalah and thence down the coast 600 miles to Aden. We settled into the high-level cruise over the great rolling red sand dunes of the empty quarter of Arabia. It is called the Empty Quarter because there is nothing, absolutely nothing, there and I sat marvelling at the silence and beauty of the scene with Tim a mile abreast of me. Suddenly, in my headset, I heard a click, just that, a tiny electronic click. Thinking it might be a 'doll's eye' magnetic indicator on the fuel panel I glanced down and saw to my horror that I had lost transfer pressure from my right-hand fuel tanks; worse still, as I looked, there was another click and the left-hand doll's eye showed a left-hand fuel failure. I had 1,300lb of usable fuel in the main collector tanks until I flamed out and then I was dead. I pressed the transmit button, "Hey, Tim, I have had a double transfer failure." Back came the words forever etched in my mind, "Sooner you than me, mate." There was nothing I could do except wait for the flame extinction followed by my own, from thirst, a couple of days later in those great red rolling sand dunes. Tim said nothing and then with my fuel down to 600lb I heard another click, the right-hand fuel system started pumping fuel back into my main fuselage tank; it failed again. Then the left side started feeding and I flew back to Aden with a stream of transfer failures and recoveries. When I got home the engineers said that there was insufficient pressure to transfer any fuel and were surprised that I made it. So was I.

Knocking the house down

During this time minor political troubles erupted, leading to minor military operations. An area had been proscribed west of Ataq due to bad behaviour by the locals. I was leading a pair and the proscription seemed to be working: there was not a camel, goat or man to be seen. Then, right in front of me, was a camel. I turned hard left through 360 degrees, my No. 2 following, sighted on the camel and touched the gun button. As soon as I had fired I pulled up and around to see what had happened. The camel was nowhere to be seen, and then I saw a huge red circle where the camel had been and now wasn't. That big red circle has remained with my conscience ever since.

On another occasion there had been trouble at Al Qara, again, and Manx Kelly and I were briefed to knock down a house. Leaflets had been dropped the day before to avoid human casualties, the wooden doors removed to avoid financial loss, and the village guns lined up to enjoy the sport. Until around ten o'clock there is little wind in up-country Arabia, making it ideal for a gun attack, as our trusty rockets were not accurate enough to guarantee precision work. Manx and I got airborne and headed north, eventually swinging into a large fast orbit to ensure that we had identified the correct house. Once satisfied, Manx turned in but, just as he was about to fire, a great ball of white appeared from behind his aircraft followed by a long white trail stretching for a mile behind. I called "Red lead you have been hit," and found that he had had no idea. I tucked up in close formation and saw that the whole of the back end of his right drop tank was missing but no other damage. The white trail was fuel being sucked out of his wing tanks. Manx said that we would finish the job with one pass, turned in again followed by me at around a mile, not wishing to put my gunsight on my leader. Manx had fired-out so I put the fixed cross well above the house to allow for the gravity drop at extreme range, assumed no wind, and dumped a full war load in one pass, and was enormously pleased and slightly surprised to see my rounds on the target. Manx called me to rejoin and we headed south; suddenly he called me into close formation and accelerated, then, applying 'g', he pulled into a loop, then another one and then a barrel roll. I had flown my first formation aerobatics while staring at a big black hole that was all that was left of my leader's 80-gallon tank.'

Mo 'Noddy' Hawkins (Junior Technician)

Noddy Hawkin completed his training as an airframe fitter at RAF Halton in 1965 and headed for his first posting with 229 OCU at RAF Chivenor.

Middle East memories
'My twelve-month unaccompanied tour in Aden and Bahrain during 1967/68 enabled me to continue my love affair with Sir Sidney Camm's Hunter. It continued for another ten years when, on my return to the UK, I was posted back to RAF Chivenor. When that station closed in 1974, I moved with the TWU Hunters to RAF Brawdy.

My earliest memory of Aden was stepping off the British United Airways VC10 into the wall of heat that was RAF Khormaksar. Having spent just over a year on 229 OCU at RAF Chivenor, it was inevitable,

I suppose, that I should join the Hunter SSF at Khormaksar, servicing the FGA.9s which at that time carried a combination of 8 Squadron and 43 Squadron markings. My job was scheduled servicing of the Hunters, and one abiding memory is standing in the cockpit of a Hunter in the SSF hangar when terrorists blew up a Vickers Viscount of Aden Airways on the adjacent pan. The aircraft was parked no more than 200 yards from where I was working – one minute it was there and a second later it disappeared in an enormous explosion. Wreckage flew in all directions, including a large panel that arced over the fence and landed yards from where we were working. The explosion was followed by Aden Airways' crews running around, starting up the engines on the DC-3s parked nearby, and taxiing them away from the burning wreck.

During the six months I was at Khormaksar, the time was divided on several detachments to the route stations at Sharjah, Masirah and Salalah. It was during a Sharjah detachment that, while on MASB duty at the end

The aftermath of an explosion that destroyed Aden Airways Viscount VP-AAV on 30 June 1967. The aircraft had been taken out of service for an engine change and subsequently placed in quarantine for twenty-four hours just in case a bomb had been sneaked on board when it was in the hangar. Clearly the security measures then in place were totally inadequate. Debris from the explosion landed on the Hunter pan but no aircraft were damaged or personnel injured. The Aden Airways DC-3 VP-AAS on the left of the photograph had been quickly taxied out of harm's way by one of the airline's pilots (*photographer unknown*).

of the runway, a Hunter FGA.9 landed rather heavily in front of me. Once it had back-tracked up the runway, I ducked under the port wing to pull the MASB safety plug, and realised that I could see daylight through the top of the undercarriage bay; the landing in fact had been so heavy that the undercarriage had been forced up through the wing, cracking the main spar and wrecking the pintle housing at the top of the leg. The engine was shut down and the aircraft towed, very carefully, back to the hangar for major repairs. I remember thinking to myself as I fitted the ground lock to the port undercarriage jack, out on the runway, "Why am I bothering to do this?"

I remember, too, stepping off a Blackburn Beverley at RAF Masirah, as a large gang of local Arabs crowded excitedly round the front of the aircraft. Moments later, the propellers were slipped into reverse pitch by the pilot and the crowd disappeared in a huge sandstorm, emerging coughing and spluttering as the aircraft backed slowly away from the edge of the 'bondu'. Whilst on the subject of the Beverley, I wonder if anyone else has sat in the front seat of the tail-boom cabin on one of these aircraft and been frightened to death as the flaps are lowered by the huge electrical actuator located on a spar, just feet from your head.

When Khormaksar closed in the autumn of 1967, I moved with the Hunters to RAF Muharraq, up the Gulf on Bahrain Island. Now the Hunters belonged to 8 Squadron alone (43 Squadron having disbanded, only to later reform on the Phantom) and we worked from a building alongside 208 Squadron, also flying FGA.9s. My one claim to fame here was to paint a huge squadron badge, complete with the yellow, blue and red bands, alongside the 208 Squadron one on the blast wall protecting the squadron building from the routinely-armed Hunters on the line. I have a single black-and-white photograph of this masterpiece, taken when it was only partially painted, in which one of my colleagues has chalked on the wall his not-too-flattering translation of the squadron motto, *Uspiam et Passim* (something about "You play ball with me and I'll shove the bat ...!"). The lettering was only about two-inches high, but my wife managed to read it when I subsequently showed her the photograph. I often wonder what happened to the paintings and wonder if they are still there. My other abiding memory of Muharraq was the chance to go flying in one of the squadron's Hunter T.7s, XL612. We flew for nearly an hour, most of it in formation with an FR.10 which took photographs of our aircraft. My one regret was not having my own camera with me; the chance of the flight came at a moment's notice and my camera was back at the block. I have always considered the Hunter to be a fantastic

One of the photographs taken from an FR.10 depicting Noddy Hawkin's flight in 8 Squadron T.7 XL612-T (*Noddy Hawkins*).

looking aircraft, and when one is flying yards off your starboard wing, it takes on a whole new dimension, a real object of beauty. But I do have some pictures of me in the T.7, taken by the FR.10, a permanent reminder of my first flight in a Hunter trainer.'

Brian Hersee (Corporal)

An armourer by trade, Brian was posted from 54 Squadron at West Raynham to Muharraq in September 1967 for his tour on 8 Squadron in Bahrain.

'At that time we were given the choice of a straight twelve-month tour or thirteen months with a month's UK leave, so I did eight months and four months. I had already spent three months on detachment in El Adem and Gibraltar defending the Rock against the Spanish that year.

Initially I was assigned to the armoury but moved onto 8 Squadron just in time for a detachment to Sharjah, along with 208 Squadron, for an Armament Practice Camp (APC). Our departure freed up space on the tarmac at Muharraq for aircraft participating in the withdrawal from Aden. No. 208 started their APC as we finished ours.

One of the problems encountered on the Hunters was that they were nearly all at different armament control modification states. To help overcome this, we kept a log of these mod states, so that we could advise

Dutch Holland is the pilot seated on the left, Rick Howse (on loan from 208 Squadron) sitting on top of the ladder and Brian Hersee is the taller of the two airmen standing in front of the intake in this view of 8 Squadron members at Sharjah on 23 February 1968 (*Brian Hersee*).

pilots as to which switches did what during their pre-flight walk rounds. Unfortunately, this did not prevent the occasional accident from occurring.

EMRU

In simple terms, the Electrical, Mechanical Release Unit (EMRU) was an electrically- or mechanically-operated bomb-release mechanism. The unit only released the store from the carrier, air pressure being used to propel the store away from the aircraft. If operated when the aircraft was on the ground, the store would just drop to the ground under the force of gravity.

ERU

An Ejector Release Unit (ERU) was a device that used a cartridge to eject a store away from an aircraft pylon with a great deal of force. The Hunter ERU was a single-piston device which protruded out from the wing directly above the pylon. ERUs were installed in the outboard pylons of the Hunter for use with the SNEB rocket pods mod.

During our detachment, a 208 Squadron armourer named Barney sustained serious injuries while preparing a Hunter for a sortie using practice bombs on the range. As he was preparing the aircraft, which was equipped with EMRUs in the outer pylons, it went unserviceable and he was given the hurry-up to prepare another. This one was fitted with ERUs. In trying to hurry, he forgot to unplug them so that when the bomb test was carried out, the ERU performed as designed. During the test an armourer had to lie under each bomb carrier and close a series of micro-switches. Both Barney and a second armourer on the other wing were struck by the carriers as they were blasted vertically downwards. Barney's skull took a direct hit from the ERU piston and his life was only saved by the actions of one of our pilots who had trained as a doctor in South America.

The 1968 Sharjah detachment was specifically geared to training some of our FGA.9 pilots on the FR.10 and was probably one of the most enjoyable but hardworking detachments I ever did. Starting early and finishing late, and with no time to spare, we made our own sandwiches in the line tent at lunchtime. Our flight sergeant would book late meals for us every night, but as the aircrew brought a crate of beer for us most nights, we were often late getting to the Mess.'

'Mac' McLauchlan (Flight Lieutenant)

'Mac' McLauchlan served his tour in the Middle East as a Hunter FGA.9 and FR.10 pilot on 8 Squadron from 1961 to 1963.

Ferry to Kemble
'During the latter part of my tour, I was detailed to lead three squadron FGA.9s back to the UK for refurbishment and, as was the norm for these long flights, the ferry was not without incident. I was allocated XF455/T with Dave Edmonston flying XJ687/E.

We chose the southern route via Khartoum, El Adem, Malta, Orange and Lyneham. In the early 1960s the first three stops were all at RAF bases, while Orange was a French Air Force fighter station with an RAF groundcrew detachment. Maps prepared with tracks, distances and times, the next task was to air test the Hunters for fuel burn with all the underwing stores. As internal fuel was a mere 400 gallons we needed all available external fuel from two 230- plus two 100-gallon drop tanks, a total of 1,060 gallons, enough for 3.25 hours flying given careful flying. This would be needed as the longest planned leg was three hours from Khartoum to El Adem over the Sahara desert. Fuel costs were generally unimportant in the Middle East, so an air test with full load was flown which proved that one of the internal tanks had a leak; the tank was replaced and, after a series of tests lasting over three hours, XF455 was cleared for the ferry.

Aden is never cold; even during the Cool Season temperatures match a summer in the Med. However, North Africa and Europe were very different, especially as the winter of 1962/3 was to become one of the coldest on record. My gallant companion ignored any advice and packed his KD uniform. Being rather more cautious I squashed a blue uniform into my flightbag. The only luggage space in the Hunter was in the unpressurised radio bay. This was shared by the battery, so any leak would leave small burn holes in the unsuspecting pilot's bag and contents. Anti-G suits were not worn for such a long ferry, but folded on the seat as a rudimentary en route massage when pressing the test switch, as three hours on a hard dinghy pack was not very comfortable.

Settting off

We left at first light. As I walked round my aircraft for the external inspection my ground crew chief said "please don't kick the tyres sir, she's serviceable", so I didn't, as old XF455 showed the wear and tear of two years' operations in a harsh climate. The first sector was from Aden overhead Asmara in Ethiopia to Khartoum, a two-hour twenty-five-minutes flight, with a brisk low-level portion along the White Nile to bring us within landing weight; the Hunter with all the external tanks went from too heavy to low fuel in a surprisingly short time. Transit with refuel and sandwiches went pleasingly to schedule, our intention being to reach El Adem before dark; no pilot enjoyed night flying in the Hunter without landing lights and with dim cockpit lighting. In the event this was to prove an aim too far. Although we had arrived in Khartoum without difficulty, departing was to prove less easy. RAF Khartoum was there to service Transport Command aircraft on their way to East Africa and Aden; thus our RAFAIR callsign was considered a transport flight, so the obvious presence of two warplanes on their tarmac produced an official objection from the Sudanese authorities which took diplomacy an hour to overcome. Eventually clearance was given to depart, starter master switches to ON, the avpin starter motor gave its usual high-pitch scream as the RR Avon lit up and we were on our way once more, now too late to reach El Adem in daylight. Heavy weight at over 20,000lb required a long take-off roll, rotation at around 150 knots with a lift off nearer 170 made close formation take-off an interesting exercise. Normal climb to 40,000 feet was 430 knots to M. 0.85, then maintaining a constant mach number of O.87 allowing the aircraft to climb to 45,000 feet as weight reduced.

Skirting Egypt

The direct track from Khartoum to El Adem was unavailable as it would have meant crossing a slice of Egypt, at that time no friend to the UK, so we routed via a point in the desert known as Nasser's Corner, which meant a dogleg, thus extra time and distance. This last was a major consideration, as a three-hour sector meant reaching our destination rather short of fuel, just fifteen minutes to dry tanks on arrival, assuming all went well. Cheered before leaving Aden that a Canberra from El Adem would be available to provide guidance over the desert turning point, we were less cheered by the news on leaving Khartoum that the said Canberra was still on the ground and likely to remain there all day. In typical single-seat fighter-pilot mode, we thought the likely reason was that the two navigators in the crew were unable to agree their position.

Cruising at M.0.87 at an altitude of 22,000 feet, breathing 100 per cent oxygen, no autopilot, no navigation aids, and no radio contact other than the wingman flying some 800 yards abreast, was of the least concern to us at the time, until passing Nasser's Corner, near Jebel Uweinat. We had used up the fuel in the outboard 100-gallon drop tanks and were cruising steadily at altitude when Dave "Loddy" Edmonston called on the radio to

A photograph taken by Mac McLauchlan of XJ687 over Libya immediately after Dave Edmonston had dropped the outer pair of 100-gallon tanks (*Mac McLauchlan*).

say that fuel was not flowing from one of his 230s. Without it, he would not make El Adem and would have had to eject once his fuel ran out, so it was unlikely he would reach El Adem before bar closing time. In those days I carried a camera in the cockpit, so offered to take a photo when, as looked inevitable, he decided to eject. He seemed unimpressed by my offer. However, before reaching this point, using what today is known as crew resource management, a rapid look at *Pilot's Notes*, and a brief discussion of the problem, a decision was reached. He would jettison his now-empty outboard 100-gallon tanks in the hope that the pressure surge would encourage the bigger inboard tank to feed. So off into the desert went the two phenol plastic tanks, in time for me to take a photo of the Hunter now flying on the inboards plus internal fuel. To our mutual, and his vast, relief the plan worked, the fuel started flowing correctly, and we were both now sure of reaching our destination by air.

The fickle finger of fate

Fate has a way of catching one out when all seemed comfortable. On contacting El Adem, with clear skies, we were cleared for a high-speed descent from our 45,000-feet cruise in the remaining daylight, direct into the deepening dusk of the airfield. As a considerate leader, I sent my wingman into land first, then followed some fifteen seconds behind. Landing checks in the Hunter were simple: air brake IN, indicator BLACK, undercarriage DOWN with 3 GREENS, then there was suddenly no point in continuing with the checklist or the circuit as the green lights remained obdurately out. A quick prod at the indicator showed that while the lights were working the undercarriage was not. Hawkers had kindly installed an emergency air bottle for such contingency, with a less kindly side effect. Once used, although the wheels would extend, all hydraulic fluid was lost, the result being a landing without power controls and only one flap selection, full down for landing. This was probably all my fault for having offered to photograph my chum in distress; one never learns to beware the fickle finger of fate until too late. So ATC was informed, the emergency services trundled out to meet a Hunter which, though not in distress, was certainly fatigued, as was the pilot.

It took three days for repairs, the weather grew increasingly colder, but, eventually our refuelled and repaired aircraft were ready to continue the adventure. A third ferry Hunter from our squadron, XE651/M with Pete Loveday at the controls, joined us for our onward leg to Malta. He had flown from the Gulf via Cyprus and would continue as our number 3 to the UK. El Adem to Luqa was a fairly short flight, low level to Benina,

Mac McLauchlan walks out to his aircraft, FGA.9 XF455-T, at El Adem at the beginning of the next leg of the ferry trip, to Malta (*Mac McLauchlan*).

then on to Malta before dark in a little over two hours.Third to land on the south-west runway, touching down at 130 knots, I saw the other two Hunters taxi off at the top of a marked slope, so it seemed to this rather unobservant pilot that they had reached the end and were waiting for their leader. Not a sound assessment, as on touchdown the brake chute promptly fell off its attachment, the anti-skid brakes were already worn to limits, and my aircraft surged relentlessly towards what I thought was a cliff, the sea and the end. I cut the fuel, mentioned the stopping problem and sat tight. My chums heard my call of brake failure, saw the chute was missing, and kindly pointed out that there was still plenty of tarmac ahead, as indeed there was once I had breasted the hill, so a quick restart was in order to avoid the humiliation of being towed and, breathing a sigh of relief, I led the formation into dispersal. The local Canberra crews were watching the arrival of three Hunters in their usual critical fashion, so it would have been very bad form to have run off the end in a crumpled heap.

One night in the transit officers' mess at RAF Luqa could have been compared to the Black Hole of Calcutta, though not as comfortable. Our local overseas allowance was a handful of British coins, Malta being

Mac McLauchlan, Dave Edmonston and Pete Loveday (left to right) pose for the camera at Luqa, Malta, on 9 December 1962 (*Mac McLauchlan*).

considered cheaper than Aden, so a quiet and sober night was spent in the bar planning our next leg to Orange in France.

Stopover in France

The Hunter could have reached Lyneham, just, from Malta, given a fair wind, or so the planning tables seemed to indicate. However, a refuelling stop in France seemed preferable to arrival over England in winter weather low on fuel. The old adage that a pilot may worry about the weather or the fuel state, but never the two together, seemed good to us, so did lunch in Orange as we arrived there in a little over two hours from Luqa. The Armée de l'Air squadrons flew Mystere IV fighters, similar in performance to our Hunters, and made us welcome with an excellent lunch. Fresh bread was a rarity in Aden, as was the French habit of a modest glass of red wine with lunch. We followed their example, not unreasonably, only to be accosted by an RAF wing commander, immaculate in No.1 dress, curious about the presence of three junior officers in shabby tropical flying kit with equally shabby Hunters now parked alongside his shining scarlet Heron of the Queen's Flight. Our account of why and where was accepted with obvious reservations about an excellent lunch with our French friends. Clearly in his opinion fighter pilots were an unreliable lot. He may have been right: five days down-route with two days of clean laundry meant we were far from being as smart as the CO of the Queen's Flight. We never learned why he was in Orange and he didn't enlighten us. With three Hunters serviceable for once, I received approval from Orange ATC to do a low-level pass to say farewell and we came past the Heron at 100 feet and 500 knots, an 8 Squadron salute to a senior officer.

Cruise climb in wide battle formation over France, well above the civil airways of the time, made for an easy leg to RAF Lyneham to refuel, clear customs, and then fly on to our respective destinations, the other two to St Athan and mine to Kemble. However, first we had to meet Customs, who regarded arrivals from the Middle East with suspicion. Inspecting my Hunter, the Customs officer wanted to know what lay behind a panel in the middle of the RAF roundel on the fuselage. I had no idea, other than the RR Avon 207, which aroused official suspicion, so my groundcrew who did know, obediently opened the panel. The triumphant look on the Custom officer's face vanished as he touched the hot turbine outer case, still at a healthy temperature after flight. Unhealthy for human hands, however, and the inspection ceased forthwith as he disappeared to seek first aid. No, neither the groundcrew nor pilot laughed – out loud anyway.

The subject Queen's Flight Heron XM296 encountered on the apron at Orange Air Base during the ferry of three Hunters to the UK (*Mac McLauchlan*).

End of an adventure

So for the last leg to RAF Kemble. Not far, but in the gathering gloom of a grey December evening it took a pilot more accustomed to the clear Arabian skies some forty minutes to find his destination. No navaids, too proud to ask for radar assistance, I found the airfield eventually, and XF455 landed smoothly on Kemble's runway, the end of an adventure and great fun at the time.'

Mike Murden (Squadron Leader)

There could not have been a sharper contrast between the job Mike Murden left behind in Bomber Command to that awaiting him at Khormaksar.

Following a nine-ship formation flypast over Khormaksar in April 1961, a beaming smile from Mike Murden in the right-hand seat of the lead 8 Squadron Hunter T.7 says it all. The pilot for the occasion, Squadron Leader Laurie Jones, is standing up ready to dismount (*Brian Griffiths via Gail Murden*).

Mike Murden, second in from the right, playing his role in an AOC's inspection of 8 Squadron at Khormaksar in 1961 (*Mike Murden via Gail Murden*).

In August 1960 he was assigned as Engineering Officer to 8 Squadron, which had just completed its conversion from the Venom to the Hunter FGA.Mk.9.

The Technician's burden

'A few hours after my arrival I was taken to meet the CO, Squadron Leader Rex Knight and his pilots. I was delighted to be made so welcome. But the next day my mood turned to dismay when I met the NCOs and airmen, many of whom seemed shattered from working long hours in an appalling climate with inadequate resources. All work had to be undertaken in the open because there was no room in the hangars except for aircraft on second-line servicing. Engine ground runs were carried out on the crowded aircraft dispersals. On my first morning a corporal engine-fitter lost control during an engine ground-run, causing the aircraft to jump the chocks and collide with the end of the hangar. Such an accident should never have happened but, to a certain extent, the man was a victim of the circumstances at Khormaksar at the time.

Then there were the duststorms with sand everywhere, the cause of much of the unserviceability problem which included engine malfunctions, brake failures, electrical and undercarriage problems. The intense heat also added to our difficulties. On one occasion we waited weeks for replacement fuel-bag tanks. Spares, sent out by ship as deck cargo, melted during the journey and fell apart when unpacked on arrival. Much needed improvement came towards the end of 1960 when the squadron moved to a newly-constructed headquarters and dispersal at the eastern end of the airfield. Even so our established strength, based on previous UK experience, was totally inadequate for operations in Aden.

Because of the exceptionally high levels of equipment failures and severe shortages of spares, an unacceptable number of aircraft were grounded waiting for AOG spares. Command staff took firm steps to remedy the situation but it was many months before improvements reached the squadron. These many problems did not stop us getting on with squadron routine, including reconnaissance, practice on the range and supporting the Army on Dhala convoys, each being accompanied by one of our pilots acting as FAC. On these occasions we had armed aircraft standing by ready for intervention.

On 13 January 1961 Flight Lieutenant Les Swain disappeared on a routine flight near the Yemen border. We were all very upset at the loss of such an experienced and popular pilot. Every available aircraft was sent out to search. Hunters, Meteors and Shackletons all returned with bullet holes. For several days the groundcrew worked incredibly hard throughout daylight hours doing rapid turnarounds and re-arming aircraft. At times like this every possible serviceable aircraft was needed, even though the majority had deferred defects. So before most aircraft could fly I had to impose limitations by making "red-line entries" in the Forms 700. I was often concerned about the airworthiness of these aircraft and the possible consequences of further failures during subsequent operations. Fortunately there were no such incidents during my time on the squadron.

When the whole squadron moved to the Gulf on exercises, our duties at Khormaksar were taken on by 208 Squadron from Nairobi or carrierborne aircraft of the Royal Navy. Groundcrew usually travelled by Beverleys of 84 Squadron. On the way we would refuel at one of the route stations such as Salalah.

Following a most welcome visit by Air Commodore Ivor Broom from the Air Ministry, the unit's manpower establishment was considerably increased. By February 1961 new hangars had been constructed, spares were more plentiful, technical manpower had been increased and pilots were getting more of the flying needed to remain proficient. At the same time, behind the scenes, contingency plans were being drawn up for VANTAGE, one of the larger exercises held in the spring of 1961 and involving all three services. Carrier-based aircraft of the Royal Navy relieved 8 Squadron at Khormaksar so that we could move to Sharjah and practise for "an emergency somewhere in the Persian Gulf." Army involvement in the exercise included the Trucial Oman Scouts and Coldstream Guards at Burami Oasis.

Kuwait Crisis – Operation VANTAGE

These changes came just in time because, by mid-1961, it seemed increasingly likely that General Kassim would send Iraqi invasion forces into Kuwait. So whilst there was still plenty of room for improvement, we were better prepared than we had been a year earlier, when, on 30 June 1961, 8 and 208 Squadrons were ordered to move immediately to Bahrain, together with 30 and 84 Squadron Beverleys carrying groundcrews and spares. For 8 Squadron that meant a flight of 1,300 miles from Khormaksar. But 208 Squadron had to fly from Nairobi and cover almost twice the distance. On arrival at Khormaksar 208 had a sandwich lunch, still wearing flying suits, before departing, "cutting the corner" over Oman, to reach their destination early that evening. There was a real possibility of a Gulf War.

The Mark 9 fighter-ground-attack aircraft carried two 230-gallon long-range fuel tanks on the inside pylons, giving the type the extended range needed for its role in the Middle East. Operation VANTAGE included the possible need for the Hunters to fly from Bahrain to the Iraq/Kuwait border and beyond, jettisoning tanks on the return leg. So, on arrival, we refuelled immediately and I sent airmen to collect more tanks and jettison-cartridges from the contingency stockpile. In the meantime we decided to paint white bands around the wings and rear fuselage of one of our aircraft to see if it could be distinguished from other RAF Hunters as two similarly equipped squadrons were operated by the Iraqi Air Force alongside their MiG-15Bs. There were 500 long-range tanks in the stockpile, so the planners must have expected a lengthy campaign. To my dismay the men returned to tell me that there were no explosive bolts in store. A few urgent signals confirmed that none could be located anywhere in the theatre. So the plan to "jettison" was out of the question. A decision was made to remove the long-range tanks fitted to the aircraft and replace them with the smaller 100-gallon version.

By this stage all bowsers were full, so they could not be used to empty the contents. We had no option other than to drop the 230s onto the sand, roll them onto their sides and empty the contents, being careful not to spill fuel on the tyres. All of these became contaminated with sand and had to be

8 Squadron FR.10 XE589 pictured outside 131 MU with the experimental white bands that would have been used to distinguish RAF Hunters from those of Iraq had the Kuwait crisis developed into open warfare (*Simon Morrison*).

scrapped. Most of that night was spent re-configuring tanks, so there was no time to finish painting any more fuselages. We had very little sleep before returning to the aircraft.

Kuwait Crisis – moving in

Early the next morning we were ordered to move into Kuwait. Together with the groundcrew, I was in the first Beverley to take off, soon to be followed by the Hunters led by the CO, Squadron Leader 'Laurie' Jones. Visibility was appalling and everyone on board the Beverley was wondering about the whereabouts of the Iraqi aircraft. The crew eventually located Kuwait civil airport and landed, but as we taxied in we were ordered to take off immediately and continue to the partially-completed Kuwait New airport. As we came to a standstill we could see helicopters from HMS *Bulwark* coming in to land. During the morning several Centurion tanks came out of hiding and moved to the perimeter. But we soon lost sight of them because the visibility remained at about 400 yards for most of the next few days. Consequently almost every take off and landing was a very hazardous business.

120

The new airport was incomplete and had never been used before. We moved into the terminal building which had no windows, doors or services. Within minutes of our arrival a Kuwait government official came to me offering over 100 cars, trucks and cranes for unrestricted use by the British forces. Petrol would be issued free to any driver wearing a British uniform. Squadron pilots were quick to volunteer to help so we soon had vehicles available to unload the continuing stream of Beverleys and other aircraft. The build-up of forces seemed phenomenal and before the day was out included aircraft from Cyprus and the UK. The whole airfield became seriously congested and matters were made worse when we realised the Hunters were sinking into the perimeter track which consisted of newly-laid tarmac that was melting in mid-day temperatures of 125 degrees F. We could not touch the aircraft. So much of the servicing, such as engine changes, had to be done at first light while it was cool. It was thirsty work and Flying Officer John Volkers was very popular when he managed to commandeer a truck load of Pepsi Cola for the airmen. By the end of the first day we found places to sleep on the concrete floors of the terminal building, but it was very hot inside and some pilots found it cooler to sleep on the aircraft wings.

On the second morning we began work very early while it was still cool. Field kitchens had been set up and were most welcome. For several hectic days I remained the senior engineer at Kuwait and soon found myself drawn into all sorts of problems well outside my official duties with the squadron. Aircraft continued to arrive all day and throughout the night from Cyprus, UK and the Far East, including commandeered Argonauts and Comets. On arrival from the UK, Britannias sometimes stayed on the runway and kept engines running because no external power was available. Operating conditions could not have been more hazardous. Most of the time visibility was down to 400 yards at ground level. On the third night a newly-arrived airman from Lyneham went out to marshal an incoming Britannia. In the dark, tired and blinded by blowing sand, he walked into a propeller and was killed. We were all deeply upset by the accident. A few days later Flying Officer 'Flick' Hennessey of 208 Squadron took off on a local reconnaissance flight using an 8 Squadron aircraft. He became disorientated in the poor visibility and was killed. It was a frustrating time for Hunter pilots because of the dreadful visibility. After the initial rush to reach Kuwait, it was at times near-impossible to carry out reconnaissance. That same morning a bomb exploded on a Beverley at Bahrain so we then had additional worries about terrorism.

That first week I was the senior engineer at the airport, so I continued to be involved in most technical activities on the base. Each morning the Oil

Company insisted on signatures for enormous quantities of aviation fuel. And during the week more than a hundred technical tradesmen from UK, and some from Singapore, reported for duty. They had no tools and were not acclimatised, so it was impossible to use them all on aircraft maintenance. Many had to be employed unloading stores and armaments.

Senior officers visited each day from Bahrain, and I usually attended daily meetings with SASO, OC Ops and sometimes the AOC, who always arrived in his distinctive white Canberra. Expatriates at the Oil Company, grateful for our intervention, offered overnight use of air-conditioned accommodation to some squadron pilots.

On the fourth day there was an early morning scramble by two Hunters after a reported intrusion by an unidentified aircraft. The pilots did not encounter any Iraqi aircraft but the incident proved a timely reminder of the need to remain vigilant. The Iraqi Air Force must have faced similar difficulties with visibility in the Kuwait area. By the time the weather cleared the build-up of British Forces was nearing completion. Initially, limited radar coverage of up to eighty miles was provided by HMS *Bulwark* as she stood close to shore during daylight hours. But the carrier had to move offshore each night as a precaution against attack. After the first few days everyone began to relax a little and a few of us visited HMS *Bulwark* by then in Kuwait Harbour. On 9 July HMS *Victorious* and her escorts arrived from the Far East and provided much improved radar cover. There were now over 5,000 men and a considerable number of aircraft there.

By mid-July it seemed that Iraq had abandoned its plan to invade Kuwait. Whilst there was a need to remain alert, settled routines were being established. Despite the order to "Minimise", signals traffic was overloaded most of the time and great ingenuity was needed to get AOG (Aircraft on Ground) parts for aircraft. The health of pilots and tradesmen suffered for each extra day spent in that dreadful climate.

After the initial build-up of forces was completed, 8 and 208 Squadrons took turns to rotate between Kuwait and Bahrain and then between the Gulf and Khormaksar. Even though facilities at Bahrain were far from ideal, pilots could resume training and it was possible for everyone to have the occasional day off work. But after the Kuwait Emergency life had changed for everyone involved, as had the continuing British presence in the Middle East.

Pilot fatality

On 22 November 1961, whilst we were in Bahrain, two aircraft took off on a routine training exercise. Only one returned, reporting that his No. 2,

Flying Officer Dick Gaiger, had overtaken him in a dive and disappeared into cloud. A subsequent search found aircraft wreckage in Qatar. Dick had been killed on ejection. The Qatar government would only allow one person to visit, identify the body and return with the remains. I was asked to go so that I could also use the only opportunity to visit the accident site and report back to the Board of Enquiry (since no one else would be allowed to visit at a later date). I flew as the only passenger on a Pembroke and was left on the runway with a promise that I would be collected the next day. I had only a few hours at the scene but managed to work out what had happened. Without a pilot on board the aircraft had hit the ground upside down, straight-and-level. I found it had suffered a nose-down tailplane runaway caused by a fault in the actuator circuit. In an emergency the pilot could use the standby trim switch, but it was first necessary to isolate the faulty circuit by pulling out the circuit breaker. Unfortunately the *Pilot's Notes* made no mention of the circuit breaker.

The next morning I returned to Bahrain with Dick's body. After the funeral I explained my findings about the accident to the pilots. That afternoon Martin Webbon took off as one of a pair. In a subsequent tail chase he found himself unable to pull out of a dive. Shortly after that we had a call from air traffic telling us that Martin had put out a "Mayday" call and mentioned "tailplane runaway". Realising that he could not pull out of the dive, Martin pushed hard on the controls using his feet and then blacked out from the negative-G as he did an outside loop. He landed the aircraft safely but had two black eyes caused by his escapade. Both tailplane malfunctions were reported immediately to Command Headquarters and to our colleagues on 208 Squadron. Local orders were issued to deal with the problem and I wrote an article which was published in the Command *Flight Safety Journal*. But, despite repeated requests from Khormaksar and Steamer Point, there was very little feedback of information from the Air Ministry during my remaining time on the squadron.

On 30 March 1962 Khormaksar held a station open day. The 8 Squadron contribution was by three Hunters. Two aircraft made low, fast passes from opposite ends of the runway whilst a third, piloted by Flying Officer Peter Blackgrove, made a supersonic dive to reach the centre of the runway at the same time. To our horror, Peter failed to recover from the dive and flew straight into the ground. Later that day we recovered the tailplane actuator from the wreckage and confirmed that the accident had been caused by a runaway tailplane.

I was not sorry to return to the UK at the end of my tour in Aden. By the time I left Aden six pilots had been killed, including John Volkers and Martin Webbon. I had been deeply upset by the loss of each of these friends and also by the death of the airman. I am not sure that life was much happier for those servicemen who succeeded us.'

Tim Notley (Lieutenant, RN)

Having completed a tour flying Scimitars with 807 Squadron from HMS *Centaur*, Lieutenant Tim Notley RN was posted out to Aden in August 1962 on an exchange posting with the RAF, for a two-year tour flying Hunters with 8 Squadron at Khormaksar.

Fair exchange

'My exchange appointment with the RAF and 8 Squadron in Aden and the Persian Gulf was a fascinating experience, despite my inauspicious start. There was something about the Middle East that truly interested me. Around the southern edge of the Arabian Peninsula there are amazing landscapes: craggy mountains, strange rock formations, and, not least, the Hadramaut. The latter is an incredibly deep and wide cratered ravine over 300 kilometres in length, more impressive to me than the Grand Canyon in the USA. It is where the Hadramis still live, some in their skyscraper mud dwellings/castles. They were the merchants who first brought eastern spices to the western world.

To the north of Aden lie the ancient lands of the Queen of Sheba, where evidence still remains of a sophisticated irrigation system of some 2,000 years ago. This was the only area that I saw once, briefly, from the ground. A pilot had to accompany the Dhala convoy army detachments, in case they were attacked on their way up to Dhala, which was on the border of the Yemen directly north of Aden. The job of the pilot was to direct aircraft against any attackers, "dissident tribesmen" as they were called. Once it was my turn to be the pilot for the Dhala convoy. Luckily for me, the major in charge of the convoy was an experienced archaeologist and it was he who pointed out the ancient irrigation systems. It was a rare opportunity to learn something of this fascinating part of the world.

Apart from flying in and out of Khormaksar, we also flew round the desert of the Empty Quarter, via Masirah, to land at either Sharjah or Bahrain where we spent two month-periods on detachment.

Living and flying round this part of the world inspired me to read more of the history of the Arabs and of how their empire developed. And, also, to read the exploits of crazy Europeans, usually British, who lived and adventured in those lands.

Off on the wrong foot!

Number 8 Squadron had a long history of operating in the Middle East. Unfortunately for me, grossly overconfident in my flying prowess having just completed my first operational tour on Scimitars, I managed to damage one of their Hunter aircraft within a week of my arrival. When on the ground, the pitot head is protected by a rubber tube-like cover to which is attached a warning flag to remind the pilot to remove the cover prior to manning the aircraft. In this case there was no flag (but there often wasn't) and I failed to notice the cover was still on. Thus when taking off, and halfway down the runway, there was no speed indication and I decided to abort the take off. Big mistake! The heavily-laden Hunter, with two 230-gallon fuel tanks under the wings, failed to stop in time and the aircraft went into the runway overshoot and the undercarriage collapsed in the sand.

My initial thought was that there was another aircraft on the flight line – I'll just nip back and get that one. Oh no, the RAF made a big song and dance about the whole episode. I was grounded for a month, severely reprimanded, and my pride suffered a severe and well-deserved, blow. Actually that accident probably saved my life during the rest of my thirty-plus years of

In a relatively minor incident, Tim Notley's Hunter drifted off the Khormaksar runway and buried its wheels in the sand. The photograph depicts EO Owen Truelove (left) assessing the situation together with Pete Loveday, as Sergeant Bob Browning inserts a ground lock and the groundcrew prepare to push the aircraft onto the metal strip (*Ray Deacon*).

flying – I was a much more careful pilot from then on. On my first flight from Aden after the accident, there was no problem in taking off the pitot head cover. The ground crew had made a large White Ensign and hung it from it.

However, after that little setback, I enjoyed a full two years flying their Hunters and obtained more flying hours per month than many other pilots on the squadron, mainly by being available if an extra sortie had to be flown; I became known as an 'Hours Hog'.

One way to build up hours was to ferry aircraft that were due for refurbishing, back to the UK. It was always something of an adventure, not only because of encountering bad weather, but also because the facilities for refuelling at some airfields on the way could be uncertain. The route that I did a couple of times was Bahrain to Teheran, to Diyarbakir (in Turkey), to Nicosia (in Cyprus), to El Adem (in Libya), to Luqa {in Malta), to Istres (in France), to Lyneham (for customs clearance in UK) and finally RAF Kemble. In all it took two days and eleven hours flying.

Keeping the peace

Apart from the normal flying exercises in the area there were a couple of 'wars' in which we were involved – the Radfan War and the Beihan Patrol. In the former, our task was to support 'friendly' Arab tribes in the rugged northern hinterland of the Aden Protectorates (as it was then) and also to provide close air support to the British Army operating in the area. Mostly our support consisted of knocking down forts of 'enemy' tribesmen; this was done in a relatively civilised manner. First we flew over the area dropping leaflets to say that we would be back in an hour to knock down their fort with rockets and 30mm cannon shells. That gave them time to evacuate the buildings and watch our return from the nearby hills. After we finished, not having always damaged the fort severely, the "enemy" Arabs would collect up our expended brass 30mm shell cases and sell them in the Aden flea-market at a useful price.

The Beihan Patrol lasted some months during 1963 and 1964. Then it was thought that Egyptian aircraft would attack the Aden Protectorate; this was before the Arabs finally forced the British out. Therefore 8 Squadron, along with 43 and 208 Hunter Squadrons, was tasked to maintain a constant patrol along the Yemen border during daylight hours and intercept any attacking aircraft. The Egyptians never came, much to our disappointment; we had illusions of some serious air-to-air combat.'

Two years later, Tim returned to flying Scimitars, this time with 803 Squadron from HMS *Ark Royal* before moving on to HMS *Eagle* in 1968 and the Buccaneers of 800 Squadron.

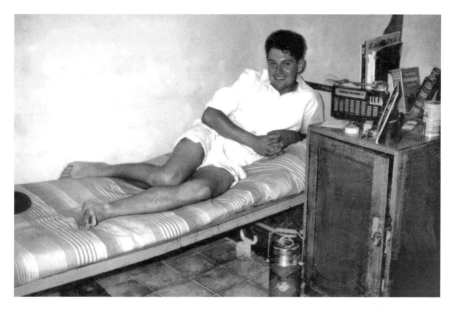

Bill Overy takes a well-earned break on his pit (*Bill Overy*).

Overy, Bill (Corporal)

Bill Overy was an airframe fitter whose two-year tour of duty in Aden began in early 1961.

Aden, the Land of Sun

'Aden. You are posted to Aden!' "Great, where the hell is Aden?" "Look it up on a map," was the reply from the station HQ clerk who did not know either. Back at the crewroom I received a lot of blank stares but one person, who did not even put his newspaper down, said, "Lots of sand, miles of golden beaches and it used to be a military prison." Great, just what I wanted to cheer me up. All too soon, I was on my way to RAF Innsworth.

After a lonely last night in England we boarded a Bristol Britannia for the flight to Aden. It was a civilian aircraft and we were a mixed bunch of RAF passengers, from officers and airmen to wives and children going out to meet their husbands. We completed the flight in one leg because General Nasser of Egypt was still upset with us over the Suez Canal episode. This meant flying south over North Africa and turning east at Nasser's Corner and on to Aden. We eventually descended into the small British colony that was Aden, thinking that it would be my home for the next two years.

I was assigned a room with three other guys in Hunter Block at Khormaksar. Next morning, dressed in khaki shorts, shirt and thick long woollen socks, I reported to station headquarters. I was told I was to report to 8 Squadron along with another new arrival, Corporal Bruce Clements. No. 8 Squadron was a fighter-ground-attack unit that was equipped with Mk.9 Hawker Hunters. Bruce had come from 111 Squadron (the Black Arrows) which had been equipped with Hunters but in the flying display role. Together we reported to the Chiefy who ran the second-line servicing.

We should then have gone through the arrival process which usually took two days but Chiefy told us to forget it, give our chits to the clerk and get outside to turnround four aircraft that had just come in. "But I have just come off Valiants and never worked on a Hunter." "No time to train; just imagine it is a Valiant with one engine; Corporal Clements will show you the ropes."

Initiation

We wondered out onto a pan that was alive with teams of mechanics checking out the engines, electrical, radios and armament. One guy was putting in new brake parachutes while others were busy with oxygen and air trolleys, refuelling bowsers, all going flat out. One person was filling up something in the fuselage with a watering can. "Don't disturb him," said Bruce, "They are pouring Avpin into the engine starter and it's a mono cycle fuel that will happily ignite at this temperature and, as it does not need oxygen to burn, is a devil to put out."

Bruce took me round doing all four turnround checks together so next time I would be on my own. The pilots sauntered out while we signed the aircrafts' form 700s and they were soon strapping in and the engines started. An interesting bit of fun was had when the engine started as the Avpin exhaust was ejected from a tube below the fuselage and would happily ignite. The airman on starter duty would then dash underneath and use his beret to beat out the flames. It actually worked but played hell with the state of your beret.

As our charges departed we realised we had a small problem. The hot sun reflecting from the concrete pan in the 90-plus degrees F temperature had turned our legs into a delightful shade of red and neither of us could bend them. One of the mechanics popped us into a Land Rover and nipped us down to sick quarters, where the medic took one look at us and with a smirk said, "8 Squadron I assume?" He gave us each a jar of cream that worked wonders and then we were whisked back to the squadron. It did not take long to get into the routine and soon we were as brown as everyone else. At last, we did not have to suffer the cry of "Mooney" because of our white skin.

Those first few days were a blur as the squadron started early in the cool of the day, as did everyone else but, when they packed up at 13:00, we just carried on. Most weekends were normal working days but we worked under the adage of work hard, play hard. This made for a great squadron spirit as everyone was in the same boat and parties abounded.

The Kuwait crisis

In 1961 the independent state of Kuwait was under the protection of the British government. This meant that when General Kassim, the leader of Iraq, declared he was going to invade his small neighbour the British government leapt into action. Well, actually it was us who leapt into action.

It was the end of June 1961 and the members of 8 Squadron were planning a goodwill visit to Rhodesia. As we were travelling to a friendly power we would dress in civilian clothes. Our bags were packed and we had listened to a briefing from the wing commander that we were on a goodwill visit and the pranks of the squadron's last visit were not to be repeated. It seems that our pilots had flown their Hunters down a railway line and played chicken with a railway engine approaching from the opposite direction, causing the train driver to put the brakes on so hard it wore flats on the driving wheels. Another aircraft flew down the main street in Salisbury and then straight up on reaching the building at the end, causing all the windows to fall in. Just a couple of stories that had become legend but, knowing our pilots, they were very believable.

However, on 29 June 1961 there we were working away like mad to bring the Hunters up to full readiness with our cases packed in flashy civilian clothes when in rushed Chiefy bellowing the instruction to go back to our billets and pick up our suitcases as we had to depart quickly.

Back at the squadron Chiefy was directing operations, handing out papers and manuals and gathering essential equipment, ground equipment, spares, oils and lubricants, needed for a panic move. I had not been issued with a toolbox, as they were in short supply, so carried mine in a small tartan hold-all; very chic. Once packed onto trailers, we were whisked off to a waiting Beverly, there to help the loadmasters transfer all the gear into the cavernous hold. Despite the appearance of disorder it was a planned operation that worked out well.

The Bristol Beverlys of 84 Squadron were our support aircraft and the perfect workhorse for desert operations. It was almost dark when we boarded and the engines were soon running. As there weren't enough seats – the upper passenger section had been cleared and filled with food and kitchen equipment – we were left to sit among the ground equipment. The trip to Bahrain took sixteen hours with a refuelling stop at Masirah en route. The old hands were not amused but to me it was adventure with a capital A. Masirah was a depressing place and we were only too happy to climb aboard once more. Imagine spending a year's posting there.

As we descended into Bahrain, we were informed that the groundcrew would be divided into two. One section would continue on to Kuwait to await the arrival of the Hunters while the second, to which I was assigned, would turn round and arm the first wave of Hunters. We would then join the first section in Kuwait just as soon as a second Beverly or 208 Squadron's Hunters had arrived in Bahrain. As the high-explosive rockets needed to be assembled and would place a heavy burden on the armourers, everyone gave a helping hand. On the next day, the first wave of 208 Squadron Hunters started to arrive from their base in Kenya, leaving 8 Squadron to concentrate on its move into Kuwait.

By the time we finished eating a well-deserved meal, it was too late to find accommodation, so we decided to sleep under the wings of our aircraft. Our wing commander arrived and was very impressed with what had been

The 8 Squadron Hunter line looks isolated at an almost deserted Kuwait New Airport in July 1961 with only a 152 Squadron Twin Pioneer awaiting its next call of duty at the far end of the apron for company (*Bill Overy*).

achieved and told us we would soon be joining the squadron in Kuwait. The spirit on the squadron was fantastic; it was what we had trained for and we were a team.

After a hearty breakfast the next morning, we continued prepping the aircraft, this time with the help of 208 Squadron's groundcrew. They told us that accommodation was impossible to find and they had been crammed into small rooms like prisons. We still had no change of clothes as all we had brought was civilian gear intended for the Rhodesia trip and, with the temperature and humidity, it was normal to change clothes sometimes twice a day. As the RAF did not like the idea of us going to war in civvies, we were told to make do with what we had. A few of us decided to find accommodation and by pure luck discovered a new accommodation building that was nearly finished but not yet open. The builders were not bothered so long as we arrived after they had left and left before they started which was not a problem.

That night we slept well and were up early next morning to prep the last of our Hunters. We then bade a fond farewell to sunny Bahrain and boarded a Beverly for the short hop to Kuwait. We were greeted by an odd assortment of vehicles driven by the rest of our groundcrew. Apparently, they had been taken downtown in a bus and told to help themselves to any truck they wanted. That is except one person who was given the bus.

Whereas Bahrain was hot and humid and you could watch your cloths turn dark with sweat when standing still, Kuwait was just HOT, HOTTER and very, very HOT. When the clam doors opened at the rear on landing, it felt like opening an oven door. The temperature averaged around 115 degrees F in the shade if you could find any. Inside the cockpit, it jumped to 140 F or more and the wings were so hot you could fry eggs on them; I know we did it.

Our new home was at the new international airport that was about fifteen miles south of the old airport. Unfortunately, it had not been completed when we arrived and, as such, was missing some of the basics. The runways had been finished but the pans were still tarmac and to stop the aircraft sinking into it, wartime metal grids had been laid. A water bowser stood in the sun to keep it warm and electricity was only for essentials.

We had to unload the aircraft quickly as it slowly inched forward to prevent it sinking into the soft tarmac. We had to make do with locally-made wooden steps that had to be pushed along to keep pace with the moving aircraft. We could handle the Beverlys but unloading Britannias as they arrived from the UK did cause a few problems. The squadron took over

Home sweet home! The large store shed at Kuwait New (above) was requisitioned by 8 Squadron airmen to meet their accommodation needs. (below) Not exactly the Hilton but at least it was somewhere to put one's head down. The close proximity of ammunition boxes might have made getting to sleep a tad difficult though (*both, Bill Overy*).

a large stores shed which was located behind the pan and next to the fuel dump; it was one of the few buildings on the airfield. Camp beds had been laid out with our spares and stores, including rockets and shells, stacked between each bed.

In the evening on my first day a local sheik arrived out of the blue to see how we were settling in. Rumour had it that we were all getting medals or maybe a Rolex watch but he only asked if there was anything we wanted. Drink and food were the most important so it was decided we would stick to chicken sandwiches and we had to explain what a chicken sandwich was. We also requested soft drinks such as Coca Cola. The next morning two large trucks delivered ample supplies of coke and chicken sandwiches. It transpired that the Kuwaiti interpretation of a chicken sandwich was two thick slices of local bread and a complete chicken in between. We could live with that.

We were so thirsty we just downed the Coke, hot or not, too quickly which proved to be a disaster; no one needed a laxative after that. As there were no toilets we had to make use of a small shovel, two rocks and a plank and disappear by truck into the desert to dig our own toilet.

There was no mess either, so we had to cook our own food. This came in a large sealed metal container that was about two-feet by three-feet and stamped "24 Hour Ration Box". In it was an unappetising mixture of tinned war rations and a small burner to heat the food. Four of us teamed up and mixed our boxes into one and shared the cooking. We decided that the best thing to do was to empty the contents of all the tins into one and make a stew.

As our kitbags were packed for the intended detachment to Rhodesia, we only had civilian clothes and the uniforms we were standing in. These were a trifle grubby already. Trying to wash them without soap did not remove the grease and oil from working on the aircraft. The local army unit defending the airport thought we were great fun and decided to teach us the art of living and working in the desert. We finished up looking like Lawrence of Arabia. I still have my canvas water bottle and headdress.

Despite all the distractions, we had to ensure the Hunters were maintained in a serviceable state. The first patrols took off at dawn which meant an early start. Everyone got on with the job as we expected to see Iraqi tanks arriving at any moment. Patrols were flown all through the day, requiring minor snags to be deferred until the evening when the rectification work could start. This often involved working way into the night despite having to be up before the dawn the next day.

On top of that, we were required to share guard duty with the army. A picquet consisted of six airmen and one soldier. Each airman was issued with a pickaxe handle and a flashlight and the soldier carried the only rifle.

Wing Commander Neville arrived to give us a briefing during which he informed us that the Iraqi Army had Centurion tanks, the same as the Kuwait Army. A road linked the border directly to the airfield, a distance of thirty miles. As the tanks could reach speeds up to 30mph, they could reach us in an hour if the Hunters could not dissuade them. Land opposition was provided by the 3rd Carabiniers, who had taken over the Kuwait Army tanks, 45 Commando and 2 Para.

The days went by in a blur and I sent letters to Edna as often as I could but it was difficult as we were uncertain as to what we could say. What I did not know was that our local paper had printed the story of our move to Kuwait including a large picture of me working on a Hunter.

After ten days we pulled out of Kuwait and flew back to Bahrain where we stayed for the rest of July. The delights of decent food and drink, and visits to BOAC's Speedbird Club made up for the hardship we'd been through.

A detachment of 13 Squadron PR Canberras had arrived in Bahrain while we were away to photograph activities on the Iraqi side of the border. A strong bond quickly developed between their groundcrew and ours which nearly came to an abrupt end. They had a stuffed owl as a mascot

Time to unwind! Having endured a strenuous and at times frustrating year, 8 Squadron airmen let their hair down on Christmas Day in Bahrain, 1961 (*Bill Overy*).

The 'Slops' has not taken affect yet judging by this more formal gathering of 8 Squadron members; Christmas in Bahrain in 1961 (*Bill Overy*).

that looked just like the one on their badge. One day it disappeared and we got the blame, but it eventually turned up as quietly as it disappeared and nothing more was said.'

Ken Parry (Flight Lieutenant)

Having completed a tour on Hunters with 1 Squadron at West Raynham, Ken Parry was posted to Muharraq as flight commander, QFI and IRE on 8 Squadron for a tour that lasted from mid-1969 to late 1970. He then attended a CFS refresher course on the "mighty Chipmunk" at Little Rissington before taking up a post as OC Bristol University Air Squadron.

Life after Khormaksar
'Both we and 208 Squadron operated out of the same hangar and used the same flight line at Bahrain. No. 208 had been there for a while and at the time of the Aden closure when 8 Squadron moved to Muharraq, another set of offices was built above the existing 208 facilities. So, we were the "upstairs" squadron and they were the "downstairs" mob. When 1417

Flight disbanded at the time of Aden closure, its FR.10s were re-allocated to 8 Squadron as B Flight, so we had eight FGA.9s and four FR.10s during the time I was there.

Muharraq was a large base (though not as huge as Khormaksar had been) with a small proportion of accompanied posts for nominally two years, but the vast majority of people were on thirteen-month unaccompanied tours. This led inevitably to some friction and bad feeling. Offensive Support Wing consisted of 8 and 208 Squadrons, a GL Section with an Army major and a couple of FACs, and an RAF Regiment squadron. Ops and Transport Wing had a detachment of 114 Squadron Argosys from Benson, 152 Squadron Pembrokes for communications duties until they were grounded for fatigue reasons, and all the facilities for the H24 staging post for transports, not just serving the Gulf but also going to Singapore and Hong Kong.

No. 8 Squadron's time at Muharraq was much quieter than the Aden days in terms of operations. There was some involvement of B Flight, which had the four FR.10s, in border problems around Oman – things were kept very close to a very few chests, and even as the A Flight commander I was not privy to what went on. As far as I know, it was recce only, with no weaponry involved. Both 8 and 208 had an air defence commitment in Bahrain. There was a GCI radar in the middle of Bahrain island at Hamala, which was also the base for the UK infantry battalion. We would occasionally fly practice

Looking down the Sharjah runway early one November morning in 1970 as a pair of 8 Squadron FGA.9s are captured blasting loose sand from the runway while heading towards the camera (*Ken Parry*).

intercepts under their control, and some of them did not work as intended – I remember once being vectored very cleanly onto an airliner in the airway into Bahrain from the south-east, instead of the intended Hunter. Ho hum.

The experience level on the squadron was very low at the time, with mostly first-tour pilots. A Flight's main flying task was taking a lot of them from Chivenor, giving them experience and building their flying skills, so they were ready to go on to the Harrier or Phantom when they went home. We had few experienced pilots on A Flight; only about three or four out of around twelve had previous Hunter tours. B Flight were more experienced; at that time FR was regarded as more demanding than the FGA role.

Regarding the airframes, you may know that Middle East squadrons' aircraft each came back to the UK every two years for refurbishment at St Athan or Kemble. That began to change during 1969, as the UK-based Hunter squadrons re-equipped with Harriers, and there were many airframe moves. Several Gulf-squadron FGA.9s and FR.10s were sold back to HSA for resale to overseas air forces; some West Raynham-based aircraft were sent to the Gulf, and so on.

The route stations

Used regularly by the Hunter squadrons for APCs, Sharjah had only one accompanied post, the Station Commander, and seemed to be a much happier place than Muharraq. Based there were 78 Squadron with Wessex, 84 Squadron with Andovers, 653 Squadron (AAC) flying Beavers,

A pair of SNEB-equipped 8 Squadron FGA.9s begin their take-off runs at Masirah in October 1970 (*Ken Parry*).

WR975-A, one of four Mark 3 Phase 3 Shackletons from UK-based squadrons allocated to the Maritime Detachment (MarDet) at Sharjah in the late sixties. A 208 Squadron Hunter T.7 can be seen on the apron in the background (*Aviation Bookshop*).

and Mardet, a standing detachment of MR.3 Shackletons from the UK, tasked with preventing smuggling, of both goods and people, into what was then the Trucial States, and soon to become the UAE. Masirah and Salalah were both wholly unaccompanied, and neither had RAF flying units based there. Masirah was supplied by a weekly Argosy from Muharraq, leading to the conundrum: why is Masirah open? To accept the weekly Argosy. Why does the Argosy go to Masirah? To keep the airfield open.

There was a rumbling insurrection in the south-western part of Oman near the South Yemen border, and my recollection is that Sultan of Oman's Air Force had some aircraft at Salalah in connection with that. We were not allowed near; there was a no-go line somewhere south-west of Masirah that defined the edge of our permitted training area.'

Ken Rochester (Senior Aircraftsman)

An aircraft electrical mechanic, Ken Rochester began his two-year tour at Khormaksar on 28 September 1963 and was put to work on Transit Flight.

Following retirement from service with the RAF, Provost T.1 WV476 was one of several converted to T.52 standard for the Sultan of Oman's Air Force. It is seen here following reassembly outside 131 MU at Khormaksar in early 1964 (*Ray Deacon*).

Unsettled times

'By coincidence, my sergeant in charge, Sergeant Scott, was at school with my dad. After just two weeks I was sent to ASF and my first job, along with an airframe and an engine guy, was to prepare the last 8 Squadron Meteor, a T.7, for a ferry flight back to the UK. On completion, it transpired there were no authorised Meteor pilots available to fly it back so it was handed over to the fire service and dumped on the far side of the main runway.

At around this time, in addition to some Percival Provost T.1s being fitted with .303 machine guns for Oman Air Force and a few USAF T-28s passing through en route to Thailand, there were three pre-production Lightnings undergoing tropical trials and we were charged with their handling on the ground. They left sometime before Christmas, each aircraft being sprayed with styrofoam and taken by road to the Marine Craft Unit for loading on to a barge and onward transfer to a freighter in the bay. The civilian working party was supplied by Shorts of Belfast.

A new challenge and some close shaves

Towards the end of November 1963 I was moved again and, despite a request to work on 37 Squadron's Shackletons, the Hunters of 8 Squadron became my next challenge. Other incidents I recall include the sudden dropping of underwing tanks due to shorting in the cables. This occurred twice if I recall correctly. On another occasion we were towing a Mark 9 from ASF back to the squadron when the towing-arm separated. Someone shouted "It's broke!" and the Land Rover driver slowed to a halt ready to re-connect. The aircraft, however, didn't have any brake pressure and continued its forward run until the inevitable collision with the back of the Land Rover. We, of course, took avoiding action, jumping over the side of the vehicle pretty sharpish.

On another occasion two of us were despatched to stores to collect a new drum of IPN (Isopropylnitrate – or AVPIN as we knew it) using a gunpack trolley as a means of transport. On the way back through the camp we were stopped by another driver who calmly informed us that there were sparks coming from underneath the drum. On investigation we found that there was insufficient hydraulic pressure in the trolley and the cradle had dropped low enough for the drum to scrape the ground. IPN generates its own oxygen on igniting and was used to start the Hunter's Avon engine and would have made a spectacular explosion had the drum ignited. I dread to think what would have happened to us if it had worn through the metal.

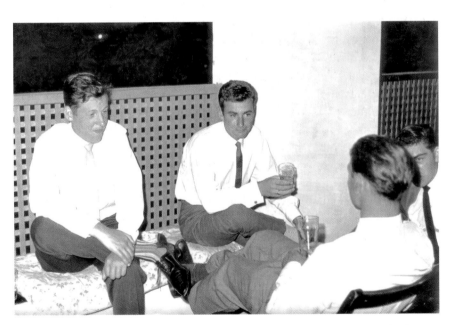

Ken Rochester and Brian Wilkinson imbibe on a glass of 'Slops' along with a couple of colleagues at an 8 Squadron function at Khormaksar sometime during 1963 (*Ken Rochester*).

I also remember an incident when we were doing a retraction test and the sequence valve failed causing the 'D' doors to raise first leaving the main wheels to crunch straight into them. On another occasion, during a detachment to Bahrain, we received a box from stores which should have contained a dive brake and much to our surprise, contained an arrester hook for a Royal Navy Hunter.'

Bill Romer-Ormiston (Senior Aircraftsman)

An armourer by trade, Bill Ormiston was one of the lucky few, along with the author, to sail out to Aden in the sparsely-accommodated HMT *Nevasa* in April 1962. Based at Khormaksar for the duration of his tour and assigned to the small-arms armoury and the bomb dump, where he prepared and armed 3-inch rockets and iron bombs, Bill found himself loaned out to all four Hunter units and the Shackleton squadron for varying periods during his tour.

That dreaded 'Cruise'!
'I remember the Bay of Biscay very well and, having thought that I had got away with it for so long by avoiding the sight of soldiers constantly throwing up, the smell finally triggered me off and I succumbed to a serious bout of seasickness. We shared accommodation with the Royal Green Jackets and Royal Marines, some going to Malta while others were heading for the Far East. They were a tough crowd who could not come to terms with the comparative casual discipline of the RAF. In the words of the Duke of Wellington when describing his troops, "I don't know if they frighten the enemy but by God they frighten me."

We stopped at Malta and went ashore. Walking through those narrow alleys and entering seedy bars was a terrific experience for me. I recall a fight between drunken soldiers and sailors had started down a side alley and I started to wander towards it. Fortunately, a couple of experienced guys I was with grabbed my arms and frogmarched me back out of the alley. As we reached the corner, MPs assigned on land patrol (both Army and Navy) arrived and just waded into the mêlée, wielding their hefty looking batons, just like a bad Hollywood movie.

At Port Said we were not allowed ashore but certain traders were allowed onboard the ship to set up their stalls, no doubt after a little greasing of the right palms. The haggling was quite intense and I watched as the more experienced old hands used a neat technique which we then adopted. With their system, a note was offered, usually a ten-bob note and the trader allowed to grab it. Without letting go of the note, a generous helping of the trader's goods was heaped and scooped towards the buyer with his free hand. The trader, deeming ten bob to be insufficient, would try to prevent this with his free hand while still hanging onto the note with the other. At some stage, one or the other would lose their nerve and let go of the note. If it was the trader, he recovered his goods and the buyer kept his note but if it was the buyer, he quickly used both hands to shield and bag the pile. Much abuse was hurled at the escaping buyer as he disappeared below decks.

Work in the Station Armoury

In the station armoury I devised a method of mass production which generated a great deal of initial scepticism and resistance. My colleague and I demonstrated our new process of servicing rifles, Sten guns, Bren

The pilot acknowledges the signal from an armourer who has just connected the MASB safety break plug under the wing of his aircraft, prior to departing for a session on the Khormaksar range. Adopted by OC 8 Squadron, Squadron Leader Laurie Jones as his personal aircraft, hence the tailcode, FGA.9 XE654 was armed with four concrete-headed practice rockets and a live gunpack when photographed in February 1963 (*Ray Deacon*).

guns and pistols and it worked so well that it was adopted into standard practice. In true forces fashion, this was not just to make Her Majesty's Forces more efficient, but to give us more time to ourselves. The higher-ups took the least line of resistance and let us get on with it.

One of our projects was to take a Mark 2 Sten gun (a better-made model than the Mk.3) and designate it the 'armoury Sten'. The weapon was stripped down and the black finish rubbed off and the steel of the receiver and the bolt polished to a mirror finish. The receiver was then treated with a chemical/ heat process to create a gun-metal blue finish (similar to a high quality English shotgun), leaving the bolt in shining silver contrast. Armourers called it blueing. I took a Stanley wood-plane and made an exact copy of the elegant curved wooden hand grip and fitted this to the front receiver of the Sten, giving it a 1920s Tommy-gun look. It was finished off with a custom stock and looked very smart. Whenever we went on guard duty, we always chose this weapon together with a customised Smith & Wesson .38 pistol. Although the Enfield revolver was a fine pistol, it was ideally suited for use in the desert and would always fire, even when unloved and seldom looked after, but it was not used by us as it was seen as 'uncool', to use modern jargon. The S&W on the other hand was a far more temperamental weapon.

The sad loss of a Hunter and its pilot
I hadn't been with 8 Squadron for more than a few weeks when I was detailed for duty on the Khormaksar firing range. The pilots of the squadron honed their skills with regular practice, firing off their cannon and rockets. The Hawker Hunter FGA.9 was armed with a gunpack of four 30mm cannon in the forward fuselage and unguided 3-inch rockets fitted to the underside of the wings. Frequently they were required to provide very close support to ground troops and any errors could have caused blue-on-blue incidents. Great accuracy was, therefore, required the closer to our troops the Hunter's fire was directed.

The range was a wide and desolate area of desert broken only by the occasional leafless thorn tree. The heat was incredibly intense and there was seldom a breath of air. The heat danced on the horizon causing mirages and the distant mountains seemed to hover over what appeared to be a shimmering silver lake. This optical illusion would be familiar to all who have served in the deserts of the Middle East. A file of camels could suddenly just disappear only to miraculously re-appear, plodding their stately way across the sands.

Our range party consisted of, as I remember it, the range safety officer, our sergeant and another airman who, I seem to remember, was nicknamed

"Ozzie". Having tested the radio in the Land Rover we received confirmation that two Hunters were on their run-in. While one aircraft remained in the circuit, the other would appear suddenly, almost silently, low and fast, streaking across the desert, the sun flashing momentarily off its canopy. The firing commenced and we were treated to the sight of the sparkle of gunfire from the gun ports as trails of black smoke streamed back along the underbelly. Of course, I may be prejudiced but the Hawker Hunter must be one of the most beautiful and elegant aircraft ever built. There followed the sound and sight of the cannon shells hitting the target. The aircraft then lifted her nose and a second later the sound of the aircraft itself would strike us like a great hand, before turning on a wingtip and barrelling up into the sky and rapidly disappearing. Through our binoculars we watched the point of impact and reported the success or otherwise of the attack to the pilot. As can be imagined there was a certain amount of friendly banter but in fact the pilots were held in great esteem by the groundcrews. Theirs was a dangerous job and they were well respected.

On this my first duty on the range, I was standing by the Land Rover when Flying Officer Martin "Cherub" Webbon sandblasted us with his jet exhaust and then hit the ground, regrettably fatally. Martin was known as Cherub due to his choirboy like features and was held in high regard and affection. By nature, while highly professional, the pilots who fly fast jets are adventurous risktakers. Cherub's range scores were consistently high because of a technique he had developed of his own. He flew lower and decreased his angle of attack relative to the target, allowing a greater percentage of his rounds to pass through the target with less waste on the over- and under-shoot, giving him a higher than average score rate. This, of course, was more dangerous but that was the nature of ground attack. He was consistently warned about his low flying and his response was always "incorrect altimeter reading".

He requested a low fly-by to allow both him and us to estimate his height. As he gently floated towards us, the undercarriage and flaps were lowered. As he approached the range officer's post, he turned his aircraft, XE600, suddenly as if to hose us down with the jet blast. The Hunter began to crab slightly sideways and, as the jet pipe slewed towards us, the air was filled with intense heat and the overpowering smell of Avgas. Sand and hot air swept across us and for a moment we actually looked into the jet pipe and could see the fierce flame deep within. As I was standing against the Land Rover, I threw myself across the front seats to avoid the debris hurtling towards me. Sadly, Martin's aircraft had lost too much

The Range Safety Officer at his post on the Khormaksar range. Part of his job was to ensure that when running in to fire their guns pilots did not descend below a stipulated height by using an array of height markers (*Roger Wilkins*).

airspeed and, even though he applied full power, the aircraft was slow to respond. Raising myself upright, I saw her wings rock as if feeling the air and the nose rose gently skywards. The tail seemed to slide away from her and the engine spooled up, rapidly screaming to a crescendo. She was now vertical but virtually hanging in the air. Slowly, so slowly, she made a little altitude before gently, as if giving up the fight, rolling over and smashing nose-first, almost vertically, into the ground. For one bizarre moment she appeared to actually enter the ground with the aircraft disappearing as if behind an object. As the wing roots disappeared there was an explosion up the length of the aircraft and she fell back against the ground like a wounded bird. The next second we were running towards the aircraft. The explosion had not been devastating and something, a sort of vain hope, made us hope that Cherub could have survived. I remember running and jumping over pieces of wreckage as we covered half the fifty yards to the aircraft in a matter of seconds. Then the ammunition started to discharge in all directions and burning fuel splashed out across the sand, followed by a second explosion. The sergeant, who was alongside us, shouted for us to stop. Ozzie and I could not accept that Cherub could be dead and the sergeant, older and experienced had to physically restrain us from advancing further towards the wreckage. I was just 19 years old.'

The Christmas spirit is in evidence at Muharraq in 1963 as 8 Squadron members Taff John, Dave Smith, Bill Sheppard and Brian Watling try their best to drink the 'Wet Start' bar dry (*Ray Deacon*).

Bill Sheppard (Flight Lieutenant)

Having previously served on 2 Squadron flying Swifts in the fighter reconnaissance role in Germany, followed by a short refresher course at Chivenor, Bill Sheppard was posted to 8 Squadron in 1963. Here he remained flying ground-attack sorties until a few months before the end of his tour, when his FR experience was put to good use by 1417 Flight. At the end of his tour, Bill was initially posted to North Coates on Bloodhounds but was quickly assessed as suitable for instructing and moved to CFS at Little Rissington for QFI training.

Ferry Flight

'In mid-December 1964 I was tasked, together with Chris Cureton, to ferry two Hunter Mk.9s from the UK to Aden. We picked them up at Kemble, where they were prepared for the flight, and the route was to be Kemble - Luqa - El Adem - Jeddah - Khormaksar. My aircraft was the venerable XE649, which had already done a tour on 8. It was coded S from 1 April 1960 until 17 August 1962, when it was sent back to St Athan for its first refurbishment.

Now, on 14 December; it was going back out for a second tour. As usual, it was chucking it down with rain when we got to Kemble and, as usual, the aircraft weren't ready in the morning, so we kicked our heels until they were pronounced fit to go that afternoon. So we were late before we'd even started!

The first leg was incident-free, and we duly landed at Luqa (Malta) in the late afternoon in somewhat better weather than we'd left behind in the good old UK. We night-stopped there, being forbidden, for some quaint reason, to continue in the dark, which put us further behind schedule, but an early start next morning got us equally uneventfully, into El Adem, in pre-Gaddafi Libya. Here Chris's aircraft started playing up. When it worked, the later Hunter starting system of a turbine turned by ignited Avpin was great, but a series of starter-bay fires ordained that we should always have the bay door open for starting, any resulting flames being 'patted out' by the attendant airman equipped with an asbestos glove – crude, but effective. This in itself was no great problem, though it did rather negate the purpose of the system, which was to effect a rapid start followed by an equally rapid getaway in the event of a scramble. The Avpin tank, in theory, held enough of the stuff for at least three starts. However, Chris's aircraft began developing another problem, when, having pushed the starter button, all that happened was the 'wheeee, phut'. Not an uncommon phenomenon. There was a little black box on the inside of the starter-bay door and standard practice on failed start-ups was to wallop it with the butt-end of a large screwdriver, and most times it took the hint and did what it was supposed to do. With the groundcrew at El Adem fully conversant with the foibles of Hunters, this was no problem as the box was duly thumped and Chris's mount sprang to life.

Soon after getting airborne, we changed to the frequency we had been given for contact with Cairo control, but when we called them for the appropriate clearances they weren't interested, telling us to call some-one else on a frequency we didn't have (of course!). After a bit of an argument, I finally called Chris over to a frequency that was for nothing in particular, and told him to spread out to a good 3,000 yards line abreast, so as to keep a bloody good lookout behind us, while opening up to a cruising speed of around Mach 0.9. Not fuel-efficient, but that was not the worry – possible Egyptian military curiosity was. We then steered a course down the dead centre of the Red Sea until within radio range of Jeddah, which luckily seemed to have heard of us, and allowed us to land there without further argy-bargy.

And this is where the story really started. We were met, in the mid-afternoon, by a somewhat bewildered gentleman from our embassy in Jeddah in his Land Rover and, after being refuelled by a marvellous Arab from Shell, who knew all about refuelling Hunters (from where?), even to banging the drop tanks at the appropriate places to get the float-switches to do their stuff, we set off to get further clearance from Air Traffic and to seek out more Avpin. The first was successful, the second not, so we had to pray we had enough for our last start ups before Khormaksar.

In those days Jeddah was a sleepy little airport, servicing the needs of a nascent Saudia with its DC-3s, plus the odd similar aircraft from Aden, and at that time of day it was virtually deserted. Air Traffic were friendly and helpful, but there was no one else around at all – just us, our two warbirds, and the embassy chappie. No chocks, no ladders, no fire extinguishers – nothing. And Chris's aircraft playing silly buggers with its starter.

His was obviously the first priority, so we concentrated on that. By climbing up via a drop tank, a wing and the spine, and dropping into the cockpit, he readied to start up while I looked after the starter bay. And, of course – wheeee, phut and nothing else. The embassy chap looked quite amazed at this display of modern military technology and was more astonished when I asked him if, a) he had a toolkit and b) if so, did he have a screwdriver, preferably a large one? He foraged about in the bowels of the Landy and found what I wanted, so I dived under Chris's aircraft and gave it another try – same result. Not only did the prospect of a night, or more, in Jeddah not appeal, but there was the not-trifling matter of diplomatic clearance to consider, the renewal of which could have stranded us there for a couple of weeks or more. So, to the bewilderment of the watching diplomat, I hammered the black box with the handle of his screwdriver and signalled Chris to give it another go. Thanks entirely to this bit of delicate technical expertise, the starter acknowledged it was up against a superior intellect and burst into life, and a modicum of flames was extinguished by waving the door about (I seldom, even in those days, wore flying gloves!), before closing it and retreating in triumph!

Now for mine. Having left the parking brake on, Chris exited his aircraft using the reverse procedure of his entry as I got into mine in like fashion. It started up first time and after Chris had climbed back into his cockpit, strapped in and we waved good bye to the diplomat, who was shaking his head in disbelief, off we went. We should really have gone all they way down the Red Sea to where it joined the Indian Ocean, turned left and up the coast to Aden, but after a while I had had enough, so we took a short cut across Yemen, figuring that their air force radars weren't likely to bother us too much. A little later we called Khormaksar and heard the welcome voice of our own ATC, before breaking into the circuit and landing – job done.

All par for the course on many a ferry trip, but it did make me wonder what would have been the outcome had something gone wrong – Chris's parking brake slipping off or a genuine fire on one of our starts at Jeddah, for instance. One or both of us court martialled or something, probably, as, of course, we had broken, if not every one, at least several, of the rules in the book. Good fun though and I bet the embassy chap in Jeddah dined-out on the story for a few weeks after that. Some consolation for what can hardly have been a plum posting.

XE649 stayed with 8 Squadron until 20 October 1966 before being returned for yet another refurbishment and back to Bahrain to serve with 208 Squadron from 17 June 1967. Having remained with 208 until 24 February 1969, it returned to St Athan for the last time. Whoever had the pleasure of ferrying it on these occasions could probably have left it to its own devices as it would have found its own way.

OK, who's for the High Jump!

No. 8 Squadron was on one of its regular detachments to Bahrain over the Christmas period in 1963 and, shortly before starting a four-day Christmas break, our OC, Tammy Syme, dined with the CO of 3 (I think) Para, who were based on the island at the time. During what was probably a fairly alcoholic evening, the para boss opined that air force chaps didn't have the bottle to leap out of aeroplanes, preferring to stay within except in emergencies. Tammy hotly disputed this, to which the colonel responded that as they were going on a jump at Sharjah shortly, why not send some of his nancy-boy pilots to jump with them – or words to that effect. "Done," said Tammy, and next day, somewhat sheepishly, he told us what he had said and asked if he could have, say, six volunteers. Pete Loveday, Steve Jarvis and I, plus another three whose names I can't recall, raised our hands. I had actually completed the abbreviated para course at Abingdon a few years before, notching up two jumps from a tethered balloon and three from a Hastings – one of a couple of types in which I have taken off several times but never landed, the other being the DH Rapide some time later.

The next day we set off for the Para camp, where we were given a rudimentary lesson on how to land and roll with it and that was that. A couple of days later we embarked in a Beverley at Muharraq at dawn, along with a number of paras in full battle garb, kitbags etc., and headed off to the Jebel Ali area, a flattish piece of desert used by the paras for training. Feeling a bit out of place in our comparatively poncy-looking flying suits, we were subjected to cynical and amused smirks from the hefty thug-like paras as they probably wondered why we were there. On reaching the target area, the Beverley disgorged its load of paras on a couple of runs at about 800 feet, before climbing to 1,000 feet for us. Despite the option of opening the

Pete Loveday, Ray Deacon and Taff John caught in a rare serious moment during an 8 Squadron Christmas bash at Muharraq in 1963 (*Ray Deacon*).

back end, we exited from a side door in quick succession and floated gently down to earth, or sand. Except, however, in my case. Having checked the 'chute was okay, I looked down, and instantly sensed where I was heading for; within all that sand was one piece of flat rock, and, of course, no matter what I did to the virtually unsteerable para-type 'chute, I dropped inexorably towards it. On impact, I executed my three-point landing – heels-arse-head in quick succession – backwards, which made sitting down rather tender for a day or two (the heels had boots, the head a helmet, the arse ... !), but otherwise no problem. The six of us then gathered up our 'chutes and awaited the Beverley's landing to pick us up and take us home.

The atmosphere on the way back was somewhat different from that on the outward flight. The paras were more friendly and pressed upon us tin mugs of their special-brew called 'Tang', a powdered orangeade drink made up to a strength that could dissolved stainless steel. It went down surprisingly well. Although they didn't hand us an honorary red beret, we had vindicated Tammy's rash boast and gained respect from those toughies in the Paras.

There was an interesting postscript to this a little while later. During the Christmas break, most units, ours included, had installed billet bars for the lads to imbibe for as long as the copious stocks lasted. Needless to say, the 8 Squadron bar ran out of beer early on the final evening, so Pete Loveday and I went searching other bars for any surplus we could buy from them. After a fruitless search amongst several, we entered one bar in which everyone instantly froze, staring at us in a distinctly unfriendly manner. Somewhat taken aback, I asked if they had any spare beer we could buy and was about to receive, I'm sure, a frosty reply, when a voice in the crowd shouted, "Hey, mate, didn't you jump with us at Sharjah the other day?" On realising whose bar we were in, I replied in the affirmative, whereupon beers were firmly pressed upon us and we left with half-a-dozen cases of the stuff. Hardly enough to quench the drought at 8 Squadron, but better than nothing. Happy days and it did a bit for inter-service relations too.

Poor Pete Loveday was killed in Malaysia in February 1966, when, with myself and three others, he was on a detachment flying Jet Provosts on a trial for forward air controllers. On one sortie, having done his bit with them, he gave them a beat-up, but sticking up above the forest canopy was a sole, leafless tree. This he hit with his starboard wing, taking it clean off. The aircraft flipped over immediately and plunged into the jungle, killing him instantly. A sad, but very quick, end to a super guy.

Sharjah shower!

It was not just the lads who lived in Tyneham huts at Sharjah, as on the late 1963 detachment there were eight (or ten?) of us "drivers" sharing one too. The day it pissed down early on a Sunday morning, we were awoken by the noise of it on the roof. I suddenly realised that it was *fresh water* – as opposed to the sea-water showers we had there, so I yelled at the rest to get outside and have a much needed freshwater shower. We all stripped off, and dashed outside, and started lathering ourselves with proper soap, not the horrid stuff you needed for a sea-water shower. Great! Then what happened? Sod's Law. It stopped raining and there we all were, covered in soap, so we had to go back into the usual showers and rinse it all off in sea water.

Cup of tea Sir?

On that same detachment, 8 Squadron OC Squadron Leader Tammy Syme told Mike Flynn, a newly-arrived pilot, and thus the junior officer, to make coffee for him and a visiting air vice marshal. He duly did so, and luckily Tammy took the first sip. Being very new, Mike hadn't realised that the normal taps gave sea water – there were special taps for fresh water – and he had made the coffees with brine'

Peter Sturt (Flight Lieutenant)

Peter Sturt was assigned to 8 Squadron for the duration of his tour which began in September 1963 and ended in August 1965. Peter recalls a interesting sortie that included formating on a Shackleton.

Shackleton escort!

'The OC 42 Squadron was flying the Shackleton while our flight of four Hunters from 8 Squadron practised some close formation on his aircraft. I was flying XF552/D. The main thing I remember from that sortie was when

Despite the premature call, the four FGA.9s perform a timely break from the visiting 42 Squadron Shackleton MR.2 somewhere over the Aden hinterland (*Chris Bain*).

we formed up in echelon port on the port wing of the Shack and the intention was for a fifth Hunter to take a pretty photo of the four peeling neatly off to the left, a la Second World War stuff. Unfortunately, OC 42 decided to call the break rather than our formation leader and he did it by saying "standby to break", "break one", "break two", "break three", etc., in that order. Our whole formation twitched horribly. I was No. 3 and when I saw the two aircraft on my right banked towards me, I heaved up and away out of it. It took some time to get us back into any semblance of order and we did not see OC 42 after that. I think he took his aircraft on to Sharjah or Bahrain.'

Mass RAF/RN balbo

Following his tour with 8 Squadron, Peter returned to the UK for a period as an instructor at Chivenor. An exchange posting to the Royal Navy flying Buccaneers with 809 Squadron ensued during which he returned to Aden aboard HMS *Hermes* in 1967. A massive flypast over Aden and the Protectorate consisting of the Khormaksar Hunter wing and Buccaneers and Sea Vixens from HM Ships *Victorious* and *Hermes* took place on 17 May 1967. The formation was lead by Sea Vixens from 892 and 893 Squadrons, followed by Buccaneers

The largest flypast ever flown over Aden took place on 12 May 1967: fifty-five aircraft comprising Sea Vixens from 892 and 893 Squadrons, Buccaneers from 801 and 809 Squadrons, and Hunters from 8, 43 and 208 Squadrons and 1417 Flight (*via Peter Sturt*).

from 801 and 809 Squadrons with Hunters from 8, 43, 208 and 1417 Flight bringing up the rear. Peter flew XT279, a Buccaneer S.2 of 809 Squadron.

'This was quite a memorable flight since the Vixen lead pilot was not that familiar with leading large formations. During the final run in to Aden he decided that he was a few seconds too early and opted to slow down from the run-in speed of (I think) 350 knots. Unfortunately he chopped his throttle too rapidly to about 250 knots and the concertina affect as this rippled down to the back end of the formation (especially the Hunters at the very back) was again quite interesting. Fortunately the whole formation achieved some order by the time it overflew Aden Harbour and Khormaksar. I suspect the comments in the Jungle bar that evening amongst the Hunter fraternity were somewhat blue!'

Tam Syme (Squadron Leader)

Tam counts himself is one among a number of pilots who twice experienced the intensity of flying in a ground-attack role with 8 Squadron in Aden. Having cut his teeth on the Venom in the mid-fifties, Tam returned to Khormaksar for a second tour in the summer of 1963, this time as squadron commander.

Policeman's baton
'A tale that springs to mind concerns a policeman's baton; not just any policeman, but one from the Crater area. During my first partial tour on 8 Squadron around 1957, an unfortunate policeman came into a bar we frequented and someone (could it have been me?) gently lifted it from the hook on the unsuspecting victim's belt. The baton then became a prized

Recent arrival Squadron Leader Des Melaniphy (left) and Squadron Leader Tam Syme pictured during the handover of the command of 8 Squadron in the summer of 1965 (*Mal Grosse*).

Tam Syme and Des Melaniphy extricate themselves from a Hunter T.7 at the end of a familiarisation flight over the Aden hinterland (*Mal Grosse*).

treasure in the pilots' crewroom. When I went back to the squadron in 1963, I was amazed to find that the baton was still there.'

Peter Taylor (Flight Lieutenant)

The author is indebted to Peter Taylor for allowing him to include his excellent article entitled 'Unforgettable Years'. Following a ground tour as station adjutant at RAF Chivenor, Peter arrived in Aden on 7 September 1965 and succeeded Graham Williams as a flight commander on 8 Squadron. Two years later, to the day, and on promotion to squadron leader, Peter was posted to HQ Transport Command as Squadron Leader Harrier Policy.

Unforgettable years
'At about 13:30 local time on 29 November, 1967, the last British forces in Aden leapt into Westland Wasp helicopters and took off from the twelfth brown of the golf course. In doing so, they left behind one of Britain's most influential bases in the hands of the local Arabs. Thus ended a British presence in that extraordinary part of the world which had lasted for 128 years.

From my point of view (and that of many others), I did not feel good about our departure. I felt I was deserting a large number of local people from all walks of life who had supported us, and then depended on us for their safety and future prosperity. It didn't happen, and after our departure some terrible things were done to anyone who had served the British in virtually any capacity. It has to be said that President Nasser's pledge that he 'would kick the British right out of the Arab world' came about in Aden as a result of the failure of political rather than military will.

This is very much a personal story of what it was like to live and operate in the Aden Protectorate in the last two years of its existence. I'm glad to be able to write about it now, some forty-two years after the events which left an indelible mark on those who were there. We, the military and our families, the politicians and officials and, of course, the local people, were all caught up in the maelstrom caused by an end-of-empire struggle and a vicious nationalist movement.

Political background

The political situation in Aden affected just about every part of our lives. Until about 1963, despite the rise of Arab nationalism, Britain seemed determined to retain a strong presence in Southern Arabia. Indeed, an uprising in 1964 in the Radfan was put down very firmly by combined British forces. However, a change of government at the end of 1963 had brought about a review of Britain's role in the Middle East and the consequent need for large military bases. And Aden was a large base, containing great numbers of soldiers and sailors, and the huge RAF base at Khormaksar.

By 1965 it became clear that the British government had it in mind to withdraw all British forces from Aden and the surrounding territories, probably within two years. This was all the encouragement the various tribal and political factions needed. By early 1965 terrorist incidents in the Protectorate were a daily occurrence and casualties began to mount on both sides. The Army was reinforced, internal security tasks were greatly increased, so that patrolling the streets, security walls and barbed wire, and stop-and-search became a familiar scene. It was against this background that I arrived as a flight commander on 8 Squadron in September 1965.

Key personalities

During my tour in Aden, we were led by some exceptional people, many of whom went on to the highest posts in the land. Our governor for the last, difficult months was Sir Humphrey Trevelyan, while the commander-in-chief was the charismatic and much-admired Admiral Sir Michael le Fanu. He was often seen, dressed in his blue issue navy shorts, pushing Lady le Fanu in her wheelchair on the streets or to the beach. He would occasionally put on his driver's hat, and drive his own car, with the driver in the back. He would also wave to all and sundry if he saw that we had recognised him.

There were two air officers commanding in my time, the fighter ace AVM J.E. Johnnie Johnson, being the first. On his departure from Aden back to England we were required to escort him out of the area and provided him with a formation in the shape of a J. He was followed by a great man, AVM Andrew Humphrey, who later became Chief of the Air Staff and then Chief of Defence Staff before dying tragically young. We also got to know the marvellous Lady Humphrey who seemed to know then, and still remembers, so many of our names. Our two senior air staff officers were Air Commodores Mike le Bas and Freddie Sowrey.

RAF Khormaksar

In 1965 Khormaksar was probably the biggest operational base in the RAF, serving the whole of Southern Arabia. Just about every type of transport, support and strike aircraft operated from Khormaksar. It was a tough station from which to operate – and it needed someone tough to run it. No problem there. Our station commander was Air Commodore Michael Beetham, who became Marshal of the RAF Sir Michael Beetham, one of our longest ever serving Chiefs of the Air Staff (CAS).

Strike Wing Khormaksar consisted of 37 Squadron with Avro Shackleton MR.2s; 8 and 43 Squadrons with Hawker Hunter FGA.9s and T.7s; and 1417 Flight with FR.10s. The wing commander was E.S. (Martin) Chandler. I once asked him why he was called Martin when his initials were E.S. Martin gave a typical answer: 'If your names were Ernest Sydney, wouldn't you change your name?' Wing Commander Chandler's Squadron Leaders Operations, were firstly Roy Bowie and then Fred Trowern. They were both great characters; Roy a former 20 Squadron CO and a very good rugby referee, and Fred, who was a hugely experienced pilot and was subsequently chosen as a member of the HS Kestrel FGA.1 (Harrier precursor) Tri-Partite Evaluation Squadron at West Raynham, Norfolk.

No. 8 Squadron was commanded by Squadron Leader Des Melaniphy, No. 43 firstly by Phil Champniss and then Harry Davidson, while 1417 Flight was commanded by Dickie Barraclough. Also on 1417 was Flight Lieutenant Richard Johns, who later became CAS and, on retiring from the service, was appointed Constable of Windsor Castle and chairman of the RAF Museum.

All three Hunter units were full of characters and in the main got on together extremely well, especially considering that the two ground-attack squadrons had to share aircraft through the imposition of centralised servicing. This meant that the units had to pool all their assets in second-line servicing. None of us liked this much because as we worked a twenty-four-hour shift, starting and finishing at midday on alternate days, the incoming squadron was unlikely to inherit a large number of serviceable aircraft. There wasn't much incentive to repair aircraft just to hand them over to the next mob. However, we all managed affairs well, and squadron life, operational and training flying, combined with a great social life, meant that this was one of the best tours of my service career.

The Hunter

I cannot imagine that anyone who saw and flew the Hunter did not cherish the experience (probably even those who flew the Armstrong Siddeley Sapphire-powered F.5). In all her guises, she maintained the original graceful lines of the Hawker design team. By the time the FGA.9 arrived on the scene, the aircraft was good to fly, maintained reasonable serviceability, and was powered by the superb Rolls Royce Avon 200 series. Weapons and weapon-aiming were still fairly rudimentary, but good training and plenty of practice enabled us to get the 30mm cannon rounds and the 3-inch rockets close to the targets. We didn't do much 1,000lb (453kg) bombing in the Protectorate, and the SNEB rocket had not yet reached us.

Ever since I had been in Fighter Command and met a few people who had served in Aden, I had wanted to go there. I heard about operations in the de Havilland Venom with its centrifugal-flow Ghost. I knew also that when the Hunter superseded the Venom, there were one or two doubts that the axial-flow Avon might not cope so well with the large quantities of sand which were inevitably ingested. Nothing could have been further from the truth; we all felt the greatest confidence operating deep in the interior at high or low level with this remarkable engine behind us. The memories all come flooding back – 7,850rpm, 680 degrees C jet-pipe temperature, 35psi oil pressure. The Hunter wing design was superb, especially after the introduction of the dog-tooth leading edge. The aircraft had virtually no vices and enabled us to concentrate on operating, which was just as well, because operating in Aden could be demanding.

Operations and daily life

So what were these operations in Aden during the last two years of the British presence? The main operational tasks were in support of our army colleagues and the local government. There was some post-Radfan activity, which intensified as terrorist incidents in the region increased.

Nos 8 and 43 Squadrons would be tasked either to attack specific, pre-planned targets or under close control of both British and Arab Forward Air Controllers. These attacks were almost always preceded by leaflet dropping to warn of impending attack, followed by pre- and post-reconnaissance by 1417 Flight's Hunter FR.10s. One such attack took place in the Radfan at a place called Khuraybah, a very rugged area and the scene of one of my first operational sorties. My logbook tells me that, on 30 December 1965, I led a four-ship formation to attack a single house which we had been told was harbouring weapons for dissident tribesmen. In classic air control style, a leaflet drop by Frank Grimshaw (who a year earlier had been my best man) warned the villagers of the proposed attack and advised them to leave the area. As Frank circled overhead, one-by-one our four FGA.9s fired four unguided rockets each at the now deserted house, while the tribesmen sat in the hills taking pot shots at us with a variety of hand-held weapons. During and after the attack, Frank took the pictures and we certainly gave it a hammering, although one would have to admit a small amount of collateral damage to next door.

While writing about up-country operations, let me tell you about the incredible community at Wilan, located about fifty miles (eighty kilometres) north of Aden, almost 7,000 feet (2,133 metre) above sea level. It was a rugged place with virtually no water. The tribesmen who lived there were very fiercely independent and lived a primitive existence. The women had to walk down a steep track to bring in water when it was scarce, which must have been most of the time. I was also told, but I cannot confirm, that the inhabitants believed that their calendar was some 1,000 years behind ours. I don't know how many Europeans have ever been there, but none of us ever wanted to upset them in case we came down nearby.

Another memorable location was Shabwah, some 150 miles (241 kilometres) north-east of Aden and on the western edge of the great Wadi Hadramaut. Shabwah, now in ruins, was reputed to be on the old spice route where the Queen of Sheba maintained a palace. Such were the places over which we flew our day-to-day operations – it was truly breathtaking.

However, to move to more mundane matters – as I have already described, 8 and 43 Squadrons operated a twenty-four-hour shift, which

Above and below: Two views of the Hadramaut region some 300 miles north-east of Aden as seen from an 8 Squadron Hunter flying low over the varied landscape (*both, Mac McLauchlan*).

began and ended at about 13:00 on alternate days. A standby of two fully-armed FGA.9s with rockets and guns was the absolute priority between dawn and dusk, ready to give immediate support to the ground forces anywhere in the Protectorate. Morning standby meant being ready to take off in the dark, if required, so that when dawn broke at about 05:15 to 05:30 attacks could be made.

Training encompassed the whole gamut of ground-attack and air-defence operations. Our staple diet was four- and six-ship simulated attacks with bounces; air combat in simulated small and large formations; practice interceptions under radar control; army and naval co-operation; and, of course, a great deal of weapons training, both at the excellent range just north of Khormaksar and at selected ranges up-country. All this was interspersed with operational sorties of every kind, not only to assist in maintaining the security of the Protectorate but also to continue to advertise the strength and determination of the British presence.

Detachments in Southern Arabia

There were also some interesting detachments to be had in the general area of Southern Arabia. For example, 8 and 43 Squadrons undertook regular ten- to twelve-day detachments to the island of Masirah in the Oman. Masirah had a large runway and was staffed by a small number of RAF personnel on one-year, unaccompanied tours. Other than superb beaches, an unsophisticated weapons range, thousands of turtles, good sporting facilities and the Golden Flip-Flop bar, Masirah did not have much to offer. However, we always seemed to have a marvellous time when there. The permanent staff seemed to like us because we were a different lot against which to compete at cricket and football. And there were always lots of memorable incidents.

On my first trip to Masirah in October 1965, over the first weekend, I flew to Beit Al Falaj on the north coast of Muscat where my flying instructor on DH Vampires, Brian Entwisle, was the squadron commander of the seconded British presence. The Omani Air Force in the area consisted mainly of Percival Provost T.52s (the piston-engined trainer) and DH Canada Beavers. While with Brian over the weekend, we flew eight sorties together, firing 3-inch rockets, low flying and landing at some extraordinary strips. The names were so romantic; Lonetree, Sayq, Hazam – but, nowhere near so romantic when you were trying to find them and discovered the words on the map, Position approximate, Abandoned, Disused, Existence reported, Elevation unknown.

I had enormous respect for the skill and knowledge of Brian's squadron, one of whom was the almost legendary Puddy Catt, who flew with me on one of my Provost weapons' sorties, for which I had to offer him a reciprocal sortie in a Hunter T.7 some months later. That sortie was the lowest I have

An overhead view of Bayt al Falaj airfield on the north coast of Muscat, home to the Sultan of Oman's Air Force (*Aviation Bookshop*).

ever flown over sand because I swear Puddy thought he was still in a Provost flying at 100 knots!

Back at Masirah, the usual round of flying, sports and evening entertainment was often enlivened by a late night trip to the beach to see the turtles lay their eggs in the sand. And they say aircrew have no soul. But, by the end of our stay at Masirah, we certainly had moustaches, since growing them seemed to be one of the obligatory competitions on all detachments. After one such sojourn, on our return to Aden we were met by our wives who normally seemed quite pleased to see us. However, on seeing Andrew Bell's ginger monstrosity, his delightful wife Victoria gave him an ultimatum, 'Andrew, I shall not shave under my arms until you remove that awful thing!' It was off that night!

Social life
In Aden, we enjoyed a great social life. The officers' mess was well run, with plenty of good entertainment. Regular film shows outside, formal dinners, excellent swimming pools and many squadron activities made for good morale. For those of us who were married, we lived mainly either in the Ma'alla flats or in slightly bigger premises at Khormaksar

Beach. Beaches and swimming pools were, of course, plentiful. The main areas used by the majority of us were at the Tarshyne beaches at Steamer Point. Occasionally we would take the eight-mile (thirteen-kilometre) trip to the oil refinery beaches at Little Aden, nicknamed the Costa Bremner, after a brigadier of the same name, one of our Army senior officers.

Also en route to Little Aden was the British Cemetery at Silent Valley, where many British servicemen were laid to rest over the final few months of our presence in Aden. It was a solitary, but rather beautiful place and I believe that it was well cared for long after our departure. Let's hope it still is.

There were also good eating places in the area and, until the end of 1966, it was reasonably safe to go to them. Air Conditioning was not plentiful and, except for the squadron crewrooms and one bedroom, we all made do with acclimatisation and the ubiquitous fan. The fan not only provided some air movement and cooling, but was a source of endless entertainment. For example, winding the fan up to full speed and throwing in empty beer cans could produce unpredictable results. Full cans were, of course, silly in all respects, and when one just missed the station commander, there was a bit of a fuss and the practice was officially discouraged. I also saw Fred Trowern stop a spinning fan with his head. There is a technique to this and if you don't know it, I don't recommend it.

The food we ate was interesting. Before terrorism really took hold, it was possible to get fresh meat (sheep, goat) from the old town of Crater. Other meat came frozen from Australia and the eggs locally apparently came from China. We seemed to eat quite well, and whenever I went back to RAF Chivenor, Devon, on one of our yearly Hunter Simulator and Emergency (HSE) refresher courses, I always brought back a leg of lamb which we shared with some of our friends (imagine trying that now).

The weather was generally very good. The Cool Season (low 80s and low humidity) lasted from October to May. The Hot Season (high 90s and high humidity) was with us for the other months. As April and May approached, we all watched the forecasts as the Inter-Tropical Convergence Zone moved inexorably south, bringing with it the extremes of temperature and humidity, and the worry of severe sandstorms. These stopped everything in their tracks and, as there were few close diversion airfields, flying operations were carefully monitored. Even without sandstorms, visibility in the Hot Season was seldom good, even up to 20,000 feet (6,000 metres).

Terrorism grows

By the middle of 1966, as the political situation deteriorated, terrorism both in Aden and up-country was growing. This affected all our lives both for us and our families. Murders of British and Arab people in the shopping and eating areas were increasing. Generally, we were not armed, although duty wardens were introduced in the areas where the families were concentrated. The wardens were temporarily issued with pistols.

At this point I shall admit something now after all these years. When my wife flew out to join me in December 1965, I had purchased a small automatic 0.25 Browning through a London store and had it placed aboard her BOAC flight in custody of the crew. When she left the aircraft, the crew handed her the package which she thought was some jewellery that I had bought to welcome her to the Middle East. I think she was just a bit disappointed when she discovered it was a gun. I tried to teach her how to use it at Khormaksar beach but, having fired it once, she yelled and dropped it in the seawater. I managed to recover it and I carried it with me for the rest of my time in Aden whenever I went shopping or eating.

As 1966 drew to a close, terrorism reached a peak and it was clear that if we, the British, were to leave Aden in 1967, evacuation of families would have to begin soon. My abiding memory of the back end of 1966 and early 1967 is of increased street patrols, grenade throwing, the odd bomb explosion and more trouble in the hinterland. The latter generated an interesting situation in the Beihan region, which led to some demanding flying for all the Hunter units.

Beihan outpost

If memory serves me correctly, in June or July 1966, the Egyptian Air Force mounted an attack on a fort or palace of one of the local sultans in the Beihan region. I think the attacks were carried out by MiG-17 Frescos and some physical damage was done to the fort, which was situated on the border area of Saudi Arabia, North Yemen and the Protectorate. All this was some 100 miles (160 kilometres) north of Khormaksar airfield.

To deter further attacks, the RAF was tasked to fly armed patrols in the Beihan area. However, we all know how expensive and generally inefficient it is to maintain airborne patrols. It so happened that there was a tarmac runway at Beihan which was used by RAF Beverleys, among others, to re-supply forward troops. As the runway was only about 1,500 yards (1,371 metres) long, at about 4,000 feet (1,219 metres) above mean sea level, and it was the Hot Season, Hunter operations were not feasible. Very quickly the decision was taken to lengthen the runway by about 300 yards. In no time at all, the Royal Engineers built the extension so that 8 and 43 Squadron Hunters could complete a Beihan patrol, land at the airstrip and carry out an armed daylight standby, though getting in and out was always a demanding affair. I believe that someone on 43 Squadron was the first to land a Hunter at Beihan, but Wing Commander Chandler and I were the first under 8 Squadron colours to land there on 15 August in the early morning.

Later that week, on 19 August, I returned to Beihan with a great friend from 43 Squadron, Neil Hayward. Again, we went at first light in the relative cool, remained on standby in the tent, and took off at last light, landing back at Aden in the dusk. During the day, the heat and dust were intense. I was never sure how we would receive enough warning to get airborne, or if indeed we could have taken off at all in the middle of the day. As I have indicated, Beihan operations were somewhat problematical and after one more landing on 22 September, air patrols once more became the preferred method of making our presence felt.

All through the end of 1966 and early 1967 the emphasis was more and more on operational flying. Patrols, flagwaves, and the occasional strike were our regular diet. On 1 May 1967 the evacuation of families began in earnest. My wife and recently-born son were on the first aircraft to leave. From that time onwards life changed greatly for all of us.

Towards withdrawal

From May until the final withdrawal in November, the pace of life quickened considerably. Once the families had gone, the flats and the beaches were practically empty. The officers' mess at Khormaksar could not cope with the large numbers previously living off the base and some of the nearer family housing had to be used instead. It was an eerie experience to drive through Ma'alla and see row upon row of deserted flats, many with empty holes in the walls where air conditioners had either been stolen or requisitioned to replace unserviceable equipment. It became commonplace to see squatters and animals in all areas previously occupied by British servicemen and their families.

As the families and eventually the servicemen began to withdraw, it was also becoming common to see abandoned cars in ever stranger places. Rather than leave the cars to the terrorists, some people had driven their cars off cliffs, left them on the edges of the desert and, towards the end, some intrepid person had managed to get his car to the top of Shamsan, the extinct volcano which encompassed the old town of Crater.

On 8 Squadron, Squadron Leader Des Melaniphy left for home in March. He was succeeded, much to our delight, by Squadron Leader Fred Trowern from Strike Wing.

In June much happened in the Middle East, not all of it in Aden. With the Hot Season well and truly established, we were all astonished at the ferocity and efficiency of the Israeli Air Force in destroying Arab air resources in the Six Day War. In the air-conditioned operations centre, we were able to follow the progress of that great air campaign. The lessons were not lost on any of us. Shortly after the war ended, the Adenis called a fuel strike which had a significant effect on our capacity to continue flying. As one result of this, it was decided that 8 Squadron should detach the majority of its aircraft to Sharjah.

Typical of Fred Trowern, he let me take six aircraft and about ten pilots with supporting groundcrew for just over six weeks. We were able to maintain normal flying training, while he and the others remained on short rations in Aden. Once the fuel strike was over, the Sharjah detachment returned to Aden. Flying operations in support of the ground forces intensified by day, and also by night. Up till now, only the Shackletons had operated in Radfan country at night, and from what I saw they were effective. Nobody likes a lot of thousand-pounders dropped on their heads, even in the mountains of the Radfan.

However, the AOC, AVM Humphrey, thought that it would be an even better idea if the FGA.9s could fire a few rockets and guns at rebel positions and road communications. Accordingly, a few of us were selected to train to fire weapons at night. It was not too bad firing on the range, because horizons and the various lights gave reasonable definition. In the mountains, with no lights, lots of haze and black as pitch, it was not a lot of fun. Add to this an artificial horizon which tended to be unreliable after a hefty (panic-stricken?) pull-out from a 30-degree dive, and temporary blindness caused by the rocket motors, and you can imagine that this was quite a sporting endeavor. I don't know if we frightened any tribesmen, but ....

The last months

Our time in Aden, and mine in particular, was coming to a close. Withdrawal was becoming a reality, with some units returning to the UK and others redeploying to other parts of the Middle East. We had a new station commander, Group Captain D.F.M. Browne, and Martin Chandler had been succeeded by Bob Ramirez.

There was little opportunity to get off-base and we tended to spend a lot of our evenings in the flats we were now all sharing. I think we were about six to a flat, and I'm glad to say I could not think of better people to be with. We had an enormous amount of fun, much of which seems a bit irresponsible now, although we were all suffering slightly from siege mentality.

I remember one evening when much damage was done to the brain and body by the six of us imbibing large quantities of Drambuie shandy. This led to long periods of fans at full speed, using the odd head in an attempt to slow them down, beer cans being spat out, and finally pillows being thrown in by the pair. Next day, we were knee deep in feathers which could only be cleared by throwing lots of water on them, before sweeping them through the windows on to the sand below.

Talking of water, I should have mentioned The Big Flood. On 1 April 1967 John Hill was due to get married. For two unprecedented days it poured with rain and there was a huge flood, turning Khormaksar into a swimming pool and most of the rest of Aden into a quagmire of mud. Huge quantities of water built up behind security walls which then broke and poured gallons of mud on to the roads and into the flats. Some people were even drowned, and cemeteries

Rainfall in any quantity was extremely rare in Aden and there was no drainage system. An occasional light shower did not cause problems but the deluge that hit the State on April Fool's Day 1967 caused flooding over the whole area. In this view an RAF Mini driver braves the waves at Khormaksar (*Ken Simpson*).

were washed away with some very unfortunate results. However, John still got married. A week or two after the flood, the desert bloomed and for a while, there were great areas of green. It really was miraculous.

It was also in the last few months that the Royal Northumberland Fusiliers, led by Lieutenant Colonel Richard Blenkinsop, suffered appalling casualties when some of the Arab Police and Security Forces mutinied. On 20 June 1967, twenty-three British soldiers and one civilian were killed. It was a dreadful time and, from that day, I have always had the greatest admiration for the way Lieutenant Colonel Blenkinsop and his men conducted themselves in the immediate aftermath. Not only did they not seek wholesale revenge, but continued to show great courage in the face of further provocation. Their last parade was at Silent Valley, where they said their farewells to their friends before flying home.

The Northumberlands were succeeded by the Argyll and Sutherland Highlanders, commanded by the aggressive Lieutenant Colonel Colin Mitchell or, as he later became known, 'Mad Mitch'. He and his troops carried out a much-publicised attack on Crater, the area from which the mutiny probably sprang.

My last weeks

During my last few weeks in Aden, life was much the same: terrorist attacks in town, rebel activity up-country, flying in support, and sharing the good times and the bad with some very good people. Perhaps there should be one last anecdote. Once the families had gone, we were left pretty much to find our own entertainment, and I've explained what that added up to. However, the *Daily Express*, which had been prominent in reporting what went on in Aden, realised that the troops were not getting much entertainment from the stars at home. To be fair, there was a problem of insurance because clearly Aden was a dangerous place. Nevertheless, the *Express* stuck at it and in a few weeks we were entertained by Hughie Green, Bob Monkhouse, Tony Hancock and Samantha Jones. I don't know if they knew how much their visits meant to us, but they were quite marvellous, often putting on four or more shows each day for three or four days. I felt sorry for Tony Hancock, who was clearly at the end of his tether and died a few months later in Australia.

On 1 September 1967 I flew my last operational sortie in Aden – an armed border patrol – with Daz James. Six days later, I packed my kit, said my farewells to the few who were left on 8 and 43 Squadrons, gave my car, I think, to Sid Morris and left Khormaksar by Vickers VC 10 bound for Brize Norton in Oxfordshire.

As you can see, Aden was an unforgettable tour for me. The politicians and officials, the commanders, the men and women, the families and friends, together forged an unbreakable bond. Nor can I forget the many Arabs who served with us and for us, and to this day I still don't feel good about some of those left behind. Finally, there was the Hunter – a masterpiece if ever there was one. She was beautiful, she could be deadly, and with that great Avon engine, she was reliable. Who could ask for more?'

Fred Trowern (Squadron Leader)

Fred Trowern was posted to 8 Squadron, at that time under the command of Squadron Leader Rex Knight, in June 1959 and joined Flight Lieutenants Tai Retief, Porky Munro and Manx Kelly on C Flight, the fighter reconnaissance element equipped with Meteor Mark 9s. A and B Flights were still equipped with Venom FB.4s.

My first experience of Aden
'After a short period we became independent, and titled 'The Arabian Peninsula Reconnaissance Flight' (APRF). Tai Retief was the officer commanding and we were subsequently boosted with the arrival of another Meteor pilot, Tim Seabrook. However, we still continued to fly each others' aircraft. During August/September both 8 Squadron and APRF pilots began their conversion training for the Hunter Mark 9. Having re-equipped, 8 Squadron continued to operate with two flights, the APRF being amalgamated as B Flight with Tai Retief as the flight commander. Squadron Leader Laurie Jones assumed command of 8 Squadron in March 1961 and my last trip of my first tour took place on 6 June 1961.

Welcome back!
I returned to Aden in May 1966 as Deputy OC Strike Wing to Wing Commander Martin Chandler, succeeding Squadron Leader Roy Bowie. Sadly, Strike Wing had by now suffered 'Centralised Servicing', both 8 and 43 Squadrons sharing the same Hunter FGA.9s with, to my horror, 43 Squadron markings aft of the fuselage roundel and 8 Squadron markings to the fore of the roundel. Squadron Leader Des Melaniphy was OC 8 Squadron and Squadron Leader Harry Davidson OC 43 Squadron. The recce element, equipped with the Hunter Mark 10 had again broken away and become 1417 Flight commanded by Squadron Leader Dickie Barraclough.

Superb study of Sandy Burns pulling his FR.10 XE589 away from a 37 Squadron Shackleton's camera somewhere above the Aden hinterland (*Sandy Burns*).

In May 1967 I assumed command of 8 Squadron. Shortly thereafter, 43 Squadron was disbanded and 1417 Flight rejoined 8 Squadron as its B Flight. In August 1967 the squadron deployed to Masirah as cover for the withdrawal of military forces from Aden. A couple of our aircraft and pilots remained in Aden to the very end. Our aircraft were repainted in their correct markings and after one or two sorties to Aden to check the situation of our chaps, we deployed to Bahrein, via a short period at Sharjah. We joined 208 Squadron, the resident Bahrein fighter squadron, also equipped with the Hunter FGA.9 and commanded by Squadron Leader Tony Chapman. My flight commanders were initially George Aylett (A Flight) and Derek Whitman (B Flight).

When I handed over command of 8 Squadron to Jock McVie at the end of October 1968, A Flight had eight FGA.9s and B Flight four FR.10s. Oh, and we also had a couple of T.7s.'

Mike Veale (Junior Technician)

An electrical fitter (aircraft) by trade, Mike arrived on 8 Squadron following a tour with 1 and 54 Squadrons at West Raynham.

'I married my first wife Pam whilst stationed there and she was pregnant when I was placed on PWR for an accompanied tour to Aden. I flew out in early 1966 and she followed in time to have our daughter in Steamer Point military hospital in September.

The Ma'alla Incident

On what was probably one of my first days on the squadron, I was walking past the compressed-air bottle storage compound when there was an almighty bang, a hiss as an enormous air bottle leapt over a fence and headed in my direction. Like a torpedo it buried itself in the soft sand, only coming to a halt when it slammed into the tarmacked road. I was so shocked that it didn't occur to me to run; I just stood there gaping at it. I mentioned it when I arrived at the squadron hut, but nobody seemed surprised. It obviously took a lot to stir 8 Squadron.

Coming from West Raynham, I knew my way round the aircraft fairly well and it didn't take long to get used to not touching anything metallic with bare flesh. Being very skinny, I was the obvious choice when an engine-starter panel needed replacing. This was a board that hung on the starboard side of the fuselage in the starter bay. Hawkers, in their wisdom, used soldered connections rather than plugs and sockets and the only way to enter the bay was to take my shirt off and wriggle in holding the panel against my back. This was a major mistake as molten solder tended to drip into my navel and I still have the scars to show for it.

Incidentally, I was doing a starter-board change when an Aden Airways Viscount exploded, as witnessed by Noddy Hawkins. I dropped out of that bay a lot quicker than I went in to see bits of Viscount still going up. I learned later that the airline had a policy of isolating its aircraft for a twenty-four-hour period as a precaution against an onboard bomb.

The structure of the Hunter required that the electrical and instrument trades needed to work closely together. We had two instrument fitters; John Cowgill (I think) and the other whose name escapes me. They looked very similar, fair hair and blue eyes, and were nicknamed "Bill and Ben the instrument men".

One day I went out to do a pre-flight check on a T.7, accompanied by Bill (or was it Ben?). The aircraft had been cooking on the pan for several hours and we decided to do our cockpit checks together. Part of my task was to lower the canopy but, having neglected to check for hydraulic pressure first, there was no response when I selected "Up". Within a few minutes the sweat was dripping from us. Finally, someone noticed our frantic hand signals and disappeared, we thought, to call for assistance. A few seconds later, we were surrounded by hysterical airmen but, by then, things were starting to become serious.

Eventually, a sympathetic soul waved a hand-pump handle and disappeared to the rear of the cockpit only to re-appear moments later to tell us he would have to get a hydraulic rig. It transpired that all were in use, not the message we wanted to hear. I had always been a bit claustrophobic and our situation was becoming increasingly desperate. It was agreed that the only way that we could get out was to start the engine. Instructions were bellowed out and the cartridge fired. As the engine spun-up I selected "Up" and the canopy rose, allowing a wave of relatively cool air to wash over us. Instructions were subsequently issued to prevent the situation arising again.

Being married, I lived off-camp in a very nice flat on the Ma'alla Straight. Our block of flats was called Basildon House and faced the harbour rather than the shabby Arab quarter. Its position was appreciated even more when Rod Carter's flat received a rocket-propelled grenade through the flimsy wall. His near neighbours, Ron and Helen Speer, decided that it was a too close for comfort and moved in with us in No. 11. Things became a little cramped, but not for long as Ron became tour-ex a short while later.

As the security situation deteriorated, the decision was taken that all dependants would be sent home and Pam and our young daughter, Sarah, were given their date to fly out. In the darkness of the designated evening, a coach took us to the departure lounge at Khormaksar and the last thing my wife said to me as she boarded the VC10 was "Be careful, don't do anything silly". There was no coach to take me back to my flat so I asked Bill (or Ben) if he would give me a lift in their open Hillman Minx tourer. As we entered Ma'alla an agitated pongo (naval slang for an Army soldier) flagged us down. His patrol had been hit by a grenade and their radio-man was severely injured. Their radio was out of action. "Would we go to the patrol HQ and summon help?" Of course we agreed but the task lost its appeal when he told us that it was in the Arab quarter. With the injured soldier on the floor and groaning in pain, we set off on our errand of mercy.

The journey took us down the straight and left into a narrow alley that was out of bounds to service personnel. A hundred yards in, we arrived at a heavily-defended building from which the sound of radio traffic could be heard. Bill stopped the car and went in to inform them of the attack while

Ben and I sat outside feeling very exposed and vulnerable, especially as Bill had taken the ignition keys with him.

Apart from the radio chatter not a sound could be heard or light seen from any of the surrounding buildings. I began to imagine hidden eyes watching us. Eventually Bill emerged and told us there was a body in the building; he didn't know whether it was alive or dead. He quickly reversed and we got out of there as quickly as possible and headed for my flat.

The following morning I handed the flat over to a grumpy warrant officer who took pleasure in admonishing me for not calling him "Sir" enough times. That afternoon I moved into the 8 Squadron barrack block on Khormaksar airfield.

Armed and dangerous

Airmen who served in Aden will remember the boring guard duties imposed on them. Patrolling the Marine Craft Unit was not a problem, but I hated guarding the MRT pans; there, the floodlights faced inwards, making it impossible to see any activity beyond the perimeter fence. Any number of FLOSY or NLF subversives could have been out there and we would never know. Our five rounds of .303 ammunition would not have made much of an impression on them. And heaven help anyone who lost a round; they would be in serious trouble while the terrorists had more rounds than they knew what to do with.

Competition Hotshot!

As events transpired, and being a member of the station shooting team, I fired several rounds during my tour. Working shifts allowed time to undertake practice shoots on the long range at Little Aden. We entered a team of four in the Inter-Unit (postal) All-Arms Competition, which required us to shoot two classes of rifle, sub-machine gun and pistol. We went on to win. News of the result soon spread and we were asked to represent Khormaksar, the RAF, the Queen and the Raj' at the annual Aden Police Rifle competition. This was a prestigious event and an honour to be invited we were informed, so how could we refuse?

Final practice took place on the long range and we were confident that we could put on a good show. Just as we were packing up our equipment an Army captain, together with his patrol, arrived, demanding to know if the range been swept. Looking rather perplexed we asked him what he meant. "Mines," he bellowed, "Mines." Standing orders stated that the range should be swept for mines before any shooting could take place. Little did he realise that we had been using the range for several months and it was a chastened rifle team that headed home that day.

On the day of the competition, and accompanied by a couple of officers, we were flown by Andover to an up-country airstrip, completely devoid of buildings. The pilot did not hang around and headed straight back to Khormaksar on the understanding that he would return later in the day. A Land Rover then appeared and took us to the range; it was not much more than a patch of flat desert with a couple of marquees. After a short while, large numbers of Arabs appeared from every direction accompanied by members of the police who began to organise them into teams according to their respective tribes. A quick scan of their weapons raised our hopes, some dating from the First World War and others homemade, their wooden bodies being strapped to the barrel with copper electrical wire. The ammunition was green with mould. With our trusty .303s we were on a winner, or so we thought.

Not long before the contest was due to begin, and much to our surprise, another Land Rover carrying a dozen or so brand-new Parker Hale target

Following the loss of Dakota KJ955 through sabotage at Khormaksar, the Middle East Communications Flight received Andover CC.2 XS793 as its replacement. The photograph captures it parked alongside a 105 Squadron Argosy in 1967 (*Aviation Bookshop*).

rifles with Vernier sights arrived. The rules of the competition were then explained. It was to be a knockout event in which two teams fired at a series of metal plates set up at a distance of 300 yards. On the word "Go", at the 400-yard point, each team had to run to the 300-yard mark, load and fire. The first team to knock all their plates down was declared the winner.

Our opponents had tucked their loose clothing into their belts, exposing skinny little bow legs that left us floundering behind. As we arrived at the 300-yard marker they were knocking the last of their plates from their mounts. A complete fiasco and humiliating defeat. As the competition came to a close, we were invited to join everyone else for a feast in one of the marquees but, having seen what was on the menu, I was happy to stick to my RAF packed lunch; a curled-up cheese sandwich, a packet of crisps and a bitter apple. How the mighty had fallen. The arrival of our aircraft could not have come soon enough.'

Graham Williams (Flight Lieutenant)

A short detour to Aden

Graham was one of only a few Hunter pilots to have had prior experience of what it was like to fly in Aden and this occurred during his tour with 54 Squadron from 1958 to 1960.

'We deployed four aircraft from El Adem, where we were on exercise, to Khormaksar in 1960. They were flown by Squadron Leader Ian Worby (OC 54), Wing Commander Bennet (OC Flying at Stradishall, our home base), Flight Lieutenant Chris Bruce and yours truly. We stayed in Aden for three days (1 to 4 April). The Boss and the wing commander flew an operational sortie with 8 Squadron whilst Chris and I remained in the bar. We had our own groundcrew with us and, unbeknown to me, they took the leading edges off my aircraft and filled them with cigarettes. I had the last laugh because Chris and I went u/s in Khartoum on the way back and the aircraft were left baking in the sun for three days. The cigarettes were totally unsmokable. I remember it all as though it was yesterday; unfortunately it was over fifty years ago.

I was posted to 8 Squadron at the beginning of October 1963. Squadron Leader Tammy Syme was the Boss and I was to take over from Jock McVie as OC A Flight. The other flight commander was Gordon Talbot and the Engineering Officer was Owen Truelove who led

Above: Time to relax for 8 Squadron pilots at Tam Syme's married quarter with from l to r, Graham Williams, Paul Constable, Kiwi Hounsell and Tam Syme (*Mal Grosse*).

Below: Dressed for a special function, 8 Squadron pilots on the pan at Muharraq in late 1963 with, from l to r; Chris Cureton, Nick Adamson, Jock McVie, David Baron, Tim Notley, OC Tam Syme, Gordon Talbot, Roy Humphreyson, Mac McCarthy, Graham Williams, Sid Bottom and Peter Sturt with Paul Constable and Owen Truelove at the front (*Nick Adamson*).

an excellent bunch of groundcrew and who managed to keep us flying when lesser mortals would have failed; no mean feat when we were a long way from home and at the end of the list for spares. We were only in Aden for ten days and then we left for the two-month detachment to Bahrein. It was the start of a very interesting and busy period in the history of 8 Squadron.

It did not take long before we were in trouble. If Aden was at the end of a long supply line for spares, Bahrein was even worse. You depended on Aden for spares and, unfortunately, the other two squadrons back at base would get their hands on the goodies first. So we often ended up flying our aircraft with some deficiencies, commonly referred to as 'red lines', as a warning was always written in the F700 (the servicing document) in red for the pilot to see before accepting the aircraft. Some of these deficiencies you would never have accepted in the normal course of events. One morning, the officer commanding engineering wing at Bahrein, Wing Commander Charles Sloper, who subsequently became the chief engineer of the RAF, decided to wander around the squadron and have a look at what we were doing. It should be said that, although he had no direct control over the squadron as such, he was responsible for the professional engineering practices as a whole. He looked at all our F700s for all the aircraft, said nothing and went back to his office. Half-an-hour later there was a telephone call requesting the squadron commander and the engineering officer to appear in his office. So I, in company with Owen Truelove, duly complied with his request. It immediately was obvious that this was an engineering spat and that I was there only as a courtesy, being the acting squadron commander. The wing commander stated his dissatisfaction with our engineering standards and a discussion between Owen Truelove and he commenced and I was left distinctly as just an interested bystander. It slowly got more and more heated until, to my dismay, I heard Owen say to the wing commander, "Look Sir, why don't you f*** off and mind your own business." I suppose I should have been grateful that he remembered to say 'Sir'. But at that stage I would have been quite happy to have been elsewhere and I was convinced that my first, albeit very short, tenure as a squadron commander was going to come to an ignominious close. I was just wondering when the court martial would take place; but, much to my surprise, the wing commander was so taken aback by Owen's aggressive stance that the argument fizzled out and we were dismissed with a warning to watch what we were doing. I could barely believe that we had got away with it.

Christmas in Bahrein was celebrated in what was the traditional RAF way overseas. Every unit on the base had its billet bar and the officers were invited to sample their wares. A prize was awarded for the best decorated bar and that involved the station commander (Big Daddy) having to visit each one in turn. And that meant having a drink in each one. Since there were at least twenty bars, the station commander's inspection was a tour de force; how he remained standing I'll never know. But he did and he never showed the slightest signs of intoxication, even though each billet bar tried to doctor his drink. It was an outstanding performance.

And further to that, we were sitting in the bar just after dinner on Christmas Eve when the station commander marched in and announced that he was closing the bar. There were some vociferous protests as he marched out of the back door which was a short cut to his house, leaving a sign on the door saying 'This way to the bar'. It was another memorable evening which lasted well into Christmas Day.

We flew back to Aden in time for the New Year's celebrations and life returned to normal – for a day or two until what became known as the Radfan campaign began. The British involvement in Radfan began during the Aden Crisis, with rebels using the Dhala road to bring down supplies for the terrorists in Aden. The British Army took the decision to deploy a garrison into the Radfan to limit the rebels' supplies and thus the Radfan tribesmen's ability to blackmail the traders. The Radfan tribesmen were aided and supplied by the Yemenis, who themselves had received aid and supplies from the Egyptians, and soon had Dhala under daily attack.

According to the commanding officer of 45 Commando the tribesmen of the Radfan were 'a xenophobic lot, equipped from boyhood with rifles, who regarded the British arrival in their mountains as an opportunity for target practice'. The tribesmen mined the road from Aden and ambushed Army convoys; they made the position of the British and Federal garrison as difficult as possible. The usual method of aerial leaflet drops and bombings could not be employed following worldwide critical reaction against similar Egyptian tactics in the Yemen, so the task of counter-attacks was left to the infantry. A large number of so-called dissident tribesmen had attacked the federal fort at Thumier and it was decided that a ground force consisting of the FRA, British Army units and the Royal Marines would move into the area to display the Federal government's determination to maintain law and order. Thus began Operation NUTCRACKER.

EVERYWHERE UNBOUNDED – 8 SQUADRON

We had only been back in Aden for a few days and we always had a pair of aircraft on standby for both air-defence duties and close air support. It was our first weekend back and since my family was still in UK – we were awaiting the allocation of a married quarter, a wait which in the end lasted for nearly a year – I said that I would take the weekend duty. I was joined by Martin Johnson as my No. 2. Stand-by was generally carried out from the crewroom on a 15-minute alert as it was far too hot to undertake cockpit readiness. Martin had been on 8 Squadron for some time and was familiar with the local area, a fact which was to turn out to be quite fortuitous, as, although I had now been on the squadron for three months, most of that time had been spent in Bahrein. My memory may be at fault but I do not think that we were particularly well briefed as we did not expect anything to happen. How wrong could we be?

In the early afternoon we got a call to scramble to provide air support in the Radfan. As we got airborne I realised that I had no idea where this was so I handed over the lead to Martin who said quite confidently that he knew where it was. We contacted the FAC who seemed to be quite excited.

Armed with eight HE rockets under each wing and a full HE gunpack, 8 Squadron FGA.9 XG256-H heads towards the Radfan for another attack on a dissident target in June 1964 (© *IWM*).

179

Every time he pressed the button to transmit you could hear the bullets passing him by; so he had good reason. It took us some time but we finally got the message that he wanted us to open fire. It had been some time since 8 Squadron had been involved in active operations and we were having difficulty in believing what we were hearing. At this stage, Martin elected to hand the lead back to me. And having got to the stage where the FAC was pleading with us to open fire on the targets he had designated, we set to with a will. We did have some difficulty in acquiring the targets because the FAC, being under a certain amount of pressure, was somewhat over-excited. Like us, it was probably the first time that he had been involved in a shooting war.

It was obvious to me, at least, that we were going to be kept quite busy and that we needed some back-up. Unfortunately the rest of the squadron was down on Tarshyne beach with their families and girlfriends and, it being after lunch, in no fit state to participate. As soon as we landed we got another two aircraft prepared and off we went again. By this time it was getting towards dusk and I shall never forget flying over the area trying to make sense of exactly who was where and doing what to whom. It was very rugged and mountainous country; spectacular but not so if you were trying to move around on the ground, especially when the enemy knew the area like the back of their hand. There was an incredible amount of tracer flying around and I have to say that I remain convinced to this day that some of our own units were firing at each other. However, it was certainly a very exciting day and it continued over Sunday. The rest of the squadron were somewhat displeased with us as we had had all the 'fun'.

Back in Aden, there were some slight changes. We were still flying close air support sorties for the ground forces but the Yemen Air Force had been making a particular nuisance of themselves in the area around Beihan again, some 200 miles north-east of Khormaksar. There had been a number of overflights by MiG-15s and Il-28s and also some incursions by Yemeni ground forces. It had happened in the past from time to time and the Hunter squadrons were tasked to provide a standing patrol in the area from dawn to dusk. There was in fact a small airstrip at Beihan but it was deemed too short for the Hunter to operate from. March 1964 saw a recurrence of the problem and we found ourselves doing these Beihan patrols. We flew in pairs and it took approximately thirty minutes to get there. We would then alternate between medium and low level. One aircraft would spend twenty minutes at low level with the other one at about 15,000 feet and then we would swap over to balance the fuel consumption, as low flying used more fuel. It was extremely tedious and, considering the amount of time that all three squadrons spent on patrol, we never caught an intruder.

The only time that we nearly caught an aircraft was during the AOC's annual inspection. This latter event involved the whole airbase. Everything that moved was saluted and, if it did not, it was painted. The air officer commanding, who was Air Vice-Marshal Johnnie Johnson, of Battle of Britain fame, came and inspected the whole base, the day starting off with a full parade on the main aircraft parking area. As the man who was in charge of the flying programme, I had naturally put myself on the stand-by roster so that I could legitimately avoid the parade and any of the other sundry unattractive activities that went on throughout the day. Much to my astonishment we got a scramble right in the middle of the parade. And it appeared that our local radar station had a positive identification on an Il-28 in the Beihan area. We were told to make all haste. That I did, using the taxi track for my take off which interfered somewhat with the parade. When we contacted the controller after take off he was absolutely positive that he had a lock on the Il-28 and I decided to cut the corner to Beihan which involved flying straight across the south-east of the Yemen. We were actually given a precise controlled interception on to the supposed intruder but when we got there he was not to be seen despite searching high and low. He had disappeared back to his own airspace. It was a great disappointment; but it was infinitely preferable to, and more fun than, participating in the AOC's parade. In fact we used to get quite a few air-defence scrambles but we never actually caught anything.

It was only some ten days later on 27 March 1964 that, having retired to bed after a session in the Jungle Bar in the mess, I was almost immediately woken by a banging on the door. Who should appear in the room but the Boss telling me that he needed four pilots for a dawn sortie. Since it was already well past midnight, there was a question as to whether we could find four pilots sober enough to participate in whatever the task was. We all lived in a bungalow with eight bedrooms in the grounds of the mess which had belonged to 8 Squadron from time immemorial. Indeed it was the only accommodation in the officers' mess which had air conditioning, contributed by some grateful soul from the past. It has to be said that the only air-conditioning unit that seemed to work was that belonging to the squadron engineer by some quirk of 'fate', or that was what he claimed. The Boss was unavailable for the task as he had somewhat carelessly managed to break his arm; so the two of us went down the bungalow, turning on the lights of each bedroom, to check on the sobriety and availability of each living-in officer. We scraped up two more besides myself, and I do not think I will ever forget the reaction of Martin Johnson. As we turned the light on and asked the question, he was already standing at attention drinking a pint of water to persuade us of his fitness to fly – even though he did not know what the task was. Nor, indeed, did I. Fortunately we did not need any more than three pilots as the wing commander, John Jennings, decided that he was going to lead the sortie, with the three 8 Squadron pilots in his four-ship, followed by Phil Champniss, the CO of 43 Squadron, with another four-ship.

We briefed at some ridiculous hour in the morning whilst the groundcrew were preparing the aircraft with sixteen HE rockets and a full load of HE 30mm for the cannon. The plot was for a Hunter FR.10 of 1417 Flight to go off and take pre-strike pictures of the target as a second 8 Squadron aircraft dropped warning leaflets just fifteen minutes before we arrived, for us then to strike the target with rockets and cannon and then for the FR.10 to take a post-strike photo. The target was to be the Yemeni fort at Harib just over the border from Beihan. I flew as No. 3 to the wing commander with Martin Johnson on my wing. To get a full load of rockets on the aircraft you had to take the outboard pylons off and replace them with a rocket rail. If you left the pylons on you could only load twelve rockets. No. 43 Squadron made the sensible decision to leave the pylons on and just carry the twelve rockets, whilst we decided to do it the hard way and replace the pylons with rails so that we could carry all sixteen. It was not a particularly easy or quick job but the groundcrew did the first three aircraft with ease.

Unfortunately for Martin, the fourth aircraft proved to be somewhat recalcitrant and, as we started up and checked in, the armourers were still struggling with his aircraft. So we taxied out without him, telling him to catch up if he could. I do not think I have ever seen such an anxious face, sitting in the aircraft, terrified that he was going to miss out. We took off just as dawn was beginning to break and the seven aircraft made their way up country. It was about a thirty-minute transit to the target, and after ten minutes we were treated to the sight of Martin approaching us at a high rate of knots and joining up with the formation.

It was a beautiful morning as we pulled up and tipped in on Harib Fort. All appeared to be quiet and John Jennings let rip with sixteen rockets fired in ripple. I had a ringside seat as I went down the dive and I saw his rockets hit the target just as I fired mine. Then the fort just disappeared in smoke and dust. We made a second pass with guns, then the FR.10, having waited for the dust and smoke to disperse, took a post-strike picture. We landed back at Khormaksar an hour-and-a-quarter after take off just as the rest of the squadron were coming in to work. For some reason we were sworn to secrecy with regards to where we had been or what we had done. This was slightly embarrassing as Gordon Talbot, my fellow flight commander who had been on the squadron far longer than me but missed what was undoubtedly a major event, was all over me asking what we had been up to. In the end I gave in and told him under pain of death and he was most put out that he had not been involved. However, there had not been time to call in the married people who lived off base. The post-strike target photos were quite interesting. No one had said anything during the briefing about air defences, not that I recollect anyway. But when we looked carefully at the photos, there were quite a few anti-aircraft guns, including ZSU23/2, in emplacements around the fort. The covers had been taken off (or blown off) but no shots had been fired as far as we knew.

A few days later I was tasked to lead another eight-ship strike on another fort deeper in the Yemen. However, this was cancelled at the last moment due, I believe, to protests by the Yemen to the UN and the UK incurring the displeasure of the Security Council and so ended the affair of Harib Fort.

The tale of a T.7 ferry

This is a little tale concerning a ferry trip carried out in August 1965. As was the custom every two months or so, we would take a couple of old Hunters back from Aden to the UK for refurbishment and pick up a couple of refurbished ones. On this particular occasion I had to pick up a Hunter T.7 (XF321) and my No.2, a certain Flight Lieutenant Richard Johns of 1417 Flight, had a Hunter FR.10 as his mount. The T.7 had four 100-gallon tanks and the FR.10 had the usual two 230- plus two 100-gallon tanks. The discrepancy in performance between the two aircraft was quite marked and the FR.10 on my wing could easily outperform my aircraft despite the significantly greater weight.

All went well for the first five legs, Kemble to Lyneham to clear customs, Lyneham to Istres, Istres to Luqa, Luqa to Akrotiri and, finally, Akrotiri to Diyarbakir. It is a long time since I have been to Diyarbakir but in those days to describe it as a dump was being kind. It was somewhere in the middle of Turkey in the back of beyond with only very basic facilities; not a place that any sane man would schedule a night stop. Some years before I had been arrested at Diyarbakir when ferrying a Hunter T.7 (XF310) out to

T.7 XF321-TZ was ferried out to Aden by Graham Williams and received the markings of all three Khormaksar-based Hunter units, 1417 Flight and 8/43 Squadron before entering service (*Aviation Bookshop*).

the Far East, when they claimed that I had landed there without diplomatic clearance. On that occasion a very stressed USAF exchange pilot – they were flying F-84s at the time – had very kindly rescued me from my predicament. He was in fact the only man who spoke English (after a fashion) and went everywhere with an interpreter. He must have done something very bad to get such a punishment posting. But I was under no illusions; this time I did not want to stop at Diyarbakir under any circumstances.

We refuelled and taxied out for take off. And that was when I discovered that I could not get the T.7 into power controls. Every time I selected ailerons and elevator into power, the dolls' eyes remained white. Flying a Hunter in manual control is an emergency situation although it cannot be said to be that difficult. The controls are extremely heavy and usually require two hands on the stick. We did practise manual landings from time to time; but manual take offs were not in the pilots' notes. So I am taxiing out and wondering quite what to do. My instinct was to avoid going unserviceable at Diyarbakir, but I did not like to say anything over the radio to Dick Johns, my thoughts tending to anticipate the subsequent board of enquiry. The less anybody knew about what I was about to do, the better.

So I committed myself to a manual take off, not a recommended practice or one that I had ever tried before. In fact I don't know of anyone who has tried it, although I am prepared to bet there are a few who have done it inadvertently. The only aspect that worried me was where to put the elevator trim. Too much tail up and I might not be able to control the pitch-up. Too little and I would have trouble getting the nosewheel off the ground. However, Diyarbakir's runway was quite long and I guessed that I would have time to get airborne even if I had too little tail-up trim. So I erred in that direction so that I would avoid the pitch up which could definitely be embarrassing. Off we went down the runway and, quite apart from the inferior performance of the T.7, it became clear to Dick that nothing much seemed to be happening with regard to getting airborne. After a while he gave up any attempt to remain on my wing and accelerated past me into the air. I actually got airborne just at the end of the concrete in a flurry of dust, sorted out the trim, raised the undercarriage and flaps and climbed nonchalantly away.

It was not until we had landed at Tehran that I was able to tell him what the problem was. And because there was no one to rectify the problem at Tehran, I had to do the next leg in manual as well. But this time Dick was prepared for the take off and I had in any case learnt from the first manual take off what to expect. When we got to Muharraq, I managed to find a knowledgeable technician who took one look at it and diagnosed blown fuses, which indeed it was. So we were able to continue our way on to Khormaksar, via Masirah, in fairly good order. It was not a trip that I shall forget. Indeed ferry trips hardly ever failed to test one's ingenuity, resourcefulness and initiative. They were always a challenge and also great fun; you never failed to learn a thing or two.

My last few weeks in Aden involved handing over to my successor and saying farewell. The latter was made a little difficult by the fact that a complete curfew on all movement after dark had been enforced, a curfew which we did our best to avoid. Despite the enforced separation from my family, it had been a challenging, enjoyable and satisfying two years. I had completed just under a hundred operational sorties, no accidents (apart from the 43 Squadron pilot), and a very professional bunch of aviators who were always willing to enjoy themselves both in the air and on the ground; it was not a tour that I will easily forget.'

Chapter 3

Glory the aim – 43 Squadron

Phil Champniss (Squadron Leader)

Number 43 Squadron arrived at Khormaksar from Nicosia in Cyprus in March 1963 when Squadron Leader Peter Peacock was the commanding officer. Two months later, his successor, Squadron Leader Phil Champniss arrived and he remained OC the squadron until his departure in November 1965.

'In June 1999 Ray Deacon, who had served in Aden at the same time as I did, was doing some research for a book he was writing on the Hunter and asked me if I could let him have some memories of my time in Aden as OC 43 (F) based at RAF Khormaksar. The following paragraphs are a transcript of a tape I sent him at the time. Trying to remember specifics of a period after some thirty-five years is not the easiest of tasks and I apologize for the inevitable inaccuracies that may have occurred.

I had flown the Hunter quite a lot, having converted to the Mark 2 in 1955 when I joined my first squadron, 257, based at RAF Wattisham in Suffolk. The Mark 2 was equipped with an Armstrong Siddeley Sapphire engine which was excellent when it was running but was prone to bearing failures which, to put it mildly, was decidedly unfortunate. From Wattisham I was posted to RAF Chivenor which housed the Hunter OCU and was equipped with Hunter Marks 1 and 4. Both were powered by Rolls Royce series 100 Avons. I was then posted as a flight commander to 14 Squadron based at RAF Gütersloh in Germany flying the Mark 6 Hunter which was equipped with the more powerful series 200 Avon. Halfway through my tour the trainer version of the Hunter, the Mark T.7, arrived, equipped with the series 100 engine.

CO's aircraft
Number 43 Squadron was equipped with the FGA.9 Hunter which I had not flown prior to my arrival. On arrival at the squadron, I was shown the

Hunter FGA.9 XE546-B, pictured on the dispersal at Khormaksar in January 1964, became the personal mount of Phil Champniss during his tour as OC 43 Squadron (*Ray Deacon*).

aircraft which was, nominally, allocated to the squadron commander. When I looked in the cockpit I noticed that there were two blanking plates on the lower starboard console covering what, in my Gütersloh days, had been a modification which allowed the pilot to test his low-level fuel-float switches. I should mention that the fuel gauges in the Hunter at that time were very reliable but tended to under-read at height but, and this was the potentially embarrassing bit, over-read at low-level. In 1960 I was a display pilot and I relied very much on the accuracy of the low-level float switches which illuminated at 650lb per side. RAF Germany introduced a modification to provide a test facility but this was removed when the aircraft was no longer serving in RAF Germany, and thus I was able to say to my predecessor that although I hadn't flown a Mark 9 I had certainly flown that particular airframe whose number was XE546. And the explanation was that a large number of Mark 6s were converted to Mark 9s and my log book confirmed that this was one such. A good start to my time on 43!

The attack on Fort Harib, 28 March 1964
When I joined 43 we had sixteen pilots but only about a dozen were deemed to be 'operational', i.e. cleared for operational sorties. It normally took about

six months for a new pilot to be trained up to operational standard. One of the earlier operational missions was what became known as the Beihan Fort task. Beihan was an area on the Yemen border about a couple of hundred miles to the north-east of Aden. The ruler, the Sharif, was very pro-Britain which made him very unpopular with the Yemenis immediately to the north of him and with whom the UK was, *ipso facto*, at war. There was a fairly large fort about a couple of miles inside Yemen territory although it must be said that the borders were very imprecise in that area. The politicians of the day ordered the destruction of the fort and, since there were no UK ground forces in the area, the task fell to the Hunters of Strike Wing; there were three Hunter squadrons, 43, 8, and 208, and a Shackleton outfit, 37. Eight aircraft were tasked and the OC Strike Wing, Wing Commander John Jennings, led the formation with the front four from 8 Squadron and I led the rear four. No. 208 were in Bahrein at the time. We each carried sixteen 3-inch rockets; they were in two rows of eight. The weather was fine and we had no difficulty in identifying the fort and, being made principally of mud, it was no match for the rockets. The pilots of 1417 flight, equipped with the Hunter FR.10, confirmed that the strike had been successful but it did excite the do-good brigade in the UK and there was quite a bit of adverse Press comment at the time.

The Aden cannon

We always flew with our four 30mm Aden cannon loaded with HE shells, and thank heavens we did because if you fired ball ammunition, which is what was used on the practice range, you've got yourself a fairly horrendous ricochet hazard which with one "donk" ("donkey" = engine) is not to be recommended. In fact in my whole time out there I only heard of one ricochet and that was when a chap was far too close. Incidentally, you could select inners and outers, the two at the bottom of the gunpack or the two at the sides or you could select all four. Selecting the whole lot was enormous fun, but my gosh if you hadn't done it before it used to frighten you as not only would it shake your feet off the rudder pedals, and that's no exaggeration – it really used to clatter – but it would knock about fifty knots off your speed, not to be recommended if you are going slowly. The good old-fashioned gyro gunsight which the pundits knock these days but was in fact extremely reliable and if you flew it properly was very accurate.

The Radfan War

A follow-on of the Beihan strike was that we had to mount CAPs (Continuous Air Patrols) over the area for a few weeks which must take the Nobel Prize for the most boring flying in the world. We would load up the aircraft with extra drop tanks and cruise around at about 2,000 feet above the ground just in case the Yemenis decided to have a go at the small Army garrison that had been deployed to the area. We had to fly at low speed to allow us a reasonable time on patrol whist still allowing us enough fuel to get back home. Hardly an operational posture. Just as an aside, we could not carry any rockets because the outboard pylons had to carry the extra fuel tanks. We never saw any sign of the Yemenis although the Army often said that they could see the Yemeni aircraft just as soon as we left. I don't think so.

But then came the Radfan campaign and that was quite a different kettle of fish. The Yemenis had been successful in whipping up a fair amount of fervour amongst the local tribesmen in an area about 100 miles due north of Aden under the banner of FLOSY, the Federation for the Liberation of South Yemen. There was a deal of mayhem and the UK decided that the 'rebellion' must be put down. Quite a large army contingent was flown in and the Hunters were tasked with providing whatever air support was needed. Unfortunately 8 Squadron was deployed to Bahrein and 208 Squadron was in Kenya participating in the celebrations for Independence. It always seemed to happen that way. The result was that 43 Squadron had to meet the task until the other two squadrons could be recovered. The task took the form of three distinctly different requirements:

Air proscription

This required two aircraft to patrol a defined area and attack anything that appeared 'suspicious'. The vast majority of these areas were just barren "rockscape" and there was no movement at all. So no action. However, on several occasions we were tasked to attack a specific target in one of the areas and this involved the use of our primary ground attack weapon, the 3-inch rocket fitted with a high-explosive head, that dated from the Second World War era and was popularly known as "the drainpipe". The rocket was a very effective weapon but was quite difficult to aim accurately, having the trajectory of a house brick. The problem was that it was quite a slow weapon and, therefore, had a very large gravity drop between firing and reaching its target. Occasionally you would have one where the fins had become distorted giving you what was known in the trade as a "twirler". Instead of going straight ahead it would start barrel rolling and if you were on the range with one of these, you would call "twirler" over the R/T and hope the Range Safety Officer (RSO) didn't think you'd just goofed when you aimed. The Hunter is fitted with a gyro gunsight and it had a specific setting for rockets which involved tracking the target with the bottom of the sight in order to raise the nose to compensate for the gravity drop. Unfortunately this tended to make the gunsight pendulous and this in turn made it essential to track the target for significantly longer than when tracking for the use of the guns. But with practice it was quite normal to deliver the weapon within ten yards of the target, though the presence of crosswinds made the task decidedly more difficult. We could fire our rockets in salvos of two or let the whole lot go at once. At one stage we ran out of HE heads and had to fall back on concrete heads used for range practice but, against a mud target, they were almost as effective as high explosive heads.

Target identification

The second type of support was when we were tasked to destroy a specific target which was causing the ground forces a problem or was deemed by the Intelligence people that it be removed. Either way, the planning was the same and we usually had photographs to aid target recognition. Quite often, for these pre-planned sorties, we had the services of a Forward Air Controller (FAC). This was, in the vast majority of cases, an Army officer of the unit being supported and who had sight of the target. He would, by reference to, hopefully, distinctive ground features, guide the pilot to pick up the target visually. Unfortunately, and this is in no way meant to be a criticism, some ground features can be very distinctive to onlookers on the ground but the absolute opposite when looking from the air. "There is a small tree just in front of the target" is all very well but if it's small then the chances are you won't see it from the air. And on the other hand the pilot may well be able to see dozens of small trees, or none at all. But safety is paramount and the golden rule is that if the pilot isn't sure that he's got the right target then he doesn't fire. There were many times when there was doubt in the pilot's mind and one way that we evolved to eliminate this doubt was to fire off a few rounds of cannon at what was thought to be the target and wait for confirmation from the FAC that it was the correct target. This sounds a bit hit-or-miss (excuse the pun) but we always knew the forward line of our own troops, so the risk of a friendly-fire incident was minimal. There was one very dramatic exception to this assurance which I will come on to later.

Close air support

The third type of mission was when we were called in for close support when the ground unit considered that only air support was the quickest way of removing a potential, or actual, risk. We kept two pilots at cockpit readiness at Khormaksar throughout the daylight hours for this task. They could be airborne within five minutes and in the target area in a further ten. Immediately to the south of the operational area was a landing strip which housed the Army HQ. A member of the brigade staff was a Brigade Air Support Officer (BASO). Throughout the Radfan campaign this post was manned by an RAF officer, Squadron Leader Roy Bowie. He had direct radio contact with the operations room at Khormaksar's Strike Wing HQ. The pilots on standby were in continuous contact with the ops room. When the BASO received a request for close air support he would, after verifying the practicality of the request, pass it direct to Khormaksar who would relay it to the pilots on standby who would immediately scramble and, at maximum speed, head for the general operational area, having selected the BASO's radio frequency. When within radio range the pilots would make contact with the BASO who would then brief them on the general nature of the request. He would then give the pilots a contact point (CP) which was one of about ten pre-briefed such geographical points on the ground which all pilots knew by heart. These points were identified by a letter of the alphabet. The BASO would pass the FAC's callsign and instruct the pilots to make contact with the FAC on a dedicated frequency. Once radio contact had been made with the FAC he would describe the nature of the target. He would then give the pilots a heading and time to fly at 420 knots. This combination of heading and time would put the pilots over a point at which to commence their pull-up to a height which would enable them to achieve a 30-degree dive angle having turned through 90 degrees at the top of the climb, left or right depending on the FAC's briefing. The FAC knew the standard distance covered in the pull-up and the turn in and adjusts the heading and time to make good the pull-up point. The FAC would select a left or right turn in depending on which direction gave the pilot the optimum chance of visually identifying the target. Once the pilots acknowledged receiving the time, heading and direction of turn information, the FAC then gave them a description of what they should see at the top of the dive. The pilots then manoeuvred their aircraft to make good the heading and speed over the designated CP. If all went according to plan, the FAC would make visual contact with the aircraft as soon as they initiated the climb. The FAC then started commentating with the aim of leading the pilot's eyes from what he could see during the pull-up until he could identify the target. It was a good system and, provided that both the FAC and the pilots, did as they had been trained to do, then it worked.

An 8 Squadron FR.10 flies low over the unforgiving peaks of the Radfan Mountains while on a routine patrol. Narrow wadis flanked by walls of rock required a high degree of skill and concentration by the pilots (*Sandy Burns*).

In the Radfan we were fortunate in that there was no air opposition and the enemy had no effective anti-air weapons, apart from small arms. So one could afford to complete an orbit if necessary and there was always the option of firing a few rounds of gunfire to confirm the position of the target. Occasionally we would run out of fuel, or ammunition, before the

A 1417 Flight FR.10 this time; XE589-RC scours the wadi floor close to Bakri Ridge for suspicious dissident activity (*Roger Pyrah*).

task had been completed, or, as often happened, there would be another task allocated to us when in the area but which we couldn't complete. In such an event we would call Khormaksar Ops to scramble another pair of aircraft to complete the task. Things didn't always go to plan and there was one very near miss when we were tasked to take out a particular house in a row of five

193

in a quite large village. I led the particular sortie and we had no problems identifying the exact house that was the target. It was a very calm morning and there would have been no excuse if we'd missed. The rockets did their job and I felt quite pleased that the sortie had gone well. When I landed I was surprised to see the squadron's ground liaison officer (each squadron had its own Army major on full-time attachment as a GLO) waiting on the pan as I climbed out of my aircraft. He was a super chap called Tom Couper and he really was excellent at the job and his knowledge of things Arabic in the area was quite incredible. He didn't look very happy. My heart sank as I dreaded the possible news that we'd knocked down the wrong house. He put my mind at rest when he confirmed that we had got the right house but he then said that immediately behind the house was a small mosque that no one had noticed and certainly no one had told me. He asked if any of our rockets had overshot and I confirmed that, if anything, mine would have been on the short side because I thought I was a bit out of range. The other pilot also confirmed that he would have erred on the short side as he, too, felt he was out of range. An FR.10 from 1417 Flight was already on the way back with the post-strike photographs and we waited in trepidation to see the results. In the event we had not hit the mosque though the house had come down very, very, close to it. But from then on we always demanded pre-strike photos of any target in any sort of built-up area.

Pilot shortage

We were working very hard and we were down to eleven operational pilots and I became very concerned that we would be unable to keep up the pace unless we could get some more pilots. One of the detached squadrons was returning within a few days but I still felt that we should bolster our numbers by at least a couple. I went to see the Station Commander, Group Captain Blythe, and explained my concern. He had converted to the Hunter but had only a few hours on the aircraft and certainly had never had any operational training. He asked me if I had any ideas and I said that I would be happy to choose three of my best non-op pilots who were still under training in their work-up phase and fly them with one of my more experienced guys on operations but under the closest of supervision. He agreed and I said I would fly with one of the best young pilots I had who was a guy called John Thomson. (He eventually became C-in-C Strike Command and would undoubtedly would have become CAS but, tragically, died whilst still C-in C.) He was, incidentally, godfather to my son. But he exceeded my wildest expectations in the trips I flew with him and I asked the station commander to listen in to the R/T whilst we completed the initial sortie so that he could hear, at first hand, what we were trying to do, and more importantly, how we were doing it. Within a week we had an extra three operational pilots which eased the load for the rest of us which, as the next few paragraphs will reveal, was just as well.

Working with the Forward Air Controller

We were normally on standby sitting in the cockpit prior to a forward air controlled sortie. A Brigade Air Support Officer (BASO) was based at an airfield which started life being called Thumeir, a little strip 1,300 yards long and about 100 miles north of Aden which for some reason was later renamed Habilayn. BASO had an HF radio link back to Tactical Wing HQ at Khormaksar and he was responsible for issuing the order to scramble. When the order arrived you would get airborne as fast as possible and when the weather was good, which it usually was, you could fly to Thumeir with your eyes shut. On arrival we would do a couple of orbits during which we were told what contact point to head for. There was a whole series of them, about fifty to sixty miles from Thumeir and all coded by letters, not very clever but it saved mentioning the name and you'd belt off there. Whilst en route the forward air controller (FAC) would come on the radio and give you a heading, a target description, a time and the speed at which you should fly. They assumed you were flying at 420 knots and would know how much ground you would cover by the time you pulled up for the rocket dive and how much more ground you would cover as you turned through 90 degrees to begin your attack. As you pulled up he would guide you to the target by reference to ground features. This wasn't as easy as it sounds – absolutely fine when you're on the ground saying "bushy top tree" (except there weren't any that you could see) but what might look like a damn great feature down there – the big hill in front of you – you can't see because, at 3,000 feet, you're above it. So we devised a system that took all the guesswork out of it. Once we knew we were on a safe heading, we would give a few little bursts of 30mm at what we believed the target to be. Although a 30mm shell would spoil your whole day if it hit you, it didn't pack the punch of a 60lb HE rocket. As your quick bursts hit home the FAC would make any correction according to the fall of shot (a gunnery term), such as, "left 100 yards" or "the building just behind the one you aimed for" or whatever. If there was still doubt, we'd go round and do another quick burst of cannon fire until we got it right. It all sounds a bit old fashioned but it was very effective. Once having established which building it was, you could then go around and do an almost academic attack, where you got your speed right and made the most of the dear old Hunter's stability, bloody great wing, to plant the 3-inch drainpipe comfortably within ten yards, half that with sufficient practice. We would keep attacking until we ran out of rockets or got deployed to another target.

Most of the time, FAC sorties were flown in pairs as hauling a four-ship around with you was a bit cumbersome and unnecessary. It was better to keep a second pair back at Khormaksar and call base ourselves – "Scramble the next pair, we're leaving and we haven't finished the job." It was not unknown to piss about for some considerable time and not actually find the target or it would prove to be not what the FAC wanted. So if we pulled off the target we would call the next pair in ourselves. And that was the pattern we flew; it was rather nice because you could be on the beach by half-past-four in the afternoon having actually having done 'a job of work' and a very exciting job of work too.

Supporting the SAS

There was one event that I shall never forget and it made an absolute nonsense of all the 'rules' that we made. I got a call very early one morning from Wing Commander John Jennings to say that I was to report to his office immediately and to bring one of my most experienced pilots with me. He wouldn't say any more on the phone, so I called a guy called Roger Wilkins who was, by far, the most experienced pilot on the squadron, having previously been a sergeant pilot for several years. We got to the wing commander's office in about twenty minutes and he told us that an SAS patrol had been ambushed at first light that morning, were unable to move from their location and that their CO had asked for urgent air support. The problem was that they would be unable to have radio contact with us and indeed their exact location was unknown as they had moved from their original, briefed, location. Roger and I were airborne within twenty minutes and headed for the operational area.

I made contact with the BASO who explained that he was not in contact with the unit but was getting his information from the SAS's HQ at Khormaksar which, believe it or not, was about fifty yards from my own Squadron HQ. The BASO had a rough idea of where the unit was but it was an area of about four miles square in the north of the operational area. I knew the area pretty well and he and I agreed that we would fly over it and confirm that the unit could at least hear us even if they couldn't actually see us. The lines of communication were tortuous to say the least but, after what seemed an age, the BASO confirmed that they could hear us but couldn't see us but thought we were to the north of them. I shifted our orbiting a couple of miles to the south and waited for a response. Again after what seemed a week the BASO said that they could now see us but we were still well to the north of them. At least we were reducing the area of uncertainty. I completed another orbit, further to the south, and waited for advice. This time we were much closer to them but I had no idea just where they were on the ground. The only thing I could do was to fire a few rounds on a northerly heading and erring towards the northern edge of my previous orbit. Success. The unit could see my fall of shot and asked me to aim about three hundred yards to the south and a similar amount to the west. Roger Wilkins had been patiently following me around but obviously there was no point in him firing until we knew that it would be effective and, more importantly, safe to do so. I fired a few more rounds and received a further correction and a request that we fire some of our rockets. I confirmed with Roger that he could see my last fall of shot and I then fired four rockets at the latest aiming point. Roger did the same and finally we got a message that the result was very satisfactory as far as the unit was concerned. But I had still no idea just where they were but if they were happy then so was I. By this time we had only sufficient fuel to stay in the area for a further fifteen minutes, so I called Khormaksar and ordered the scrambling of a further pair of aircraft to replace us. As soon as I was in R/T contact with them I explained the situation and confirmed that they could see where my rockets were landing and that they were to use that as an aiming point. Roger and I then left and headed for home for a rapid refuel and re-arm.

We were back in the area in forty minutes which worked out well as the pair who had relieved us were just about to leave. And the sortie followed the pattern that had been set and the unit seemed very pleased with our efforts but we still couldn't see them, or their attackers for that matter. We were able to keep aircraft overhead for the rest of the day although it was hard work for us, and even more so for the groundcrew. But obviously we would be unable to provide any support once the light faded and I had to make sure that the unit was aware of that fact. I flew the last sortie that day and left with a very heavy heart as I felt we were letting the beleaguered unit down but there really was no more we could do. And we still hadn't seen them. Tragically my foreboding was justified. The unit had to make a run for it and in the process lost three of their number including their CO, Captain Edwards. As soon as it was dark, the remaining five (or it could have been seven) managed to escape and headed for Thumeir, some seventeen miles away. But there was an extraordinary act of heroism by one of their number, Corporal Baker. He had been shot in the knee and yet managed to run about twelve miles back to the Army's HQ. He couldn't run as fast as his mates so he, obviously singlehandedly, did a sort of 'Ramboesque' act and sprayed the pursuing tribesmen with his Armalite rifle as they rounded a corner and then made good his escape whilst the attackers sought to 'regroup'. Baker did this on at least a couple of occasions.

About three days later I was sitting in my office when my adjutant told me there was someone in the crewroom who wanted to see me. I went to the crewroom and there was this very fit-looking soul with one knee heavily bandaged. It was Corporal Baker who had discharged himself from hospital and just wanted to come and say 'thank you' to the squadron. It was a very emotional moment for me. During the course of our discussion he told me that our rounds had fallen about twenty yards from their position at one stage and it was probably just as well that I didn't know that at the time. But he had been in Malaya three weeks previously and I asked him which country he preferred. He said that he preferred Malaya because he felt much more comfortable fighting in the shade. One of the most impressive men I've ever met. But the whole episode amply demonstrated the absolute necessity of having reliable communications. I've often wondered since that time how things might have been so different if that had been the case.

A bit of family fun

We decided to have a Families' Day so that, hopefully, the wives and kids could come onto the base and see what their husbands and fathers actually did for a living. I decided that we would not actually fly but we would try and make the hangar look "interesting" with bits of ground equipment and a weapons display. We always had at least one aircraft in bits and this particular Saturday was no exception and it formed a good static display complete with commentary.

Bear in mind that this was the mid-sixties and to own a car was the exception rather than the rule. But everyone needed wheels of some kind and most of the pilots, certainly those on their first tour, bought Vespas or a similar type of little 50cc bike. We had about a dozen of these and someone suggested that perhaps their owners could work up a little formation display for the Families' Day. No sooner mentioned than the owners were off and riding. John Thomson was going to lead it and there was frantic activity with the briefing board and dozens of sticks of chalk as various formations were studied and positions allocated. All good stuff and at least it would be something different. But there was only a week before the day itself so rehearsal time was a bit short and the only sensible practice time was at the end of the flying day and that only left a couple of hours of daylight at the most. John came to see me with about three days to go and said that they had settled on the format and the display would last about ten minutes and conclude with a drive-past at which he asked me if I would take the salute. He said they would drive past from left to right in an echelon starboard and then he would lead the 'break' and circle to have them all lined up in front of the "dais" and then do a formation engine switch off, salute, and dismount.

It did seem to be fun and I said I would be delighted to take the salute. John said that the final practice was to take place on the Friday and asked that I be there for that one. The practice was fantastic and I've never laughed so much as John was bellowing orders for the various formation changes but every now and then his orders were swamped by one of the riders missing a gear; a 50cc at full throttle in neutral is very, very noisy, and no one knew what to do next. But they got through to the end and the drive-past was absolutely perfect, and very funny. And so to the day itself. I must say that it went off very well and we sold gallons of tea and stickies which swelled the squadron coffers. And so to the formation demonstration. It was even funnier than the rehearsal that I'd watched. One manoeuvre involved riders approaching each other from two opposite corners of a square, a la Household Cavalry at the Horse of the Year Show. Two of the riders got the timing slightly wrong and collided. No problem; quick remount and rejoin the fray and they went past again to tumultuous applause from the crowd. Then came the formation drive-past, break and dismount. Well, that was what was supposed to happen and the first part certainly did. The actual drive-past was immaculate and I saluted at the appropriate time. But they just kept on going and no attempt was made by John Thomson to lead the break. If he didn't go then nobody else could. I watched in disbelief as the entire formation rode off the pan into the sand and all crashed. They were only going slowly and nobody was hurt. The audience were in absolute hysterics and even more so when they heard John Osborne, the number two, ask John Thomson why the **** he hadn't led the break. "I couldn't turn because my clutch lever was jammed in the pocket of your overalls." A great day and one I will never forget.

An uninvited trip to Saudi

A quick story about XE546 and Saudi. In late 1963 No. 43 Squadron was detached to Bahrein for the regular roulement. One Saturday morning I got airborne early to do some gunnery practice on a target being towed by HMS *Gurkha*. My number 2 had gone u/s on start-up so I was on my own. The weather was superb but when I'd finished my ammo I started to return to Bahrein but was informed that the airfield had fog. I was still in the clear at ten miles and certainly couldn't see any sign of fog. I said I would join for a visual circuit and noticed the odd wisp of fog which could only have been about thirty-feet thick. On finals I ran into it and overshot but thought I'd have another go but flying a higher circuit and finishing with a steeper approach. Silly boy! Got myself into a bit of bother and came remarkably close to clipping an aerial that was on top of the officers' mess. So I said I was diverting to Dhahran which was the nominated diversion for the day and I knew that the weather was fine there, and it was. I explained to the British ATC guy (they were all employed by International Air Radio Limited, IAL) that I was diverting due to bad weather at Bahrein and he cleared me to land. I taxied to a deserted ramp and was met by a USAF major who was the remnants of a training mission that had converted the RSAF to the F-86. Unfortunately they had run out of spares and the aircraft had all been put into long-term storage. He took me to his crewroom and gave me a cup of coffee.

I had been there about twenty minutes when a very pleasant RSAF major came in and asked me if I was the pilot of the Hunter. I said I was and he asked me to go with him. We drove for about five minutes to a rather tatty hut and he ushered me into one of the rooms. He then astonished me by saying, "I'm afraid that you are under arrest for violation of Saudi airspace, flying a warplane over the Kingdom of Saudi Arabia with guns that are still hot and having a camera on board." I tried to explain that I had diverted from Bahrein because of fog but he was having none of it. He said that he had to go and speak with *higher authority* and would be back shortly. And he locked the door as he left. It was now about 9.30. At about 11.30 he returned with an Army colonel who looked all of eighteen but he did speak superb English. He repeated the allegation and I repeated my explanation. He said that he would have to check with Riyadh and I then said that I wished to see the local representative of the British Embassy. He completely threw me by saying that the nearest British diplomat was in Jeddah, over a thousand miles to the east and there were no phones. After another couple of hours he returned and said he was sorry for the confusion and I was free to return to Bahrein. Great, but please could I have some fuel. He replied that I could, provided that I paid for it. This was in the days before credit cards and the only money I had was four English pennies that I'd carried in my overalls since Wattisham ever since one of our number baled out and couldn't use a handy telephone box.

I went back to my aircraft and I had about fifteen-hundred pounds of fuel which I reckoned was just enough to get me home provided I had absolute priority to land. I phoned the station commander at Bahrein and told him that I would be airborne in ten minutes and could he make sure that I did have priority as I was a bit short of fuel. He replied to the effect that they had closed the airfield and so it was all mine. I took off from the taxi track as I didn't want to waste any fuel trundling all the way down to the runway in use. Probably the shortest take off run I've ever had. And sixteen years later I was back in Dharhan but I kept very quiet about my previous visit.

Political targets

Towards the end of the campaign we had to deal with an increasing number of what I shall call 'political' targets. These were always buildings of one sort or another and always had a connection with an individual whose loyalty to Britain was, shall we say, doubtful. It was considered, at that time, that a salutary 'message' could be sent to any others of the same persuasion by destroying the selected target but, of course, it was absolutely essential that we didn't knock down the wrong one. To reduce the risk to an absolute minimum we devised a procedure that worked very well. We would despatch a member of 1417 Flight about fifteen minutes ahead of us and he would positively identify the target with the FAC, using his guns if necessary. We would then approach at about 6,000 feet above ground. We obviously knew the rough area in which the target lay and when we had about ten seconds to go I would call the FR.10 pilot who would then pop over from behind the nearest hill and illuminate the target with his guns. We then started our dive and had all the time in the world to track the illuminated target. The procedure worked a treat and certainly surprised the FAC who, literally, never saw us coming until our rockets struck.

It wasn't always that straightforward. I was involved in an incident which shouldn't have happened. I was leading a pair of aircraft and my wingman developed a problem en route and had to return to Khormaksar. It was a straightforward air proscription sortie which involved searching a relatively small area looking for anything that seemed out of the ordinary. Whenever we did this the ground forces would stop operating their guns and so the area was known as a 'guns tight' area. I was poling along minding my own business when I heard, and I mean *heard*, this loud bang and my aircraft actually shook. I though at first that I'd had some unserviceability but the

A superb image of a Hunter swooping low over an up-country village as at least seven pairs of eyes can be seen anxiously looking skywards. Quality photographs such as this, captured by an FR.10's forward-facing camera, enabled the ground attack pilots to identify clearly the correct building selected for 'demolition' (*Sandy Burns*).

aircraft was flying perfectly normally and then I noticed some smoke on the ground. I immediately climbed to get out of any possible danger and saw another puff of smoke on the ground. I called the BASO and he said they were unaware of any offensive activity. I decided that, as I was about to leave anyway, I would save any further investigation until I was on the ground back at base. I was debriefed by my GLO and related the incident and he said he would investigate. About ten minutes later he came back to me and was looking decidedly embarrassed! Apparently "guns tight" didn't apply to mortars. I pointed out that a mortar-shell strike on our aircraft was pretty terminal and we would have to think again if the mortars were going to be cleared to fire when we were in the area. From that day onwards "guns tight" applied to mortars.

Ferry trips
My last endearing memory of my time in Aden had absolutely nothing to do with "Operations". It always seemed very odd to me that when one of our aircraft reached such a decrepit state that it was beyond the capability

of our local Maintenance Unit to repair, then we would ferry the aircraft back to the UK for a total refurbishment. I did a couple of these ferries, in both directions, and one was truly hilarious. We always ferried in pairs for obvious reasons. This particular trip involved staging through Jeddah for the first time and involved me returning my own aircraft, XE546. The actual route was Aden-Jeddah-El Adem-Malta and then the UK, or a stop in Nice if the weather was dodgy. The specific route I was given by our illustrious HQ involved us in backtracking about 150 miles south once we'd left Jeddah. I never knew the reason why but apparently it was a condition of the diplomatic clearance for entering Saudi Arabian airspace. That was all very well but this extra mileage meant that we would have to complete the last 100 miles or so to El Adem on foot. I explained this little difficulty to our HQ but they said that I'd have to negotiate with the Saudi authorities once I got there. Helpful. The diplomatic clearances only lasted for twenty-four hours, so it was essential that we got to Malta on the first day.

I'd planned to leave at 09.00 but when I came to start my aircraft, it wouldn't. This was not unusual and the Avpin starter would fail to get up to the required revs and would automatically shut down, known in the trade as a 'whee-phut'. Correctly it was known as an 'A' failure. Normally it would behave at the second time of asking but mine wasn't going to play ball. You're allowed one more try but clearly my aircraft didn't want to leave Aden and the third attempt was unsuccessful. One had to wait forty-five minutes for everything to cool down so I and my wingman, Cliff Middleton, climbed out and returned to the crewroom for a pint of squash. At the next attempt my aircraft started but Cliff's didn't. Back to the crewroom.

About a couple of hours later we tried again and this time both aircraft behaved and we took off en route to Jeddah. This is only about an hour and a half's flight and we arrived at about midday to be met by a USAF top sergeant and an eighteen-year-old chap in a very smart suit who was an under-under first secretary at the British Embassy. The USAF man was a technician with a couple of USAF C-123 Providers, which was like a twin-engined Hercules. He sorted out a fuel bowser and I confused him by saying that we couldn't refuel until I had released the air pressure in the fuel system by loosening a screw in the top of one of the 230-gallon ferry tanks. This was a perfectly standard procedure and the American offered to get me a screwdriver but I said I didn't need one because I had a penny coin which would do the trick, and it did. The American gave me rather an odd look. I then said that I would need some oxygen to top up the aircraft but he said they hadn't got any. We checked our aircraft again and the gauges said that we had more than half a tankful so I decided to continue on the grounds that the next leg was only slightly longer than the first. I then asked the American if there was an area radar at Jeddah and he said that there was only an airfield radar that had a range of about fifty miles and even that range could only be obtained if the aircraft was above 10,000 feet. That piece of information solved the backtracking problem. I was anxious to get going but my aircraft wasn't so keen again. I could tell by the sound of the starter that I was short of internal electrical power. I didn't want to risk another aborted start so I told Cliff to keep his engine running whilst I conferred with the American technician. I explained that I needed an external power supply and he immediately said that he could use the output of one of the Providers. But they were a couple of hundred yards away and so I thought that it would not be possible to adopt his idea. Wrong. He was authorised to taxi his aircraft so that's exactly what he did and lashed up a connection to my aircraft. I've never heard the starter going so fast and my aircraft positively leapt into life. We took off towards the west and I had briefed Cliff that we would stay at low-level for about eight minutes heading west and then climb on a north-westerly heading to clear Saudi Arabian airspace as soon as we could. Saudi ATC wished us a good flight.

The leg to El Adem must be the easiest navigation task of all time. Just keep the Red Sea on your right and when you hit the coast line to the Med, turn left. In fact one can cut the corner and we made El Adem with no problem and we hardly seemed to use any oxygen at all. The turn-round at El Adem went well and I was getting really anxious to continue as the possibility of having to land at Malta's Luqa airfield in the dark was becoming very real. And we weren't supposed to ferry at night. But the dreaded Diplomatic Clearance problem was ever with us although the further west we went then the more 'sensible' the authorities became. But we were still in North Africa. Both aircraft started at the first attempt and then my aircraft decided that it liked El Adem and so refused to let me motor the canopy shut! This sometimes happened when the micro-switch in the hood rail stayed shut, so the whole thing thinks it's already shut and cuts off the power to the motor. But I could see the switch protruding so this wasn't the cause. One can de-clutch the canopy and I did this hoping that sliding it manually shut and then immediately re-clutching it might just do the trick. I would know because the hood seal would inflate if the canopy was in the shut position. I slid it forward as hard as I could and I've never been so pleased to see, and feel, the hood seal inflate!

The leg to Luqa is relatively short and we went there as fast as we could and beat dusk by about ten minutes. We stayed in the transit mess and were feeling extremely tired. But we had to pay the Gut the obligatory trip for a few beers but we really didn't do it justice since sheer fatigue caught up with us. We both had a cracking night's sleep and were in no hurry to depart the following morning on what should have been the last leg. But with the following morning came the news that although the weather at Luqa was fantastic the same could not be said for the UK generally and Kemble in Gloucestershire, our destination, in particular. The forecast was for things to remain bad for the entire day but improve the following day. I decided that we would make an overnight stop in Nice, which would at least get us closer and give us more fuel to cope with any diversion if we were prevented from landing at Kemble the following day. But then my aircraft threw a real wobbly. It just refused to do anything when I tried to start. Dead as a dodo. We climbed out and a corporal of the starter crew asked me what the problem was and I explained that I couldn't start and relayed the problems I'd been having since leaving Khormaksar. He then astonished me by saying that it was probably my starter box and that the box was exactly the same as the starter boxes on the Canberra PR.9s based at Luqa. I should mention that wasn't the only astonishment that I was experiencing at that time. This corporal was a native Maltese and was a locally recruited member of what was, in effect, a Maltese Air Force. He said that he was sure he could 'cannibalise' a Canberra starter box and make mine serviceable. And, within an hour, he had. So off we set only this time I had to get Cliff to give me a hand with my canopy as I couldn't slam it shut hard enough to depress the micro switch.

The leg to Nice is very short and we arrived at about midday in the middle of summer, and the tourist season. Taxiing around Nice in the middle of the tourist season is a very distracting business. There are balconies full of very 'comely wenches' and keeping one's eyes on the taxi track, particularly when one doesn't know where one is going, is not an easy task. But we were to be parked in an area which I can only describe as a scrapyard. Actually this wasn't altogether inappropriate judging by the state of our aircraft. We shut down and climbed out and I immediately noticed that my starboard Maxaret braking unit was having a fit of the sulks and was weeping all over the place. Cliff and I looked at it and I said that I thought my part of the ferry might just have come to a grinding halt. I then noticed a chap walking towards us who was wearing a pair of white overalls. I thought that was all we needed – a Frenchman coming over to gloat over an Englishman in a spot of bother. But he then said, in perfect English, that we appeared to have a problem with the Maxaret unit and he asked whether I remembered him. He was English and an ex-RAF junior technician who had been on 14 in Germany when I was there. A small world. But the great thing was that he said that he could tighten up the unit and stop it leaking, albeit it might only last a couple of trips before it might start leaking again. I explained that I only had to complete one more trip before the whole aircraft was due to be refurbished. But I asked him what he was doing in Nice and he explained that he was with a couple of Bristol Freighter aircraft from Channel Air Bridge based at Southend and they were detached to Nice for the summer, ferrying cars to and from Corsica. He immediately began to work on the troublesome braking unit and after about ten minutes he had stopped the leak and pronounced it to be OK for at least a couple of trips. Fantastic!

At this stage a local rep from BEA turned up, on a bike. He was our 'agent' and said he'd booked us into a local hotel and had a car waiting to take us there. We got our overnight bags and he went off to fetch the car. He took us to the Hotel Roxy, in one of the sleazier parts of Nice, and which would have been pushed to rate a single star. But it was in the middle of summer. Our involvement with things technical followed us into the hotel when my wash-basin decided to retain all the water in it. A call to reception didn't help since the plumber had finished for the day. I used Cliff's basin and we contributed a fair amount to help France's balance of payment problems that evening and retired a little the worse for wear.

The following morning, having confirmed that the forecast improvement at Kemble had materialised, we tried to get going but, once again, my aircraft wasn't going anywhere. There are two quick fixes for a misbehaving starter and the guy who fixed my Maxaret unit knew both of them. One is to pour boiling water down the air intake of the starter and the other is to blow compressed air up the exhaust of the unit. Neither fix worked on this occasion. There was nothing for it but to call the UK for help and I sent a telegram to RAF Chivenor asking them for assistance, explaining that I needed an engine mechanic. Four hours later a Hunter T.7 arrived flown by a guy called John Walker, later to become Air Chief Marshal Sir John Walker, together with an engineer, an armament officer!

I suggested that they go back to the hotel and book themselves in and at least the engineer could have a look at my wash-basin problem. Meanwhile I went to ATC and explained that I would have to cancel my flight plan as we had a technical problem and I didn't know when we would be leaving. I went back to the aircraft to retrieve my bags and said to Cliff that I was going to have one more go as I really had nothing to lose. And obviously my aircraft was impressed by my determination and promptly started. This was too good a chance to be missed so I told Cliff to help me with my canopy and then get into his aircraft and start up and I would make my peace with John Walker later. I re-filed my flight plan over the air, not really legal, but the ATC officer was the epitome of helpfulness, and we were given priority over the scheduled airline traffic and set off for Kemble. The weather was gin clear all the way and I was very pleased to see Kemble from at least 100 miles. Which, frankly, was just as well, because one of my generators was on the blink and my starboard fuel gauge had given up all pretence of being in the slightest bit interested. And just to make the point my brake chute fell off as soon as I deployed it on landing. I didn't need it but thought I'd use it because we rarely did. Silly me.

And that was just about the end of my time on 43. I had an absolute ball and although I had the privilege of commanding two Harrier squadrons later in my career nothing could match the fun and sense of achievement that I had during my time in Aden. Mind you, I often think that it was just as well the rules in those days were not quite so strict; there must have been at least a dozen times when my actions would have warranted court martial in today's climate. Hey Ho!'

Mike Gill (Flight Lieutenant)

Having completed his training course at Chivenor in 1960, Mike was posted to 43 Squadron which at that time was based at Leuchars. When General Kassim threatened to invade Kuwait in July 1961, 43 Squadron was relocated to Nicosia in Cyprus as a precautionary measure. The Squadron remained on the island until March 1963 when the deteriorating situation in Aden required a further move, this time to Khormaksar. Mike soon found himself flying his Hunter in operational conditions.

'Cyprus was the most wonderful of islands and fortunately antagonism from the Greek and Turkish communities was not directed at the British forces but only between themselves. I would have stayed contentedly at Nicosia for much longer than we did, but in spring 1963 the Squadron was again relocated to RAF Khormaksar where I spent the remainder of my time with 43 Squadron until my tour ended in July 1963.

Whilst in Aden with both 8 and 208 Squadrons, detachments were completed on a rotational basis at Bahrain and it was whilst on temporary location there, that the following events occurred.

Mike Gill climbs the ladder attached to his 43 Squadron Hunter FGA.9 XJ683 (*Mike Gill*)

As a prelude to the story, I need to explain that it had become part of an initiation process that new pilots joining the Squadron would have some sort of jest or prank carried out on them, and when it was learned that two new members were to join us in June of 1963, it was suggested that I might like to attend to their arrival procedure.

Their names were John Thompson and Martin Herring. They arrived in Bahrain via Aden and were met in the Officers' Mess by Flight Lieutenant Chris Golds, dressed as a Corporal behind the Reception Desk. Having signed them in and with no one else around, Chris told them that it was normal procedure to greet newcomers with a stiff drink and pulled out a bottle of whisky from behind the desk and poured them out a couple of enormous slugs, which he hurriedly encouraged them to swallow in one gulp after Chris purported to have seen a senior officer passing the main doors.

They and their bags were then shown to their bedrooms, where they were told that unpacking is undertaken by local Arab women. Sure enough, almost immediately, two of the Officers wives appeared, heavily disguised in burkhas and proceeded to unpack the bags. To the embarrassment of John and Martin, much tittering took place as underpants were shaken open and thrown in disgust in a corner with sign language from the Arab women that Arab men did not wear such garments in Bahrain and they should be thrown away.

Martin and John appeared shortly thereafter at the outside Mess bar to meet the Squadron Commander and other pilots including myself. I quickly briefed them to say that their arrival could not have been better timed as the Sheik of Bahrain was shortly to arrive to say hello. I told them that he would be seated and only be talking with the Squadron Commander at the two chairs adjacent to the bar and that we other pilots would be politely seated two or three metres away from them and that we were not to speak to the Sheik unless he spoke to us. I also mentioned that the Sheik did not drink alcohol and would be having a glass of water and that in deference to his habits we would also appear to be drinking water. I told them that we had to follow the Sheiks mannerisms so that if he had a small sip of water, everyone else had to have a small sip at the same time and if he had a large sip everyone else had to copy with an equally large sip.

The Sheik turned up a couple of minutes later to be greeted by the Squadron Commander and they sat themselves down, as we then did. The Sheik was regally dressed in flowing robes and head dress, aged about 50 years, well tanned, greying hair and a very florid complexion and large reddening nose. Such was also the appearance of our Squadron Engineering Officer delighted to take over the role of the Island's Sheik.

The Mess Corporal, alias Chris Golds, then arrived with a large tray of drinks, the Sheik and the Squadron Commander being handed two glasses of water. All the other pilots were then handed their pre-filled glasses and when the Corporal arrived at John and Martin, with a big wink, he told them that all the pilots were in fact drinking gin, but were having to pretend that their drinks were water to keep the peace with the Sheik who was unaware of the subterfuge and would be happy in the knowledge that everyone appeared to be on water the same as him.

Over the next 10-15 minutes the Sheik had an occasional sip of his drink and John and Martin certainly appeared to be able to cope with their small sips of gin. They became disconcerted, however, when suddenly the Sheik threw down the remainder of his drink in one massive gulp and signalled for another glass. All the pilots seemed to cope well with this large gulp apart from John and Martin who clearly had not expected gin to be downed in this large quantity and did an admirable job of containing their strangulated gasps. The Corporal then reappeared with

A pair of 43 Squadron Hunters led by Mike's FGA.9 XJ683 lift of the Khormaksar runway in the early summer of 1963 (*Ray Deacon*).

glasses even more full than previously and with another wink at John and Martin, said that he hoped they were enjoying themselves.

The Sheik seemed to be getting on well with the Squadron Commander chatting quietly between themselves and as seen by the rather larger mouthfuls of water that he had started drinking. All the other pilots were still coping well although John and Martin were struggling with the amount of neat gin they were having to down. I blandly commented to them that as Squadron pilots, they would soon be used to these levels of alcohol when they had been with us for a while.

To the relief of John and Martin, with another final surge the Sheik threw back his last half glass of water and declared that he must go. All the pilots followed suite, swallowing their drinks with straight faces and the Sheik was barely out of sight, when Martin disappeared into the bushes retching violently and John still seated with a very pale face. Naturally, they were unaware that the Sheik, Squadron Commander and all the other pilots were in fact on water, whilst they were the only two drinking neat gin. The pair were excused squadron duties the following day.

Sadly Martin Herring lost his life shortly thereafter when he failed to pull out of a dive whilst firing rockets on a target in a wadi somewhere south of the Yemen whilst back at Khormaksar. John Thompson went on to have an illustrious career in the RAF and Chris Golds is now retired and he and his wife live in North Devon.

My three years with the Fighting Cocks was a memorable time for a young man and I can barely remember a better time of my life whilst I look back at aged 80 years at the fun and camarderie that I shared with all the other pilots.'

Alan Pollock (Flight Lieutenant)

Following four years flying Hunters in Germany, Alan volunteered to become a Qualified Flying Instructor (QFI) and joined thirty colleagues for the 150-day course at "the summertime retreat and well-known Cotswold village-cum-airfield community that was the CFS at Little Rissington" in 1961. Having gained a reputation for being both the fastest-ever Clarkson Trophy disqualification (before he had even started) and the instigator of a prank to brick up the ground-school entrance, Alan undertook instructing roles on Jet Provosts at Cranwell and Gnats at Valley before "escaping Flying Training Command and joining 43 (F) Squadron to fly Hunter FGA.9s in 1964". Throughout his fifteen years of service Alan was "imbued with great respect and admiration for the RAF's backbone of technician airmen, providing thoroughly serviceable aircraft for us mere drivers".

All fired up in Aden

'For my second sortie on 5 April, 1966 I was detailed to fly an air test on FGA.9, XE609/S-Sierra. Some two minutes after take off, while flying under brilliant Aden sunshine over the sea to the east of Khormaksar, I slowly became aware of a dull glow in the fire warning light. I immediately throttled right back and pulled up into a steep climbing turn to port to establish whether there were any signs of smoke and flames trailing from the back and headed back towards terra firma. Pushing full top rudder to skid and visually cover the poor downward rear visibility below the tail, always the Hunter's vulnerable blind spot for a defensive lookout, there was no trace of smoke. It was only later that I found out that the Pan call I made was not received by Khormaksar ATC due to R/T failure, nor had I heard their warning to me on take off that I had was trailing vented fuel and smoke.

I was soon flying a very high down-wind leg on a frequently practised forced-landing pattern, as the increasing potential of an emergency stop-cocking looked imminent should the fire warning remain on. I was also fully aware that I was above Sheikh Othman township, a hotbed of insurgent activity, as the recalcitrant fire light went out only to re-appear with any opening of the throttle. With a safety-first reversion to manual control, a light crosswind and 3,000 splendid yards of runway, there was certainly no need nor wish to write off any Adeni families below by releasing the full 230-gallon drop tanks. What an international incident that would have caused. Having supreme confidence in our Martin-Baker letdown option, there was plenty of time and opportunity to drop the 230s over the desert sand when turning on high finals, should a dangerous lack of control occur. Thankfully this didn't happen and the expected 'dutch roll' effect was quite minimal. We regularly practised manual forced landings so there was no great drama even though my R/T was useless. Having made a safe landing, I immediately turned off Khormaksar's solitary runway and jettisoned the brake 'chute a few yards onto the peri-track, by then fully aware there was a steaming fire cooking the rear fuselage. I hastily applied the parking brake and, with everything swiftly shut down, stood up and replaced both ejection seat pins, before unceremoniously abandoning the aircraft by slithering back over the hood and spine, onto the wing and off via a drop tank. The fire, more cruddy smoke than fulsome flames, was quickly extinguished by a rapidly attending airfield fire crew. The memory of those five or six minutes have remained firmly with me ever since.

For some reason I was away for a few days after the incident and was not able to follow up on the cause, nor was I that fussed really. It was the first air-test flight after a fair amount of maintenance work and engine change carried out by the Aircraft Servicing Flight (ASF). Retrospective analysis revealed that the aircraft had caught fire on take off. Once airborne, radio transmissions between myself and the tower on both local and approach frequencies were non-existent. Due to the bright midday sun, it was only very slowly that I realised that the crazed and dim fire-warning light was not only on but had almost certainly been on for a long time. There was never an assumption during Hunter flight-simulator or emergency drills that a fire warning light could come on and stay on without being immediately noticed by the pilot. A modification was subsequently devised that ensured fire-warning lights would be more easily detected in strong sunlight conditions.

As may be seen in the photograph, the fire was mostly centred on the starboard side of the rear fuselage and provides a good illustration of why I couldn't see any signs of fire at the back end despite banking high to the left and yawing up to the right while looking left to check for smoke.

Groundcrew inspect the damage to 8/43 Squadron FGA.9 XE609 following a fire in the rear fuselage. As subsequent inspection also uncovered severe damage to the centre fuselage section, Alan Pollock was a tad fortunate not to have experienced a more uncomfortable departure from the cockpit. The aircraft was scrapped (*Alan Pollock*).

The photograph was probably taken after 'Sierra' had been towed back to ASF as there is no evidence of foam on the ground.

The 'LULU'

In Aden Strike Wing parlance, a 'LULU' referred to the immediate scramble of the first pair of standby Hunters, each armed with 3-inch rockets and full gunpacks, following an urgent request from an Army unit in trouble up country and requiring immediate close air support. These calls were invariably directed by a forward air controller but could, on rare occasions, be called to strike at a clearly defined target area. Aircraft on standby were held on the pan at five-minutes' readiness by each squadron, their cockpits prepared for a call to scramble. Each pilot would have carried out a thorough pre-flight, walk round aircraft inspection and completed his weapon, external and internal pre-starting checks, with the parachute straps and harness, the ejection seat height and rudder pedals pre-adjusted to individually suit. A ciné magazine would already be loaded in the gyro gunsight or zipped in the right thigh pocket of his lightweight flying suit.

213

43(F) Squadron pilots at Khormaksar in February 1966 with, standing: l to r; Wally Wilman, Tony Hughes-Lewis, Andy White, Mike Fernee, Brian Waters, Ron Burrows, Jack Jennings. Seated: Neil Hayward, David Malin, OC Sqn Ldr Harry Davidson, Geoff Taylor, Alan Pollock. At the front: Tony McKeon and Rod Dean. Nigel Ashley, Pete Griffiths and Jim Lawton were away on courses or leave (*Alan Pollock*).

Finally, having signed the Form 700 and authorisation sheets, the pair would be declared 'on state'. The pilot briefing would have included any relevant operational conditions on the ground and standard pair attack procedures. Once a pair had been scrambled, a second pair of aircraft and pilots would be brought rapidly onto state.

Close air support

Normally the close air support was co-ordinated by a trained Forward Air Controller (FAC) on the ground or, more rarely, in an Army Air Corps (AAC) Beaver or helicopter in the particular area under attack. This was invariably in the Radfan, literally five minutes flying time from Khormaksar. The regular use on operations of HE/SAP rocket-loads for close air support on targets so close to such a large main base, represented a most unusual situation in the history of air power. On arrival in the target area, the pair would normally split into a mutually supportive, opposing racetrack pattern – the second Hunter would be at 1,500 feet or so, flying in the opposite direction. As one aircraft fired a short marking burst of three or four rounds the second rolled in to fire a further marking burst, having carefully watched the first fall of shot and made any adjustments given by the FAC. The leader would then call the FAC, "In sighter for marking attack" followed by either "Permission, in Live RP" or "In Live Guns". Clearance would be given if the marking attack line and position had been accurate. On pulling out from a marker burst up in the Radfan, I vividly remember one particular adjustment call from an accomplished FAC; "Five yards beyond on the other side of that rock". As we often fired our guns so close and above our own troops, a substantial spew of 30mm shell cases would be ejected on them. They affectionately called this "brass rain". Our troops were extremely appreciative of our support, even effusive, but the praise surely should go to that flexible operational workhorse, the Hunter FGA.9. I am sure I was not alone in preferring to be one of a pair rather than as a singleton which occasionally happened following an unserviceable start up, purely for the ambivalent feelings when the casualty results were given on the following day. When one was in a pair, one halved, not always with a faultless logic, the degree of perceived responsibility for the opposing lives taken. Even before arriving in Aden, I would make a conscious effort to avoid carelessly hurting small creatures and insects but after Aden this policy was taken to obsessive extremes.

Operating out of Beihan

Lulu sorties, though demanding in their sense of responsibility for a safe and accurate delivery of weapons, were much more enjoyable than the monotonous Beihan patrols as the latter usually required pilots to loiter in the area and the flight to and from the border was a bit of a drag. The monotony diminished somewhat following the provision of an extended runway suitable for limited Hunter operations at Beihan in 1966. Surrounded by an impressive backdrop of jebels and a big tooth-shaped crag, noticeable distractions in themselves, made one's curved final approach more unusual to say the least. My first landing on that hot, high (approximately 3,600 feet) and short 1,800-yard runway, code-named Operation KIMAR ZAYN (a close-run thing), was by no small margin, the bumpiest runway surface which I encountered anywhere in a Hunter. The oleos compressed and extended at a rapid rate on the rough, compacted surface making the brake 'chute an essential asset here and not just a desirable accessory to save brake and tyre wear. On touching down, the Hunter behaved like a bucking bronco, making one extremely reluctant to apply the brakes in the normal fashion. Due to its altitude and the extreme heat, the touchdown indicated air speed was a considerably higher true air speed and landing ground speed. Landing a Hunter was normally so straightforward a process its Maxaret braking bringing you safely to a halt, even on short smooth surfaced runways.

Heat, Djibouti diversion, maps and key memories

Besides so much enjoyable flying and the theatre itself, there are three things which I and many Hunter pilots remember from our Aden days. Firstly, and perhaps shared with everyone arriving by air, was the initial searing blast wall of heat which hit you when stepping out of the aircraft on arrival. Secondly, an easily remembered twin set of three figures engraved on each Strike Wing pilot's brain – 235 degrees (magnetic) and 135 nautical miles – the signpost to Djibouti. At 135 nautical miles distant and reached by steering 235 degrees magnetic from Khormaksar, this was the nearest and only viable diversionary airfield for the Hunters. On the rare occasions that a great turbulent, angry-looking, mountainous wall of a sandstorm could be seen rolling in from the north, one needed to be mindful that the closest diversion runway was a long way across the Red Sea. On my only visit to Djibouti, not in a Hunter, one of the two French Armée de l'Air technicians who refuelled our RAF aircraft had lit cigarettes dangling from their francophone mouths, having first consumed a large quantity of red wine; routine lunchtime fare.

Thirdly, the 1:500,000 'half million' maps of South Arabia provided for pilot use comprised two halves. One covered the area to the west of a north/south line of longitude a mile and a half from the western end of Khormaksar runway which was pasted and taped to a second section covering everywhere to the east of the line. The challenge when using the unified map was that spot heights of mountain tops were registered in feet on the western half and metres on the rest – the main operational area around the Radfan and beyond straddled across both maps. A few miles over the then Yemen border to the west of Dhala, the Jebel Jihaf rose to 10,720 feet while on our side of the border, to the east of the Wadi Bana, several peaks exceeded 8,200 feet. These were marked on the conjoined map as merely being in the 2,000s (metres)!'

Roger Wilkins exchanges positions and armaments with an Aden Levy soldier (*Roger Wilkins*).

Roger Wilkins (Flight Lieutenant)

Roger Wilkins served on 43 Squadron from 22 July 1963 to 30 August 1965.

By Brit to Aden

'In 1963 trooping to Aden was generally contracted out to civilian operators. I was lucky I suppose in getting a non-stop Britannia. When Margaret came out the following January with the children it was on a piston-engined DC-6 which had to carry out a technical stop for fuel in Rome. It was midday on 22 July when the doors opened on the civilian pan at Khormaksar. The temperature must have been around 37 degrees C (100 F) with a humidity of over 70 per cent. It was worse at night.

I was met at the steps of the Britannia by a couple of 43 Squadron pilots who happened to be back at Khormaksar carrying out some admin tasks. Harry Gill and Tim Robertson soon put me in the picture. It was then that I discovered that the rest of 43 Squadron were up at Bahrain on a two month detachment. The reason was the need to provide a squadron

217

of ground-attack aircraft in Bahrain to repel Iraqi tanks if they were to invade Kuwait for the oil. Shades of the first Gulf War. In order to fulfil this commitment each of Khormaksar's Hunter FGA.9 Squadrons (8, 43 and 208) spent two months up at Bahrain and four months back at Aden. As this detachment was unaccompanied (no wives or children) it was most unpopular with all concerned except for the bachelors.

I was quickly installed in the mess at Khormaksar which was a substantially built pre-war edifice. Unfortunately none of the public rooms or bedrooms were air conditioned, with the exception of No. 8 Squadron accommodation, more of which later. When I moved into my room I found I would be sharing with Harry Gill who was en route back to Bahrain. The rooms were on the first floor and were huge, with a ceiling fan and large balcony. At this time Khormaksar was probably the largest station in the RAF in terms of numbers of Squadrons, and when I arrived the station commander was Group Captain Michael Beetham.

Settling in

As I had arrived at midday, and RAF Middle East was still working pre-air-conditioning hours (07:00 to 13:00 and then sleep or beach) I could not start my arrival procedure until the next day. Physically, Khormaksar was a huge airfield and with no transport it took several days to do the rounds and sign in at all the appropriate offices. Having finally sorted the admin, I then had to get on a flight up to Bahrain (RAF Muharraq). After another couple of days I was finally allocated a seat on an Argosy of 105 Squadron which was the 'airline' of that part of the Middle East and arrived in Bahrain in early August. Bad mistake – if Aden was hot, Bahrain was indescribable, much hotter and much more humid. I don't know how our airmen managed to service the Hunters; just to touch the metal skin of the wings or fuselage would have given severe burns. On the social side, even the station swimming pool had to be cooled. Fortunately, unlike Aden, all the bedrooms and some of the public rooms were air conditioned. The squadron commander was Squadron Leader P.G. Peacock who had brought the squadron over to Aden from Cyprus in March 1963. The Khormaksar Hunter squadrons had an establishment of twelve aircraft each, which with 1.3 pilots per aircraft meant around sixteen pilots.

Back to Bahrain. I flew my first flight with 43 on 16 August 1963 in T.7 XL613. This was an engine air test followed by two circuits. Then on the 21st I carried out a dual-handling check, again with Squadron Leader Peacock, which consisted of practice forced landings and more circuits.

Pictured soon after arriving at Khormaksar in September 1963, T.7 XL612-X was allocated to 1417 Flight and regularly loaned to the FGA squadrons as and when required. It had the distinction of being the last Hunter to fly in RAF service when withdrawn by the EPTS in August 2001 (*Ray Deacon*).

Then the detachment was over; we left Bahrain in the capable hands of 208 Squadron and it was back to Aden. My first trip from Khormaksar was yet another flight in a T.7, XL612 this time, with Squadron Leader Peacock on a sector recce to introduce me to the delights of the Aden Protectorate. Unusually, the four Hunter 7s belonged to 1417 flight and were lent to the Hunter 9 Squadrons as required.

Now for the FGA.9
At last on 5 September I had my first flight in an FGA.9 – XE546. Not surprisingly it was equally as pleasant to fly as the Mark 6; the additions and modifications had not spoilt the performance at all if one allowed for the effect of the higher ambient air temperature. The FGA.9 had an Avon 207 with a little more thrust so the performance was virtually identical to a Mark 6, except that the Aden air temperatures increased the time to height somewhat. However, as we were generally flying at low level this did not cause problems.

In the event I was not given long to get used to Aden as just over a week later the squadron was off on yet another detachment, this time to RAF

Eastleigh in Kenya. This time it was purely ceremonial – the squadron was to carry out a formation flypast at the Royal Kenya Show as part of the celebrations for the imminent Independence Day handover. As a new boy I wasn't one of the Hunter party and instead had to go down to Nairobi in a Beverley with several other pilots and the groundcrew. This was a most uncomfortable trip, which took nearly seven hours lumbering along at 160 knots at (for us) a pretty low level.

I only had two flights at Eastleigh, one a triangular cross-country Eastleigh-Mount Kenya-Nundawat-Eastleigh. The following day I was in a flypast over Eastleigh and then, shortly after that, the squadron flew back to Khormaksar without me. I was left behind with XE623 which had gone seriously unserviceable. I had to wait nearly a week for it to be fixed but that was not all. The distance back to Khormaksar was more than 1,000 miles, passing over Northern Kenya and Ethiopia, some of the most inhospitable and desolate terrain in the world. A crash landing would have been fatal and using the good old Martin-Baker would have produced the same result, only taking a little longer. However, the ruling was that a single-engined aircraft on this route must be accompanied by a twin with a navigator, a) to make sure we were going the right way and b) to mark the spot where/if we went down. In my case I hitched a 'lift' with a Canberra and so we were pretty compatible. Even so I was glad to see the Gulf of Aden coming up, with Djibouti on the left, and even more so when I was within gliding distance of Khormaksar.

Shortly after the squadron's return to Aden, Squadron Leader Peacock was tour-ex and he was succeeded by Squadron Leader Phil Champniss. This also coincided with the start of our operational flying. It was not our job to worry about the politics of the situation. We were there to support the Army, to be their 'mobile artillery'; that was what we had trained for and that was what we looked forward to doing. What seemed to have started it was a civil war in North Yemen (the baddies) spilling over into South Yemen (the goodies). For some years the Egyptians had been fomenting trouble in North Yemen and stirring up the local tribes to the north of Aden with promises of 'freedom'. This eventually culminated in the Radfan Campaign. But more of this later. One other interesting arrival was in October 1963 when Air Vice-Marshal 'Johnny' Johnson was appointed AOC RAF Middle East Command.

Captured Crate
However, as a result of the Egyptian presence in the north, the RAF received an unexpected Christmas present in the shape of a Yemen Air Force IL-14

(Crate) transport. On 2 December 1963 this aircraft became lost and landed at Lodar (Lawdar), a small up-country airstrip to the north-east of Khormaksar. It was quickly surrounded by the Aden Protectorate Levies and prevented from leaving. The Egyptian crew were subsequently returned to North Yemen but the aircraft was retained. It was flown to Khormaksar for a short while but eventually ended up on the fire dump. Lodar was one of the small airstrips used by the Twin Pins and Beverleys for the re-supply of the army and local 'friendlies'. There were no roads connecting with the outside world and the only transport was by foot, donkey or camel.

But before launching into the flying side I will say a little about the domestic situation as pertained before Margaret and the children came out and before the terrorism started (it wasn't called terrorism then, we called it 'the troubles'). As mentioned above, Khormaksar was a very large station. The officers' and sergeants' messes were attractively built of large, chiselled stone blocks and some of the airmen's accommodation was of equally high standard. Many of the admin blocks were also permanent buildings but down at squadron level we were in single-storey pre-fabs (Twynehams), albeit air-conditioned. None of the public rooms or bedrooms in the mess

Having been flown from Lodar to Khormaksar by two test pilots from Boscombe Down, the captured Egyptian IL-14 (Crate) was parked behind the SAR Flight/Shackleton hangar for several months before being towed across the airfield to the fire dump (*Roger Wilkins*).

were air-conditioned, but all of the office accommodation of Flying Wing, Tech. Wing and Admin Wing had the air-conditioning humming twenty-four hours per day. The only exception was the sleeping accommodation of the 8 Squadron pilots and the reason was that some time previously one of their pilots had been killed while carrying out an attack on the air-to-ground firing range. As a very useful memorial his mother had provided funds to equip sufficient air-conditioned bedrooms for all of 8 Squadron pilots. The mess public rooms were as to be expected – large, high-ceilinged and airy with multiple ceiling fans. But the main attraction was the Jungle Bar, outside, open to the stars with thatched roof and palm trees all around. The only slight drawback to all of this was that the electricity generating power station was just inside the main gate and only a couple of hundred yards away. As it was powered (reputedly) by a Rolls Royce Avon similar to the one in the Hunter, it was difficult to ignore. One rumour had it that it had been intended to be placed on the northern edge of the airfield where it would only have bothered the odd passing camel, but that Works and Bricks had held the plans upside down when constructing it!

When I arrived the station was on a peacetime footing, Middle East variety. Although it would have been quite realistic to work a normal 9-5 day as all office accommodation was air-conditioned, the working day was from 07.00 until 13.00 and then back to the mess for lunch and a zizz or down to the beach. The distance from the mess to the flight line was a mile or more and it was no fun hiking it twice a day. For some reason there was no transport provided and so it was either buy a car, motorcycle or Shanks's pony. At first I used to hitch a lift to both the squadron and to the beach but as I would need a car when the family came out I bought a second-hand Fiat 600 from one of the pilots who was tour-ex and returning to the UK. In fact it wasn't only cars that got handed on like this as, later on, just before Margaret arrived I employed a children's *ayah* in much the same way. Because of the climate the single officers didn't need four wheels and so it was fashionable for the bachelors to buy new Honda 50 motor cycles. At that time Honda and Fiat seemed to have the monopoly in Aden.

Apart from driving to the squadron the only other places to go on a daily basis were shopping at Steamer Point and to the beach at Tarshyne a mile or so farther on. So here is a typical day – woken at 06.00 by the batman, a local citizen, with tea followed by a shower and down to breakfast. Dress for a flying day would be khaki shorts and short-sleeved shirt with normal UK blue officer's peaked cap, long khaki socks and, officially, black lace-up shoes. However, there are two stories here. Before going to Aden we were advised to ignore the recommended RAF shorts ('It ain't half hot Mum' in style) and nip down to the Indian tailor's shop just outside the main gate where he would produce short shorts, made to measure in twenty-four hours. The black shoes which we were expected to wear not only to and from work but also while flying would have been useless in the event of baling out. So the move here was to pop down to the Bata shoe shop on the Ma'alla Straight and get a pair of desert boots for thirty shillings. In fact this was one of the few battles that the pilots actually won, as later on we were allowed one pair a year, paid for by the RAF. After breakfast it was down to the flight line for Met briefing at 07.00 which was a communal affair for the two Hunter Squadrons and 1417 Flight. The briefing did not usually take long as there was rarely any cloud and it only rained once at Khormaksar in the two years I was there. The main problem was in the hot season when strong winds would whip up the sand into duststorms at very short notice. It is worth noting that in the event of such a storm or maybe a crash on the runway there was no nearby diversion. The nearest was the French Air Force base at Djibouti, which was 140 miles away across the Gulf of Aden, to the south west.

Met briefings

After the Met briefing the pilots returned to their respective squadrons where the flight commanders would lay down the flying programme for the day. As we were a fairly small squadron we did not operate as two flights but all worked together with the flight commanders taking turns at planning the flying programme and authorising the flights. The type of training was similar to that of the day-fighter squadrons I had previously been on with the exception of air-to-air firing. We had no capability to tow flags and, anyway, we were principally ground-attack. We did, however, practise high-level battle formation and dogfighting, just in case a MiG appeared.

With twelve Hunters on strength there were usually about six or seven available at the start of the flying day. On a none air-to-ground range day this would usually mean a four-ship going off either to practise high-level battle formation followed by a dogfight and tail chase, or a low-level route to a practise target simulating a rocket and cannon attack. The remaining aircraft would be sent off as a pair or solo on cross-countries, aerobatics etc.

On arrival at the squadron after Met briefing, the duty flight commander would detail the four pilots on the four-ship and outline the task. When the task was to train newly-arrived JPs (junior pilots) the formation would be led by an experienced pilot with another as number three. We were still flying the 'finger four' which the RAF had copied from the Luftwaffe in the Second World War as it was ideal for both high-level and low-level operations. The nominated four pilots would go into the briefing room to go through the proposed flight using a blackboard and other aids such as maps and photos of the targets which had been supplied by 1417 Flight. Sometimes, however, in order to train the JPs the positions would be reversed and the experienced pilots would fly as Nos 2 and 4 in order to monitor the conduct of the trip and provide a debrief on return.

Working up

The length of time it took to go operational depended on many factors. The shortest time was taken by pilots who had flown the same role in another ground-attack squadron. Next came pilots with plenty of single-seat jet time, i.e. on day fighters, and finally junior pilots who had just come through the training system and who had very low total flying hours. For a 20-year-old JP with about 260 hours experience it would take about three to four months to become operational. With someone like myself with two previous fighter tours it took about a month, this was mainly to learn the squadron SOPs (Standard Operating Procedures). It is interesting to note that, when transferring from one squadron to another, even in the same role, the first thing one was told was 'forget what you learnt on your last squadron, this is the way we do it here'. On becoming operational, the next step was to become Op. 2 and then Op. 4. This meant that you were qualified to lead formations of two or four aircraft on operational sorties. Generally only the most senior pilots became Op. 4 and of course the JPs rarely made Op. 2 until near the end of their tour. It must be emphasised that the training flights and operational flights were being carried out during the same period, with the ops obviously taking priority. This highlighted the difference between training and actual operations. We trained for low-level missions to fly below radar cover and avoid SAMs but, luckily for us, the other side did not have these weapons. Thus a typical practice low-level strike would be flown in a finger-four battle formation at 250 feet and 420 knots. The route would be planned to fly up wadis to stay below the assumed radar cover and so would involve many changes of course on a typical 200-mile route. When nearing the target an IP would have been chosen about a mile from the target and at 90 degrees to the track flown. At the IP the leader would open up to full power, pull up sharply to about 3,000 feet, roll over, drop the nose into a dive and hopefully line up with the target. With the Aden cannon the pipper in the gunsight display was placed smack on the target and the gyro gunsight compensated for wind effect. However, the enormous gravity drop of the 3-inch drainpipe meant that the bottom diamond of the display had to be placed on the target in order to raise the nose to compensate. On actual operations it all changed as the enemy had only small arms and an occasional heavy machine gun. In this case the sorties were still flown in battle formation but at between 3,000 and 5,000 feet. This not only kept us above small-arms fire but also made navigation much simpler.

Apart from range-firing sorties, the aim was to despatch one or possibly two sections of aircraft to practise RP and cannon strikes. Any singleton aircraft left over would be despatched immediately on low-level navigation exercises or high-level aerobatic practice. This would introduce a 'stagger' into the programme to prevent the groundcrew from being overloaded. After a briefing which took about thirty minutes, the 'four-ship' would launch which meant that those not on the first wave could relax and have a coffee or a pint of orange squash. It was during one of these breaks that an 'eggy round' might be unleashed. An eggy round was one of those pointless, almost stupid ways that 43 Squadron pilots had of letting off steam. If an individual suspected that those present were too lethargic he would fetch an egg from the fridge, sidle into the crewroom and shout 'eggy round' and at the same time lobbing the egg towards one of the other pilots. That person had to catch the egg and immediately toss it to someone else. When eventually someone dropped the egg he had to clear up the mess. An eggy round could also occur in someone's flat or house during a party but was understandably most unpopular with the wives.

Front-line batman

The liquid loss due to the heat in Aden was so great that the docs recommended drinking at least ten pints of liquid a day. When in the crewroom this was served by our 'boy', Salah, who came from North Yemen. He was a little chap, although probably middle-aged, who had been working for the RAF for many years. His job was to keep the squadron clean and tidy and serve orange squash, coffee and light snacks. He was married but his wife was in North Yemen so he didn't get home to see her very often; in fact he told us it was about once every four years. It just so happened that one of his visits home was due in mid-1964. He was granted leave of absence by the squadron commander and then made a very surprising request – he asked for a letter from the CO to help him get across the border to North Yemen. Of course we could not understand this as the letter would say that he was employed by his country's mortal enemy, the RAF. However, he persisted and was given a letter stating who he was, who he worked for and asking all concerned to give him help where possible. We awaited his return with interest, expecting that the North Yemen Army would give him a hard time but in fact it was just the reverse. He used his letter to hitch rides up to the border and then, when he produced the letter to a North Yemen officer at the crossing point, he was treated like a VIP and put on a truck which took him all the way home. His return was in a similar vein and he was a happy little chap when he returned to us.

One of the more unpopular duties for the most junior pilot was tending to the 'Fighting Cocks'. It has been a tradition since the First World War that, wherever 43 Squadron was stationed, there would be at least two genuine fighting cocks kept as mascots. This normally posed no problems in the UK but the climate in Aden was hardly conducive to a long life for the cockerels and the turnover proved to be very frequent.

The endurance of the Hunter FGA.9 was such that most sorties, except firing on the range, lasted for about one to two hours and so, with a turn-round, each aeroplane could fly twice in a morning provided it stayed serviceable. Thus each pilot would get either one or two trips per day. This serviceability was a factor of the complexity of each succeeding generation of aircraft. When a section of four Meteor 8s (as I flew on 1 and 63 Squadrons) landed they would invariably all still be serviceable. With the Hunter usually one of the four would be unserviceable. With the Lightnings they would all have snags which would prevent them flying again straight away.

Navigating the Protectorates

In early 1964 I became the Squadron Navigation Officer and, as I had always been interested in maps and charts, the Aden Protectorate and its rugged terrain proved to be my biggest challenge so far. There were virtually no roads away from Aden town and so the salient features used for navigation were the coast line, the wadis and up country, the escarpment and unusual rock formations. Unlike the Hunter 10, which had one NDB (Non-Directional Beacon receiver), the Hunter FGA.9 had no electronic navigation aids. The only means of navigation was the Mark 1 eyeball, a topographical map and a stopwatch. In fact when the Hunters arrived from the UK there was a stopwatch fitted on the instrument panel, but this was removed immediately on landing in Aden, locked in a safe, and only replaced when the aircraft was returned to an MU (Maintenance Unit) in England, the reason being that stopwatches were V & A (valuable and attractive) items and would most likely have been stolen. Hence we all had to buy our own stopwatches and I still have my Minerva Majex to this day.

In any event the position of the watch located down at the bottom of the instrument panel was of no use as we flew most of the time 'heads up' looking out of the cockpit. To house our own stopwatches the engineers made up an aluminium bracket which was bolted on top of the left-hand coming and so was easily viewed whilst looking out of the windscreen. The basic map in use was a 2 million (1:500,000) topo (topographical) map which provided an excellent depiction of the terrain features. This map was used for all high-level work and also low-level as far as the IP. These maps were supplied by the Air Force but, for the final run into the target, we relied on larger scale 1:100,000 maps which we obtained from the Army. The 2-mil maps were from the same series that we had used in the UK but the army maps were very detailed, brown in colour and extremely accurate. The 2-mil maps had to be covered in clear fablon as coloured chinagraph pencils were used to mark the route to be flown. As practice flights were flown at 250 feet (AGL) and at a speed of 420 knots, it was necessary to put minute (time) marks along the route, i.e., every seven miles. Turning points were chosen over or near good landmarks such as distinctive rock formations or bends in wadis (dry rivers). The map, of course, had to be folded to a size manageable in the small cockpit of the Hunter and was usually perched on the left thigh. The right thigh had a built-in knee pad for recording the position and details of targets and radio frequencies, etc. Once airborne and settled down at 420 knots the stopwatch was started and the minute marks on the map compared to the ground. Even at that speed and height it soon became second nature and pilots were rarely unsure of their position. Of course it would have been easy to pull up and get a much better view of the ground but that would have been cheating. The formation leader was the only one navigating; the others flew in a wide battle formation (the finger four). When approaching the IP the maps would be swapped and the army brown job replaced the 2-mil. The leader would call "Approaching IP" as a warning to the rest of the formation and then "Pulling Up". This was the signal for the formation to pull up to about 2,000 feet and for the No. 2 to ease out and drop back, with Nos 3 and 4 further in trail. The run up to the IP was displaced laterally from the target to allow the leader to roll through 90 degrees before dropping his nose to put the gyro gunsight on the target. Ideally the other three aircraft would attack line astern with about 300 yards spacing. After the attack there was the problem of finding the leader again. In clear weather this was fairly easy but when it was hazy it could be a problem. Usually a prominent landmark some distance from the target was briefed as a rendezvous point as a last resort.

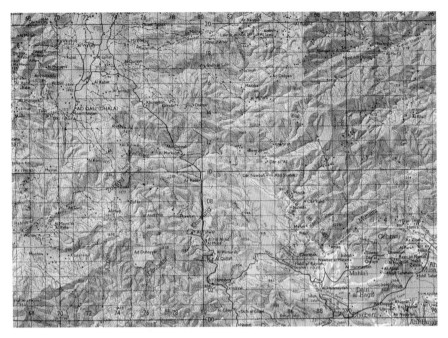

A copy of one of the highly detailed brown Army Air Corps maps also used by Hunter pilots in Aden (*Richard Grevatte-Ball*).

The hi-lo-hi technique was used where the target was outside the radius of action at low level. This involved climbing the section to possibly 40,000 feet, cruising at that level, in battle formation, to a pre-arranged point followed by a swift descent to a point just short of an IP. Thereafter the attack was made at the familiar 250 feet and 420 knots. After the attack the section would reform and climb to height in battle formation for the cruise back to base. The use of this technique roughly doubled the radius of action of the Hunter FGA.9. However, this was never used on actual operations as the target areas involved were all relatively close to Khormaksar. Where real ops were concerned, in the knowledge that the other side had no radar and was restricted to small arms, it would have been foolhardy to fly at ultra low level in range of rifle fire. In addition flights were flown at medium level to ensure accurate navigation to be able to pinpoint the targets precisely. This was most important where we were laying down fire as close as twenty-five yards to army positions or where the target house or fort was in close proximity to houses inhabited by non-involved civilians.

When fairly close to Khormaksar there were many civilian cars and vehicles to be seen on the local roads and tracks, particularly on the Dhala

Road, the main route north to Sanaa. However, up-country it was a different story as, before the days of the 4 x 4, the only vehicle capable of tackling that inhospitable terrain was the huge Mercedes truck. These were always open or canvas-topped, and were covered in garish coloured flags and cloth patches which stood out like a sore thumb in the desert terrain. They were always packed with humanity clinging to the outsides and top and usually had a fair cargo of goats and sheep in addition.

Air-to-ground firing on the range

Firing on the air-to-ground range, which was very close to Khormaksar, was usually organised in periods of about a week at a time. This gave the armourers a chance to get into the swing of things and also the logistics of the range party needed quite a lot of effort. The only two weapon systems we had at that time were the four 30mm Aden cannon and the 3-inch drainpipe rockets. The Aden gun was a superb weapon, extremely accurate and lethal when using the HE (high explosive) rounds, with a rate of fire of 1,200 to 1,400 rounds per minute. This equated to a total firing time of 7.2 seconds but, of course, the guns were never used this way. Each burst was probably around half a second in length. On the range we fired only ball (solid) shells, otherwise the range party along with all of the targets would have been decimated. The use of the Aden gun in the Hunter demonstrated that there is no substitute for real wartime conditions for testing weapons. All the firing done previously in the Hunter 6 and earlier models had been under 'peacetime' conditions where very few rounds were fired on a range sortie and so when, later on in the Radfan campaign, we were firing four guns with 135 rounds apiece, one of the frames in the structure of the fuselage adjacent to the Aden guns began to crack. In order to prevent this, an order was issued that in future only two guns at a time were to be fired. This was achieved by using the gun-selection switch which was just outboard of the anti-G control cock. The guard had to be raised and the switch set forward to Inner, whereupon only the two inner guns would fire. When the Inners had exhausted their ammunition the switch was returned aft to All, and then the two Outers could be fired.

For political reasons we were not allowed to drop bombs or napalm (which would have been ideal against tanks if we had gone to Kuwait) so we were left with the 3-inch drainpipe, so called because that is what it resembled and it was just about as effective. Its official title was the 'No. 1 Mark 3 RP'. It was first used by the Fairey Swordfish in 1936 and throughout the Second World War, and in particular by the anti-tank Typhoons in

Normandy after D-Day. The Hunter carried four Mark 12 rocket rails under each wing (except when the outboard 100-gallon tank pylons were fitted when one rail each side was replaced by a drop-tank pylon). The RPs could be hung up to three tiers on each rail, thus giving a maximum of twenty-four (or eighteen with drop-tank pylons fitted). The main draw back of the 3-inch drainpipe was gravity drop; after about 200 yards the RP had lost its forward momentum and started to curve gracefully to earth. The three types of warhead available were:

- 60lb solid shot head (actually made of concrete). This was the round used on the air-ground range.
- 60lb HE/SAP (High Explosive/Semi Armour Piercing). This was the version we usually used on operations.
- 60lb HE/HC (High Explosive/Hollow charge). This head was designed for penetration of armoured targets. Fortunately for us the other side did not possess any.

The targets on the range were fifteen-feet-square, canvas on a wooden frame. These were used for both Aden guns and the rockets and there were usually four or six of these targets erected in a row some yards apart. The range party was under the control of a senior NCO armourer with a couple of airmen and a team of local Arabs to do the work. Also present was a pilot from the squadron as the range safety officer (RSO) and to record the scores. On a firing day, a truck would pick up the pilot at the officers' mess and proceed to the airmen's mess via the sergeants' mess. The airmen's mess would provide rations for the day's outing including the 'wads' (sandwiches) and great urns of tea. All of this involved a very early start as the range had to be ready for the first aircraft's arrival at around 8 o'clock. The locals were picked up at a nearby village and were always the same Arabs. For them it was a desirable job. On arrival the labourers would set up the targets and the pilot, the RSO, would climb up into the wooden control tower to try out his radio.

The attacking aircraft arrived in pairs, spaced out so that there were only two on the range at a time. First the leader would dive on his attack and as he pulled up to go around for his next attack, the No. 2 would go into his dive. Each attack had to be cleared in by the RSO and a radio failure meant RTB (return to base). The attacks were made from 2,000 to 3,000 feet and the angle of dive was about 30 to 40 degrees but it felt a lot steeper. For range work, the Aden gunpack was loaded with 60 rounds per gun,

Local Arab workers are pictured unloading equipment and targets at the Khormaksar range. Located a mere seven miles from the airfield, the sight and sound of Hunters attacking the targets was a common occurrence (*Roger Wilkins*).

but wired off so that only one would fire on each sortie. Unlike the system we had used at home on the air-to-air flags, the shells were not marked. Instead, after each pair had completed firing and the range was safe, an NCO would run out to the target and poke a stick which had been dipped in coloured paint through each hole and then count the holes and record the scores. Thus if the target was relatively unscathed it could be used several times. This system saved reloading after each sortie and so four pilots could go to the range in turn before the gunpack had to be changed. If a pair had been particularly accurate the target would be lowered for patching or replacement of the canvas and a fresh target allocated to the next pair. As an indication I see from my log book that I often got between thirty and forty-five hits out of sixty fired at the target. The rockets were a different matter and scores were either a DH (direct hit) which was very rare, or marked by the number of yards by which one missed. The marking was again by the range NCO who plotted each round and estimated the error by means of white concentric circles painted on the ground.

Due to the gravity drop mentioned above, average errors with the 3-inch drainpipe were around ten to twenty yards. There is an amusing story about

The stirring sight of 43 Squadron FGA.9 XE611-X unleashing a salvo of 3" rockets on the Khormaksar range in June 1964 (©*IWM*).

the range party which was told to me by one of the range NCOs. As with most aircraft, the brass cartridge cases were ejected once the round had been fired. The Arab range party were allowed to scavenge these cases as there was a considerable amount of brass involved which was very valuable to them. The cases would fall along the track of the aircraft in its dive and this is what happened with the single seat FGA.9s. However, for some reason, the two-seat Mark 7 retained its cases and so the Arabs used to call the two-seater Mark 7 'the Jewish one'.

In the meantime, squadron life carried on with the most interesting flying I ever experienced. It was noticeable that the operational sorties were increasing and changing from patrols and flag waves to actual close support for the Army. Interspersed with this flying were detachments to Bahrain and Sharjah, the latter for yet more air-to-ground Aden cannon and 3-inch rocket firing. As Christmas 1963 approached the squadron commander, Squadron Leader Phil Champniss took pity on me and sent me home to do the HSE (Hunter Simulator and Emergency) course at Chivenor.

Ferrying to the UK

After two years of operations in dusty Aden, the Hunters would become very 'tired' not to mention sandblasted. As there were no facilities for major rebuilds in Aden, the aircraft had to be ferried home to a British maintenance unit to be refurbished and repainted. This was carried out at Kemble or St Athan. For safety reasons two aircraft at a time were despatched and so when my turn came to carry out a ferry home I was very relieved to be allocated a Mark 10 of 1417 Flight. Despite the fact that the Mark 9s operated over thousands of miles of hostile terrain they were not equipped with any navigational aids, whereas the Mark 10 had a single ADF receiver; luxury indeed. I was tasked to ferry home Hunter 10 XE614 and my No. 2 was Flight Lieutenant Al Liddle in 43 Squadron Hunter 9, XF421.

Due to the political situation in the Middle East, Colonel Nasser was being very unfriendly and refused to allow the RAF to overfly Egypt which was the shortest route home. Instead we were faced with an eight-leg excursion by way of Masirah, Bahrain, Tehran, Akrotiri (Cyprus), El Adem (Libya), Malta, Nice and finally the MU. With two 230- and two 100-gallon drop tanks the Hunter's range was a respectable 1,850 nautical miles. But even so the leg from Tehran to Cyprus was a bit touchy if the weather was bad. The trip normally took four days but I see from my logbook that we scrounged an extra two days at Akrotiri.

Date	Itinerary		Flight time
17-06-65	Khormaksar	Masirah	2 hrs 20 mins
	Masirah	Bahrain	1 hr 40 mins
18-01-65	Bahrain	Tehran	2 hr 05 mins
	Tehran	Akrotiri	2 hr 55 mins
21-01-65	Akrotiri	El Adem	1 hr 30 mins
	El Adem	Malta	2 hr 00 mins
22-01-65	Malta	Nice	1 hr 40 mins
	Nice	St Athan	2 hr 05 mins

Ferry trips were usually combined with an HSE course at Chivenor, thus allowing a little time to visit parents and other relations. Ideally there would have been two refurbished Hunters waiting to be returned to Aden but in our case this was not so and we returned courtesy of a Transport Command Britannia.

Hunter (HSE) course – RAF Chivenor

All Hunter pilots had to do the Simulator and Emergencies (HSE) refresher course once a year and so this time it worked very well and I was home for Christmas. The course itself was a week long at RAF Chivenor in Devon, and consisted of simulator rides with every conceivable emergency thrown at one, followed by real dinghy drill off the south coast. By today's standards the Hunter simulator was pretty crude and, of course, there was no visual or motion. In fact it felt nothing like flying a Hunter at all but it was the best we had and at least you could practise engine fires. Unfortunately, December was the wrong time of the year for real wet dinghy drill but I had to take the rough with the smooth. The deal was that we (there were about ten on the course) were taken out to sea about five miles offshore in an air-sea-rescue launch and then had to leap overboard attached to a one-man dinghy by a lanyard. We were wearing only swimming costumes under a suit of denims (a one piece coverall used by airmen when carrying out their work). The sea temperature was about zero and the denims gave no protection against the cold so there was a great incentive to get into the dinghy pretty smartly, put out the sea anchor, and erect the hood against the chilly wind. Having dropped us off one at a time about 300 yards apart, the launch left us for a while to play with the various goodies onboard, trying out the tins of boiled sweets and firing off the flares, before slowly coming around to pick us up again. At first we were very glad to be back on board but the combination of the swell of the sea, the hot engine-room and a tot of rum was enough to give the fishes a good meal!

In the drink!

We were driving in our little Fiat 600 along a road which bordered the inner harbour and, as we rounded a bend, there was an Argosy, for all the world like a flying boat, lying in the water not fifty yards from the shore.

The sorry sight of 105 Squadron Argosy XP413 being recovered from the shallow waters off the western end of the Khormaksar runway (*Roger Wilkins*).

It turned out that it was a 'feathering' classic. The Argosy (XP413 from 105 Squadron) had been up on a training mission for a newly-arrived pilot and one of the exercises was a practice engine failure on the approach to land at Khormaksar. The instructor pilot had shut down the port inner expecting the trainee pilot to feather that engine. Unfortunately, in his anxiety to cope with the emergency, the co-pilot feathered the port outer. The Argosy did not fly well on two engines, particularly if they happened to be on the same side. As there was not enough time to relight the port inner or un-feather the port outer, the captain had no alternative but to ditch the Argosy in about three feet of water.

On the flying side there were frequent detachments to Masirah Island, Sharjah for the Armament Practice Camp and Bahrain to impress Iraq.

RAF Masirah

Masirah Island lies just off the north-east corner of Oman and the RAF had maintained an airfield there since 1929. It was originally an unmanned staging post between Aden and Iraq but during the war assumed great importance as a base for anti-submarine operations and also as a staging post to the Far East. In the 1950s and 60s it resumed its task as a re-fuelling point for us between Khormaksar and Bahrain. In addition, aircraft from all three Hunter squadrons used to be based there for short periods to give a change of flying location. Apart from the RAF base, the island supported a few fishermen and there was absolutely nothing to see there except the turtles. Masirah is host to the largest nesting population of Loggerhead turtles in the world and is one of those mysterious places where, at certain times of the year, turtles come ashore to lay their eggs. Enlisting the aid of a resident officer and Land Rover we were taken to the beach to see this amazing sight. At about 10 o'clock at night the females start to come ashore in their thousands and scramble about twenty feet from the sea. Then, after digging a shallow hole with their flippers, they each lay about a hundred eggs. Nothing seemed to deter them, such was the biological urge to reproduce. Even idiots like us running around with torches made no difference. As soon as they had finished laying, they retraced their route back to the sea and disappeared. Their impression in the sand was most distinctive, rather like the wheel marks made by a tractor. We did not have time to stay to watch the eggs hatch out as it takes sixty days but apparently only a tiny percentage make it back to the sea to become adult turtles. By far the vast majority succumb to predators such as seabirds and small mammals.

A couple of photographs depicting five 8/43 Squadron FGA.9s and a T.7 on detachment to Masirah in 1966 (above) while an additional Hunter has joined the line for the second view (below) which also included Vulcan B.2 XM645 on detachment from the UK (*Bob Machin*).

Another magnificent sight off Masirah Island were the manta rays. As we flew low over the clear blue sea we could see these thirty-foot monsters gracefully 'flying' through sea with steady sweeps of their giant wings just like enormous skates.

RAF Sharjah

Sharjah is on the west coast of the United Arab Republic, just north of Dubai in what is now the United Arab Republic. When we were based there for APCs we were accommodated in prefab-type huts, with the beds all lined up along each wall. My abiding memory of Sharjah is of the millions of flies which infested the place, which is all the more unusual as we rarely saw any insects at all back at Khormaksar, except for the occasional cockroach. Every time someone went in or out of the hut those left behind would spend an hour swatting them with plastic fly swats.

I had one minor scare at Sharjah whilst returning from a live RP sortie on the Jeb-a-Jib range. I had been carrying eight RPs but one of them hung up and so I had to land with it still on the rail. I informed the tower and came in to land but despite a very gentle touch down the RP dropped off and skidded down the runway in close formation with me before sliding off onto the bondu. In fact there was little danger as it was a solid 60lb concrete head but it could have caused damage if it had hit something.

RAF Muharraq – Bahrain

The kingdom of Bahrain is a small island, farther up the Gulf between Qatar and Saudi Arabia. The Ruler has always been very friendly toward United Kingdom and so it was whilst we were at RAF Muharraq. Even in the 1960s there was the threat of Iraq invading Kuwait to get their oil and so a fighter ground-attack force was positioned there, hopefully to deal with Iraqi tanks. Initially, 8 Squadron handled this with 208 but, in 1963, 43 Squadron was posted to Aden to beef up the defences. As explained elsewhere in this narrative, the three Hunter squadrons rotated the Bahrain detachments, two months up and four months back at Aden. However, this was most unpopular with all concerned and so, in June 1964, 208 was sent permanently to Bahrain and 8 and 43 remained at Khormaksar. This did not, however, preclude short detachments to Bahrain which averaged two to three per year.

The weather in Bahrain is even more extreme than Aden. The temperatures in the summer are far higher but it is the humidity which is the real problem. As opposed to Aden, which normally only had air-conditioning in bedrooms, every room in the mess at Muharraq had air-conditioning for which we were eternally grateful. On the flying side, in the summer, the humidity caused a thick mist to form every morning which did not burn off until after 09:00. This naturally curtailed the flying programme somewhat. When off duty we rarely went off base except occasionally to a beach for swimming. In those days, unlike in Aden, Bahrain had no restaurants catering for western tastes and so we did our socialising in the mess. As the pilots were all 'living in' (the mess) during these detachments there was a tendency towards exuberant behaviour in the evenings and apart from the usual mess games, it was not unknown for full cans of beer to be thrown up into the revolving ceiling fans with predictable results. And then on one particularly heavy night, the mess upright piano was taken out onto the beach and demolished with some plastic explosive borrowed from the SAS. The station commander was naturally most displeased and our CO, Phil Champniss, had to fly down to Khormaksar to be reprimanded by the AOC. While he stuck up for us, we suffered his full displeasure when he returned and we had not only to pay for a new piano but put on denims and clean up and re-decorate the bar into the bargain.

The ground crew
Prior to centralised servicing, the squadron groundcrew numbered between seventy-five and eighty-five NCOs and airmen. In charge of all the technicians (tradesmen) was an engineering officer, usually a flight lieutenant or flying officer although on occasion this post could be filled by a warrant officer. The only NCOs and airmen not under the command of the engineering officer were a few administrators who dealt with the paperwork and who reported directly to the squadron adjutant. Each trade was represented by a senior NCO, who was nominally responsible for other SNCOs, junior NCOs and airmen in that trade. A senior NCO in charge of a particular trade was generally known as 'Chiefy'. The number of airmen on strength in a particular trade depended on the role of the squadron. In Aden the most numerous were generally airframe, engines and armourers, the latter being responsible for servicing the cine, guns, rockets and ejector seats. The ancillary trades, which comprised electrics, radio, radar, instrument mechanics, plus a few photographers, not only had to carry out first-line servicing of the aircraft on turnrounds but also assist with marshalling aircraft in and out. No. 1417 Flight of course had far more photographers to deal with the three F95 cameras in the Hunter 10.

Up-country with the Army
Every so often it was felt by the folks on the Hill that a Hunter pilot should go up-country with the Army to see how the other half lived. When my turn came I was flown in a Beaver of the Army Air Corps to an army camp on a 6,500-foot-high plateau in the Radfan, some seventy-five miles north-east

of Aden where there were some minor skirmishes with the dissidents. I felt very like John Wayne with my six-shooter strapped to my waist (we did not usually carry side-arms as the Air Ministry obviously thought, that if we did, we would present more of a danger to our own side.) The idea was that we would work with the FACs (Forward Air Controllers) and advise them on the Hunter's tactics and capabilities. Although Hunter pilots were not trained FACs I had a go several times and quite enjoyed being on the other side of the action. The only problem was that the Army had a very rigid manner of speaking on the radio. Possibly because of their radio set's poor performance whereas we were used to crystal clear UHF (Ultra High Frequency) radios. The RAF stopped using "Wilco" and "Out" many years ago, although "Roger" (I have received and understand you) was still used as it saved transmission time.

As usual the Army looked after themselves very well and I was not surprised to find a fully kitted out officers' mess, albeit under canvas. The only things to beware of, my batman warned me, were scorpions and camel spiders. In particular, it was very important to check one's boots before putting them on in the morning. Camel spiders had bodies nearly as big as a tennis ball and the sting was reputed to be lethal. During my stint up-country I had a couple of trips in the Beaver and noticed that the Army Air Corps pilots were generally NCOs; only the flight and squadron commanders were officers. After a most enjoyable and unusual week on the plateau, my return to Khormaksar was in a five-seater Scout helicopter which had been tasked to convey a captured dissident to the Army headquarters in Aden for interrogation. Rather unwisely, the take off was scheduled for midday when the temperature was at its highest and, with the pilot, myself, two escorts and the prisoner, the poor Scout was struggling to get airborne. Eventually the pilot unloaded us all and positioned the Scout on a gentle downward slope on the edge of the escarpment overlooking the sheer drop. We then clambered back on board and the pilot opened the throttle to maximum rpm and eased forward over the edge of the 6,500-foot drop. To me it was frightening enough, but to the prisoner who had never even been close to an aeroplane before it must have been terrifying. I swear our reluctant passenger turned white.

Another trip up-country in a Beverley of 84 Squadron was a visit to Beihan airstrip by a group of 43 Squadron pilots to assess whether there was any possibility of putting a section of Hunters there to confront the Egyptian MiG-15s. I produced a report to the squadron commander which said that I was prepared to have a go but would prefer the runway to be lengthened by 300 yards.

Above: The 653 Squadron Beaver XP777 that flew Roger Wilkins high into the Radfan hills for his initiation into Army life on the ground (*Roger Wilkins*).

Below: A party of Hunter pilots survey the scene at Beihan during the trip to ascertain whether Hunters would be able to safely operate from the short unsurfaced runway. Clearance was subsequently given after an extension was added to the runway. 84 Squadron Beverley XB266-V waits to take the party back to Aden (*Roger Wilkins*).

The proposal was that we would take the drop tanks off and fly up to Beihan with a reduced fuel load which would help to cope with the short landing run. The idea was discussed up at the Hill but nothing came of it due to the almost certain FOD (Foreign Object Damage) to the underside of the wings and fuselage and even ingestion of rocks and stones by the engine with probably fatal results. But the real clincher was the realisation that a MiG could catch us on the ground and write off two Hunters, not to mention the pilots.

Hunter accidents

It must be remembered that our normal training had to proceed hand-in-hand with the operational requirements. New pilots had to be trained up to operational standards and the more senior had to keep their hands in. Thus it was that, on 17 April 1964, Flying Officer Martin Herring was leading a practice four-ship formation up-country on simulated rocket attacks. Together with Flying Officer John Thompson and Flight Lieutenant John Batty, he was being tutored by Flight Lieutenant Glyn Chapman, flying in the No. 4 position. It would appear from the eye-witness accounts of the other three pilots that, as Martin was pulling out of the dive, one of the 230-gallon drop tanks came off causing the aircraft, XG136, to become uncontrollable and crash into the ground. Martin was killed instantly. Coincidentally this was the second of my personal Hunters, which I first flew on the 10 September 1963 and subsequently another seven times, the last flight being on the 13 April, just a few days before Martin went in.

There was one other fatality on 43 during my time but this came much later in 1964, after the merging of 8 and 43 Squadrons. There was a short detachment to Masirah Island involving four aircraft of the Khormaksar Strike Wing. The pilots were from both squadrons which was unusual in that we rarely ever flew together. At the end of the detachment, on 16 October, a four-ship formation led by an 8 Squadron pilot took off and, once in battle formation, commenced a climbing turn onto the track back to Khormaksar. The weather was fine but, as usual in the mornings, was very hazy. Unfortunately, in the turn, Flying Officer Ian Stephens, who was flying XE592 in the No. 4 position, became disorientated, crashed into the sea and was killed.

There were two other serious accidents which fortunately had happier outcomes. On 11 August 1964, Flying Officer Ron Burrows was No. 2 in a formation led by Flight Lieutenant John Osborne. After take off they turned to fly at low level up the coast to the north-east in battle formation. At about ten miles from Khormaksar, Ron experienced an engine flame-out caused by a failed fuel pump. He immediately pulled up to 2,500 feet and turned back towards the airfield. Several attempts at re-lighting were unsuccessful and he was obliged to eject when down to 800 feet. The aircraft, XE623, crashed in the station aerial farm and was remarkably intact for a pilot-less landing. Ron suffered the usual 'Martin-Baker' back but made a quick recover and was back on flying after only three weeks.

The other accident was even closer to home. Flight Lieutenant Glyn Chapman arrived in the circuit one day but found that one of his undercarriage legs refused to extend. He re-cycled the undercarriage several times to try to get the leg to lower but to no avail. The advice from the duty officer in the tower was to climb up and bale out over the airfield but Glyn declined and put the Hunter down gently on the remaining main wheel and nose wheel, holding the wing up on the affected side for as long as possible. Of course there was no foam available at Khormaksar which meant the possibility of fire when the wing finally met the runway. However, in this case all was well and at a very low speed Glyn eased the wing onto the ground and the Hunter did a pirouette before coming to rest. Fortunately I had my cine camera with me and took a fine shot of the hood coming back and Glyn doing the 100-yard sprint in record time.

Operations

Although 8 Squadron Hunters (and previously Venoms) had carried the burden alone, the deteriorating situation up-country required more air power and, in November 1961, 208 Squadron was moved down from its long detachment to Bahrain and then, in March 1963, 43 Squadron was posted in from Cyprus.

When I arrived in July 1963 the only operational sorties were battle flights, RANJIs and flagwaves. Battle flights were intended to be standing patrols over Beihan, a fertile area with a small airfield on a 7,000-foot-high plateau about 100 miles north-east of Khormaksar. The small airfield at Beihan was used by the short-field transports like the Beverley and Twin Pin but was unfortunately too short for the Hunters. The threat at that time came from Egyptian flown MiG 15s and 17s which crossed the border to bomb and napalm Army positions and local villages that were friendly to the British. We soon found, as did the RAF in the Second World War, that standing patrols are incredibly inefficient and very expensive in flying hours and so these were soon discontinued. There was a radar station at Mukeiras and we responded to incursions by scrambling a pair of Hunters from Khormaksar but by the time we reached the Beihan area the MiGs were long gone. I did once spot a MiG 15 while on a training exercise but as I dived on him he scooted back across the border and safety. And in case you are wondering, we always flew training flights with the four Aden cannon fully loaded. With two squadrons of Hunters plus 1417 Flight screaming around all day at low level, the dissidents were very aware of our air power. However, we could not carry out ops at night and this is where the last component of Khormaksar's Strike Wing came into its own. Most nights, one of the Shackletons of 37 Squadron (for obvious reasons we called them Shackle-bombers) would be loaded with small bombs and cruise around the dissident areas releasing one at irregular intervals. The idea of this was to make sleeping difficult, thus reducing their effectiveness the following day. We had no idea if this scheme was in any way effective, but it may well have helped the Army a little.

RANJIs were intended to prevent the dissidents smuggling arms and other supplies into the Aden protectorate by sea by patrolling the coast to the east and west of Aden. Intelligence thought that small coastal vessels or dhows might be used and a lot of fuel was expended on these flights but I don't think that much of value was ever discovered.

As the name suggests, flagwaves were intended to impress the local inhabitants with the might and strike ability of the Royal Air Force. Acting on intelligence supplied by the Army, sections of two or four were despatched to known trouble spots to make a lot of noise and buzz the offending villages. This was all great fun and quite harmless as no live firing was involved. However, by early 1964 the civil unrest up-country was starting to increase and activity in the Radfan, a mountainous area sixty miles north of Aden, began to intensify. In addition, the Quteibi, Ibdali and Bakri tribes who traditionally supplemented their income by looting travellers on the Dhala road which connected Aden to the state of Yemen also intensified their activities.

Thus the main Radfan-based tribes, backed by Egyptian and Yemeni troops and weapons, mined the Dhala road and began regular ambushes. I missed the first Radfan offensive, code named NUTCRACKER, which started on 4 January 1964, as I was on the HSE course at RAF Chivenor. I believe this was the first time that the twin-rotor Belvedere helicopters of 26 Squadron had been used to transport troops into action. Up to this time in Aden, choppers were generally used only for re-supplying formations already in position and casevacing out casualties. The units involved in NUTCRACKER were the 2nd, 3rd and 4th Battalions of the Federal

Roger Wilkins was one of a number of pilots who took their cameras aloft to photograph the rugged landscapes and townships over which they regularly flew. Here are a couple of examples from the lens of Roger's camera, depicting sheer cliffs that hugged the wadis (above) and tall buildings in a compact village (*Roger Wilkins*).

Regular Army supported by a troop of Centurion tanks from the 16th/5th Queen's Royal Lancers and artillery from the 3rd Regiment Royal Horse Artillery. Assisting the Belvederes were four Wessex helicopters from 815 Squadron Royal Navy (from a carrier which was in Aden at the time). In addition to landing formations of the FRA into the battle area on the ridges above Rabna Pass, the Belvederes also airlifted the 105mm guns of the 3rd RHA, apparently lowering them facing in the right direction to save the detachments struggling to turn them in the confined space. Khormaksar-based Hunters and Shackletons of course also carried out numerous sorties in support of the NUTCRACKER operation.

As well as stroppy locals, the Army had two different groups to contend with, FLOSY and the NLF. North Yemen, which was backed by Egypt, was fomenting unrest in the South mainly through FLOSY (Federation for the Liberation of South Yemen) and the NLF (National Liberation Front). In those days the term used was 'dissidents', not terrorists. The two groups initially hated each other and were fighting for supremacy between themselves as well as with the British, but towards the end of my time in Aden they joined forces, which helped accelerate our final withdrawal. In addition to the strikes called down by the Army in the field, we were starting to carry out patrols in well-defined proscribed areas, where the

Number 26 Squadron Belvederes, XG457-D and XG463-B, lift off from Khormaksar in company with a SAR Flight Sycamore (*Ray Deacon*).

Hunters were tasked to shoot anything that moved, be it man or beast. The idea was to deny the dissidents access to their food supplies and generally make life miserable for them. Each of the proscribed areas was well leafleted by 1417 Flight to ensure that 'honest' locals would keep well clear. On one occasion I was leading a fairly new junior pilot, on his first operational flight, in the Wadi Bana area. Wadi Bana was a large river running almost due south, from the Hadraumat in the north down to the sea. It marked the eastern edge of one of the proscribed areas and was an extremely good landmark in almost all flying conditions. On this occasion we had some trade, a lone camel grazing on the river bank completely unaware of our presence. Before I continue with this story I must return to my teen years when I read a novel about a Spitfire squadron in Burma in 1944. One of the passages haunted me for years as it described the hero, in much the same situation as ourselves, firing at an elephant with his four 20mm Hispano cannon, which virtually disintegrated the animal. The description was very graphic and when I saw the camel I knew I didn't have the heart to do the same thing. I therefore told my No. 2 to go down and shoot the camel while I flew top cover overhead. This was all part of my cunning plan as I knew this particular chap was a lousy shot. Sure enough on his first pass he missed by a mile but the camel quickly became aware of the Aden cannon's high explosive shells. Galvanised into action he leapt into the Wadi Bana and made like a speedboat for the far shore. After pulling up from the first attack my No. 2 circled around and I sent him down for another go. The second attack was no more successful than the first and I saw splashes all around but none of them hitting the speeding camel. As this was happening, I saw to my relief that the camel had reached the centre line of the river, still going like a train, and was therefore out of the prescribed area. This gave me a valid reason for calling off further attacks and so, although I didn't do my exact duty that day, at least my conscience was clear.

An incursion too far

In March 1964 the Radfan campaign started in earnest and we commenced live air-ground strikes with our four Adens and our 3-inch drainpipes. The targets were mainly forts or sangars (small circular fortifications made of piled-up rocks) where the dissidents were known to be hiding or storing weapons and ammunition; fortunately in those days the intelligence supplied to us was very good. The most interesting sorties, however, were the 'Lulus'. These were requests from the FACs on the ground with Army units. If they were in trouble they requested air support and we would scramble a pair or four Hunters at very short notice to give close support with cannon and rockets.

On 13 March 1964 Yemeni armed helicopters and MiG-17s made an incursion across the border and attacked the village of Bulaq and a frontier guard-post with bombs and machine guns. This was a serious escalation of the already tense situation and demanded some action in reply. The Hill (RAF Headquarters) signalled London and asked for permission to retaliate and on 28 March a strike was carried out on the fort at Harib, a few miles into Yemeni territory near Beihan. This was a combined effort by 8, 43 and 1417 Flight with the two FGA.9 Squadrons led by Wing Commander John Jennings, OC Strike Wing. As usual, 1417 carried out the pre-strike and post-strike photo shoots. The stone fort at Harib was almost completely destroyed by cannon and RP fire and was judged successful as the enemy attacks in that region suddenly ceased. Unfortunately I missed this op as I was engaged in ferrying a FGA.9, XF456, back from Nairobi to Aden at the time.

However, just after I returned to Khormaksar I was involved in a most exciting and strenuous operation. About thirty miles north of Aden, in Wadi Taym, an Army patrol involved in Operation CAPBADGE had been surrounded and pinned down by an overwhelming force of dissidents. The patrol was situated in a valley which would have been no problem to us except that it was a very rare day in Aden where there was complete cloud cover sitting right on the top of the surrounding hills. Fortunately, the patrol had a FAC with a radio and so he was able to describe accurately the layout of the situation and position of the patrol and call for a Lulu. On arriving overhead it looked very much as though there was no way of getting down below the cloud. On closer examination there appeared to be a 'saddle' in the mountain ridge and so I told No. 2 to orbit while I went through into the valley. As I got into the valley the patrol fired off smoke and it became apparent that there was not enough time or distance to push the aircraft forward into a dive before having to pull up back into the cloud. Unfortunately the valley was too narrow for a Hunter to circle under the cloud base and carry out an attack. As I circled round above cloud and found the saddle again I decided on a desperate measure. I approached the saddle at a fairly low speed and just before reaching it rolled inverted and went through the gap upside down. This enabled me to pull hard and stay with the contour of the mountain until almost to the bottom where I rolled over and fired at the attacking dissidents. (Note that in a fighter it is always easier to change attitude by pulling back on the stick than pushing forward in a bunt.) I tried the same manoeuvre another couple of times and then briefed my No. 2 to have a go. We carried out several attacks until our ammunition was exhausted, by which time a second pair, who had been scrambled from Khormaksar, arrived on the scene. My pair returned to the airfield to re-arm; it was so close that we did not need to refuel, and then returned to have another go. All in all, we spent the best part of a morning laying down fire, sometimes as close as twenty-five yards to our troops and were very pleased when an Army rescue force arrived.

Another notable operation was in the case of an SAS patrol which was cornered on 30 April 1964 and where the troop commander and the radio operator unfortunately lost their lives. On that occasion, 8 and 43 Squadrons provided dawn to dusk cover, firing thousands of rounds of 30mm Aden cannon shells and rockets but, of course, we could not continue at night.

Official records show that during May and June 1964 the two ground-attack squadrons, together with 1417 Flight, flew 642 operational sorties and fired 2,508 rockets and 183,900 rounds of 30mm Aden cannon ammunition.

Centralised servicing

Just as the Radfan operation came into full swing in June 1964, someone in the upper echelons at Khormaksar came up with the brilliant idea of centralised servicing. This was probably meant to facilitate the servicing effort of Tech Wing and provide more aircraft hours for the

No sooner had 8/43 Squadron FGA.9 XE530-O been retrieved from the runway following a wheels-up landing at Khormaksar on 5 August 1965 than airmen from the central servicing pool set about making the necessary repairs (*Roger Wilkins*).

operational requirements by merging 8 and 43 Squadron aircraft into the Khormaksar Strike Wing. In fact this did not involve 1417 Flight (although the Flight's ground crews were initially involved) or the Shackletons of 37 Squadron, so it was a bit of a misnomer to start with. Number 208 Squadron had moved to Bahrain permanently, thus obviating the 'two-months-up/four months-back' saga, but the pooling of aircraft and loss of virtually all of the NCOs and airmen to Tech Wing was extremely bad for the morale of both pilots and groundcrew. As one of the Hunter squadron commanders, with classical understatement, wrote in the June F540, "The results are most discouraging." The other squadron commander was even more scathing: "The new servicing system has yet to provide adequate aircraft for even one day's flying." In essence it did not affect our flying effort as the two squadrons continued to operate independently but the greatest effect was the pooling of the Hunters which meant having both 8 and 43 markings painted either side of the fuselage roundel. Thus we also lost our distinctive Fighting Cocks on the side of the nose.

Terrorism

By mid-1964 the dissidents realised that taking on the British Army in conventional warfare was not a good idea and, on 18 November 1964, the last remaining dissident tribe sued for peace. Although there was still plenty of flying on operations up-country, the emphasis by the NLF and FLOSY gradually changed to what we now call terrorism and the enemy shifted to attacks on service personnel and families living in Aden. It took the form of lobbing hand grenades into our flats and married quarters and even a bazooka fired from a car on Ma'alla Straight most evenings. I went out and scrounged some wood and wire netting to put over our windows as we were on the first floor but whether it would have been very effective I fortunately never found out. In November 1964 the Oasis bar on Ma'alla Straight was attacked, probably with a grenade, and two servicemen killed and one injured. However, one of the worst incidents occurred on Christmas Eve 1964 when a terrorist threw a grenade into a married quarter at Khormaksar, killing the daughter of the principal medical officer of Middle East Command and injuring several teenage children of senior officers. Very young children were also targeted, their booby-trapped school satchels and toys being washed up on Tarshyne beach. One incident which raised our morale a little involved the officers' mess at Tarshyne and one of the servants who had worked there for years. Apparently he had been persuaded

A view of the Officers' Mess bar at Khormaksar (*Keith Webster*).

by one of the terrorist groups to set a bomb in the officers' mess timed to explode at breakfast time when the mess would be crowded. The device was fairly crude and involved sticks of dynamite and a wind-up alarm clock. Unfortunately, for him, in the early hours of the morning, he tried to set the time for the explosion but wound the hands round too far and succeeded in blowing himself up. The mess was damaged extensively but there were no RAF casualties.

On Khormaksar airfield the RAF aircraft dispersals were always well guarded but the civilian apron was not. On 29 May 1965 an RAF Dakota (KJ955) of the Middle East Communications Squadron was blown up and destroyed.

By June the Lulus were decreasing and the main effort was on Flagwaves and air-defence scrambles. One interesting flagwave was a Hi-Lo-Hi to Shibam, some 280 miles north-east of Khormaksar. This was an Arab town that had probably never seen a motor vehicle but was composed of dozens of skyscrapers, some of them ten-storeys high, built entirely of mud bricks. At that distance it was getting near the limit for a low-level sortie and we unfortunately did not have much time to look around. However, 1417 had been there previously and I made a point of scrounging one of their nine-by-nine photographs of the skyscrapers.

One of Roger Wilkins' last flights in Aden was in his allocated aircraft FGA.9 XE649-R. The photograph is one from a series taken by George Cole who accompanied him in his 1417 Flight FR.10 (*Roger Wilkins*).

August produced only two op sorties for me. On the 2nd, I flew a flagwave over Muffid and Kharabah villages in XF445 and on 18 August a most unusual exercise. Number 43 had been tasked with carrying out a funeral flypast near the town of Nisab for a friendly Sheik who had just peacefully passed away. A formation of two Hunters was requested and so I went with the Phil Champniss. Due to the distance we had to fly a Hi-Lo-Hi and on arrival carried out a few low runs over the cortege in close formation and at a respectable low speed, just the opposite to a normal flagwave.

One of my last flights in Aden was on 24 August 1965, in my own aircraft (at that time R Romeo/XE649) when I flew up-country in company with Flight Lieutenant George Cole in his 1417 Flight FR.10. He took many photographs but my favourite is a close up of XE649 over the incredibly terraced fields where the local farmers eked a precarious living from the barren soil.

Due to the normal changeover of pilots, I was now the longest serving member of 43 Squadron. On 26 August I carried out my last flight, a low-level 'navex' in XJ689. And so, after just a little more than two years, my 43 Squadron tour was over. My time on 43 Squadron in Aden provided the best flying I had ever experienced during my RAF service. The rugged terrain, the fantastic scenery over which we flew and, above all, the chance to really do what we, as ground-attack fighter pilots, were trained for – the chance to carry out real operational live firing sorties. In addition, shortly after I returned to the UK, I received the General Service Medal with the purple and green ribbon and Radfan Clasp, to add to my solitary Coronation Medal.

Return to the UK

Very little could be taken home on the Transport Command aircraft and so all belongings had to be packed in wooden crates (scrounged from Tech Wing). These would be sent home by sea and we would not see them for several months. The journey home was scheduled a few days later and this time the family travelled together. The VC10s, which were just being introduced, halved the journey time to about six hours but we drew the short straw and got a Britannia, which by this time was getting a little long in the tooth. Our take off was at 20:00 and as we rolled down the runway I said to Margaret "he is not going fast enough, we won't get off at this speed," Sure enough, the reverse thrust came on with a howl and we began to decelerate. Fortunately Khormaksar has a very long runway and we stopped before the end. The Brit then taxied back to the terminal building and we were off-loaded. As with airlines today, we were never told the reason for this incident but, after a few hours in the transit building, we trooped back on board and this time successfully got airborne. The journey home to Lyneham was a lengthy twelve hours but, as we had all been up for nearly twenty-four hours, it was not difficult to sleep on board the aircraft.

When we left in August 1965 the military situation in the field was well under control but the terrorism was beginning to affect the families and civilians. It would have been possible to evacuate all of the families and civilians and the British services were well able to contain the dissidents, but the British government of the day made a political decision to quit Aden and the final pull out was completed on 30 November 1967.'

Chapter 4

Vigilant – 208 Squadron

David Drake (Flying Officer)

David Drake was attached to Jufair HQ from April 1967 until the end of the Aden evacuation where he assisted Transport Operations.

'When the final Hercules lifted off from Khormaksar, there was a jingle outside in the corridor and Sir Andrew Humphrey, the former Governor General, entered with champagne for everyone involved. I then joined 208 Squadron without the benefit of a refresher with the OC, Squadron Leader

Above and next page: Two views depicting 208 Squadron FGA.9s en-route from an APC in Sharjah to their home base at Muharraq in 1968, composed of a neat four-ship formation and a close-up of XK140-D (*both, Dave Drake*).

Tony Chaplin, suggesting that next they would be sending civilians. So I was with 208 from November 1967 until December 1968.

Ground Incident at Rashid Range

It was time for an APC (Armament Practice Camp) which would be carried out at RAF Sharjah and so we deployed all serviceable aircraft en mass. The following day I was tasked to drive out to the range at Rashid. I took a Land Rover accompanied by two junior pilots. The range was some twenty miles beyond Dubai and the tarmac road quickly became a graded gravel track. Approaching the range tower, disaster struck as the gear lever separated from the transmission, leaving the vehicle stuck in first gear.

The tower was opened up and checked as necessary; sadly the SSB radio which I had hoped would have enabled a rescue vehicle to be sent needed a trained operative to set up. We continued to check the targets and lead-in markers and finally decided to make the drive back to Sharjah.

First gear in the heat of the desert meant that it took only a few hundred yards for the engine to overheat. This therefore made our progress to the main graded highway very slow. Finally we made it.

We were now on the main graded highway and had stopped for yet another cooling down when a truck loaded with long metal construction rods stopped to give assistance. The friendly Arab driver who spoke some

254

Above: Following the closure of Khormaksar, the Hunter pan at Muharraq was extended in the form a V shape due to the proximity of the runway, in order to accommodate two squadrons. 208 Squadron aircraft dominate this 1969 view in which T.7 XL566-Z and FGA.9 XJ632-B plus a pair of Kuwait Air Force Hunters can be identified (*Aviation Bookshop*).

Below: Number 208 Squadron Hunters, 152 Squadron Pembrokes and a mix of 30 and 84 Squadron Beverleys were the main occupants at Muharraq when this photograph was taken in 1964. The two Pembrokes parked beyond FGA.9s XE645-M and XE654-J are WV744 and XL956 (*Gordon Macadie*).

English grabbed one of the rods and managed to connect our vehicle to the rear of his truck. By this means we made it back to base.

Leaving our vehicle outside the base I went into admin and asked what I should do. I was told to give the driver the address of the base and tell him to submit a claim. With this information our rescuer quite happily went on his way. I drove the broken Land Rover into the MT yard and thought no more about it.

Some months later, back at Bahrain, the Boss summoned me into his presence. 'Just received this from Sharjah, can you explain?' It was a claim form made by the "friendly Arab" for the cost of recovering my vehicle. Sharjah seemed to wish to pass on the claim to 208 Squadron. He was obviously extremely savvy. When I recounted the tale of our range detail, the Boss laughed and dealt with Sharjah in his own way. He agreed that the Arab was a worthy rescuer. He now probably owns most of Dubai.

Stab me Vitals

On 10 July 1968 I was flying FGA.9 XK140 on a live mission on the Yas Island range. The aircraft was armed with six 3-inch SAP HE rockets (3-inch drains) and 540 rounds of 30mm HE cannon shells.

As a pair I led the squadron boss and once airborne and achieving 370 knots climbing speed I suddenly experienced severe vibrations. The instruments showed normal settings for the engine. However, when the Boss closed to give my aircraft a visual check, he reported that my starter door had opened and with the DME aerial had stabbed the fuselage to maximum depth with unknown consequences. He advised me to jettison the drop tanks, still full with 460 gallons of fuel. By now we were at 15,000 feet and it was quite a mesmerising sight to watch the pair tumble all the way to hit the sea just north of the airfield. Two great big blobs were all that was left in the calm sea.

I set up for a forced landing, uncertain of what would unfold, and therefore would be able to cope with anything more serious.

Touchdown was good and the brake chute deployed and the engine stop cocked. All safe I thought, time to relax. WRONG! The deceleration had over-ridden the latch system of one of my rockets and it now detached and was free to continue under its own inertia. My deceleration enabled the ugly war-headed rocket to slowly move further down the runway. I had limited braking due to having shut down the engine, but I decided to get as much space between that rocket and myself. Then the rocket snaked and went off the runway tarmac into the gravel, tumbled and stopped dead. I now let go of my braking and willed my inertia to get me as far past the ordnance as possible.

It was important to exit the cockpit as at this time of the day the temperature climbs very quickly. The hood mechanism did not unlatch and neither would the electric motor work. Without panicking it seemed to take an age to sort it out.

Later it was discovered in the engineering manual that it was possible for the electrics to take up to two minutes for the hood mechanism to activate. The hood normally motored open immediately.'

Les Dunnett (Senior Aircraftsman)

An armourer by trade, Les arrived at Khormaksar from the A&AEE at Boscombe Down in December 1961, and spent his two-year tour in Aden with 208 Squadron.

The sedentary route to Aden

'On 18 December, 1961, sixty-two airmen congregated at Salisbury railway station ready to travel on to Southampton Docks and the troopship *Oxfordshire* prior to setting sail for Aden. It was a cold and bleak start to a journey none of us wanted to undertake. Tales of Aden were legion and none favourable. Accompanied by all the (now nostalgic) sounds of a steam locomotive the next leg of the journey started – next stop Southampton Docks.

We were to be bunked-down alongside a battalion of the King's Own Scottish Borderers (KOSBs, or Kosbies). Surprisingly there was no trouble between us. I think both sides were too wrapped up in what lay ahead and thoughts of families left behind. On the first morning at sea all the airmen were assembled and told

Les Dunnett enjoying a post-Christmas lunch drink in Bahrain (*Les Dunnett*).

257

that we would be given daily tasks to undertake throughout the ten-day journey. "Those that don't volunteer will be given the worst jobs," was the warning. And so the tasks were allocated. Pat Devlin and I hung back and said nowt. Eventually the duty NCO said that all the duties were covered and we all had jobs, so that was that. So, each morning Pat and I would grab our greatcoats and head for the engine-room outlet which we found on the uppermost deck. Huddled up in the warm exhaust air we read all morning whilst everyone else was hard at work. Nobody ever found us.

Whilst sailing through the Bay of Biscay there was a horrendous storm that had the ship actually cork-screwing. Staying on your feet was next to impossible. I loved it but I would guess that 90 per cent of those on board were violently seasick. As we sailed into the Straits of Gibraltar it still hadn't subsided so we hove to, waiting to see if it would calm enough for us to make a visit ashore. But it was not to be, to everyone's bitter disappointment. After three hours the anchor was raised and we pushed on across the Med, bound for Egypt. Only now did it become warm enough for us to change into KD (our tropical wear). White legs and knobbly knees!

Christmas Eve was a really boozy affair with a lot of drunkenness, particularly amongst the 'Jocks'. No trouble, but very boisterous. On Christmas Day the bars remained shut, not an alcoholic drink to be seen. We were not happy bunnies. Christmas morning we were all allowed to go onto the upper deck where there were lots of activities for the married families and children, including a fancy dress competition. It was fun to watch but oh for a pint of beer!

Egypt proved to be great fun and a most welcome break from the daily monotony. Numerous 'bum boats' came alongside and a roaring trade with local Arabs ensued, our first experience of bartering. We were instructed not to deal with them as 'officially approved' traders would be coming aboard, but this was totally ignored. Their merchandise included many items unseen in England. About twenty traders came aboard accompanied by three or four Egyptian policemen. During the proceedings, we spotted the policemen trying to take a cut from the traders' sales and despite a lot of arguing and shouting, they each coughed up, except for one. The officer involved called one of his colleagues over and between them, lifted him up and threw him over the side of the ship. We were staggered. He was lucky to survive the drop from that height. Welcome to a different world.

With the exception of the ship's crew the journey through the Suez Canal was very much an adventure. This was our first view of the Middle East. Mile upon mile of featureless sand, broken only by the occasional village

Gliding through the Suez Canal at what felt like walking pace, the HMT *Oxfordshire* makes her way south towards the Red Sea in December 1961 (*Les Dunnett*).

comprising a small oasis with palm trees and greenery. At some point, the canal opened into what seemed to be a big lake full of ships at anchor, waiting for north-bound ships to clear the southern section of the canal. The silence was quite eerie and it was possible to hear anchors being dropped by other ships half a mile or more away. We also had our first sight of flying fish – incredible.

On leaving the canal behind our thoughts turned to Aden. Nothing was known of our destination apart from vague and exaggerated stories garnered from those who had served there. All we knew was that it was incredibly hot with an unbelievable high level of humidity and that it was possible to spend two years there without seeing rain. I had been told that I would be joining 208 Squadron at RAF Eastleigh in Kenya but that changed as the squadron had relocated to Aden. A bitter disappointment.

And so to Aden
On the morning of 31 December 1961 we arose and went on deck for our first sight of Aden. Oh my! Extremely hot and humid – yes, but dull, drab and overcast. Not exactly what we hoped for. After being unceremoniously dropped outside a three-storey stone-built tenement block, I found the only

259

empty bed, dumped my kitbag and other gear and went in search of the toilets. Easily found, but they were damp and dark. Sitting on the toilet, I felt something run across my foot, just above the shoe level. Looking down I was horrified to see the floor was covered with the biggest cockroaches I had ever seen in my life. Imagine 'big' and treble it! I quickly learnt that a "sit-down" operation in the toilets meant continuously drumming your feet on the floor to keep the blighters at bay; but it made the whole thing extremely difficult.

Returning to the room I found it was still empty – no sign of life at all. Wonderful, all on my own and there it was, New Year's Eve. The large ceiling fan barely stirred the air and the perspiration dripped off me. Being early in the evening, I changed into my pyjamas and just lay on top of the bed, not realising that it would be the last time I wore pyjamas and the last time I drank gin for thirty years. I had started to doze off when a voice said, "What are you doing there mate, c'mon upstairs we've got a bar up there,". I never found out who he was but followed his instruction to "come as you are." The room had been partially converted into a well-stocked bar. My new friend explained that a bar was constructed in each block every Christmas and the station commander would visit each in turn and award cases of 'Slops' beer to the best.

My first two weeks at Khormaksar were spent in the "bomb dump" waiting for the arrival of 208 who were in the process of being transferred from Kenya to Aden. I was stunned at the rows and rows of 1,000lb bombs. They seemed to stretch out of sight. When I questioned the NCO in charge he informed me that we were bombing villages in Yemen on a daily basis. What truth there was in that statement I didn't know but certainly bomb trolleys were loaded up daily and taken to the Shackleton squadron. It was staggering that there was never any mention of hostilities in the British press at the time. The two weeks soon sped by and my new squadron duly arrived and I had company in my room at last.

During our two-month stints at Khormaksar each landing on the block had its own *dhobi wallah*. This was a young Arab lad who would take your laundry each day and return it the next – all neatly pressed. He would also clean the rooms and make cheese-and-tomato rolls when wanted. For this we each paid one shilling and six pence per week. Good value for money.

Steamer Point had back streets that were forbidden to service personnel, where the abject squalor had to be seen to be believed. Locals lived in "homes" made of flattened-out cardboard boxes that stretched from the back streets up the side of Mount Shamsan. A few of us often wandered into the "forbidden zone" to visit a cafe (for the want of a better description), our favourite meal being a mixed grill consisting of two meats of an unusual but not disagreeable flavour. What they were I shudder to think but I suspect it was either goat or camel.

Detachments to Bahrain

Every two months the squadron flew up to Bahrain to relieve 8 Squadron on the Kuwait stand-by. This was a permanent rotation that prevailed throughout my two-year tour. Bahrain had a more palatable climate in the winter, although it was hotter than Aden in the summer and more humid. The winters could be cold with even a touch of ground frost some mornings.

The air traffic control tower attached to the terminal building served as both a military and civilian airport centre but I can't recall there being much civil traffic, mainly visiting RAF aircraft. On my first visit to Bahrain I was given a stint on night-time guard duties, introduced after dissidents walked onto the airfield and blew a huge hole in the side of a Beverley transport aircraft. RAF personnel were scattered around the military section of the airfield during hours of darkness. I recall that seemingly endless night

Following a sabotage attack on 84 Squadron Beverley XM110, the hulk was placed on a mound of sand for the Parachute Regiment to practise unrestrained para-drops from the exit in the tail-boom section (*Ray Deacon*).

quite clearly – squatting under the wing of an aircraft, head leaning on my rifle while dozing on and off. Fortunately I was awake each time the duty officer's patrolling Land Rover came round.

One incident I remember well as I took a solo walk around part of Muharraq Island outside the camp, something which was strictly out of bounds due to the possibility of being attacked. Nevertheless, I set off one afternoon along with my new Pentax camera to see if I could take some interesting photographs. It was incredibly hot and it took some time to trudge across the featureless flat sand to the first village. On reaching the outskirts a number of young boys appeared and ran around me laughing and smiling, calling out 'baksheesh, baksheesh,' the recognised begging call. I had a fair number of coins on me so I spread them out as far as possible. Their value amounted to peanuts but it appeared like they had made their fortune. At this point I became aware of a number of teenage boys and young men approaching the crowd and the mood suddenly changed. Two of them made lunges towards my camera which I managed to avoid. Then another lunged at me, pushing hard at my chest. Stepping backwards I went flying over, not realising that one of the youngsters had come right up behind me with his bike. I began to feel seriously worried, not so much for myself but for my precious camera. In the nick-of-time, a dozen or so lads rode up on their bikes, all of them wearing red blazers from a nearby school. They were soon shouting at the yobbish crowd around me and when things started to get hot I just gripped my camera firmly and got the hell out of there, my dignity intact, just. Needless to say that was my last excursion into the wilds of Muharraq Island.

I considered myself a "good" drinker in that, no matter how much I drank, I would always be able to walk steadily back to my room and fold my clothes neatly before climbing into bed. One particular morning I awoke to the sound of voices laughingly enquiring if I'd had a "good night last night?" As I lay there in bed and having managed to open my eyes I realised I was not in my bed but spreadeagled on the path midway between the NAAFI and the billets. The voices were those of my mates as they stepped over me while on their way to the mess for breakfast; it may have been a good night but it certainly was not a good morning.

Of all the flights we made backwards and forwards to Aden, Bahrain and Sharjah, we only had one that was hairraising. It was on a return trip to Khormaksar. As the Britannia gathered speed down the main runway on take off, a window panel blew in. How nobody got hurt was a miracle as it hurtled back through the cabin, bouncing off the tops of the seats as it went. As this was happening a quick-thinking chap near the front dashed up and entered the flight-deck, shouting to the pilot. Lift off was aborted, just in time, and we turned and taxied back to the apron. The co-pilot calmly entered the cabin, retrieved the window panel and reinserted it in the main frame. "We'll test it on take off" was his only comment as he returned to the flight-deck. I've never known such silence from the guys as we sped down the runway once again. No problems this time.

Sharjah and sick again

On my first visit to Sharjah I was to be taken into hospital with sandfly fever within twenty-four hours of arriving. Memories of that week are vague as I had a raging fever and was delirious most of the time. I do recall that they were unable to bring my temperature down, so I was repeatedly stripped and bathed with iced water. It felt like having a red-hot iron applied to your skin. Very unpleasant. I was released from hospital in time to join the lads and return to Bahrain. On my second visit, the same thing happened. Within a day I was back in hospital with the same infection. This time, however, it was less severe and I was out and about four days later. I had obviously built up my immune system as there were no recurrences over the next two years.

Thinking back, there was an incident when a pilot activated his brake 'chute before touching down, causing minor damage to the undercarriage due to the heavy impact. The pilot left the squadron shortly after and it was rumoured that he had lost his nerve.

Due to the excessive heat the working day began early and finished around lunchtime. The afternoons were generally spent dozing on our beds after a few lunchtime beers in the YMCA in preparation for the earnest drinking in the evenings. There were occasional "outings" using a three-ton open-backed truck and, on a trip to a medieval fort some way out into the desert, we encountered an Arab and his young daughter signalling they wanted a lift. We hauled them up and into the back of the truck and asked our local Arab guide to talk with our newly-found passengers. After a few minutes the conversation became quite animated and the guide shouted for the driver to stop to allow the father and daughter to get off. We sat there bemused. After we set off again the guide explained that the father was on his way to sell his daughter at the next town. Angered by what they heard, some of the chaps were for going back to lynch him. A few miles further on we came across a village built up the side of a small hill with a stone tower at the top. Apart from numerous goats it seemed to be deserted. On spotting someone by the base of the tower, we made our way up the hill to be greeted by an old, toothless villager armed with an ancient blunderbuss-style rifle.

Above: The Bahrain detachments offered pilots and ground crew an opportunity to unwind from the everyday pressures of operations in Aden as exemplified in the photograph above. Christmas dinner in 1962 has been washed down by an ample supply of liquid refreshment for this group of 208 Squadron airmen (*Les Dunnett*).

Below: The end of another Bahrain detachment sees a happy band of 208 Squadron airmen waiting to board an RAF Britannia for the flight back to Khormaksar (*Les Dunnett*).

We deduced that the women and children were hiding from us in their mud huts while the men were away fighting an endless feud with another village.

Open Day at Khormaksar

The Khormaksar open day was to start with two 8 Squadron Hunters diving towards one end of the runway, breaking the sound barrier as they descended, as a third Hunter dived from the opposite end. The aircraft were timed to cross in front of the control tower, halfway down the runway. Having broken the 'barrier', they began their pull out but one aircraft failed to complete the manoeuvre and crashed in a fireball in the middle of an Arab army barracks on the opposite side of the runway. The 21-year-old pilot was killed instantly. A tragic sight I hoped never to witness again. The show continued as planned but nobody had the heart to enjoy it. A sombre note on which to end this resumé of my two-year tour in the Middle East and the beginning of a new chapter, a posting to the V-bomber base at RAF Marham.'

Ted Lambe (Senior Aircraftsman)

Having arrived in Aden as an air radar mechanic on 3 January 1963, Ted Lambe was assigned to 208 Squadron to work on Hunters. Due to the escalating troubles in Aden and the increasing numbers of transport aircraft bringing in reinforcements through Muharraq, Ted was posted to the Muharraq Handling Flight a year later.

'My memories of Aden are stepping off the aeroplane into the heat … and it was the cool season; the smells and flies, and the speed of sunrise and sunset. Being on a Hunter unit, we regularly moved between Khormaksar, Sharjah and Muharraq and made the most of the cards we'd been dealt. Like the time when a 43 Squadron Hunter was in the hangar for servicing and one of our riggers repainted the Fighting Cocks emblem to show it lying flat on its back and KO'd with stars around its head. Their CO was not amused.

On one detachment to Muharraq, we modified a large packing case to use as the line office to improve conditions over the tent that served as our crew room. While down at Sharjah, a 3-tonner was "requisitioned" for a trip inland where we encountered an old Portuguese fort, abandoned but truly "Beau Geste", an isolated lookout post manned by a guard with an antique rifle which no doubt was still lethal, and a picturesque village by a small oasis between the ever-present dunes. I was a member of a team

A view from beneath the wing of an RAF Britannia at Muharraq, looking towards the 8 Squadron line. Members of the Visiting Aircraft section are standing by ready for the engines to be started on the 'whispering giant' (*Ted Lambe*).

planning to climb Kilimanjaro but had to withdraw because of "a little local difficulty" up-country. My long-time friend, Neil Richards, who was also based at Khormaksar, took my place.

In December 1963 I was flown down to Embakasi, Nairobi, in a Shackleton as part of a detachment to support the celebrations marking both Kenya's and Zanzibar's independence days. Two flypasts were flown by the squadron during our stay, on the 10th in Zanzibar and 12th in Nairobi. We were billeted in the Spread Eagle hotel on the road to Thika for the duration of the detachment and, while there, four of us clubbed together and hired a car which I drove to Naivasha to see the lake filled with flamingos and to watch an amateur car race. We then moved on to the Menangai Crater for the view of its enormous crater and signpost on the Equator. We also stopped at the small chapel on the Kikuyu Escarpment, skirting the Rift Valley, built by Italian PoWs engaged in building the original road. On the way out we were passed by a convoy of lorries packed with former Mau Mau fighters, still armed, as they were leaving the Aberdare forests and heading for Nairobi as free men at Uhuru (freedom day). Our natural anxiety passed when some of them waved.

On another trip we all popped down to Dar es Salaam for the day as this was our base for the Zanzibar 'do'. At the end of the festivities the Mayor of Nairobi presented the squadron with a commemorative scroll.

At Muharraq as I was about to leave for the UK and no longer part of 208 Squadron, Flight Lieutenant Trevor Copleston AFC gave me a squadron tie as a memento – which I have to this day.'

William Lonergan (Flight Lieutenant)

Having joined the RNZAF in 1954 as an engine mechanic, William worked on a number of interesting aircraft including the Avenger, Harvard, Devon, Mustang and Dakota, and flew dogfights in the back seat of an Avenger. 'They were the days when aeronautical hooliganism was encouraged,' he recalls. William joined the RAF in 1959 and became a creamed-off QFI on the Jet Provost. There followed a tour on the Hunter with 208 Squadron at Muharraq from 1965 to 1967. William spent some time at Khormaksar and is proud to have become the last RAF officer to be banned from Aden for life.

Every one a winner!

'During my time in Bahrain, the 230-gallon drop tanks for the Hunter 9 were being modified to enable 7G to be pulled with them full. This was being done by the MU at Khormaksar. We would fly down from Bahrain with un-modified tanks, swap them for modified ones and fly back to Bahrain. It usually meant two nights at Khormaksar. I was tasked to fly one aircraft with another aeronautical hooligan, Jock Watson, flying a second. We arrived at Khormaksar only to find that Group Captain Beetham was holding his arrival party and that the main bar was closed for the night. Also in the Mess that night was a bunch of Army guys down from the Radfan and some Navy pilots who had flown in by helicopter from *Ark Royal* steaming off Aden. Plus all the 8 and 43 Squadron folk.

At about 18:00 we all assembled in the Jungle Bar for a few Carlsbergs and games of Carlsberg draughts. This went exceptionally well until about 22:00, after we had put away a significant number of tins of Carlsberg, and we all retired to the inside bar which had, for some reason, opened. Now there were two fans on the ceiling in the bar and at some point a person or persons unknown lobbed a beer can at the fan. One thing led to another and it became a contest as to which squadron could hit the fan the most times. It turned out that I was deadly accurate and it became a contest of your hero standing alone defending the honour of the "Two Hundred and Eighth Fighting Pursuit" against all comers. My buddy, Jock Watson, had gone off with some friends for a meal so I faced 8 and 43, the Army and the Navy alone. I was so accurate, and pissed, that people were handing me a Carlsberg can, which I would throw at the fan; Bingo another Direct Hit. Every time a coconut as they say.

Almost equals my achievement of getting the highest ever guns' score on 208, sixty hits from sixty rounds. It was the first sortie of the day, the wind had not started to blow and it was as smooth as a baby's bum. At some point the disaster happened; some idiot, still unknown to this day, handed me a dumpy Carlsberg bottle. I took aim and tossed it towards the rotating fan, which it struck with a satisfying crunch. Fortunately the dumpy bottles were made of toughened glass and broke up into lots of crystalline pieces, rather like a car windscreen, so nobody was cut by flying shards. For some reason people kept handing me Carlsberg bottles and I kept smashing them in the fan – 208 1, Rest 0. At around 02:00 we departed for bed, a good time having been had by all.

Later that morning, around 07:00, the Mess houseboy was busy sweeping up the detritus when the orderly officer, an admin or stores nerd, walked in and said in shocked disbelief, "Oh my God, the pilots have smashed up the bar," panicked and called the duty officer, another admin nerd, who called the admin squadron leader, who called the wing commander admin, who came over to survey the damage to the bar (bent cans and lots of small lumps of dumpy bottles). Meanwhile the houseboy cleared up the rest of the mess in a few minutes.

Now the *tragic* bit. Nos 8 and 43 had buggered off to Masirah for an exercise, the Navy had gone back to *Ark Royal* and the Army had been

XK151-D, the 208 Squadron FGA.9 flown down to Khormaksar by William Lonergan and, for reasons explained in his narrative, returned to Muharraq by a different pilot (*Ken Simpson*).

loaded into a Beverley and gone back to the Radfan. Leaving your hero as the only person on Khormaksar who was present during the "Destruction Derby". By 10:00 Group Captain Beetham, not a man known for his sense of humour, ordered a board of enquiry, placed your hero under house arrest and generally lost what sense of humour he may have had. Jock Watson laughed his socks off as he waited for a replacement pilot to come down from Bahrain so he could get the aircraft back.

I spent a week at Khormaksar with this farce of a board of enquiry and returned to Bahrain in an Argosy. Waiting my arrival was a bollocking from Tony Chaplin, the Boss of 208, and the station commander who had received a letter from Group Captain Beetham stating that "under no circumstances is this officer ever to go back to Aden". I also refused to pay the fine of £30 imposed on me.'

Doug Marr (Flight Lieutenant)

In support of Operation THESIGER, twenty-seven sorties were flown from Masirah over Dhofar State in 1966 by a detachment of 208 Squadron FGA.9s from Bahrain and a pair of 1417 Flight FR.10s from Aden. Doug Marr helped make up the 208 Squadron contingent involved in the operation which was top secret at the time.

Tracking arms smugglers
'At the end of February 1966 208 Squadron was once again at RAF Sharjah for its routine APC when, out of the blue, we received tasking by HQ RAFPG to mount an immediate operational deployment to Masirah for "reconnaissance duties". Our boss, Squadron Leader Chaplin, briefed the squadron, sending half back to our base at Muharraq to get ready for deployment before leading the first detachment of six aircraft, each fitted with two 230-gallon and two 100-gallon drop tanks to ensure maximum endurance, straight from Sharjah to Masirah. There he was joined by two Hunter FR.10s from 1417 Flight. According to intelligence sources a group of six trucks carrying rebels and armament were believed to have left the Gulf area en route for the Dhofar province, south-west of Oman and north of Salalah. It was suspected that they would follow the 'route of wells' across the inhospitable Empty Quarter.

Rebel fighters had been a threat to the Sultan of Oman and to the airfield at Salalah which was a staging post and storage facility for the RAF and whose security was of concern. The task was to fly a programme of high-

In addition to its trials work with the SNEB rocket system, 208 Squadron took the opportunity to practise dropping napalm on the Jeb-a-Jib range using water-filled 100-gallon drop tanks on the outer pylons (*208 Squadron Association*).

low-high reconnaissance sorties over the desert in the hope of intercepting the convoy before it reached its destination.

For those of us who flew our aircraft back to Muharraq it came as a shock to learn that the Central Flying School (CFS) Standardisation Team had arrived to check out our pilots to make sure our handling and knowledge of drills and procedures was up to scratch. What timing! So I and others dutifully flew our standardisation sorties before setting off in our jets for Masirah. I arrived on 5 March and went straight into a briefing for my first operational sortie. The format was for a formation of three aircraft to climb to height, let down to low level north-west of Thumrait (Midway) airfield, and then search for dissidents along routes to Dhuqu, Mugshin and Haima before climbing back up to height to return to Masirah. The low-level part of the sortie was led by one of the recce experts on 1417 Flight, these being Flight Lieutenants Dick Johns and Ken Simpson, whose expertise at identifying vehicle tracks and their freshness was part of their specialisation. When at low-level they would fly at fifty feet where the 208

Squadron Hunters would fly as an escort pair at 250 feet, scanning a wider area. This inevitably led to questioning about what we did if we came across the rebels. On asking if they were armed it was suggested that they might have Vickers guns mounted on the backs of their vehicles. We were to be armed with full Aden gunpacks but without the fuses in. Opening fire could only be approved by higher authority which was no use if the fuses were out.

During this two-week operational deployment a total of fifty-six operational sorties was flown to the enormous credit of our hardworking groundcrew. Each sortie lasted two hours on average, with almost all operational pilots gaining experience in the area, seen as some of the most inhospitable in the world. Though we did not find the convoy we learned that ground forces did, so perhaps we helped. In fact it was hard to imagine anyone in their right mind wanting to drive across the Empty Quarter, which invited the question "if you were determined to carry out such a mission wouldn't you want to do it at night when it was cooler?" And from our point of view it might have made identifying a convoy easier, especially if they had their lights on. Night flying at low level over an empty desert was, however, not seen as a sensible option.

SNEB trials

No sooner had 208 Squadron returned to Muharraq than it was tasked to carry out the much anticipated SNEB rocket trial that would lead to the introduction of the weapon into RAF service. Although there were fifty-five operational launchers on the station, there was no flying clearance or training policy. The operational pod carried nineteen rockets, which could be released as a salvo, and had a frangible nose cone which shattered as the first rocket of the salvo left the pod. Much time had been lost due to the slow pace at which the squadron's aircraft were modified but, on 4 April, I flew as the chase aircraft for a Hunter carrying a SNEB pod to observe what happened to the nose cone in normal flight. As speed built up it shattered. So the operational nose cone had to be strengthened. In the meantime we needed to train using this weapon one at a time and this required a training launcher which carried fewer rockets, did not need a nose cone and was reuseable. Suffice to say that it wasn't until December 1966 that we finally started firing SNEB rockets at targets on Rashid range near Sharjah. And what a fabulous weapon it turned out to be. We could fire it using both the gyro gunsight or a fixed sight with far greater accuracy than before, and this weapon was to give the ground attack squadrons the teeth they deserved in the anti-armour land battle.'

Peter McLeland pictured following a photo shoot over Mount Kilimanjaro with the 208 Squadron Aerobatic Team in 1961 (*Peter McLeland*).

Peter McLeland (Flight Lieutenant)

Peter McLeland joined 208 Squadron at Eastleigh in 1959, the start of a two-and-a-half-year tour in Middle East Command. Once settled in, he became a member of the MEC aerobatic team, initially flying Venom FB.4s before moving on to the Hunter FGA.9 in March 1960.

Swansong for the Venom

'In March 1960, the pilots of 208 Squadron gave up their Venoms and returned to the UK to collect their replacements – Hunter FGA.9s. As the Hunters could not be operated from RAF Eastleigh, due to the short runway, we were based at Embakasi Airport where, much to the delight of passengers and civilian employees, we carried out most of our practice displays.

The Kuwait Crisis

The date in my logbook is 30 June 1961. My previous flight was on 23 June and, unusually, it was a high-level battle, close formation and tail chase involving nine aircraft. I was flying my Hunter FGA.9, XE609 or 'Echo'. The aircraft was "mine", only because it had my name on the left side of the cockpit. I can remember nothing whatever about this flight and that was probably because things were about to change, dramatically ….

272

I had been preparing to go home to the UK as my tour on 208 Squadron in Kenya was coming to its end but suddenly my 'Tour-Ex' was cancelled. Someone called General Kasim in Iraq had laid claim to Kuwait and the squadron was to proceed immediately to Bahrain.

I see from my logbook that I flew three sorties on 30 June in Hunter FGA.9 'Oscar' (XE647);

Nairobi to Khormaksar	2 hours 35 minutes
Khormaksar to Sharjah	2 hours 40 minutes
Sharjah to Bahrain	50 minutes

Bahrain was very busy as 8 Squadron with their FGA.9s were already there and all the aircraft were being armed ready to proceed to Kuwait New. This airport was not on any map as it was still a building site.

I was the Squadron Weapons Officer (SWO) and we had been briefed that our principal targets were likely to be tanks moving across the Iraq/Kuwait border. I noticed that all our aircraft were being armed with rockets with 60lb HE heads and what we really needed were hollow-charge heads as these were more suitable for tank targets. I pointed this out to the Bahrain Armament Officer, but he was resistant to changing them as the hollow-charge heads were all stored away somewhere in wooden boxes with screwed-down lids. He was persuaded to change his mind and the rocket heads were changed. The Aden gunpacks were armed with 30mm shells belted with alternate pairs of HE and SAPI (High Explosive and Semi-Armour Piercing Incendiary).

The next day, 1 July, we were ready, and I was briefed for my first sortie. I was to lead a pair in 'Oscar' and the good news was that we were to give top cover to the other chaps who were getting their aircraft into Kuwait New. The exercise was called Armed Recce and Standing Patrol Kuwait. We were told to shoot down any military aircraft that crossed the Iraq border into Kuwait. The bad news was that they had run out of gun fuses, so I and my wing man only had one of our cannon armed with a fuse. The flight lasted an hour and forty minutes and we landed back at Bahrain at the end of it. Fortunately, we did not see any hostiles to shoot down.

The next day, 2 July, was the same: Armed Recce and Standing Patrol Kuwait to give top cover to the remaining Hunters getting into Kuwait and this time I was flying "Alpha", XG134. The sortie continued the same as the first in that we saw nothing to shoot down and again we landed back at

Bahrain after an hour and forty minutes. This time we were immediately refuelled and sent back to recce Kuwait and land at Kuwait New. Next, they had a little delivery job for me on my own. I was to take a new Hunter FR.10, XE579, from Kuwait New to Bahrain for 8 Squadron and then on the next day, 3 July, ferry 8 Squadron FGA.9 XE600/Golf from Bahrain to Kuwait New and recce Kuwait.

At this stage, I should say something about conditions at Kuwait New. In 1961 it was not on any map, and was a building site. Many of the buildings had not yet got a roof and there was no such thing as air conditioning. A searing hot wind blew in from the desert and things were grimly uncomfortable. Sleeping conditions in buildings were impossibly hot and many of us dragged a mattress out to a Hunter wing and got what sleep we could manage under that. The nicest place to be was airborne in a Hunter with the air conditioning on cold. On landing one would normally open the canopy to taxi in. However, we quickly discovered if we did that it was exactly like sticking your head into a hot oven. So, we kept the canopy shut and the cold air running till we were stationary and needed to get out. The ground crews fitted a cockpit sunshield on the aeroplane once we had got out. This prevented the inside getting unbearably hot while it was standing in the sun. One day, one of these sunshades blew away and after a scramble to get airborne the pilot of the subject aeroplane was roaring down the runway on take off before the heat from his seat cushion got through to his backside. The seat cushion is a square rubber water container for desert survival use and, after being unshaded for a long time, was full of near boiling water. He thrust with his feet on the rudder pedals to lift his bottom slightly clear of the seat, but he did have an extremely uncomfortable flight and back in the crewroom afterwards he discovered that his backside was badly blistered.

My next flight was on 9 July in XE643/Kilo and it was an Army exercise with FACs (Forward Air Controllers). It was just a forty-minute flight and I remember nothing about it. Later that day I flew a border recce of an hour in XE544/Lima, but there was nothing to report.

I should mention here that a long line of parked vehicles of all sorts had appeared on the airfield. They ranged from Willys Jeeps through Toyota cars to 40-seater busses. All these vehicles were parked in a very long line beside each other and all had the ignition key in the lock. The system was that if anyone of any rank had need of a vehicle, he could just select the one he needed, jump in and drive it away and when he had finished his task, put the vehicle back in the line and leave the key in the ignition.

By now pilots were beginning to get short of sleep and a new shift system was introduced. I can't remember the exact numbers but each week a shift of pilots got two days off in a nearby guesthouse at Ahmadi. It was beautifully air-conditioned and very cool, with lovely comfortable bedrooms and an outdoor swimming pool. Two wonderful days of comfort and swimming till it was back to the hot hell of work, where one started to count down the hours till the next two days of bliss. At this time the wind was still blowing red hot from the desert and the strange thing in the pool was that you could dive in and get a real cold shock as you entered the very warm water. Then, when you got out, you would be shivering with cold as the water evaporated almost immediately from your body in the hot, dry wind. Later when the wind changed its direction and came in from the sea, the humidity went up like a rocket to about 90 per cent. Now it was completely different in the pool. You could dive in and feel absolutely no change of temperature as you entered the water; you just went from a thin medium to a thick one. When you got out again you could do what you liked with your towel, but you just could not get dry.

On 11 July one of our pilots went off in a pair to do some practice ground attacks. The weather was very poor with visibility severely reduced by dust in suspension. It was not suitable for this exercise and one of the pair aborted and landed back at Kuwait New. However, Flick Hennessey pressed on in XG134/Alpha and later flew into the ground and was killed. We were all very sad. Flick had not been with us for very long and was well liked by all of us. I had flown him recently on 21 June in our Hunter T.7 and the exercise was practice rocket-projectile firing and 30mm strafing dual. These were just dummy attacks back in Kenya as we had nowhere there where we could practise live attacks.

Well, General Kasim didn't seem to be doing anything and we were starting to think that he had chickened out. We carried on training with various exercises; border recce, FAC exercises, dawn recce, dusk recce, simulated strikes. On one of the dusk-recce sorties, in my log book I noted 'Flag Wave Raudatain'. I have no idea what that means.

On 28 July, I recorded an exercise: "High-level battle formation, boom, tail chase." I was flying my Hunter, "Echo" on that one and I think that "boom" means a supersonic boom.

On 31 July we took part in Exercise FIREBIRD III in which we devised a method of getting a continuous stream of Hunters attacking targets over a reasonably long period. The sortie time was short at twenty-five minutes and I flew two of them. Both squadrons were involved, and we had our re-arming teams at both ends of the runway. I think the re-arm was just for the rockets

The 208 Squadron aerobatic team was based at Eastleigh and comprised Squadron Leader 'Pancho' Ramirez (leader) and Flight Lieutenants Cohu, McLeland and Biddiscombe (*Pete McLeland*).

and no fuelling was required. We flew either pairs or fours and took off, flew to the target, carried out a dummy attack, landed back on the runway in either direction, ran on to the re-arming station at the end of the runway, re-armed and took off again in the direction opposite to which we had landed.

I was very impressed by the way it all worked and felt that the targets were constantly under attack for the whole exercise period. We were all excited and pleased with ourselves. We felt that we had invented something new and achieved our aim. However, the AOC was watching at the target site and was not impressed. He said he wanted to see large formations breaking in a peel-off down into attack, like he had seen with Spitfires in the Western Desert in the Second World War.

It was now August and there seemed very little chance of any war developing, so we started to run things down a bit. I flew five sorties in the first three days of the month. They let me fly 'Echo' on the last one and I have recorded it as "Aerobatics, Ahmadi, Magwa Area", my last flight in an FGA.9. Forty-five minutes of great pleasure.

The 1961 British Forces Arabian Peninsular display team was formed with four Hunter FGA.9s from 208 Squadron and is seen during a photoshoot near Mount Kilimanjaro (*Pete McLeland*).

Later that month my 'Tour-Ex' was re-instated, and I flew back down to Kenya, before returning to the UK in September 1961.

Lesson learnt

When you suddenly move into a very hot climate, there are certain precautions that you should take. Firstly, do not rely on thirst to tell you when to drink; you must keep drinking water frequently to keep you sweating. Secondly keep taking the salt tablets at breakfast.

It seems that I neglected one or both of these because I was standing on a corner and suddenly passed out with no warnings at all. I do not even remember hitting the ground. I woke up in a tent with a couple of medics at the bedside administering. They wanted to get some salt into me and were offering strong salty water. I settled for lots of clean water and some salt tablets. I was as right as rain in a couple of hours.'

Jock Watson (Flight Lieutenant)

Jock Watson was an IRE and A Flight Commander on 208 Squadron at RAF Muharraq from 1964 to 1966.

Welcome aboard!

'Being stuck on a desert island in the Persian Gulf, with nothing much other than swimming and drinking to while away the hours, we had to provide our own entertainment and not just during our leisure time. Whenever a new pilot arrived straight out of Chivenor, he was strapped into a 152 Squadron Pembroke and taken for an instrument rating test. On informing them that it didn't matter that they had never flown pistons, the IFR panel was the same, so just get on with it, they often panicked and nearly always fell for the spoof.

It got worse! The GLO, a major with a stutter, would dress up as the Boss and tell them that he wanted them to do a night parachute jump, that night! All 208 pilots had to be para qualified before they could fly in the area he would say. Being straight from the OCU, many new pilots were quite naive and showed signs of an impending heart attack, but we soon put them out of their misery later in the bar, where Tony Chaplin would greet them in his Boss's uniform.

On one APC at Sharjah, a new arrival was talked into swinging on the fan as an initiation into the squadron. As soon as he grasped blades, the stool was kicked away from him and he fell and broke his arm. He spent his first three months on 208 as ops officer. When it healed, he went into

Percival Pembroke WV700 pictured at Bahrain in 1962 was one of five of the type to serve with 152 Squadron throughout the 1960s (*Ray Deacon*).

the bar at Muharraq and asked me to break away the plaster, which I did. Unfortunately, I managed to break his arm again. Poor chap, another three months as ops officer. Gordon Lewis, our Boss at the time, gave us all a stiff bollocking for un-officer-like behaviour before marching us off towards the bar. On arrival, Tim Webb appeared with a hosepipe and soaked the lot of us. He hadn't listened to the brief.

It must have been you; it's always you!
On returning from the IRE course at Chivenor, I was put under close arrest and marched in to the boss to be reprimanded for throwing fireworks at a dining-in night on the previous Saturday. When I explained I was in the UK at the time, Gordon said he'd been told to give the person responsible a reprimand by the station commander and that I deserved it more than the culprit. So I got the squadron reprimand. The Boss was God and he dished out punishments ad-lib, mainly to Tim Webb and myself, although a chap called Lonergan got his fair share.

Misplaced talents!
It was always too hot to work after 13:00 so the squadron repaired to the mess bar. One day new pictures appeared on the wall of Loch Ness which

were clearly missing the monster and pipers on the hills, so I thought it appropriate to add them with my chinagraph pencil. Unfortunately the station commander's wife had bought them and he was not amused, resulting in my being barred from every bar in the Gulf for one month. Not for the first time!

Tony Chaplin, the Boss, told me to fly two hunters down to Aden for the weekend so I could enjoy a beer there. The condition was that Bill Lonergan was my wingman as the long-range flights were over the empty quarter with only one non-directional beacon at Masirah to navigate on. All ferry flights had to be in pairs and daylight only as most of it was out of VHF range. Lonergan was in the Boss's bad books again and Tony wanted him out of sight for the weekend. As we were on standby for a possible war with Iraq he wanted both aircraft back on the Monday.

We flew uneventfully to Aden and Shawn O'Shea, the RC padre, met us on arrival and generously gave me his car for the weekend. Shawn was a great character who used to dance into the mess bar arm in arm with the Protestant vicar spot on midnight every Sunday night. He felt that the Sabbath was sacred and no beer during Sunday was his rule.

After a summer ball which extended beyond midnight on a Saturday he became very upset, borrowed my lighter and set fire to the marquee, ending the dancing and drinking. Being a man of the cloth he owned up to his evil deed and didn't mention that I had encouraged him. Resulting in his swift posting to Aden. Anyway, I drove off to spend the weekend with one of the nurses at the hospital saying to Lonergan, 'see you Monday A.M. for the flight back.

The danger of dallying with the SAS

Unfortunately, Bill had a few beers with two SAS guys who were enjoying a weekend in the mess and became involved in a game where empty beer cans were thrown into the overhead fans. The rule being that you weren't allowed to duck when they whizzed down and took your hits like a man. Silly SAS humour. Lonergan said, "On 208 we play the game with full beer cans." The resulting damage, blood, broken glass, etc., resulted in Bill being put under close arrest and threatened with court martial. On Monday morning, no Lonergan! I had to get the jets back to Bahrain so I asked 8 Squadron to help. They offered Mackenzie Crooks as my wingman as he was in his boss's bad books.

Tony Chaplin met me on landing back at Muharraq and I asked him if he wanted the good news or the bad news first. The good news was that both jets were back safely and serviceable, the bad news was that I left Lonergan in Aden under close arrest .... I enjoyed the weekend, Bill did not!

No brakes!

I was tasked to ferry a hunter FGA 9 solo to the UK via Aden as Iran had closed its airspace. The no-solo rule regarding crossings of the empty quarter were waived by HQ In Aden as the diplomatic clearance was about to run out. On landing to refuel in Masirah I experienced hydraulic failure and rolled off the runway on to the sand. An 8 Squadron flight commander said his engineers were too busy to fix it. Jock Kennedy then persuaded him to fix it ASAP as the diplomatic clearance expired the next day. The engineers worked all afternoon on the jet and it was fixed as darkness fell. Jock Kennedy then authorised me to fly solo at night to Aden. Not nice flying at night over hostile territory as it was then.The radio failed en route and I finally landed at Khormaksar and rolled off the runway with another hydraulic failure. No. 43 Squadron engineers patched it up and the 8 Squadron boss pinched my UK ferry but agreed that I could fly with what was left of 8 Squadron while he was gone.

One Christmas and I had been banned from the mess bar again. Mike Jones, who was the captain of HMS *Bastion*, a tank landing craft parked in the harbour, invited me and the squadron to open my mess bill on board. John Henson locked himself in the bridge and serenaded the harbour with off key Christmas carols on the ship's loud-hailer with the captain locked outside begging him to please stop. I continued to enjoy the *Bastion* mess until the end of my tour. Happy days! Mike gave the squadron the ship's foghorn as a souvenir after the ship was decommissioned and it is still with the squadron.

I became an officer of the watch onboard when transiting to Yas island and as air controller to run an air to ground-bombing exercise. Mike talked me into playing a card game which he called Mickey Mouse. I quickly realised it was called another name in the RAF, kept quiet and played dumb. Then when the stakes increased I magically became an expert and took £40 from them. Later I took the mess out for drinks and a meal at the Speedbird Hotel and repaid all my winnings, warning them not to con an RAF officer in future.

I later had a meal at the Speedbird with a sergeant major in 2 Para who was also a piper. One of his privates started swearing at the next table, so the sergeant major took him outside to sort him out then returned with a fork stuck in his stomach. Tough guys 2 Para! He apologised for the interruption and carried on as normal as though nothing had happened with the fork still stuck there. Bahrein in the 60s, exciting times.'

Chapter 5

Eyes in the sky – 1417 Flight

Ralph Chambers (Flight Lieutenant)

Ralph is a Canadian who joined the RAF in 1961 at a time when the RAF was short of pilots and the RCAF had a surplus. In July 1964 he was posted to RAF Khormaksar where he flew Hunter FR.10s with 1417 Flight and, on 28 August 1965, was promoted to OC 1417 Flight, taking over from Flight Lieutenant Roger Pyrah.

Learning the ropes
'The final phase of my instructors' course at Little Rissington in 1961 was to gain experience of flying a front-line fighter and so it was that on 15 August

The Hunter in which Ralph Chambers flew supersonic from Kemble. XF944-A was one of three F.4s operated by the CFS Type Flight and was photographed during a visit to its home unit at Little Rissington in June 1961 (*Ray Deacon*).

I was driven over to the CFS Type Flight at Kemble by RAF minibus. A familiarisation trip in T.7, WV318, with Master Pilot Trigg was followed by two solo flights in an F.4, XF944, and this provided much amusement for those watching as I had never used handbrakes in an aeroplane and only got to the take-off point with great difficulty. As I recall the flying went well and I was pretty impressed – this was 1961 after all and this was a 'hot ship' with swept wings. We were expected to go supersonic over the Bristol Channel and this I did on the first flight; aerobatics comprised the bulk of my second flight.

My CIRE and a testing test!

Having hardly had time to settle in at Khormaksar, I returned to the UK in August for my IRE course at Chivenor. On my return I clearly remember that my first task as CIRE (Command Instrument Rating Examiner) was to renew the instrument rating of Group Captain Blythe, who was Station Commander of Khormaksar, and that I failed him. This happened on 13 October 1964 in T.7 XL612. We flew again on the 14th, 15th, 16th and finally on the 20th when the good group captain was able to pass his check ride. Incidentally he, too, was a Canadian but in his case a left-over from the Second World War, and that's all I remember about him. He was relieved by Group Captain Michael Beetham who eventually became CAS, I think, and who also used to fly the RAF Lancaster at air shows.

Family matters

Those were truly very trying times with demanding military roles in the protectorate and a constantly deteriorating internal security situation. I had my wife and two kids there and the kids learned to distinguish between the sound of an ordinary hand grenade and that of a bazooka!

Taking the shots

On the FR.10 there was no aiming device for the cameras. By endless training the pilot simply had to learn to "see" through the camera lenses. Incidentally, the real recce exposures were almost always made using the left-facing oblique camera. Pilots just seem to like looking left and the metalwork of the cockpit was cut down on that side. The Mark 10 actually had five cameras; three 70mm Vintens in the nose, a 16mm camera buried in the top of the nose which operated whenever the guns were fired and a 16mm camera that could be clipped on top of the gunsight for assessment of training. This camera was known as the GGSR, gyro gunsight recording camera.

Interpreting the negs!

One of the tasks undertaken by the FR pilots was to analyse the photographs they had taken in the quickest possible time. We always viewed the film as negative-stereo pairs. With a bit of practice the stereo viewers gave a real impression of the third dimension, and after a prolonged period of negative viewing the brain accepted this as normal and usually the prints only confirmed what had already been assessed on the basis of the negative viewing.

Further on negatives, the reason a lot of the Hunters were later given white wing tips was that the cine film (16mm) used in the GGSRs was always viewed in the negative and often kind of fuzzy, but the white wing tips stood out well as black on the negative.

The gunsight

The Mark 9, and all the earlier models I presume, had an arrangement whereby the gunsight could be driven electrically several inches towards the pilot as required. The Mark 10 had no such motor and if the gunsight was required the pilot simply had to lean forward and make the best of it. Actually it did not seem to make much difference. The Mark 10, of course,

The offset gunsight fitted to the FR.10 is clearly visible in this view taken at Masirah in 1967 (*Ken Simpson*).

had no radar-ranging for the gunsight; this was controlled manually by a twist grip on the throttle.

Early in 1966 I was given the added responsibility for the Wing Photo Section, with a staff of one SNCO, three corporals and nine airmen and it was subsequently discovered that not all the processing carried out on the unit was of film taken from the Vinten cameras. Some of these guys were making photos of subjects not to be shown in polite company, much to the displeasure of the station commander who had some harsh words for the culprits. And for me!

Target marking

Target marking was done with one long burst of 30mm from an FR.10 followed immediately by a Mark 9's rockets. The procedure then involved the marking aircraft doing a post-strike recce and photo run, before rushing back to Khormaksar to have the film developed. If there was a big rush the film would be viewed in the negative format using stereo pairs' viewers. After a while you learned to reverse the way your brain worked so that the stereo negatives looked perfectly natural. We only printed if we wanted a long-term record.

All operational live missions were thrust upon us by MEC top brass "on the hill" at Steamer Point. We could authorise all sorts of training exercises but anything involving the possibility of shooting was the responsibility of others and came to us by 'signal'. However, from time to time "the hill" would want information but would be unable to get approval from "whoever" to send the tasking signal. Medium-ranking officers would then come to drink our coffee and to casually enquire if we intended to do some training in area "X" and if so could we keep the cameras running and, furthermore, how long would it take before we had wet prints. Get the picture??

Just part of the job

Flight Lieutenant Ken Simpson came to us on 1417 with a reputation for being bold and, as CO, I can assure you he was. There was a running competition to see who could get the largest image of a Land Rover wheel on 70mm film taken from a Mark 10 oblique camera. Ken always won, his wheel photos seeming to fill the frame completely.

Ken's reputation grew when, on 10 May 1966, he hit a griffon vulture at 420 knots in XE589. All tanks were dropped and he managed to stagger back to Khormaksar with Cat 4 damage.

Then, on 3 September that same year, we received a desperate request for photos of something quite close to base so Ken hopped into XE614 which was sitting with fuel state of full internals, two full 230s, and two full 100-gallon underwing tanks. The photos were duly taken and Ken hurried back to Khormaksar. Believe it or not since 1417 (and only 1417) was authorised to 50 feet, you had to pull up to join the circuit. Anyway in Ken's view the urgency was such that he landed downwind and did not stream the brake chute since that would have caused further delay. XE614 hit one of the barrier stanchions, the net having not been raised because no emergency had been declared. Cat 4 was the result. Ken was duly hauled in front of officers of increasing rank until he finally reached AOC level. At every stage he humbly confessed his guilt and promised to be more careful. You can imagine the rest of the story – as the top brass became bored with the topic and it just went away. Ken was later sent to the USA for Phantom training and became one of the first RAF Phantom pilots (his boss was, I think, ex-8 Squadron pilot Ken Hayr).

A very special Hunter

At the beginning of 1965 I returned to the UK to collect a refurbished FR.10 from 5 MU at Kemble. On arrival at the station I was presented with a shiny new looking Hunter, its glossy camouflaged paintwork gleaming as it stood on the pan in the wintry sun. XE589 was its serial number and, on 6 January, I took it for an air test to ensure everything was ready for the long flight east. Accompanying me on the return trip was another pilot in refurbished FGA.9, XJ689, which was destined to join 43 Squadron, and we departed Kemble for Luqa via Lyneham two days later. After a light lunch we flew on to El Adem and a good night's rest. With no time to spare, we took off early the following morning and headed for Jeddah and reached Khormaksar later that afternoon. There was some grief in Jeddah since whoever was supposed to meet us didn't show and it was in the middle of Ramadan.

The aircraft then went into the hangar for acceptance checks and for unit markings to be applied. The next time I saw XE589 was on 20 January when it was parked on the pan, minus underwing tanks, and looking every inch a 1417 Flight aircraft with crest on the nose and my initials, "RC"', on the tailfin and nosewheel door, ready for me to air test her. There must have been a problem or two as my log book shows that I did two more air tests on the 22nd and 26th, and it was 18 February before I finally flew a fully serviceable aircraft. My first 'op' flight in '589 was over Urqub Pass on 24 February and lasted just over an hour.

Above: Ralph Chambers relaxes on one of XE589's 230-gallon tanks following the ferry flight from Kemble on 9 January 1965 (*Ralph Chambers*).

Below: With his initials proudly emblazoned on its fin and 1417 Flight markings on the nose, Ralph is in his element flying his beloved XE589 high over the Aden hinterland (*Ralph Chambers*).

Thus began an attachment to an aircraft that has lasted over forty years and I would like to be able to locate its current whereabouts. Having sustained Cat 4R damage in 1966 it was sold to Hawker Aircraft Ltd and rebuilt as F.Mk.76 701, for the Abu Dhabi Air Force with which it served for many years. Upon withdrawal, it was sold on for further service with the Somali Air Force as CC701 and was finally grounded in the early nineties. It was last noted at Hageisa airfield in 1993.

Aircraft tailcodes

It was standard practice on most RAF fighter squadrons for aircraft to have individual tail codes, usually comprising a single letter. On 1417 Flight our aircraft were coded with two initials of the pilots on the unit. It was also generally the case that no two pilots on a fighter squadron could have the same first name, the reason being that in the heat of air combat pilots might use names instead of callsigns. Consequently, quite a few young pilots found themselves with new first names for a couple of years. On 1417 Flight, for example, we had two Rogers; Pyrah and Neal. After suitable discussions that Roger Neal was not a party to, we decided to call him Fred. Then some joker, maybe me said, why not spell it in the British way Phred. Thus his aircraft received the unique tailcode 'Ph N'.

Every drop counts

On 8 March 1965 yours truly and Flight Lieutenant Graham Williams, from 8 Squadron, sat in a fully fuelled (full internals and four 100-gallon underwing tanks) T.7, XL566, as it was towed onto the east facing runway at Khormaksar. Our task was to ferry the aircraft to Masirah and 'tribal knowledge' had it that the flight was very marginal for fuel. We threw our service hats behind us, donned bone domes, hit the start button and launched in a hurry. It immediately became clear that this was not going to be a routine flight. Fuel really was going to be a problem and there was a constantly flickering red pressurisation warning light just to add to the stress level.

On reaching the roughly halfway point over Salalah we decided to continue because we knew we had the "right stuff". We arrived at Masirah "on fumes" and I recall that I was a bit caustic to the groundcrew about the T.7's pressurisation. A straight-faced warrant officer then made quite a ceremony of presenting me with my service hat which had a neat round hole in the top where it had rested athwart some part of the pressurisation system and reduced the airflow. I had to buy all concerned a lot of beer.

Of the seventeen ops flights carried out in Mark 10 aircraft in March, three were flown at Beihan by 43 Squadron pilots owing to a shortage of Mark 9s on their unit, most of their aircraft being on detachment at Masirah. And, in addition, owing to a general shortage of Hunter pilots in Aden at the time, 1417 Flight pilot Frank Grimshaw was required to fly two Beihan patrols in a Mark 10. One of our daily commitments was to search for hostile shipping on the coast line from east of Perim Island, located in the straights where the Red Sea becomes the Gulf of Aden, to Mukha, searching for Russian freighters carrying SAM missiles to the Vietnam conflict. I remember these patrols very well, some three hours of solitude banging around at 420 knots TAS gave us all sore backs from the constant turbulence.

"Dead ants"

It was mid "hot' season 1965 or 66. The pilots on one of the ground attack Hunter squadrons, 8 or 43, I am not sure which, constantly played a game called "dead ants". The rules were quite simple: one of the pilots, regardless of surroundings would call out "dead ants" and all squadron pilots in earshot had to fling themselves on the floor with legs and arms extended vertically. This was held to be very good for morale.

So the scenario was that the great Lord Shackleton was visiting and we were all ordered to the officers' mess bar in best bib and sweaty tucker to meet the minister. As I recall there were two plots. The surface plot was that some squadron pilot was to jump the lord as he arrived and complain about the heat and defence policy, etc., etc. The secret plot was that the squadron pilots would put on a demo of "dead ants" for the great one. So, of course, *he* was late and we were all soaked in sweat by the time he arrived. The first nominated person cruised up to the lord to complain about heat and defence policy, etc., etc. The great lord, who was obviously nobody's fool, forestalled this attack by saying in a loud voice, "I like this heat". The nominated pilot slunk away. It was then time for the secret plot. The other chosen pilot waited for a bit of space, then called out "dead ants" and flung himself to the ground, legs and arms extended vertically. No one else moved. The great lord looked baffled as the pilot was hustled away. The station commander who, unusually, was an air commodore looked pained and names were taken and careers were terminated. The air commodore became CAS.

My lovely car!

My farewell party was held on Khormaksar Beach and we drove onto it in my faithful old car. Sadly, it sank in the soft sand when driving it back up the beach at the end of our bash; a long story but one of the final insults as I left the Colony.'

Peter Lewis (Flight Lieutenant)

Flight Lieutenant Lewis was posted to 8 Squadron on 17 June 1962 from Aberdeen University Air Squadron and subsequently became the first OC 1417 Flight. It was in this role that he completed his tour on 12 July 1964, returning to the UK to take up a post as Schools' Liaison Officer for the Inner London Education Authority based at RAF Kenley.

1417 Flight Commander

'Some time around the end of March 1963, Wing Commander John Jennings (OC Tactical Wing Khormaksar) sent for me and announced that the Hunter FR.10s were to be hived off 8 Squadron to form 1417 Flight, and that I was to command it. I would be given the four Hunters, the four other recce-trained pilots, and some dozen groundcrew drawn from the three DFGA (Day Fighter/Ground Attack) Squadrons (8, 43 and 208).

The pilots were Johnny Morris, a veteran from flying Mustangs in the South African Air Force in the Korean war, Jim Dymond, a PAI (Pilot Attack Instructor), Tony Rimmer, a past member of the 'APRF (Aden Protectorate Recce Flight)' which had flown Meteor FR.9s until 1961, and Geoff Timms, a solid, quiet, ex-Halton apprentice. We were all over six feet tall, all thirty or over, all married with children, and all were second or third tour pilots. All the groundcrew were very experienced on the Hunter and were those that the squadrons didn't want because they were difficult to manage.

So we had it all: a QFI/IRE (Qualified Flying Instructor/Instrument Rating Examiner – me), a PAI, someone who knew a lot about aircraft maintenance, and, most importantly, someone who had seen real combat and knew a bit about recce against opposition. And we had a set of highly competent groundcrew, who liked to work as individuals, co-ordinated by an extremely wise warrant officer who was a Fitter 1 in his time.

The first task was to get the FR.10s back into shape. The FR.10 was undoubtedly the most beautiful of the Hunters. It weighed less than the FGA.9 which had to carry ballast to keep their centre of gravity in the right place when carrying a load of external weaponry. It was a thoroughbred. Number 8 Squadron had used these lovely aircraft as "hacks", scorning them because they were not equipped to fire rockets or drop bombs; they had

290

With his initials adorning the top of the fin, OC 1417 Flight Peter Lewis is seen at the controls of his Hunter FR.10 XE614 in 1964 (*Peter Lewis*).

no DME (Distance Measuring Equipment) and, worst of all, had a funny instrument layout – the compass was where the artificial horizon should be and vice versa. The radio compasses didn't work, and the 230-gallon drop tanks, the contents of which could be incorporated into the internal fuel gauges, were rarely fitted as they incurred minor flight limitations which clashed with ground-attack manoeuvres. The cameras were a mess; many were polluted with sand which scratched the negatives, and some of the nose-camera lenses had been sandblasted because their protective "eyelids" had not been serviced regularly. And last, but by no means least, the harmonisation of the guns was way out on most of the aircraft, and the switches which allowed two or all four guns to fire were "iffy".

So there was a lot of work for the groundcrew; the WO said it would take at least a fortnight's damned hard work to get those lovely jets back to the thoroughbred status they deserved. Which was a blessing in disguise as we reckoned that we needed at least that time to get the rest of the flight into shape. We were allocated a drop-tank store as our accommodation. With a lot of help from the station 'works and bricks' we did DIY and set to building partitions to give us a groundcrew room, a pilots' crewroom, an office for the engineering WO, a little store, and, somewhat against my wishes, an office for the CO – 'we don't want him breathing down our necks all the time … '. I got a nickname of "Prussian Pete" and, some months later, two little notices appeared on the door to that office: one read "Be reasonable, do it his way", and the other "Diplomacy Department. He says and does the nastiest things in the nicest way."

To facilitate all this, there was some distribution of duties. Geoff Timms kept a close eye on how the preparation of the FR.10s was coming along; Jim Dymond, who was a very good artist and photographer as well as a PAI, was put in charge of harmonising the guns and getting the cameras running properly. He and the groundcrew came up with the idea of keeping the cameras in plastic bags in an old fridge – a primitive but effective 'dust-free environmental control'.

I annexed one of the wing T.7s (two-seat Hunters) whenever possible, and flew with each pilot on a 'QFI/IRE' check ride. A bit laughable really – they were all damned good flyers, but it did demonstrate that we could follow as well as read the dreaded *Air Staff Instructions*. Johnny Morris, meanwhile, gave us all a very hard time on visual recce techniques, and had some masochistic variations on "Kim's Game" with which he sought to tune our ability to remember and reproduce on paper what we had seen. One of his favourites was to stand each of us on a chair whilst he sprinkled mapping pins on the floor behind us. Then it was "turn round" and you had fifteen seconds (about the time taken to run past a target) to count the pins and memorise the pattern they had formed. It was amazing how good we all got at instinctively working the difference between looking and seeing. We designed cardboard "prayer wheels" which we could use for fuel calculations in the air, and for speed adjustments to ensure a correct time on target. Johnny taught us the importance of planning a good IP (Initial Point) which would give the best photographic run past the target whilst maintaining whatever element of surprise was going to ensure a clean getaway; the desert is a very quiet place, and the Hunter will have been heard long before it appeared.

Know your enemy!

I met one of the Arabists who normally worked in the Lebanon and was lucky enough to be able to convince him to spend a day with us talking about the Arab culture: the way they approach life and death; the honour of the Bedouin; and a mass of little things which came out in discussion in the flight and later in the bar on the general theme of "know your enemy". Something which was particularly interesting was his view that the "Goolie Chit" and the gold coins were useless to the point of being an incentive to do away with their carrier. In his view, if we came down in the desert,

The attractive 1417 Flight pennant was designed by the unit's pilots and applied to both sides of the forward fuselage on its FR.10s and, later, the T.7s (*Peter Lewis*).

food and water were much more important, and to offer them as a sign of friendship and submission would be more likely to succeed. If the Arab accepted the food and water then you were "on his face", and he would see you back to your own tribe. If not … .

Our final flourish was to design a distinctive mark for all our Hunters. Everyone had an input and we eventually went for a sort of arrowhead with a crinkly front end to represent camera bellows. The colours were those of Aden Protectorate (yellow, green and black), and the station commander agreed that we could use the Khormaksar crest as a centerpiece, so as not to annoy any of those chaps in the College of Heralds who have weird names. Last of all we decided that we would not have fin codes; we'd use our initials instead. All this make-over was plotted to happen overnight; the groundcrew were up for surprising the DFGA squadrons. So the morning when the shiny FR.10s, resplendent in their new insignia, were wheeled out onto the pan they caused quite a stir all round. Quite right too!

Training
Johnny Morris devised some testing training sorties for us, involving finding and photographing unlikely 'targets' like watering wells way out

in the desert, derelict buildings in the bottom of steep-sided wadis, watch towers, desert landing strips, and, the most difficult of all, complexes of caves recognisable only by the black holes in the sides of hills. He also seemed to have a secret line to the army, and whenever there was a convoy going up to Dhala he'd want photos, and a vehicle count which had to include the various vehicle types. The 'operational' test was to get a picture of a target at a predetermined time with Johnny sitting somewhere over it without getting bounced by him. One frame of GGS (Gyro Gunsight) camera cine film with you in the frame represented a 'fail'. We got a bit cocky about this ability, and challenged the DFGA boys to the same game. As far as I remember, none of them got the vital frame of cine, but Chris Golds of 43 Squadron did see the 1417 Hunter on one occasion.

The secret we had worked out was to fly low over the flattest terrain we could find on the run in to the target. Nine times out of ten, it is not the aircraft that the 'defenders', saw, but its shadow 'bouncing' along uneven terrain. Flying so that the shadow doesn't "bounce" involves going down to 25 to 30 feet which, at 420 knots, is very low indeed, and every so often one pilot would fly chase to the other sitting out at four or eight o'clock and judging the height of his buddy. Interestingly, getting down to that height is hard work as the tendency is always to creep up to around 40 to 50 feet and these buddy checks were needed about once a fortnight to keep our eyes in. Another ruse was to fly over where the waves were breaking on the shore. The motion of the water under the aircraft at roughly 90 degrees to the line of flight is sufficiently distracting to put off the all but the cutest.

Because our role was to get the information and bring it back, we would do all we could to avoid shooting or being shot at. So Jim Dymond and Johnny Morris dreamed up an interesting air-to-ground shooting sortie for whenever one of the DFGA squadrons was on the range. We would ask for a 'slot' and whatever we were offered, we'd take. But we only allowed ourselves one pass, and that had to be made on time after a navigation/recce training sortie lasting at least forty-five minutes. And we were not allowed to go above 250 feet on the run in to the targets. This was realistic, but meant that the gyro gunsight was unreliable as turbulence affected the gyroscope in the sight; but Jim had worked out a way of using the 'fixed cross' (the spot where the guns were actually pointing) to good effect, and provided we used his method we usually picked up a decent score. The flight average on air to ground was around 60 per cent, a fact of which we were proud, but quiet; there was enough banter about "the Kodak Kids" without our trespassing on the expertise of the DFGA boys.

We had a nice party piece for visiting VIPs taking a march past or a salute. With a little connivance from the control tower, as "General Salute" was called, an FR.10 would make a low photo pass and land. By the time the VIP had inspected the parade and was back on his dais, say ten minutes, the film would have been developed and printed by the MFPU (Mobile Field Photography Unit) and he would be presented with his picture as he left the parade ground.

By the end of April, I was able to tell the wing leader that we were ready for ops.

Operations

Until the war in Radfan really warmed up, 1417's main task was Operation RANJI. This involved a sweep of the coast from Riyan to the straits of Bab el Mendeb looking for 'gunrunners' landing weaponry for the insurgents inland. We found a few, but not many. However, RANJI was also a catch-all for other recce ops, and three were especially memorable. At this time, the Russians were sending warships out to Indonesia, and the Shackleton squadron would patrol the south end of the Red Sea watching for them.

This low-level photograph, captured at high speed on one of Peter Lewis's F.95 Vinten cameras on 13 December 1962, reveals the exposed nature of the 75-mile-long Dhala Road. It was the source of many dissident attacks on Army convoys (*Peter Lewis*).

On one occasion, they spotted a Skoryy-class sub-chaser which had hidden amongst the little islands off the east coast of Ethiopia whilst it refuelled. The Russians did not have a resupply-at-sea system as the RN have, and they re-supplied whilst stationary. The Shackleton spotted the sub-chaser on its radar going like hell out into the Indian Ocean. They were low on fuel, having been up all night, and could not catch it to take a picture. Could 1417 help? We would try. The Shackleton climbed to keep the Russian on its radar for as long as it could, and gave us its course and speed (about thirty-two knots I think) and I plotted an intercept some 180 miles out to sea and scrambled, probably in XE614/PL. Some accurate flying was required and when I estimated that I was some forty miles (six minutes) away I let down to as low as was sensible. The Skoryy appeared on the horizon roughly where it should have been and I lined up for a pass down its port side for happy snaps. Piece of cake!

The photos were developed, and produced a nasty surprise: every gun on the port side was leading me, and the covers were still on the guns on the starboard side! If that had been for real ... . They'd seen me coming from way out.

What at first glance could be mistaken for a Russian spy ship, the *Sinoutskerk* was a Dutch cargo vessel capable of 18kts. Peter Lewis captured it moving at speed through the Red Sea using one of his nose cameras while performing an Operation RANJI sortie in 1964 (*Peter Lewis*).

Exceeding the Hunter's ceiling!

A similar sortie in XE614/PL involved looking for a suspected Russian warship off Hodeida. The weather on this trip was unusually poor, with a lot of cumulonimbus about. I was about to throw the game away when I spotted a ship about ten miles away under a very black cloud. I turned towards it, and was delighted when the cloud base started to lift. The ship turned out to be an innocent cargo ship, but I simultaneously noticed that suddenly there was no horizon; big cumulonimbus bases are like an inverted saucer, so grey sea, grey cloud, no horizon: time to climb. Up I went, and for about the first 5,000 feet it was a bit bumpy (to be expected). But then everything went mad. There were flashes of blue and yellow light, and the aircraft began pitching and rolling all on its own; I reduced to 'penetration' speed, clamped my feet on the rudder pedals, and clamped the stick in both hands supported by both knees. The accelerometer was 'off the clock' in both directions (minus 4 to plus 12); the artificial horizon had toppled; the G4 compass was rotating gently – like a roulette wheel slowing down I thought at the time; the radio compass was swinging wildly from one bearing to another, sometimes going through all 360 degrees; the airspeed indicator was fluctuating plus or minus 30 knots, and the climb/descent indicator was bumping against the "up" stop. The only stable instruments were the turn-and-slip indicator (and even it was having its moments) and the altimeter which was climbing at an alarming rate. I've no idea how long all this lasted, except that it seemed to be a long time; but it all stopped as suddenly as it had started and I was in blue sky with that towering white mountain behind me. None of the instruments looked trustworthy, and I could not see any land, so I just turned towards the sun (home was in that rough direction) and concentrated on level flight to relax and think; I then noticed that I was at 56,000 feet so began a descent to something more sensible. Eventually, the compass and the radio compass came back; the artificial horizon (now I didn't need it) re-erected itself, and I headed for home. A very gentle straight-in approach and landing and the aircraft went straight into the hangar for a stress check. The fatigue meter showed that it had been a very rough ride indeed but, that apart, the thoroughbred was just fine.

RANJI was also used for surveillance of the port at Hodeida. The Intelligence men on the hill (Steamer Point) were very interested in what was being landed there, particularly some large crates that they had heard of. One of them came down to the wing, and in John Jennings' office it was suggested that some photos would be a great help; not that they were telling us to go of course: that might cause an international incident, but it would be nice. JJ agreed that it would be nice, but quite out of the question ... . But he had an idea ... . So I took off without signing for anything, telling the tower it was an air test – or something – and off to Hodeida. I 'sussed' the area from about 10,000 feet and ten to fifteen miles out, taking a couple of shots with the starboard facer (just in case we had to do this again sometime) and decided on the photo-run direction; north to south at about 500 feet looked good with a long burst of port and nose cameras. Let down, gentle turn to starboard, and line up. No problem, but then I saw an airfield a couple of miles inland which no one told me about. And as I got abeam the port, snapping away happily, I saw a pair of MiGs turning on to the runway. The photo shoot was all but over, so nose down and out to the coast, low over where those waves are breaking over the shore, flat out. Pure funk! I didn't see the MiGs again and I guess they didn't see me again either. Back to base to some very sideways glances from both ground and aircrew – what on earth is the boss doing buggering off without signing up?

The port and nose films were developed and printed – no title strips – and delivered to JJs office; I didn't even see them. But the starboard facers come back to me – and they were useful to others on a couple of occasions, I think. We never discussed these missions with anyone, not even the other pilots. But there was an interesting aftermath. One afternoon on the beach, one of the air traffic controllers (a Pole, who, in his time had been a Second World War night-fighter ace) confronted me and in a very loud voice asks what the hell 1417 is doing breaking air traffic rules – their radar was telling them that we were not doing what we'd said we would. I told him to shut up, and eventually pulled rank in a very grotty manner until, by the look on his face, the penny dropped.

To Kenya for Independence Day

In December 1963 twelve FGA.9s and an FR.10 were sent down to Nairobi ostensibly to provide a flypast for the independence celebrations - Uhuru. The Hunters were based on the small military complex on the dual civil/ military airport; but on the far side of the airfield there was a Beverley transport full of weaponry, just in case. All the Hunters flew with full 30mm gunpacks on every sortie. Two days before Uhuru, I was ordered to carry out a sweep following the railway from Nairobi to Mombassa to photograph and note any gatherings that might be the least bit hostile looking. Nairobi airport is some 5,300 feet above sea level and the recce was to be at midday; this would be an interesting take off. And so it proved. At maximum all-up weight, I went right to the very end of Nairobi's enormous runway, resolved to put down 10 degrees of flap once I was rolling (we never really needed to do that in Aden, even at midday), and ran up to full power before letting off the brakes. Poor PL began a gentle crawl down the runway and rolled and rolled and rolled with the airspeed increasing very slowly. Dropping the flaps at the last possible moment, I just got airborne at the very end of the runway, but despite a very rapid undercarriage clean-up, was in a more or less stable flight condition. Raise the flaps and I'd sink into the ground; raise the nose up and I'd stall. But the Riff Valley came to my rescue; the ground drops away dramatically a couple of miles from the end of the runway, and I was able to put the nose down, get some airspeed, clean up the flaps and begin to fly normally.

Exercise BILTONG was, on the face of it, a communication exercise mounted out of Bahrain. In fact, it was a thorough recce of an area to the east of a line running south from Abu Dubai down to Masirah. It was something to do with illicit oil prospecting I think, but provided Johnny Morris and I with some interesting navigation problems. There were no maps of the area at all, so we'd cross in over Abu Dubai and fly an accurate speed and heading to trace out a very elongated and narrow rectangle. If we saw something, we'd note the time and then create a sort of plot of its bearing and distance from Abu Dubai after the flight. The other would then fly that bearing and distance and if he found the something too we'd say 'that's where it is'. On one of these sorties, Johnny had found something well to the south, and there was just enough light left to check it out. Sure enough, he'd found an unusual encampment with what looked like some pretty technical vehicles which were duly photographed. The low sun would have given the PIs some good shadows to work off, and one very low pass would probably have given them mug shots of the people on the ground, most of whom looked surprisingly oriental. I finished the sweep, by which time the sun was setting and, as fuel was getting a bit tight, (all that showing off for happy snaps) I started a climb out to return to base at high level. As I climbed I followed the setting sun, with all the marvellous colours that come with sunset over the desert. Beneath was the dark and, gradually, in what had seemed in daylight like an empty wilderness, little pinpricks of light began to appear; the Bedouins, I supposed, cooking their evening meals. At 40,000 feet with the sun all but gone, the sky turning purple, the pinpricks of lights of humanity below, the stars not quite out yet and a light frost forming on the canopy there came a strange sensation as if a little voice was asking 'who the hell are you, and what are you doing here?' Some have labelled moments like this a "nearness to God". I would not argue with them, and some lines from the Rubaiyat came to me: "One moment in annihilation's waste, one moment at the well of life to taste …".

At the end of BILTONG Johnny Morris came up with a ruse. Why didn't I fly back across the Rub al Khali alone? We'd take off as a pair, he'd have radio failure and I'd carry on. So that's what we did. I used the cruise climb technique allowing XE614/PL to drift up to some 50,000 feet as the fuel burned off. When I eventually switched to the Khormaksar frequency, there was obviously anxiety about my fuel state. When I told them that I might have to burn off before landing, they were relieved, but disbelieving. In fact, the big 230s emptied on the descent, and I landed with damn near full internal fuel. Two hours thirty-five minutes, and I could have gone on for another forty-five minutes (at altitude). The first crossing of the Empty Quarter in a single-engine jet I like to think. The next morning XE614/PL, which had brought me back the day before, refused to start. There were sand blockages in some of the transfer valves apparently; the thoroughbred had showed her mettle again.

Harib

The attack on Fort Harib on 28 March 1964 was arguably the highest profile incident involving the Hawker Hunter during its eight years of operational service in the Middle East. The operation caused a political storm back in the UK and in the United Nations.

The strike on Harib fort began as an RAF classic. The wing had a standdown for two days apart from one recce Hunter and four DFGAs at two hours' standby. So there was one hell of a party at someone's house which went on a bit. At around 04:00 there was a beating on the door, and there was Roy Bowie, the Wing Ops Officer, saying "get down to flights, we're going to start some nastiness". The Wing Leader, John Jennings (JJ), had laid on a mass of toast and coffee but, as the briefing started, the adrenalin took over; I'm convinced that it is the best hangover cure there is. The fort was to be leafleted fifteen minutes before eight Hunters led by JJ struck. Sid Bottom (8 Squadron) and I were to carry the leaflets in our raised flaps and I was to photo Sid's leaflets going down on the fort. We were then to pull up to 30,000 feet and keep an eye open for any opposition which might choose to join the party. Once the strike was over, I was to photograph the fort again. It all went smoothly until, whilst filming Sid's leaflets, I saw at least one and probably three AA guns on the

Fort Harib was a solidly-built structure located some three miles inside Yemen. The pre-strike photograph (above) was taken by Peter Lewis from his FR.10 shortly after he and Sid Bottom had dropped leaflets informing the occupants that they had fifteen minutes to evacuate the stronghold. The post-strike photograph (below) was taken shortly after the smoke had cleared and shows the extent of the damage (*both, Peter Lewis*).

ground just to the south of the fort. There followed an agonising fifteen minutes: break radio silence and warn the strike boys, or keep quiet? As the strike was going in from 20,000 feet, the gunners would have to be pretty good to get a result, and they probably weren't that good; so shut up and sit tight. I need not have worried. JJ led the eight Hunters down and his salvo was a 'pickle barrel' shot. I guess he must have hit a magazine or something as there was a huge yellow flash and a mini mushroom of dirty brown/black smoke. I reckon that the other seven could only fire into the smoke and hope for the best, but there were no more big explosions. I told Sid to join the others and go home as it was going to take some time for the smoke to clear and allow a decent photograph. The smoke cleared after about half an hour, and I made the second pass. The fort was an awful mess, and there were several bodies lying about around where the guns were. The thought occurred that JJ's salvo had probably blown bits of the southern end of the fort all over the poor sods. So far so good. I reckoned that I hadn't exposed too much film (a short length of film

Photographed leaving the Tactical Wing hangar with the C-in-C Middle East, General Sir Charles Harington, are Wing Commander John Jennings on the right and Flight Lieutenant Peter Lewis on the left (*Peter Lewis*).

gives the MFPU a chance for a really quick turnaround) and that I'd got the line about right on the second run. So now it was just wait and see. The MFPU did a smashing job, and the film was on the light bench by the time I'd walked in and signed up. The photos were good, and I marked the two I wanted printed up and went into the debriefing with them. I handed them to JJ and his face lit up with a smile which was a mixture of pride and relief. All he said was "Thank you 1417." That was enough; and in the eyes of the DFGA boys, we'd arrived.

Finding our way

The Radfan War was to strengthen the links between DFGA and Recce considerably. The root of this was the maps – or lack of maps. By and large, the only large-scale maps we had were the 'White Maps' which were originally surveyed by Philby in the late 1940s. These were supplemented by 'chocolate maps' (so called because they were mainly brown) which were just reproductions of the aerial photographs taken by PR Canberras overlaid with minimal information of place names, roads and tracks, and wadi beds. There was the odd spot height, but no contours, so we all had to learn to translate the shading on these maps into what a hill, plateau or wadi would actually look like when we got there. But the most crucial factor was place names and their locations. Often, the place name had not changed, but the location had; the locals had just moved the whole place anything up to fifteen miles from where it last was – perhaps in Philby's time. The army or the SAS would call for a strike and name the place (no grid references, they didn't have our maps) and, unless there was a FAC (Forward Air Controller), the DFGA boys could not find the target. Even when there was FAC control, they often had to be talked in from positions many miles away.

So 1417 often went looking for the missing villages. We'd make some assumptions about where it might be, and then just fly from where it was supposed to be to where we thought it might be with bursts (to make the film last) from all three cameras. If we found the village, we'd give the DFGA boys the key pictures and a briefing to supplement the chocolate maps on what to look for. This raised the success rate considerably, but didn't work every time. Early in the campaign, attempts at "proscription" were made. This involved dropping leaflets on specific areas warning the inhabitants that they were in an area which was, or was about to come, a war area; this (political) device had worked successfully in Iraq and India in the days of empire, as it denied insurgents sustenance.

One morning I was ordered to leaflet a plateau in Radfan where intelligence had reported a massing of potentially active insurgents, and it was due to be struck by the DFGA later that day. If I was fired on, which was considered unlikely, then I was to fire back. I approached the area at low level (below the height of the plateau) by way of a wadi which led to it and, as I climbed to make my run across the area, I saw a crowd of people. As I got closer, I saw that they formed a rough circle. In the middle of the circle were three tripod-mounted 18-mm machine guns – a very effective AA weapon – surrounded by some twenty to thirty civilians of all descriptions, including women and children. But outside them were nine or ten others with Kalashnikov assault rifles all pointing inwards. The concept of "human shields" existed in 1964, long before the First Gulf War. Then the 18mms opened up on me; subsequent events are best forgotten. As the war hotted up, the SAS would often find caves where the opposition was hiding out. As the DFGA boys used to tip in from 15,000 to 20,000 feet for these strikes, they hadn't got much time to acquire the targets which were little more than black holes on a hillside. So 1417 went and found them first, and using the telephoto nose camera, produced a 'gunsight' picture which was given to every pilot on the strike. This helped them a lot, if only because it relieved them of working out the best IP and attack direction. Quite what the effect of a strike on a cave was, I never asked.

Helping hand
There was a visit to Aden by a party of MPs and, on the day they came to Strike Wing, things were pretty busy up-country; the DFGA boys were going at it hammer and tongs and 1417 was supporting them with pre- and post-strike photographs. Returning from one of these missions, I saw a civilian hanging about 1417's flight line. Now 1417 had an Arab "sweeper" – a lovely little man who kept the offices immaculate; made coffee for everyone – including the ground crew; and was a general "go-for". As the ground crew got to know him, they would let him help on turnarounds; nothing technical – pushing trolleys, unreeling the heavy refuelling hoses, passing tools and so on. To him, this was a real treat.

On this sortie I had fired the guns – at what, I can't remember; so when the armourers saw the smoke on the gun ports, they geared up to change the gunpack. (The Hunter was designed for fast turnarounds, so a magazine full of ammunition replaced the used one which was then taken away for reloading.) The sweeper delighted in helping with this activity whenever he could, and so it was on this day. The MPs ignored me as I got out of the aircraft, and one of them walked up to the sweeper to ask him if he was not ashamed of himself helping the RAF to fight his people. He got a surprise; the sweeper glared at him fiercely and said "No! Boss Pete is fighting the enemies of my tribe." Collapse of stout party – labour/pacifist perhaps? The next day, we found the sweeper out on the line polishing the nose camera eyelids; he'd really shone them up, and was a bit hurt when we told him that they might reflect the sun from a long way away, and that was not good. Some time later, there was a timid knock on my door, and the sweeper appeared with a roll of newspaper in which there was a *Kunja* – the traditional

Baz, the trusted Arab helper, cum cleaner and tea maker, enjoying a prank with the armourers (*David Barnes*).

Arab knife of the area. It differed from the better known *Gambia* as its scabbard is curved, not hooked. The knife was fairly primitive in appearance but had a lovely horn handle. The scabbard was made from silver, almost certainly smelted Maria Theresa dollars. The knife, he informed me, was a gift from his tribe, but I must pay for the scabbard – 500 shillings; that was the custom. He was a bit upset when he noticed that I did not wear it when flying, but time and a lot of patient explaining eventually soothed him. I couldn't remember his name until someone recently reminded me that it was Baz. I often wonder what happened to him.

The Army soon wised up to the benefits of having photographs of the terrain they were to fight over, and became regular customers. On one occasion, they asked for complete cover of a wadi some nine miles long which involved using all of XE614/PL's three cameras at about 200 feet. As our cameras only had fifty seconds of film in them this meant that, even at maximum speed, we would not get the whole of the wadi, although the nose camera with its

When the Army requested the destruction of dissident targets, Strike Wing Hunters and Shackletons were ready to oblige. When the rebel-held watch-tower in Wadi Ruqub (above) was listed for demolition, Peter Lewis was despatched to take pre-strike photographs of the slender structure on 18 October 1962. Following a visit by a force of FGA.9s, Peter returned to photograph the resulting damage (*both, Peter Lewis*).

telephoto lens would give something at the end of the run. Because the .
bed was about 1,000 feet below the plateau, the sortie had to be flown between
13:00 and 14:00 when the shadows would be at a minimum. At that time, up
there, the air became very turbulent so it was going to be a bumpy ride at 540
knots. And the final piece of grief was that at Mach 0.9, the Hunter undergoes
a nose-down trim change which at a sensible altitude is not a problem as you
just switched in the "flying tail" which effectively turned the tailplane into a
slab which could cope perfectly well with transonic aerodynamics. Too well
in fact, as it made the aircraft very frisky in pitch and it was madness to use it
much below 500 feet. So the prospect was one of riding this trim change on a
bumpy day and an interesting trip. And so it turned out; some twenty seconds
into the run the accelerometer was off the clock (again!) in both directions; so
back in the hangar for a stress check. And again, XE614/PL the thoroughbred
was fine, apart from a hole in the fin where someone had taken umbrage at
being photographed.

Occasionally, we were sent out into the open desert when there was a
rumour of a meeting of the opposition, or the collection of weaponry. On
these occasions we were told that if fired on we should fire back, provided
that that would not interfere with the mission which was a picture of the
event. On one such mission I was certain that a group of some four Land
Rovers and a fair few camels had opened up on me as I went past – guns
pointing in my direction and little yellow flashes. So rather than just go
home, I turned through 180 degrees, and gave them the benefit of all four
Aden guns firing alternate HE/ball for about three seconds – probably around
150-160 rounds. Unless the airspeed is 300 knots or less it is unlikely that
you see your rounds strike, and at 480 knots you most certainly do not, so
what effect I'd had I'll never know. The vibration of all four guns is quite
noticeable, and they knock the speed back a bit; as I opened the throttle and
pulled up, horror of horrors, the fire warning light came on. The drill for
this is, basically, eject as there is a fuel tank sitting around the jet pipe. But
there was no way I was going to join the crowd I'd just visited as there was
every probability that they were a bit angry.

So, no smoke in the rear vision mirror and normal JPT (Jet Pipe
Temperature); a gentle turn and still no smoke in the mirror. Then an
inspiration: I felt back to where the fire-warning test switch is to find
that the 'desert survival pack' had come loose from its mounting with the
vibration from the guns, and had fallen on the switch. Lift it off, and the fire
went out. Thereafter, these packs were taken out of all the FR.10s. If you'd
ejected they'd be nowhere near you, and no one in his right mind was going

Wadi Ruqub was typical of the hostile terrain through which FR.10 pilots would fly seeking out dissident activity and to photograph prospective targets, no matter how obscure. Four prospective targets have been marked up for attention by the ground attack squadrons on this print (*Peter Lewis*).

to crash-land in the sort of terrain we were flying over. We recommended that the DFGA boys did the same thing.

Quite often these missions involved taking off just before dawn, and I loved those flights. Flying low over the desert into a rising sun is a truly beautiful experience, and again, the Rubaiyat had the words:

> Awake, for Morning in the Bowl of Night
> Has flung the Stone that put the Stars to Flight:
> And Lo! The Hunter of the East has caught
> The Sultan's Turret in a Noose of Light.

Supporting the SAS

The SAS were very active in the Radfan and did a lot of surveillance of the enemy re-supply routes. One morning there was a message that a camel train had been spotted the previous night, and was resting up near the Yemen border. I was sent up for a look-see but, despite being pretty sure I was in the right place, saw nothing. Then a voice (on the R/T operational frequency) said "they're there"; that's all. So I looked more carefully. There was a sort of a track which followed the dried-up bed of a stream and which went through the odd pool of water which had not dried up. I noticed that the colour of the track above these pools was different to that below them and remembered some of Johnny Morris' training – the camels' wet feet had probably washed the sand off the path below the pools. And then, suddenly, what had appeared to be just rough boulders, turned out to be couched camels; but no sight of any humans. Time to help the Army; I turned round, and gave the camels no more than a two second burst of four guns, then turned again to photograph what I'd done. There was that brown/black smoke (as at Harib) all over where the camels had been, and no hope of any pictures. On return to base, I asked Johnny Morris to go back up there and do some pictures, but he came back without any; he said that there were so many vultures in the air and on the ground there was no way he was risking a bird strike just for my photo album.

There was a strange aftermath to this episode. Many years later, when I was out of the RAF and holidaying on the west coast of Wales with the family on Dinas Head, I was having a lunchtime pint in a pub called The Sailors Safety when a voice said, "It's Peter Lewis isn't it?" "Yes, but do I know you?" "Better than you know; do you remember some camels up in the Radfan?" "Yes." "And someone telling you 'they're there'?" "Yes." "Well that was me." The speaker was the local postman.

Not all missions were 100 per cent in their execution, notwithstanding the fact that they were successful; luck sometimes intervened. One such mission involved getting some nose-camera shots of some caves in the end of a wadi, the bed which was some 1,500 feet below the Radfan plateau. I knew the wadi fairly well having been there several times before and, in the usual good weather that Aden offered, the mission would have been purely routine. But this was February, when there is often a layer of cloud sitting over Radfan and the surrounding hills; only about 1,500 feet thick, but covering the plateau. When I got to the wadi, I saw that I would be flying into a wadi the tops of which were in cloud, through which I would have to pull up once the photos were done. I decided to fly at 300 rather than

420 knots as the camera would need to be slowed right down to make the most of the (for Aden) poor light and in I went. The run was only about half complete, perhaps three miles out from the target, when self preservation took over and I pulled up through the cloud thinking "abort". But then pride took over, so I went out to the edge of the cloud, let down to low level again, and made another run. This time, I got a bit closer but once again "chickened out" and set off for home. But halfway home, pride cut in again: I just had to go back for one more try. This time, I would fly at 320 knots with 10 degrees of flap to give me the sharpest rotation into a climb that the Hunter would do, and I went. I got my photos and rotated up through the cloud and back to base. But the photos were under-exposed (although the best achievable) and not much good for the customer.

The next day, the cloud had gone, so I went back again and got some decent shots. But in getting them, I realised that the day before my pull up through the cloud had taken me through a V-shaped depression in the wadi end, and that had I been twenty yards left or right I would have flown into the wadi wall. I then came to know what "fear in retrospect" really means.

What would probably have been the most interesting op of all was as bizarre in its conception as it would have been challenging in its execution. There was some trouble in or around Zanzibar, and there was to be a pacification exercise involving landing marines to secure the airfield, followed by the army who wanted their close support Hunters with them. The problem was that no one knew if the airfield was operational, or if the runway had been obstructed. So, 1417 would take off about an hour before the show was due to start and go and have a look at the airfield. If it was okay, the marines would secure it and the DFGA boys who were airborne but not up to their point-of-no-return would keep on coming. The 1417 Hunter would hang about making its fuel last as long as possible, and then land on the newly-acquired airfield and await the arrival of everyone else. If the airfield was not serviceable, then Nairobi if there was enough fuel, which was unlikely, or find one of Her Majesty's nice warships and eject beside it. The latter option also applied if the marines could not secure the airfield in time. But it never happened.

There is a little cameo from this whole thing which Liz and I still smile about. The beginnings of this episode involved my being knocked up at some ungodly hour, and told to pack some kit as I'd be away from home for a bit. This I did, and when Liz drowsily asked when I'd be back, all I could say was "I don't know," to which she said, "Have you got enough handkerchiefs?" We were kept on the base at Khormaksar, incommunicado, for some three days before the whole thing was called off and we could go home again. At the time, I don't remember ever thinking about what Liz, and the other wives, went through at times like those; it must have been miserable for them, miles from home and beset by uncertainties. But go through it they did, never complaining about that side of their lives. Late back with the shopping, or from the bar – that was a very different matter.

It was odd, to say the least, to get up at 04:00, fly four or five missions, some of which involved shooting and probably killing people, and then sit down with a wife and three children for a late lunch. The 'switch off' from violence had to be complete – until tomorrow. I now firmly believe that wives and families have no place in war zones. In all I flew 112 operations in Aden, most of them routine and uneventful, but some quite character forming. The flight had been tasked for 601 operations, 600 of which had been successful; the one which was a failure was when the last sortie of the day had to be abandoned when the aircraft refused to start. Towards the end of the tour I realised that something strange was happening: when it came to having completed an 'op', I couldn't remember walking out to the aircraft, transiting to the target, or coming home. But from the IP through to the break-out, I could give a faultless frame-by-frame debrief of everything. It was as if I'd been converted into an automaton programmed for perfection. A bit spooky really.'

And the Navy joined in

Although the bulk of the operations in the Protectorate were carried out by aircraft of the RAF, the Royal Navy played its part whenever it was in the area. Not only did this enable the hard-pressed Khormaksar Hunter units to take a breather but allowed carrierborne aircraft to gain invaluable training and experience in an operational theatre. During his time in Aden, Peter made several trips to carriers passing through.

'My first visit to HMS *Centaur* was to brief the crews on what to expect up-country, and to give those flying with their recce-pod a few tips on getting good results. Needless to say, I got lost below deck on several occasions, and once managed to get out of synch by twelve hours turning up for breakfast dressed for dinner. But I didn't spot any 'Danger! Crab Aboard' notices and the Navy were their usual hospitable selves.

Watching them fly their Sea Vixens off that tiny carrier at night was awesome, as was seeing them launch during the day in calm conditions

Two photographs from a selection taken by Peter Lewis during his visit to HMS *Centaur* to brief Sea Vixen crews on operations in Aden. (above) Fairey Gannet AEW.3 XP225-425 prepares to launch from the steam catapult as (below) recovered Sea Vixen FAW.1 XJ522-202 is marshalled into its parking bay (*both, Peter Lewis*).

when poor old *Centaur* was trembling violently to give them the 30 knots (I think) over the deck that they needed. On more than one occasion, I saw jet wash on the surface of the sea, and silently appreciated that we had it soft flying off runways.'

The Allsops drinking song

Sometime during his tour in Aden, Peter Lewis adapted a popular South African song, 'Ag pleez deddy' by Jeremy Taylor, to produce something more appropriate for life on the Khormaksar Hunter squadrons. The chorus, being repeated after every verse, made for a rousing rendition at parties as the effects of this branded lager took command. The original song sold more copies in South Africa than those of Elvis Presley.

> Ach please Bossman won't you take us down to Tarshyne
> We're hot and sweaty and we're hacked off too.
> The rocket range is out with haze,
> We haven't flown for days and days'
> We've got no spares, but there again,
> That's nothing new.

> Chorus Allsops, Brandy Dry, Tiger Beer and ASIs
> Saltpills, Aden Gut and S.O.R.s,
> Apart from blokes at Steamer Point,
> This really is a pleasant joint,
> With sandstorms, prickly heat
> And duty-free cars.

> Ach please Bossman, won't you come with us to Dhala,
> It's only ten hours in a five-ton truck.
> A flying programme was arranged
> The bloody thing has all been changed,
> We've twenty Hunters up on jacks
> It's just our luck.

> Ach please Bossman, need we really go to Bahrain,
> It's hot and sweaty and the Island's dry,
> The Mess serves only double tots
> The Watneys gives you awful trots,
> And everyone goes hairless if you try to fly.

Ach please Bossman, can't we do a strike on Shu yaiba,
We've got no aircraft but the idea's fine.
A simulated rocket strike
Using Chiefy Turner's bike
It's authorised and all we have to do is sign.

Ach please Bossman, if we cannot go to Tarshyne,
Or leave Bahrain, a place we bloody well hate,
We'll smash up Tac-Ops talky box
Belt the CO's car with rocks
And thump the living daylights out of 208.

Ach please Bossman, won't you come with us to Beihan,
One hour forty down a 'maginary line,
It really is a bloody bore,
And your ass gets bloody sore,
I s'pose the Hill would stop it if they had the time.'

Footnote: An account of his service in Aden was compiled by Peter Lewis in 2003 at the request of his children and grandchildren. In 2008, Peter became aware that XE614/PL survives in the Queensland Air Museum (QAM) at Caloundra, Australia. This abridged account was prepared at the request of QAM and is reproduced here with the author's kind permission. Where log book evidence exists, specific references to XE614/PL have been retrospectively included.

Roger Pyrah (Flight Lieutenant)

Having completed a tour in Aden flying Venoms with 8 Squadron in the mid-fifties, Flight Lieutenant Roger Pyrah found himself back at Khormaksar in August 1963 at the beginning of a two-year tour flying Hunter FR.10s with 1417 Flight.

'Nearly the whole of my period in Aden was of a life of excitement. It really started in October 1963 when I was asked to go as Forward Air Controller and RAF Liaison Officer with 600 men of the Hadramaut Bedouin Legion (HBL), to set up a form of administration in an area 500 miles north-east of Aden. Up until then, it was occupied by a race of Mahra people who had never seen white men before, apart from merchants passing

314

Strapped in and ready to go, proud OC 1417 Flight Roger Pyrah photographed in the cockpit of his Hunter FR.10 in 1964 (*Roger Pyrah*).

through. The area was the only remaining part of southern Arabia that did not have any form of administration.

The plan was to sweep from Fort Thamud, a remote HBL outpost, approximately 200 miles north of Mukulla (250 miles up the coast from Aden) to a place called Murait in the middle of the area, where the force was to divide in two. Half was to stay at Murait and half go to a place called Al Ghaidha on the coast, just north of Ras Fartak, 500 miles from Aden. The whole journey was 480 miles over the roughest, dustiest, and driest desert imaginable. While on route, and after establishing the two camps, each force was to cultivate good friendly relations with the population and an Arab-speaking and experienced civilian went along to help with this. While all this was being arranged, messages were sent out to all tribesmen in the area to warn them that the Sultan would be arriving from his home in Socotra and to ask them to come to Al Ghaidha to talk with him. My part in all this was to advise on air matters – air transport, air supply, building airstrips and offensive support if necessary.

The SAS break-out
The country in the Radfan area is extremely mountainous and rugged and the only way to control the area was from the high ground. Even then the

dissidents still made a nuisance of themselves and were very difficult to catch. They spent the day hiding up in tiny caves, shot all night and mined the roads. Whilst the battle of the Radfan was still at its height, our troops were frequently ambushed and cornered, whereupon we were scrambled to go and help. On one occasion they were so hard-pressed that the troops were directing our fire by radio to positions only twenty-five metres away from their own positions. This was the day that the SAS were cornered while on one of their expeditions, when they lost two of their comrades. The remainder slid away during the night and re-appeared two mornings later with a full report on enemy positions, having spent two days watching from the middle of enemy-occupied territory. They were as hard as nails, cool, calm and calculated when in trouble, but at the same time they were all very intelligent instead of the "blood and guts" as one would imagine. On this occasion, a shepherd boy saw them and shouted to the dissidents they had been watching 100 metres away. They remained under heavy fire all day and could not even raise their heads to shoot back most of the time. We gave air support all day and Captain Edwards, who was later killed, directed our fire almost onto their own position. At nightfall, after the Hunters could no longer carry out their attacks, the nine surviving SAS troopers made a run for it. They were fantastically cool to get away with it. A week later we were talking to them and they were so keen to get back to the mountains. They were in fact on

Using his portside nose camera, Roger Pyrah captures Johnny Baines at the controls of 1417 Flight FR.10 XE599-JB as it swoops low over Fort Ataq (*Roger Pyrah*).

their way back to Thumier. One of them had three holes in his leg, one hole through his arm while another had a two-centimetre groove across his back. They told us about it only because we asked – one was limping a bit and had to sit down most of the time. I admired these men tremendously, as did we all – and yet they genuinely thought that we were the bravest men alive to fly fast jets through such hostile terrain.

Running the ship

My most exciting event occurred in July 1964 when I took over command of 1417 Flight. The job was similar to one I had in Germany – fighter reconnaissance. The only difference flying over desert was navigation which was quite a problem, particularly as the maps were very inaccurate, and also the fact that in Aden it was the "real thing" most of the time. It was great to be able to do what we had trained for in earnest. We had six pilots and five Hunter FR.10s and were housed in excellent air-conditioned accommodation equipped with a telephone each. Because our job was to get information and photographs most of the time, we also needed to know why the information was wanted in order to plan how to take the pictures (how close, how high, etc.) and this meant that our tasks were

One of the many tasks assigned to the fighter-recce pilots was that of seeking out gun-running camel trains. In the photograph above a number of rebels and their heavily-laden camels can be seen crossing a dried-up river bed. (*Roger Pyrah*).

Prior to the attack on Fort Harib in March 1964, Roger Pyrah was given the task of obtaining photographs of Qataba Barracks well inside the Yemen as it was earmarked as a target for a Hunter strike but politics intervened (*Roger Pyrah*).

doubly interesting due to our being given advanced notification of moves and future plans.

Agreements were being negotiated with local leaders to keep troublemakers out of their territories. Even when these were completed, there was still a lot of work to be done in other areas because, under the direction of the Yemen and Egypt, dissident tribesmen moved into those areas to stir up trouble. I found it surprising that, despite living in terrible conditions and their weapons being old and dangerous, they never knew when to quit. Many lost their lives because their guns, mines and grenades exploded unexpectedly. One other surprising thing was how Egypt and the Yemen could afford to fight against the royalists and still pay out so much money to cause unrest in the Aden Protectorates.'

A unique view of the southern-most tip of Arabia taken from Roger Pyrah's FR.10 in 1965. The Aden Peninsula with the dominant Shamsan towering over the townships of Crater, Steamer Point and Ma'alla, and stretching out beyond to the large Khormaksar military complex and airfield beyond (*Roger Pyrah*).

To speed up the dispensing of processed prints to Army personnel on the front line, 1417 Flight devised various methods of delivering them, the most successful being described here by Roger.

Your prints are ready Sir!
'With reference to the delivery of photos to the guys up country, I can't recall it being done by putting the pictures in the flaps but that may have been the case after I left. It could have been a reason for photos getting spread around the sky which could easily happen if not properly contained and parachuted in.

When I was in command we were very restricted on training hours due to fuel shortages. We normally each got forty hours per month but this dropped to fifteen hours with ten hours allowed for operational sorties. I asked Wing Commander Jennings (OC Strike Wing) what would happen if the recce requests meant exceeding the ten hours, to which he replied, "The ten hours was purely budgeting and we could press on." So I persuaded the chaps to share stocking our fridge with beers. I got a supply of time-expired ejection seat drogues and some small sacks. Four iced beers exactly fitted in the

319

In addition to fulfilling his job in the fighter-recce role, Roger Pyrah was a keen photographer in his own right and occasionally took his own camera aloft to capture high-level images of the Aden hinterland. Here, the hilltop town of Al Qara was the subject of his attention (*Roger Pyrah*).

airbrake metalwork and acted as ballast for the dropping of the photos in the sack which was attached to the drogue. We imagined the effect the delivered photos would have on the recipient – i.e. word would soon get around on return to their base. The plan was that two pilots would get the briefing, one to fly the mission. On return the engine was kept going to avoid a turn-round check, cameras were quickly removed and raced by bicycle to the MFPU where the second pilot would mark off the pictures required on the quickly processed film negative. The prints were placed in the sack, weighted with four iced beers, and carefully planted in the airbrake. With a thumbs up, the first pilot then belted off and delivered to the troops up country. I think we got the turn-round time, on-to-off chocks, down to fifteen minutes once or twice, but this depended on the number of pictures required. Flying low and slow, the package of prints could be dropped within twenty yards of their intended recipients. After a short period of time, as expected, the photo requests started to increase and our individual monthly flying hours increased considerably. I achieved a maximum of thirty-one hours and one of us, I forget who, got close to forty. After the delivery sortie the pilot, already briefed, would then carry out a training mission so we didn't lose any training at all. Of course this was possible because of the two 230-gallon and two 100-gallon fuel tanks the Hunter Mk.10 carried, giving us around two and a half hours at low level.

Centralised servicing - and its effects

When I took over the Flight we had our own servicing crews and mostly there were five aircraft on the line ready to go, because those guys worked their socks off. However, I reckoned that serviceability was much affected by the heat and working conditions for the men were not good. The temperature of the aircraft metal was unbearable to the touch. So I had white canvas covers made with attachment points to fit the top of the rudder, each wingtip and a loop attachment at the nose. Perfect! The aircraft and the men were kept cool. Serviceability and morale improved. Then it was all change – politics reared its ugly head. Centralised servicing was brought in, the men were assigned to Engineering Wing, the canvas covers were never used again and the men didn't feel they belonged quite the same as when they were part of the Flight. Esprit de corps vanished with 9 to 5 working: serviceability – maximum of two aircraft on the line. When will a Labour government ever learn that men need to feel an important part of the action and that they and what they did mattered towards the attainment of the aim.'

Ken Simpson (Flight Lieutenant)

Having completed a tour as a fighter ground-attack pilot with 1 (F) Squadron at West Raynham, Ken Simpson undertook a reconnaissance course at Chivenor before being posted to Aden in mid-1965 and the beginning of a tour with 1417 Flight at Khormaksar. During his time in Aden, Ken took several thousand photographs using the FR.10's F.95 Vinten cameras and, fortuitously, retained copies of many interesting subjects.

Operation THESIGER

'Named after a traveller from earlier times, Operation THESIGER, took place in August and September 1965 and again in March 1966, and required pilots and aircraft of 1417

Ken Simpson takes a break during Operation THESIGER in 1965 (*Ken Simpson*).

Flight to be detached to Salalah and Masirah respectively. Highly classified at the time, the first THESIGER sorties were flown from Salalah by Ralph Chambers and I and involved our Hunter FR.10s flying long-range missions into the Empty Quarter, seeking out convoys bringing arms and supplies to dissident tribesmen in the EAP and Oman, and searching for illegal oil prospecting. The second series of Operation THESIGER sorties was flown from Masirah by Richard Johns and I and were accompanied by FGA.9s on detachment from 208 Squadron.

Operation RANJI

Operation RANJI took place three times a week and involved flying along the South Arabian coast, over an area ranging three nautical miles out to sea to several miles inland, searching for and photographing ships (mainly Arab dhows), trucks and camel trains, with the objective of detecting and discouraging the illegal supply of guns and ammunition to dissident tribesmen in the South Arabian Federation.

Bird strike

While flying an up-country sortie on 9 May 1966 a griffon vulture struck my aircraft, FR.10, XE589, in the starboard intake. The huge bird entered the intake and, although much of it smashed its way out through the upper skin of the wing, the remainder entered the engine causing it to surge. As the rpm stabilised in mid-range I left the throttle and, by dropping

As the man on the rear camel follows the Hunter through his binoculars, Ken Simpson photographs the small camel train as it crosses the desert during an Operation RANJI sortie (*Ken Simpson*).

Operation RANJI sorties demanded skilful flying for, in addition to observing and reporting what they encountered, the FR.10 pilots had to position their aircraft accurately in order to align their cameras with the subject. In the never-ending pursuit of arms smugglers, the photograph of the Arab dhow will be thoroughly examined for suspect cargo by photographic interpreters at Khormaksar and Command HQ (*Ken Simpson*).

my external tanks, managed to nurse the aircraft up to 10,000 feet on a heading back to Khormaksar where I was able to carry out an emergency landing. The damage was initially assessed as Cat 4 and XE589 was transferred to 131 MU where the category was revised to Cat 5. It was subsequently shipped back to the UK where Hawker Siddeley rebuilt it to help fulfil an overseas order.

No brakes!

On 3 September 1966 I was tasked with a recce mission to Perim Island, some ninety-five nautical miles west of Aden, followed by a "photo-drop" to the troops deployed there. In line with the now common practice, I had enough fuel after the recce to allow for a rapid turn-round with the engine running, the film to be processed and selected prints bagged and installed in the airbrake, and to fly back to Perim Island for the drop. Unfortunately, it was not to be. On my initial landing the aircraft overshot the runway, the starboard undercarriage all but shearing off when it struck a hidden object in the overrun, causing Cat 4 damage to the aircraft. It transpired that the brake pads, which would have sufficed in normal, low-fuel, circumstances, were not up to the job for a heavyweight landing.

Formations various

Apart from the period when 208 Squadron provided a four-ship display team for the Command, there was very little call for formation flying in the Middle East, except on special occasions such as the Queen's birthday, AOC's inspection, or the arrival and departure of assorted dignitaries or units. In the final few years of Britain's tenure in Aden, it was the norm for 1417 Flight to take airborne photographs of several formations, large and small.

With the disbandment of 1417 Flight in September 1967, I transferred to 8 Squadron for a few months and at the completion of my Middle East tour in late 1967, still as a flight lieutenant, I went to Davis Monthan AFB near Tucson, Arizona, to do a three-month conversion course onto the F-4 Phantom. On my return from the USA, I became an instructor at RAF Coningsby, converting RAF pilots onto the Phantom.

Another of the many formations captured by the Vinten cameras of 1417 Flight FR.10s, this one depicting 8/43 Squadron FGA.9s XE550-X, XG296-B, XJ680-E and XF435-H in box-four formation in 1966 (*Ken Simpson*).

Hot Seat!

While performing a flagwave in February 1967, Flying Officers Lawton and Sowler thought they were being shot at while flying over the village of Dhi Surrah as Flying Officer Sowler's aircraft, XF440, began to lose its services one by one. This may not be exactly what happened but it was a great story over a beer or two.

Eventually Sid lost R/T contact with everyone because the damage to the aircraft caused by ground fire had ruptured hydraulic lines which then caught fire and destroyed the radio bay. His No. 2 used hand signals to try and get him to eject as he could see the fire was very serious. Shortly thereafter, Sid went from power controls into manual and with a strong smell of burning, he reluctantly ejected near Al Ittihad, about ten miles short of Khormaksar. His aircraft crashed about three miles in front of him. His ejection was seen by a passing Army officer and his sergeant who went to his assistance. Sid was fine and said the rescue helicopter would be there shortly to pick him up. The officer insisted that he could do something and Sid eventually (to get some peace and quiet) let him roll up his parachute and then drove off to leave Sid sitting on his parachute to wait for the helicopter.

Meanwhile the helicopter had landed at the crashed Hunter thinking that Sid was nearby. Once they had established he was not in or near the aircraft they started searching the area. Not surprisingly it took some time without the parachute to spot.

Having averted disaster in the air, he nearly sustained injury back at base. As the helicopter landed in its compound (next to Strike Wing), his mates were watching over the fence to see if he came out in bits, on a stretcher, or walking. As he climbed out of the helicopter he saw them and raised his hands above his head by way of a victory salute – nearly losing his hands to the helicopter blades which were still rotating.

The officers' mess had a limited number of rooms with air conditioning and there was a strict waiting list. I arrived in mid-1965 and my turn to move in came on 31 March 1966. I had waited a long time for this moment. It rained like hell that night and the whole airfield was flooded, so much so that the generators went off – no electricity therefore no air conditioning. I think it lasted a month or two.

The same day an aircraft was calling Khormaksar for landing instructions only to be told to divert to Djibouti. As it was April Fools' Day the pilot didn't believe it and he had a long and acrimonious discussion with air traffic before diverting.

Ken Simpson keeps a watchful eye for suspicious activity while flying his FR.10 low across an up-country plantation (*Ken Simpson*).

On a rare occasion when Khormaksar came under fire, bullets started to zip over our heads in the bar. There were no stone walls behind which we could take cover and the mess and outbuildings were pretty much made of papier-mache. It was decided that if we were going to die then best done with a beer in your hand. So we stayed put.'

Chapter 6

From different perspectives

Although the Hunter squadrons were responsible for a high percentage of air operations in the Middle East theatre, it is worth recording some of the recollections contributed by crews who played a big supporting role. These include the daring exploits of the Shackleton and Beaver crews, their squadrons being able to attack targets hidden out of sight of Hunter pilots. Number 37 Squadron and 653 Squadron (AAC) worked closely with the ground-attack squadrons in the common endeavour to maintain law and order in the Protectorates.

Roy Bowie (Squadron Leader)

This account is taken from Squadron Leader Roy Bowie's book *Lost Voices*. Roy was Squadron Leader Operations during 1964 and 1965 and reported directly to Wing Commander Jennings, OC Strike Wing at Khormaksar.

The Radfan

'The emergency was officially declared in the Radfan two months before we got out there in February 1964, but I don't think we quite understood how violent the tribal reaction to our presence would be.

The Radfan is a mountainous tract of country about fifty miles north of Aden. The Radfanis are a fanatically independent bunch and warfare between the various tribes was a way of life. The caravans that passed through the Radfan along the Dhala road to Yemen – one of the traditional routes to Mecca – were made to pay [tolls] and this was a constant source of friction. New laws were brought in forbidding the levy of tolls and the Qutaibis, the main tribe of the Radfan, began to cause trouble on the Dhala road. They began shooting at the caravans and mining the road. All this happened to coincide with the civil war in Yemen. So the authorities decided to do something about it. In response to the Aden federal government request, a makeshift Aden brigade was formed, plus a squadron each of ground-support Hunters, Shackleton bombers, and Twin Pioneer transports as well as seven Belvedere helicopters. I was to act as the Brigade Air Support Officer (BASO) with David Whittaker. The general task was to stop the tribal revolt and the attacks on the Dhala road.

At last light on 30 April, 45 Commando set out to capture the high ground in the Dhanaba Basin, and that same night, the 3rd Battalion of the Parachute Regiment was to drop from Beverleys on to the Wadi Taym. The SAS were to mark the drop zone for the Paras. Unfortunately some chap with his goats stumbled into their hide and all the locals started shooting at this nine-man patrol.

Captain Edwards, who was leading the patrol, got his signaller, Warburton, to contact their boss, Major Wingate-Gray at the SAS headquarters at Thumier, where we were also based. Major Wingate-Gray asked for Hunters to assist the withdrawal of his men. They were ordered in and, as they attacked, he was on the telephone to Whittaker and me relaying messages from the SAS patrol. While we gave fire orders over the microphone to the Hunters, 8 and 43 Squadrons were going flat out all day until it got too dark to fly. Earlier the SAS had arranged for another troop to go in by helicopter, but they had been badly hit by machine-gun fire, so they pulled that troop out and changed the plan.

That night, as the SAS patrol tried to break out, first Warburton, and then Edwards were killed. The remainder of the patrol had to leave their bodies behind. Those bodies were mutilated and decapitated, and the heads were displayed in the Yemen. But we did recover their bodies later.

The Marines then went in at night and the Paras went in on foot. When dawn came, the Paras were still on the wadi floor and the Marines were up on Cap Badge. The Paras took the village at the bottom of Cap Badge and cleaned the place out. Then they were heavily fired upon and had a battle for about an hour, and two of them were killed. I called in the Hunters and they strafed the enemy and that quietened things down.

From then on the action was like the North West Frontier of India of the 1920s and 1930s. An area would be leafleted and the locals would be told that this is an area of military movement, clear out. They'd be given twelve hours' warning which meant there were very few casualties on either side. But if we got information from our agents on the ground we'd go and knock an odd house down – put a few rockets in to keep them busy, but always after we'd leafleted. The Shackletons would keep the Radfan on the move. They'd go up at night, and would sit over the top, and every time they saw a fire lit, they would drop a 25lb practice bomb at it. This meant that they couldn't cook their food and it really made life very miserable for them, which was the object of the exercise. But we weren't just going out and blasting people left, right and centre.

Of course the local political officers, who were a bit like Lawrence of Arabia, used to go round with a couple of Arab guards on the back of a camel. They were incredibly brave. They used to go out and deal with the tribes and try and keep them in order. They had a very, very big say in what was going on. They knew the score; they knew who was causing the trouble and who wasn't. The whole object of the exercise was to try and get people back to law and order.

But of course the internal security situation developed as the word came out that we were leaving. Everybody who had been friendly with us was now trying to show how unfriendly they were. At Christmas time 1964 we had a grenade thrown into the open-air cinema at Waterloo lines. It hit somebody on the knee, rolled under a seat, and someone shouted lift your feet, and nobody was injured, which was incredible. After that I was walking back up through the camp one day, and a guy said to me, "Ha, sir, you're a cricketer, aren't you?" I agreed but wondered at the same time what he was up to. He said, "Take this dummy grenade, walk back fifty yards or so, and see if you can throw it into the cinema." I kept going back until I could no longer lob it into the cinema. He then said, "Thanks very much, sir, that's where we are going to put the fence up."

We had a quarter about three doors down from us where there was a teenagers' Christmas party going on. Somebody threw a grenade in and killed one of the teenagers. There was also another one thrown into the mess at Steamer Point. So it was a bad period. The internal security situation worsened towards the end of the time that I was out there and there was a curfew on all the time, so you couldn't be out after midnight. You couldn't have more than twelve people in a party in your quarter.

But all in all, it was a fascinating tour; some of the places we could visit out there were tremendous. I suppose the great joy of flying out in the Radfan was to fly the Hunter. She was a beauty, a lovely aeroplane to fly, a lovely one to look at. It was very, very strongly built and handled very nicely. You felt when you sat in it, that you were part of the aeroplane – it was wonderful and really could shift. It had problems – it wasn't the greatest turner in the world – but a joy to fly. I flew my first Hunter in 1955 and flew one on my last day of service in 1984.'

Richard Grevatte-Ball (Lieutenant)

Commissioned into the Army from Sandhurst in 1962, Richard learned to fly with the Army Air Corps (AAC) in 1965 at Middle Wallop and was posted to 15 Flight AAC in Aden in early 1966 as a lieutenant. He served there as a DH-C 2 Beaver pilot until the withdrawal of the AAC in October 1967 when he flew one of the last three Beavers to leave Khormaksar to Sharjah.

Scout crew murdered

'The Operational Record for 1417 Flight's FR Hunters refers to their being tasked between 4 and 7 September to look for a missing AAC Scout AH.1 helicopter, XT641, which had disappeared on a flight from

Ataq to Mayfa'ah on the 3rd, and that on their last recce sortie they had spotted scorch marks on the ground which were interpreted to be an aircraft destruction site.

I, too, was involved in this sad operation, where, together with one other AAC Beaver, I piloted a Beaver from Khormaksar up to Ataq on 4 September 1967. Both aircraft then conducted a low-level search down the usual flying route from Ataq to Mayfa'ah. As we neared Mayfa'ah we were soon suspicious as we could see groups of Arabs firing at us from the ground with their rifles. This was confirmed when a bullet hit the other Beaver, entering through the door window panel, narrowly missing a middle-seat observer (who luckily had just turned

Ready for his next operation, Richard Grevatte-Ball with his faithful Beaver (*Richard Grevatte-Ball*).

AAC Scout AH.1 XR635 lifts off from its base at Habilayn in 1967. Although vulnerable to ground fire, the Scout gained an excellent reputation in helping to fight the war against dissident terrorists (*Richard Grevatte-Ball*).

towards the centre of the passenger area to 'relax his neck') and passing out through the cockpit roof just behind the co-pilot's seat – without causing serious damage to anything vital.

Soon after reporting back, the Beavers were recalled (as was the Hunter top cover) to Ataq as it was by then believed that the Scout helicopter had at least been captured, if not destroyed. Subsequently it was learnt that the Scout had been destroyed while on the ground at Mayfa'ah in a wadi bed used to collect building sand, the crew murdered, and the whole covered by sand, using a bulldozer, in an area where there were many such sandpiles. This explanation seems to agree exactly with the Hunter unit's photographic interpretation. A piece of the Scout was handed over to the authorities in Aden some weeks later as proof but, alas, it was so near to the British withdrawal from Aden and the peace talks going on in Switzerland that no attempt, to my knowledge, was ever made to recover the pilot's (Staff Sergeant Baulcomb) and passenger's (Foreign Office intelligence officer) bodies. Shameful, though, realistically, with that whole area having changed sides to the NLF, it would have required a major punitive expedition and there were no longer adequate UK forces in theatre (or enough time remaining) to undertake such a venture.

DFC

The 8 Squadron ORB for 4 May 1967 records a 'large group of dissidents attacking an Army road-repair party on the road to Habilayn and a helicopter-borne FAC co-ordinating a successful FGA.9 RP-attack on a cave mouth. An AAC Scout, armed with one fixed-firing general purpose machine gun (GMPG) on each skid, operated by the pilot, plus a side-door-mounted co-ax GPMG operated by a crewman, was flown that day by Lieutenant David Ralls, attached to the AAC, and he was subsequently awarded a DFC for the coordination of the Hunters and the aggressive attack using his Scout's guns on the Arab dissidents. It was one of the few times when such a "skirmish" had a clear "win" for British forces. The Scout's crew spotted the dissidents, chased them into the cave and kept them cowering there until the Hunters arrived. Then an accurate "target ID" by the Scout, now in the FAC role, ensured that they were literally entombed therein by the Hunter RP attack.

Withdrawal of British officers from up-country

In the last few months of 1967 it became clear that the locally-enlisted Arab Forces, especially those to be found in "Area East", would change their allegiance to FLOSY or the NFL before the final withdrawal of UK forces. These Arab units were led by British Army officers on secondment (normally a CO, a second in command and a quartermaster) and the Aden staff arranged that an AAC Beaver would be on "standby" to fly to the relevant up-country camp airstrip, often some 250 miles distant, to evacuate them when the expectancy of a mutiny arose. For a Beaver that was roughly three-hours flying time, but for a Hunter it was much quicker. The Aden staff always tasked a pair of Hunters to be "overhead" the area whenever a Beaver was due to make a landing, just in case there was any shooting on the ground. The Beaver pilot carried a hand-held SARBE UHF radio so that he could retain communication with the Hunter pilot whilst on the ground and away from his aircraft. On one of these "evacuations" I was talking to the Hunter pilot over the radio and asked him what his "battle plan" was. "Not much fuel – just enough for one pass and I'll fire at wherever I perceive the trouble to be coming from," he said. Luckily there was never any trouble, although I'm certain that the sight of Hunter high above was enough to ensure my and the British officers' safety. I well remember that on one such occasion the British officers were close to tears. They had been living with their Arab battalion for three years and just could not understand how Arabs, whom they believed to be close comrades, could so suddenly "turn their backs" on the British. In retrospect it is obvious; we were neither of their faith, nor would we be their future paymasters.

Observing the Hunter's firepower

The ORBs for both 8 and 43 Squadrons have many examples of "flag wave" and "firepower demonstrations". For example, on 24 September 1967, in the Wadi Hadramaut area, I flew some Arab dignitaries from Riyan airfield to an airstrip in the Wadi Hadramaut. Because of the extreme range, the 43 Squadron Hunters decided that they would fire off all their RPs in one pass. The air was still with expectancy and, indeed, some of the Arabs were getting a little restless as time was getting on. A large white circle had been painted on a rock face as the intended target. Suddenly there was a terrible "roar" of a jet engine and the whole rock face disappeared in a cloud of smoke, followed shortly after by the sound of the explosions. As the air started to clear there was no longer a painted rock face, but a small silver dart climbing rapidly away at height. Having no idea from where it was coming, many of the Arabs were so terrified at the sound of the approaching Hunters that they fell facedown on ground as if to take cover. It was a simply marvellous demonstration of the might of British airpower and more dramatic, through the lack of "loitering over target" time, than a series of individual attacks. The pilots were spot-on with their aim, but that was to be expected from Hunter pilots based in Aden as they certainly knew their job.

Beaver 'bomber'

Falaise Camp provided our headquarters and aircraft servicing facilities and was the HQ for 24 Brigade, an armoured car regiment and an infantry battalion. In the last few months leading up to the 1967 withdrawal from Aden, large areas up-country were declared as "no-go" zones by the British forces and, elsewhere, any armed Arab encountered could be attacked, even if they hadn't opened fire first. I think that the powers-that-be had little idea exactly how these last few months would pan out, especially the level of fighting that could have been anticipated in the hinterland surrounding Aden town, its port, and a few remaining forts still manned by British personnel. A serious concern was the gradual rundown of RAF strike elements as part of the drawdown process.

The AAC Beavers were all fitted with underwing light series bomb carriers (an RAF-issue item), which were used to carry parachute stores

Another excellent workhorse, 653 Squadron Beaver XP818 is seen on the ramp at the AAC airfield at Falaise, near Little Aden, in 1967 (*Richard Grevatte-Ball*).

(five jerrycans plus a parachute, two of these under each wing. In addition, Beavers delivered to the AAC were equipped with nose and tail bomb-arming circuits. Always made me smile. These parachute stores (or bombs) were launched by arming the electrical circuit and then pressing a button on the control yoke. The bomb carriers could be fitted with 25lb practice or fragmentation bombs. We were trained under RAF supervision and my log book shows that I was signed-off as qualified to drop either bomb type. The only snag was that we didn't have a bombsight – so it was trial and error; chinagraph-plus on the Perspex window.

Luckily we were never called upon to put these newly-found skills into practice and, to my certain knowledge, Beavers were never adopted for this role during their service with the British Army. I am, therefore, one of just seven Army pilots to hold this qualification in their logbooks.

The Beavers withdraw from Aden
As the Aden campaign moved towards the closing stages; all British troops were withdrawn from the interior to the security of the bases surrounding

Aden and its port. The Army Air Corps element was rapidly reduced; 8 Flight and its Scout helicopters had already returned to the UK, leaving the Scouts of 13 Flight to prepare for a move to Sharjah in the Arabian Gulf. No. 15 Flight was endeavouring to coax four of their Beaver aircraft into RAF Belfast transports for the move back to the UK, leaving three Beavers, together with three Beverleys of 84 Squadron, as the only aircraft to continue flying up-country in support of the rapidly mutinying South Arabian Army. These trips were now flown with the nagging doubt as to which side the Arab troops would be on; the Government, National Liberation Front, or Front for the Liberation of Occupied South Yemen. The final up-country sortie by the AAC was flown by a Beaver on the evening of 12 October.

At last, on 13 October 1967, the day arrived when the last Beavers were to leave Aden. Loyalties were exchanged between 15 Flight with its "witch on a broomstick" and 13 Flight with its "black cats". Of 13 Flight's six Scouts only one was serviceable for a farewell salute before flying off to HMS *Fearless* with a suspect main rotor gearbox. The three Beavers were fully serviceable and equipped with long-range ferry tanks and loaded with 'free' gifts from RAF Khormaksar. It was with a somewhat bloated take off that we took off and headed for Sharjah.

Saved by a Hunter!

We were transiting in three legs, the first from Khormaksar to Salalah, the second to Muscat (Bait) and finally up to Sharjah. It had been well planned in advance for, six months earlier, my squadron commander and I had flown the route up to Sharjah and then up to Bahrain (to do a flagwaving event and drop parachutists for the Sheik of Bahrain) and then fly the reverse route back to Aden.

On approaching RAF Ryan – to overfly as we knew it was now in enemy hands – one of the Beavers experienced a propeller oil-seal failure. When this happens, a lot of oil is pumped onto the outside of the pilot's windscreen and necessitates an immediate landing before the engine seizes up. I instructed the affected Beaver pilot to land and told the third Beaver to fly back to Aden to radio our misfortune. I then landed behind the prop oil failure aircraft. It took about half an hour to replace the seal (each Beaver was carrying a mechanic as a passenger plus a good stock of small spares) but we were soon surrounded by rifle-waving Arabs. It suddenly dawned on us that a DC-3 standing nearby was the Air Djibuti aircraft that they

The wrong place and the wrong time to experience an oil leak! Two of the last three Beavers to leave Khormaksar were forced to land at Riyan due to an oil-seal leak on XP774. With armed locals uncomfortably close behind him, a mechanic sets to work on replacing the defective seal. The Air Djibouti DC-3 F-BGOU had been hijacked by the gunmen and was being used to smuggle arms to fellow dissidents fighting in the Aden hinterland. The date is 17 October 1967 (*Richard Grevatte-Ball*).

had hijacked. Daylight time was fast running out, the Arabs were getting more restless – you cannot go their leader said until our boss arrives. It was getting ugly. Suddenly, very high in the sky I spotted a Hunter that had been scrambled from Khormaksar to come to our aid. Quickly, into my UHF radio, I explained our somewhat dire predicament. "OK," he replied, "I've only got fuel enough for one low pass. I'll fire my cannon and if I hit your Beaver as well – my apologies."

Well seeing that Hunter changed everything. "You can go," the Arabs shouted and with that our two Beavers "scrambled,", not even taking the time to buckle up our seatbelts. Next morning, after we had recovered from a celebratory drinking session in the mess the evening before, a post-flight aircraft inspection of our aircraft revealed that one Beaver had bullet damage to its port elevator torque tube, evidence that the Arabs must have shot at us as we took off. We were fortunate that it had not broken in flight. So a belated "thank you" to that unknown RAF Hunter pilot.'

Terry Kingsley (Flight Lieutenant)

Terry Kingsley was assigned to the Ferry Squadron at Benson whose task it was to ferry aircraft of all types to and from RAF bases across the globe. Although not assigned to a Middle East Command unit, Terry flew several ferry flights through the Command's territory. The extract below is taken from Terry's excellent biography, *In the Red*, and is reproduced here with my grateful thanks.

Ferrying the Hunters

'When the Hunter Marks 9 and 10 were fitted with the 230-gallon underwing tanks, the Ferry Squadron was tasked with exploring its range flying characteristics. This we did, after Hugh Merryweather flew direct to Malta, missed it and made it to somewhere in North Africa. They had 660 gallons of external fuel, and made some special flights possible. We did much of the development work, including evolving the long-range techniques. It was found that the range barely altered at speeds between Mach 0.70 and 0.85. However, there was a large time difference and you nearly froze to death at the low power settings, which did not pass enough heat to the cabin.

It literally fell apart!

My contact with Aden et al was through ferry flights through the area. I did return a miserable 208 Squadron Vampire T.11 from Eastleigh, through Aden, but only got as far as Teheran before the ravages of termites did it in. My good friend, 208 Squadron pilot Derek Bell, was in the UK from Kenya for conversion onto the Hunter FGA.9 at the time and it so happened that I was scheduled to go to Nairobi to pick up a Vampire trainer for return to UK. We met in UK and renewed our friendship before flying out to Kenya by Transport Command Comet. It was my first trip to East Africa, and so I did all my Vampire test flights in the Rift Valley and around Kilimanjaro and Mount Kenya. Fantastic scenery, but now to get this ancient machine home.

I flew in formation with a number of returning 208 Squadron Venoms to Mogadishu in Somalia where a short stroll by the sea renewed my fear of sharks. The beach is steeply shelving with large breakers. A large shoal of small fish appeared out of a breaker. By the time my brain had worked out that something must be chasing them, the shark had smacked down in the shallow water, just a few feet from me. My departure was rocket assisted.

337

The second leg was to Aden across some very inhospitable country. Slowly I began to lose sight of the other formation members as the canopy iced up. My heating system had failed, probably from lack of use in a tropical environment. In trying to clean a hole to see through I inadvertently squeezed the brakes which promptly locked on. It would be more than warm enough to burn off the ice in Aden, as long as I had enough fuel to wait. We descended with me looking out of a tiny hole in the ice, and they landed first. I could only try to free the locked wheels by touching them gently on the runway. If they were locked it would burst the tyres. I used up the remaining fuel flying as fast as I could to heat up the airframe. The touch and go was gentle but unsuccessful as all the tyres burst. Now for a bumpy landing on burst tyres.

It was very hot in Aden and the only place that was air-conditioned was the bar. The change of temperature for me had been close to 100 degrees C; minus 56 degrees C in the aircraft to plus 45 degrees C in Aden. Couple this with drinking 'jungle juice' undiluted and my body said enough. This juice is available in most tropical messes, being a concoction of salt, sugar and vitamins. Usually it is diluted and placed on the tables, but not this time. I drank a full glass before my taste buds sent reject messages to my head. It was like drinking hot lead, and it cleaned out my system from both ends instantly. We delayed whilst I recovered and the Vampire was fixed.

Several short legs up the Oman coast followed to Sharjah in the Gulf. From here we had a decision to make. Teheran was really marginal, but Abadan was rarely used and prone to flooding. The airport was right at sea level and could be unusable very quickly. We set off for Abadan to be informed that it had flooded and we diverted to Teheran. This was now an extreme range trip in aircraft that we did not know thoroughly. We started the descent with the fuel gauges reading empty. The formation opened up and we left room to glide in if the engines stopped. The landing was an anticlimax, but I was a little drained as we were guided into the military parking. We refuelled and I had to move to another parking spot. It would not start! Great, now what? The batteries appeared weak, and so the large ground-power unit, used to start Comets, was brought up. "What amperage would you like?" I was asked. Not a question usually faced; I guessed at 700A. The start was again attempted, and this time the Goblin wound up to 200-300rpm. Not enough to start, so I asked for 1,000A. Again only 350rpm, so I requested 1,300A, but was told that 1,350 was his limit and I knew that we were in deep trouble. Still no start and so I started to climb out. The Iranian mechanic was undoing panels before I realised it. The words

There being no proper refuelling facility at Mogadiscio, airfield workers had to resort to using petrol drums and hand pumps on this Vampire T.11 (*Peter McLeland*).

choked in my mouth as I tried to prevent him from touching the high energy igniters. These multipliers of all those amp/volts were dangerous for hours after a start. There was a flash and he flew through the air like a rag doll. The impact on the concrete was a horrible sound. I knew that he was dead – from the fall, if not from the electric shock. We walked, not ran to the body, for it was pointless. He sat up and shook his head looking at his fingers. His only mark was the polished skin of his fingertips where he had touched the igniter. I climbed back in to collect my stuff and placed my foot where the step should be. It did not feel right and on looking down my foot had gone through the side of the Vampire's cockpit. Tropical beasties had reduced the wooden fuselage to powder. There was no way that this aircraft was going to make it to UK, and so I was again left on my own in Teheran.'

Little did Terry realise that seven years later he would be flying alongside Derek Bell with the Red Arrows under the leadership of Ray Hanna.

Sandy McMillan (Flight Lieutenant)

Following tours with 61 Squadron, the Development Squadron at Watton, 206 Squadron, the Staff Nav Course, and a spell at HQCC Northwood,

Sandy became weapons leader on 37 Squadron at Khormaksar in January 1960. He was newly married and their time in Aden was very happy, shaping the rest of their lives. His wife, Jan, was commissioned to paint the portraits of the Federal rulers and they became particularly close friends with Sharif Hussein bin Ahmed Al-Habili, then Federal Minister of the Interior. Having learnt Arabic, they regularly travelled to Beihan and the other Federal states, were welcomed into the warm and hospitable Arab society, and have kept many ties with it since their departure in April 1962.

Bombs away!

'In 2006, through a series of coincidences and serendipities, I came into contact with Stephen Day, who had been a political officer in Lower Yafa' State, Western Aden Protectorate, in the 1960s. One of his responsibilities was to recommend the action that government should take against dissident tribesmen, and in July 1961 he commissioned a Shackleton bombing mission from 37 Squadron at Khormaksar.

It's about 06:00 on Friday, 20 July 1961 and just getting light. I park outside 37 Squadron's HQ, a cluster of long low buildings, and go in to meet the crew for today's sortie. Keith McDonald is my captain, a friend and flying colleague for the past five years; we "best-manned" each other at our weddings and I'm a horribly inadequate godfather to his first child. We trained together on Lancasters at Kinloss and then served in Shackletons on 206 Squadron in Cornwall. We're a farish cry here from jolting up and down over stormy Atlantic wastes in search of Soviet submarines or lost mariners, but at ease with each other in an enjoyable friendship and professional partnership.

Peter is the co-pilot and Rick the second navigator. Dodd the air electronics officer and two of the signallers, Bas and Josh, are also about and Mike the engineer has just arrived. We've been crewed together for a month or so, have come to trust and respect one another's competence and are melding into the mutually-reliant group that forms a good operational crew. Keith, Peter, Rick and I are officers and the others NCOs, but rank disappears in the air and we call one another by abbreviated roles – 'Captain, Cap', 'Eng', 'Nav', 'Sig'.

A cheerful young Arab is circulating; this is Mohammed, always called 'Chico', who enterprisingly runs an unofficial snack bar for the squadron. He has a rusty fridge and a ramshackle table in one of the corridors, provides cold drinks and Nescafé, and makes delicious sandwiches with fresh local vegetables and rolls, and the strong cheese that's flown in from Kenya.

"Steem, Bebsi, cheese-tomato?" he offers us. "Stim" is an Aden-produced range of soft drinks; they also make Pepsi under licence, but there's no 'p' in the Arabic alphabet. The squadron's catchphrase for "Excellent!" is "Very cheese-tomato."

Our tactical function in the Aden Protectorate is "Colonial Air Policing", a term betraying many underlying attitudes. This "uses operations which are psychological in intent to maintain or restore order within an area which is dissident or potentially so" (from the training manual I wrote for 37). And "It will be seen that air policing, aimed as it is at the preservation of peace, must be designed to avoid conflict, rather than seek it … all possible non-violent approaches are tried before resorting to the use of force." Well, yes; but I'm less comfortable with this now.

South Arabia, like Gaul, is divided into three parts: the vast and barren Empty Quarter or Rub' Al Khali where we sometimes hunt for gunrunning camel trains, and which we flippantly call the GAFA (the Great Arabian F*** All); then the coastal strip that runs from Oman in the north, turns the corner at Aden on the southern tip, and extends north-west to Jordan in the Red Sea. And, sandwiched between, a great V of mountains, rainy, green and fertile in the Yemeni west, dry, barren and almost impenetrable in the Aden Protectorate east. This last is our main operational area, where we and 8 Squadron's Hunters attempt to subdue rebellious up-country tribespeople. In the Protectorate there's no shortage of people who are "agin the Guv'mint" for reasons varying from general cussedness and a tradition of arms to a preference for levying their own customs duties on passing travellers. There are also people with an honest desire for independence from what they see as colonial occupation, but we in our Hunters and Shackletons don't know this [at this time]. We're told that the up-country political advisers have identified recalcitrants who are rejecting the benefits of British advice and its civilising influence. They must be taught lessons by destroying their property while going to great lengths to avoid actually hurting or, God forbid, killing anybody.

So we drop leaflets on these allegedly frightful baddies telling them that they must be good chaps or "Government will not be responsible for its actions." This splendid euphemism means "Come in number 7, your time is up – or we'll huff and we'll puff and we'll knock your house down." In both the Shackletons and the Hunters we have become adept at finding tiny villages, and even individual houses, in the harsh and confusing mountains and wadis of the Protectorate. We've also got quite good at using rockets or bombs to modify the stone-and-mud buildings. Not every aircraft finds the right target, and not every target is actually struck, but we mostly manage, thanks to directions from the political advisers on the ground.

None of us thinks to question the underlying premise, that military force will convince people to change their attitudes and actions. Nor the corollary, that if this doesn't work first time round then an application of greater force will persuade them to say "Ah, I see that I was wrong all along." These propositions now seem debatable.

In the Ops Room this morning, the briefer isn't the irascible WingCo Ops (known for mysterious reasons as "Bubbles"), but the less abrasive squadron leader. He takes us through the *Form Bravo* that orders the operation. I start to fill in the Ops Bombing form that details who we are, what explosive devices we're carrying, and how they're disposed in the bomb bay. The Met man tells us what he thinks the weather will be: an informed guess, since there are few local reporting stations. Sandstorms are an occasional hazard, but he thinks they're unlikely today.

Today's target is a village called Farar Al Ulya in the Wadi Sarar. We know it well: we were there last week and yesterday to deliver its mail, a fluttering cascade of leaflets that warned people to leave their houses lest ill befall them from the actions for which government declines to be responsible. It's near Al Qara, a spectacular village on a pinnacle to which we've also delivered leaflets and bombs. We've been told that it's the home of Mohammed Aidrus, a serious dissident who needs to be taught a particularly sharp lesson.

It's many years before I discover that Mohammed Aidrus is actually a member of the ruling family of Lower Yafa', and one of the founders of the South Arabian League. The league is an early political and mainly peaceful movement and is almost the start of the pressure for independence that later builds so strongly. It all ends in the bloody internecine battle between NLF and FLOSY, the National Liberation Front and the Front for the Liberation of Occupied South Yemen, as British forces give up and escape; but that's all a long way ahead of us today.

Nobody in our crew this morning knows that Mohammed Aidrus has been deputy ruler of Lower Yafa' but was forced into the mountains because he refused to be docile and compliant. One man's terrorist is another's freedom fighter, in 1960s Aden as elsewhere. We also don't appreciate that we're about to attack Muslim property on a Friday, the holiest day of Islam's week. For us, this morning presents a series of fairly demanding technical tasks: put a fully-armed and serviceable Shackleton over a tiny village that looks very like many others, and then destroy as much as may

The impenetrable fortress town of Al Qara, pictured from a low-flying 37 Squadron Shackleton, was a notorious dissident hideout and arms store (*Sandy McMillan*).

be with fifteen 1,000lb HE bombs. Our view is apolitical, and focused on working together as a professional crew to do what we're told as well as we possibly can – the justification of military men everywhere and everywhen.

I have many close Arab friends, so have an extra perspective which is largely ignored by my crew and squadron colleagues. I've contrived to compartmentalise this so that I can continue to work professionally. It will be some years before the conflict between what I believe and what I'm doing forces me to resign.

I'm first navigator, so can pull rank on Rick to oblige him to do the first transit navigation: his job is to get us within visual contact of Farar Al Ulya, not that easy in this ill-mapped and confusing terrain. I'll be bomb-aimer today for the first seven bombs of the strike, relishing some demanding technical challenges. Rick will aim the other eight bombs; I pull his leg gently with "Well, you need the practice" and he gives me two fingers. Finding Khormaksar again at the end of the sortie isn't difficult – we just keep going southwards until the land comes to a point. We chat briefly about the route; it's quite a short transit time, we flew it yesterday and the maps, such as they are, are already marked up, so no worries.

Now we're walking out to the aircraft, slightly delayed by several small annoyances – a slow fuel bowser, late delivery of the rations box, a re-check to make sure one of yesterday's unserviceabilities has been fixed. The morning sun glitters off the sand and flashes from the windscreens of parked aircraft and passing vehicles; the day is warming fast. Groundcrew and servicing vehicles cluster round our aircraft.

WR959 is a Shackleton MR 2; she's seven years old and came to 37 Squadron in October last year. Affectionately described as '10,000 rivets flying in close formation', Shackletons are primarily anti-submarine and air sea rescue workhorses, with a normal endurance around eighteen hours at a stately 160 knots. The cavernous bomb-bay and pair of 20mm Hispano-Suiza cannon make them ideal for 37's colonial policing role. Shacks vibrate drummingly in the air and are noisy enough for "Shackleton high-tone deafness" to be a recognised medical condition. One Army passenger was reminded irresistibly of "an elephant's bottom – wrinkled and grey outside and dark and smelly inside".

The inside of '959 is a cramped corridor of scuffed metal, sharp edges and obstructions, cluttered with equipment and projections to stab, cut or bark the unwary. Modern air travellers might find it claustrophobic. It smells of a blend of glycol, engine oil, aviation fuel, hot aluminium, worn leather

Flying low across Aden Harbour in 1961, a nicely composed photograph of 37 Squadron Shackleton MR.2 WR959-F, taken from an accompanying Shackleton (*Sandy McMillan*).

and young men, with just a soupçon of Elsan fluid. But Shacks are robust and solid, their four Rolls Royce Griffons are a great comfort, and aircrew regard them with exasperated affection, trusting them to get everybody home deafened but safe. Keith and I got used to the greater comfort and lower noise of the later Mark 3 aircraft on 206 Squadron, so returning to Mark 2s is a slight comedown for us.

Keith is already walking round inspecting '959 in the pre-flight ritual of "kicking the tyres" to check that we've got everything we should have and nothing we shouldn't. I climb the ladder into the back of the aircraft and pass the obstacles down the long tunnel with the certainty of practice – left foot just here, sidestep past Bas unloading the ration box in the galley, left hand grasps rack, vault over the main spar, duck roof projection.

I stow helmet and nav-bag on the navigation table, move further forward past the engineer's position and between the two raised pilot seats. Drop down into the nose and check the bomb-aimer's panel: all bomb-selector switches off, jettison bars and clips in place; clamber back to the nav's position and check that his console is similarly safe, with his changeover switch set to "Bomb aimer". Back through the aircraft, repeating the entry acrobatics in reverse, and walk under the open bomb doors to check the bomb load.

The armourers who bombed up the aircraft at first light are waiting for me. I'm Squadron Weapons Leader, so have a lot to do with these seasoned professionals. I've started a campaign to improve our bombing results and safety procedures, writing manuals and training people, and the groundcrew are vital to this. I've been encouraging bomb-aimers and armourers to get together more often and share problems and solutions, so relationships and standards are improving. I'm astonished to turn up in a New Year Honours List a couple of years later. Only a Queen's Commendation, which is as far down as you can get without actually falling off the List, but it's nice that people noticed what I was doing.

The corporal armourer and I work through the bomb bay, checking that the fifteen 1,000-pounders are on the allocated stations, and that they feel secure and aligned. Now I have to go back inside the aircraft again to check the camera in its floor housing aft of the door: yes, it's aligned for vertical shots, the circuits operate, the magazine is loaded, two test exposures fire OK. We should now get high-quality photographs every time I click the switch, so I close the camera hatch. Now I must repeat the obstacle-course entry process till I'm back in the nose and can work through the checks on bomb-sight and bomb-dropping mechanisms. Lights flash when they should, the distributor arm rattles over, Connell pre-selector works, the bomb release checks out on test. Everything works and the drum switch is back on "Safe except for jettison".

Nearly finished: One more trip back through the aircraft and out to the armourer in the bomb bay. Together we pull the safety pins from their tail fuses, arming the bombs, and I take charge of the pins to prove we've done it. Fifteen-thousand pounds of high explosive is now live and primed: enough to create a respectably large hole in the dispersal pan and make a number of eyes water. The corporal's responsibility now ends, and mine begins; he wishes me luck and sets off for his well-earned cuppa char.

One final time for the obstacle race; Keith passes me as I get back to the nav station so I say formally "All safety pins out, bombing equipment and camera checked and serviceable". "OK," he says and makes for the left-hand pilot's seat. I settle into my seat beside Rick, who is checking through his instruments and gear, put on my helmet and plug in the intercom. This is noisy with the familiar litany of pre-start checks as the pilots and engineer

The obstacle course presented to the crews, the cramped interior of the Shackleton MR.2 (*Richard Grevatte-Ball*).

work through their lists and make us ready for today's tasks. It's already very hot inside '959, and everyone is stripped to shorts, desert boots and flying helmets. We're supposed to wear our flying suits, but Authority sensibly turns a blind eye when people don't, perhaps because heat exhaustion is not a desirable condition for operational crews. The two pilots' windows stay open until just before take-off, as does the rear door, but it makes little difference to the increasing heat. We're all darkly tanned, for none of us has heard of skin cancer and the aim on any overseas posting is to "get yer knees brown" as soon as may be. We're also mostly slim, another effect of the heat: I'm a stone down on my already light UK weight, and will stay that way until the end of my tour.

Now the four Griffons are bellowing and we're taxiing, but the delays have lost us the coolest hour at the start of the morning and put us into the danger zone for engine temperatures. Everything has got much hotter in the twenty minutes since we first got into the aircraft. Ahead of me Mike the engineer raises his left arm to check something on his panel, and I see water running like a tap off the point of his elbow. There's a squadron competition for hottest Shack on the ground, currently held by another crew at more than 125 degrees F. On the taxiway we're parallel to the runway but pointing downwind, so the engines are breathing their own exhausts and Keith, Peter and Mike are anxiously monitoring cylinder-head temperatures. Be forced to wait too long while others take off ahead of us, and we could start to melt Rolls Royce's finest products. Luckily, there's only one Aden Airways DC-3 in front and he's away quickly, so we're unimpeded.

As we approach the end of the runway, Keith seeks to save time and cool down people and machines. He tells Peter he doesn't want to pause to line up and hold at the end of the runway while we wait for clearance. "Khormaksar, 959 requests rolling take-off," Peter says, and the tower comes back "959 clear for rolling take off." Bas slams and locks the rear door. We turn off the perimeter track onto the runway, Keith lines her up, and opens the throttles full, punching everybody hard with the acceleration that always exhilarates me. "959 rolling," Peter says, the tower responds "959, roger" and all our 10,000 rivets thunder down runway 08 Left and climb out eastwards over the sea.

Immediately, the temperature inside drops mercifully as draughts blow through the leaky old aircraft; suddenly, it's bearable. Wheels are up and flaps in, power is back to normal climb, and we're turning port. "Heading please, Nav," says Keith, and Rick responds "018, Captain"; we straighten out on course and start climbing to the 8,000-feet above sea level that we'll need as our safety height for bombing. The target area is about sixty miles away, so our transit time is less than half an hour; I unplug my intercom, grin at Rick, pick up a marked route map and go forward into the nose.

We're over the sands of the coastal plain; Sheikh Othman and the road to Lahej are on our left and we're just inland with the beach and coastal track on our right. I plug in my intercom again and relax: nothing to do for a bit except keep an eye on the terrain and be ready to help Rick if we start drifting off track. After five minutes or so the coast has curved away from us to the east and I can see the cotton plantations of the Abyan delta and the villages down it to Zingibar. Jan and I were there not long ago with Sharif Hussein and a big party of retainers after an exhilaratingly hairy drive at speed along the beach. Ahead is the abrupt division between sand and the foothills of the mountains that rise up steeply across our track; as we pass over the join we level out at operational altitude.

Most of our intercom speech is curt and businesslike, with quite long silences, but today Rick says "Eighteen minutes to target, Captain." Then, "Something hidden. Go and find it. Go and look behind the ranges – Something lost behind the ranges. Lost and waiting for you. Go!"

A baffled engineer says "Do what?"; I cut in with "Don't you like Kipling?"; Peter says "He wouldn't know – he's never Kippled", which prompts Bas into "Ah, the old jokes are the best." "Enough, enough," warns Keith, and we fall silent.

A little later I spot a village we know and say "Nav, I've got Sarar on the port side, a bit too close. We're about two miles port of track." "Roger," responds Rick, goes quiet while he calculates, then "New heading 030, Captain"; "030," confirms Keith and the Shackleton turns.

We track over the mountains and steep wadis for a little longer; we're so close that I can switch on the bombsight and make ready to run in. There's always a friendly contest between Keith and me to be first to spot the target, and today he wins with "Target is visual – lining up." Now I'm about to start directing us, so I say "Bomb-aimer, first run for target photographs and wind-finding. Nav, stand by with WFA (Wind Finding Attachment, a device that calculates local wind direction and speed from an accurately timed circuit). Captain, stand by for timed WFA run." Both acknowledge and I start sighting for the run.

Farar Al Ulya is a typical mountain village of about twenty mud-and-stone houses crammed close together and perched on a mountain ridge – stray too far from your back door and you'd fall a couple of hundred feet. People build defensively hereabouts and much prefer to look down on anyone approaching. It's also easier to shoot downhill than up, so such villages are hard to invest from below; it didn't occur to the founders that somebody might be able to command even greater height. The ground falls away steeply into the wadis below and the slopes have been laboriously terraced into long narrow fields a few yards wide for the villagers' crops. It's around 150-feet long by 50 wide, about one-sixth of a football pitch, so not an entirely easy target from 4,000 feet above. A few yards undershoot or overshoot, or a few yards left or right, and the bomb will explode deep in the wadis under the village; it's much easier to miss than to hit.

There's nobody to be seen in the village, for they've responded to yesterday's leaflets by climbing up to the nearest mountaintops for a grandstand view of our efforts. They don't seem to have bothered to take their weapons today, for there are none of the little sparkles of muzzle-flash that we often see. Aircraft occasionally come back with neat little holes from ancient Martini-Henry rifles. One startled navigator did find a spent round embedded in his seat cushion, having narrowly avoided emasculation. Wing Commander Bubbles sometimes threatens us with rumours that the tribes have acquired Egyptian anti-aircraft weapons, but we've met nothing larger than .303 calibre so far.

On one of the mountaintops is Stephen Day, the political officer for Lower Yafa', who commissioned today's strike. We don't know that he's watching with interest while we deliver his message to the unruly tribesmen, and it's more than forty years before he and I are in touch.

There's little danger in our operations, other than the normal hazards of flying with things that go bang. Though several Hunters sadly went down with their pilots, no Shackleton was ever lost in the Aden Protectorate. Keith, flying with Alan, another bomb-aimer, came close one day. The aircraft had an unsuspected electrical fault in the bomb-bay electrics. Turning in for their first run over a mountain peak close to the target, Alan called "Bomb doors open." As the doors parted the fault kicked in and fifteen 1,000-pounders jettisoned in a single salvo. Freed of the weight, the aircraft leapt crazily and, seconds, later there was the flash of a huge explosion that threw it around the sky. The safety height for 1,000-pounders was 2,790 feet, and fifteen had gone off on the peak a few hundred feet below, peppering the aircraft with stones and shrapnel. It was a quiet and thoughtful crew who returned to Khormaksar. As luck would have it, we heard later that the unintended jettison caused a landslide that engulfed a hostile camel train. "It's an ill wind that blows nobody any landslides," observed Alan.

Today the houses have started to slide under the graticule of the bomb-sight and I now have effective control; "Left-left, left-left … steady," I say, firing the camera for some "Before" shots, and Keith steers to respond. "Steady … steady … right … steady … steady … . On top … Now!" Back at the nav station Rick starts the WFA and his stopwatch and Keith takes us into an accurate left-hand circuit. I can shut up and let him expertly get on with it, so I wait for the target to swing into view again some four minutes later, then talk us on until I can again say "On top, now!" Rick stops the WFA and stopwatch and starts calculating the wind velocity over the target while Keith takes us into a wider orbit to stay in visual contact.

I'm propped face-down on my elbows on the worn leather of the thinly-padded floor. The Mark 14A bomb-sight in front of me looks forward through the V-shaped Perspex sighting panel, and the banks of switches and bomb-control gear are on my right. The vital bit of the bomb-sight is the collimator head (looking rather like a modern xenon overhead desk lamp) which projects a sighting cross of yellow light (the graticule) down onto a gyro-stabilised reflector glass. The aircraft's airspeed, altitude, and nose-up/nose-down attitude go into the sight automatically. The bomb-aimer adds the target height (to give the distance the bombs will fall), the aerodynamic characteristics of the bombs and the wind speed and direction over the target (hence the WFA fiddle of a moment ago). Now the fore-and-aft line of the graticule should track in the same direction as the aircraft is travelling, and its cross-line should show exactly where a bomb will strike. None of this will be right unless the groundcrew instrument fitter levelled the sight accurately at the last service, so we depend on his skill.

"Co-ordination between the members of the Bombing Team – Pilot, Navigator, Bomb Aimer, and Instrument Section – must be of a high standard" says my manual, adding "Personal idiosyncracies count highly in bombing teams". Keith, Rick, the 37 Squadron groundcrew and I are good at this; on the actual bomb-run Keith and I are attuned. He knows how fast to turn when I say "Left-left … steady", moderating to a tiny alteration for "Left-left steady"; we depend on his ability to hold a heavy aircraft straight and level for minutes while the turbulence buffets us. We trust one another, and our results are good and improving. Some crews never quite manage to reach this pitch: the bomb-aimer doesn't quite have the judgement, "the eye", the pilot struggles to keep the Shackleton stable and responsive, the navigator's winds aren't entirely …. But we do all right.

Bombs theoretically obey a complicated formula with lots of variables but, apparently, behave rather oddly to the eye. They seem to fall straight down below the aircraft for most of their drop, but then look as if they're racing ahead as they get near the ground. If I lean forward I can see some of this happening, but the bomb-sight is in the way and mustn't be nudged or jarred even slightly or we'll go home as failures. It's hard to call the strike accurately, so one of the signallers often goes back to the tail cone to observe results.

Rick gives me the local wind velocity from the WFA circuit and I set it on the sight. "Stand by for live run," I say and hear Keith acknowledge with "Roger, live run, turning on." Down in the galley helpful Josh says "Want a tail observer, bomb-aimer?" 'Yes, please," I say and, a moment or so later, Josh says "Tail-cone, intercom," as he checks in. He has crawled into a tail-cone entirely of clear Perspex and this can give a sudden unnerving shock of having "no visible means of support." For a second or two one feels suspended in space and vertigo has given many of us a queasy shudder – but it's a superb viewpoint.

Keith has taken us some way out so as to give plenty of time for adjustments and we're now swinging onto an attack heading, the jagged mountains sliding under me in the turn. He can see the target ahead, though shortly it will go out of his sight under the nose, so he calls "Running in"; "Running in," I acknowledge, and "Target sighted, bomb doors open."

The dissident village of Farar Al Ulya is about to be demolished by a Shackleton's load of fifteen 1,000lb high explosive bombs (*Sandy McMillan*).

I hear the whining growl as the doors start to part, and the draught past me increases. I flick the selector switch for the bomb on station 1, front-right of the bomb bay. We're dropping singly today; a stick of four or five might increase our chances of getting at least one 1,000-pounder onto the hilltop but the village is so narrow that any line error would waste all of them.

I watch the little group of brown houses start to slide in under the graticule. We're pretty well aligned already, though the aircraft is bouncing a bit; "Steady … steady … Right steady," to get a tiny starboard correction, "Steady …". The bomb release is sweaty in my hand and I'm concentrating hard. "Steady, steady, steady." At the last second, just as I press the release, the aircraft judders and the target slips infuriatingly off the right-hand side of the graticule. "Number one bomb gone, bomb doors closed, switches off … probably a miss," I say. A moment later Josh confirms from the tail cone, "Overshoot, one hundred yards port; tough titty."

We turn away for a second run, and something similar happens with the bomb from station 5 on the other side of the bay: the aircraft bumps at the last minute, despite all Keith's efforts, and this one is an undershoot and 150 yards starboard. Now our blood is up and we're determined to get a hit. We line up early and settle into the groove; everything goes smoothly and as I press the switch I think "Good one!" There's a pause while we hold our breaths, I crane to watch the bomb racing over the ground dead in line with the village but lose sight of it before the burst. Up comes Josh from the tail cone "Cheese-tomato! Direct hit, Bomb-aimer, dead lucky." "Actually, we rely on skill," I say, and somebody blows a raspberry on the intercom. As we go past the village on the downwind leg for another run we can see that the bomb has damaged several houses. "Reckon you posted that one through Mohammed Aidrus's roof," says Peter.

In one of those uninventable coincidences I'm chatting to my Bedu companion in an evening party some years later and we establish by chance that his house was one of those I knocked down. I needn't be worried: he's very amused and highly complimentary, retelling the story to everyone in the room. "Most of those pilots weren't very good," he said. "We'd sit on the hills and watch them missing. Lakin Saiyid Sandy … wallah, hu azim!" (But Mr Sandy, by God he was wonderful!).

The sortie continues, with pauses to level the bomb-sight. As 1,000-pounders leave us and fuel is burned up 959 gets steadily lighter and her flying attitude changes. When this happens her nose goes up, though she continues to fly straight and level or as much as Shacks ever do (they actually tend to hunt gently about a specific heading and altitude, being directionally

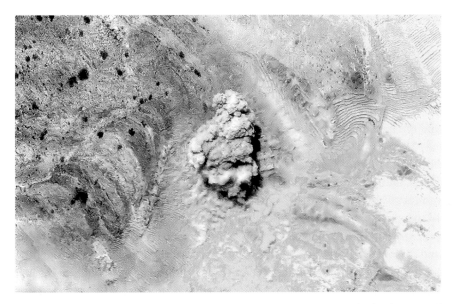

Bang on target! Seconds after the previous photograph was taken, Farar Al Ulya is peppered by several bombs ensuring that it will no longer provide cover for rebellious tribesmen (*Sandy McMillan*).

and aerodynamically unstable). If we didn't do anything about these attitude changes then we'd get increasing overshoot errors, and every so often we take time out for a levelling run.

The morning goes on; I get another direct hit and a couple of very near misses out of my other four bombs. Then it's all change; Peter and Keith swap seats, Rick comes into the nose and I go back towards the nav station, pausing in the gangway to stretch muscles cramped by long concentration and an awkward posture.

I wander back to the galley for a coffee. It's an unlikely rehearsal room, but Dodd is back here practising his trumpet. "Cherry Pink" is mostly submerged in the uproar of four Griffons, so nobody can hear him and he avoids the usual complaints from neighbours in his mess. Peter and Rick start methodically disposing of the remaining eight 1,000-pounders; Rick gets one direct hit, one large undershoot, which people jeer at, and a couple of honourable near misses.

When the last bomb has gone we fly one last overhead for an "After" photograph. It's plain that we've knocked the village about considerably and even Rick's major undershoot has coincidentally taken out a tower that was on a nearby hilltop. The near misses have also wiped out many of the terraces, so that fields, crops and their old walls have all fallen a couple of hundred feet into the wadis. The villagers will have to do much laborious work to rebuild their terracing by hand – no machine could get here, let alone work on those near-verticals. It doesn't occur to us that this may mean people will starve unless they can find another source of food. We're conscious of having done very efficiently what the briefing required of us and the legendary Martian would probably find us rather smug.

"Heading 190, twenty-four minutes to base," I tell Peter, we turn for home and I write "Off task" in the nav log. People are starting to think about lunch, and perhaps a bottle or two of Carlsberg in the mess bars. In twenty minutes we're calling for clearance to re-join Khormaksar's circuit, then letting down across Aden Harbour and over the ships at anchor to round out over the end of 08L and touch down with a screech of tyres. I log the time and "Landed". Immediately, the Shackleton starts to heat up again and by the time we're turning into dispersal everybody's running with sweat and eager to shut down and get out. The marshaller lines us up on the pan and Peter locks the brakes on and opens the bomb doors; two groundcrew duck under the wings and chock the wheels.

People complete their after-flight checks, switch their equipment off and start packing away their gear into flight bags; one by one the Griffons run down; we're pulling off our helmets into a silence that seems very loud, and clambering out of our seats; Josh has opened the back door and the ladder is in place; '959's long corridor is full of people queuing to get out into the fresher air and the chance of a breeze, even if it's almost as hot outside.

Somebody arrives from the photographic section and takes charge of the camera magazine for immediate processing. Later that evening Keith and I will stroll into Ops and delightedly discover that the photographs show how very successful we've been, but for now we can put '959 to bed and debrief our sortie. By the time we've stowed our gear away and told our story it's just on 14:00 Aden time and the light is glaring. Keith, Rick, Peter and I could just make it to the Jungle Bar in the Mess for a couple of cold beers and we debate the temptation briefly.'

John Severne (Squadron Leader)

The author is indebted to AVM Sir John Severne for allowing him to include extracts from his excellent book *Silvered Wings*.

Where to start! A mountain of paperwork faces John Severne as he sits at the 'Ops 2' desk in the Steamer Point headquarters of Middle East Command (*John Severne*).

To HQ Middle East Command (MEC)

'Having arrived in Aden in early 1966, my job was to be "Ops 2" in Headquarters Middle East Command (Steamer Point) which was a unified command with well-integrated staffs of the three services working very closely together. The Command covered a huge area from Kuwait to Botswana and Uganda to Madagascar. My job specification rather grandly said that I was to be 'responsible for the policy and operation of the Fighter, Maritime Reconnaissance and Helicopter Force in the Command'. This involved working closely with the Army in order to provide day-to-day support from 78 Squadron flying the Wessex, the ground-attack aircraft from 8 and 43 Squadrons flying the Hunter Mark 9, Photographic Reconnaissance from 1417 Flight operating the Hunter Mark 10 and maritime reconnaissance from the Shackletons of 37 Squadron. I also looked after the RAF Marine Branch unit and the Search and Rescue Whirlwind helicopter flight at Khormaksar which provided the Air Sea Rescue cover.

The Hunters were, of course, fully converted for ground attack with four 30mm cannon and the ability to carry sixteen 3-inch rocket projectiles (RPs). They provided air defence, close support for the Army and also flew in the more traditional air-policing role which included house demolitions, firepower demonstrations and 'flag waves' up-country. The latter were sometimes effective by simply providing a presence overhead. One specialist form of this was to disrupt the dissidents' rest patterns by planting sonic booms on the target areas to provide the illusion of operations at night. The RPs were Second World War weapons which were difficult to deliver accurately because they had a slow velocity with a consequent large gravity drop. They also required very accurate flying by the pilot for about four seconds before releasing the weapon, not an easy requirement in the turbulent conditions often found in the mountains.

The Shackletons were used in the theatre to provide a capability for maritime patrol and for search and rescue. The long endurance of the Shackleton gave it a good capability for providing top cover overland for troops or convoys moving through areas where there was an internal security threat. It could provide effective suppressive firepower using the nose turret's twin 20mm cannon, and also by dropping bombs of various weights. In the press releases of the day these were euphemistically referred to as "aerial grenades".

A familiar sight for land-borne forces operating in the Radfan area, Strike Wing Hunters demolishing a pair of houses and arms caches belonging to a prominent dissident troublemaker in a village near Wilan in 1966 (*John Severne*).

While making a landing run at Habilayn on 21 June 1967, 84 Squadron Beverley XM106 ran over a land mine, blowing off the starboard undercarriage and badly damaging the starboard wing and fuselage. It was dragged off the runway by Army engineers who blew it up after reusable parts and equipment had been removed.by 84 Squadron groundcrew (*John Severne*).

Flying in the Arabian Peninsula at that time was serious aviation. During 1966 and 1967 no less than twenty-three aircraft were destroyed or damaged by hostile action in the air or on the ground, including a Hunter which caught fire in the air after being hit by a rifle bullet, and a DC-3 of Aden Airways which was blown up.

Terrorist activity increases

The year 1966 saw a massive increase in terrorism and a difficult time with the National Liberation Front (NLF) and the Front for the Liberation of South Yemen (FLOSY) trying to push us out of the Federation and the Crown Colony of Aden itself. The Arabs had never been particularly fond of us and once we said we were going anyway, there was little reason for them to remain loyal, either to us or the Federal rulers whom they were always being told were our stooges and puppet successors. This was driven home by a carefully planned programme of assassinations, and any Arabs who showed loyalty to Britain tended to be bumped off and left with a label tied to their necks saying "the fate of all traitors". They naturally concentrated on the local intelligence staff, police and Special Branch. There were thirty-six such assassinations in 1964 and no less than 1,250 in 1967. There had also been a number of nasty murders of British personnel and a few small bombs, mostly hand grenades thrown around. The huge car bombs of today, thank goodness, had not come on the scene at that time. We all had to take reasonable precautions such as searching our quarters and our cars daily, never going downtown alone and never advertising parties by displaying invitation cards in our homes.

The military areas were well protected, but that did not stop a bomb exploding in the Officers' Mess at Steamer Point, the home of the Headquarters. Our local staffs were mostly Arabs or Somalis who had worked for the British for years. They were excellent people whose loyalty was not normally questioned, but we knew they could be put under intolerable pressure from the terrorists who might threaten their families if they didn't do the terrorists' bidding. Our own bearer, Said, was a Yemeni and a delightful fellow. He had worked for the British for many years and found it difficult to believe that we really were going to leave. Even when he finally accepted that we would be leaving Aden he said he would continue to work for the British. After I explained that the nearest British presence would be in the Gulf he said that was no problem, he would walk there with his family and his goats. He could not get his head round the fact that he would have to walk 1,500 miles or so across the desert.

In May 1967 strikes closed the harbour to commercial shipping and the situation was compounded when in June the Arab-Israeli War resulted in the closure of the Suez Canal. Although the Arabs were badly defeated by the Israelis our locals managed to put the blame on Britain, so the slogan of the day became 'a bullet against the British is a bullet against Israel' – which increased the resentment against us.

The front line – from a safe distance

The Army was busy controlling dissident tribesmen up-country and providing us with security at the base. A typical task might be for me to arrange for helicopters to position urgently needed army support, or for the Hunters to carry out a rocket attack to destroy a known terrorist's home. On one occasion I flew in a two-seat Hunter to witness the squadron carry out a rocket attack with eight aircraft targeting two houses and two arms caches belonging to a well-known dissident leader in a village near Wilan. The cockpit temperature was closer to that of the centre of the earth than to that of the sky we were flying in, but it was very exciting flying. On landing my pilot, Squadron Leader Fred Trowern, said, 'And to think we get paid for this as well.'

Ground-attack pilots are often directed to their targets by Forward Air Controllers (FACs), who were Army or RAF officers operating from the ground or in the air. On one extraordinary occasion, I was a passenger in a Beverley which carried an Army FAC to direct Hunters onto three separate targets. I found it almost bizarre to be slowly flying over hostile territory, relatively low, in such a huge lumbering transport aircraft. In fact, it was quite safe because, unlike today, the terrorists did not have hand-held surface-to-air missiles; we only had to keep out of range of their rifles.

The Beverleys of 84 Squadron did a marvellous job when the local workers went on strike at the oil refinery at Little Aden. In order to keep the Hunters flying, the Beverleys ferried jet fuel in their own fuel tanks from Djibouti to Khormaksar. And talking of strikes, we witnessed a most amusing situation when the Aden bank workers went on a go-slow. We were drawing out some money from National Grindlays when we watched a bank clerk pushing a trolley full of files across the room. He was indeed going slow – literally. He gradually put one foot in front of the other, an inch at a time, and he must have moved fully six feet during the ten minutes that we were there.

The Army Air Corps
I worked closely with the Army Air Corps and enjoyed several interesting flights in their Scout helicopters. Low flying with the Army is always quite an experience and one particularly exciting flight took us up the narrow mountain road to Dhala, in the north of the Federation and close to the Yemen border. There is a rough strip at Dhala where I had previously landed in a Twin Pioneer and had witnessed a novel way of starting a reluctant engine. The ground crew wound a rope round the spinner of the propeller – rather like starting a toy top – and attached the end of the rope to a Land Rover which then drove off. The engine had little option but to start, which was a good thing because Dhala would not have been a sensible place in which to be stranded. Back in 1964, Claire Hollingworth, a well-known war correspondent, visited Dhala and subsequently wrote in *The Guardian* about an interview she had had with a tribesman from the Radfan. He said that the reason they attacked the road to Dhala was the fact that they hated roads because they hated wheeled vehicles. These were depriving the tribesmen of their trade in camels and all sorts of other things associated with travel by four-footed animals. But he went on to say that they considered aircraft to be all right because, after all, the Prophet travelled on a carpet. However, that didn't seem to stop them from shooting at every aircraft they saw.

I subsequently accompanied our AOC, Air Vice-Marshal Andrew Humphrey, to witness the first landing of a Hunter at Beihan to see if it was a safe strip for them to use. There had been several incursions by MiG-17s from the Yemen and the local ruler had asked for our protection. The MiGs

One of two Westland Scout AH.1 helicopters delivered to 653 Squadron AAC in March 1964, XR600 was parked on the Belvedere pan at Khormaksar when photographed later in the month (*Ray Deacon*).

were operated by Egyptian pilots flying from San'a, the capital of the Yemen, the aircraft and the finance also being provided by the Egyptians. The Hunter, piloted by the Officer Commanding Strike Wing, Wing Commander Martin Chandler, landed and departed safely.

The RAF has always run survival courses for aircrew likely to fly over water, arctic, jungle or desert terrain. Since I was responsible for the Desert Survival Course in Aden I thought I had better see what goes on. I therefore joined a course which began when one of our Air Sea Rescue launches dumped us on the remote island of Perim at the foot of the Red Sea. We had emergency rations and kit to distil water from the dew – not very much, but enough for survival. It was a relief to be picked up several days later and to be able to quench one's thirst. I learned several good lessons from that short course, one of which was that I had not realised how incredibly unpleasant it is to be really thirsty.

Planning for the South Arabian Air Force
Not long after I arrived in Aden I was appointed air adviser to the South Arabian Government, the federal government set up by us at Al Ittihad, just

outside Aden, to run the country after we left – at least that was the intention. I was told to form a South Arabian Air Force (SAAF), by independence, consisting of a balanced force of transport, communications, helicopters and ground-attack aircraft – all for £2m. Although I already had a heavy workload, I had no staff to assist me in this extra commitment, presumably because this was deemed to be just a secondary duty.

The MoD contracted Airwork Services Ltd who had considerable experience in this field and they found the aircraft for us. The Crown Agents on behalf of the British Government bought four Dakotas with new engine life and fully refurbished for a mere £25,000 each. The Dakota, although an old aircraft, was ideal for rough up-country transport work. New and much smaller Skyvans were offered at £500,000 which we could not possibly afford. I wanted to buy six Alouette helicopters from France, but since all purchases had to be made in sterling we had to buy the only option available, the Westland-Bell 47 Sioux, despite its pathetic performance in hot conditions and at high altitude. Although our first choice for strike aircraft was the Strikemaster, none were available, so BAC refurbished and modified four ex-RAF Mk.4 Jet Provosts to Mark 52 standard, capable of carrying weapons. Finally six Canadian-built Beavers were purchased, the Beaver being a rugged single-engine aircraft designed for bush operations. I was responsible for approving the design of the aircraft markings and also the uniforms. Wing Commander Barry Atkinson MBE DFC RAF was seconded as the commanding officer and Airwork recruited the pilots and civilian engineers.

Choosing the right weapons was a problem because the requirement was to put a missile through the front door of a terrorist's house. The old 3-inch rocket projectile still being used by the RAF was not exactly a precision weapon and I therefore looked around for something better. The RAF at that time was introducing rockets called SNEB, but they were too expensive a weapon for us because, to be sure of hitting a small target, the whole pod of nineteen rockets needed to be released in a ripple. Airwork then came up with the SURA rocket, a remarkable weapon made by Hispano Suiza of Switzerland, which Boscombe Down tested for me. Boscombe confirmed that SURA was so accurate that if there were any target errors, they were the pilot's. I subsequently learnt that the neighbouring Sultan of Oman's Air Force (SOAF) was so impressed with the weapon when they saw us using it that they also bought it – so at least I suppose I did SOAF a good turn. This was a period when a number of cases of corruption concerning the sale of aircraft had been exposed, although I did not expect them to offer me a cash handout because I like to think that they knew it would not be accepted by a Brit. I was, however, delighted when Hispano Suiza offered me a small Swiss Army knife as a thank you for buying their weapon. A gift which, I hasten to add, I gladly accepted.

Britain gave South Arabia £5m for the running of their armed forces and by Independence all the aircraft except two of the Dakotas were in place, as were the eighteen pilots who were all British except for a Belgian, a German and a Czech. The engineers were British civilians and all were under contract to the South Arabian Government. Squadron Leader "Rags" Barlow, an RAF navigator who had taken early retirement from the service, was appointed as the Operations/Intelligence Officer; he also acted as adjutant to the CO.

Nearly forty years were to pass before I was able to find out what happened to the SAAF after independence. I was recently giving a lecture to the Taunton and Tiverton Branch of the Aircrew Association when one of the members attending the meeting happened to be Rags Barlow and he was able to tell me about their unpleasant experience in the hands of their new masters.

On the granting of independence on 30 November 1967, the Federation of South Arabia was immediately renamed the People's Democratic Republic of Yemen (commonly known as South Yemen). The Air Force was renamed the People's Democratic Republic of Yemen Air Force (PDRYAF) and within days the old South Arabian markings were removed and replaced with the new markings of the Republic. At the end of February 1968 the South Yemen defence minister, after visiting Moscow to seek financial aid for their armed forces, gave a distinctly anti-British broadcast in which the South Yemen Air Force was accused of passing information concerning every move of the government to the British Embassy. The British government had previously instructed the South Yemen Government that the air force was not to operate outside its own border. British pilots were flying for Saudi Arabia and our government wanted to avoid the possibility of Brits fighting Brits. This was considered by the South Yemen government as intolerable interference. On 27 February all the British personnel of the Air Force were ordered to assemble in their crewroom for an address by the Minister of Defence. Speaking through an interpreter he said that the Air Force had been controlled by the British Embassy and not by himself. He therefore had no further use for their services. During the address the building, hangars and aircraft had been surrounded by Arabs with machine guns, some being pointed through the crewroom window. They were promptly arrested.

Two buses took them to the British Embassy, but they were later allowed to go to the officers' mess, under armed guard, to collect their belongings. Rags Barlow had the uncomfortable experience of having to open all the safes with a gun in his back. Some of the families had arrived the month before and they were given one hour to pack and be prepared to leave. The following night was spent in a compound at the airport before they were all flown back to the UK early the next day, their contracts terminated without compensation. Subsequent protracted discussions with the Foreign Office failed to result in reasonable compensation for the breaking of the contracts and the financial penalties suffered by our personnel. To this day they still feel they were badly let down by our government. Soon after the dismissal the first Russians arrived with some MiG-15s and they were subsequently to form the mainstay of the South Yemen Air Force.

While the Foreign Office had announced that we were to give the Federation independence in 1968, the date was being kept secret for security reasons. When George Brown finally announced to the House of Commons, some two weeks beforehand, that the date would be 29 November 1967, the shooting stopped immediately, indicating that the terrorists were well controlled by NLF and FLOSY. This was just as well because plans had been made for us to make a fighting withdrawal if needs be.

Final departure from Aden
The plan was for the heavy and bulky items to go by sea and that people, including the families, would go by air, together with the smaller valuable items. Equipment not needed elsewhere was to be sold locally. Since Khormaksar had already suffered several terrorist attacks it was thought that it might be too dangerous to operate a large number of troop-carrying flights out of the airfield. If necessary we would therefore be evacuated by sea to Masirah Island and flown home from there, a withdrawal that would be executed by a task force of the Far East Fleet. Shortly before Withdrawal Day (W-Day) the impressive task force assembled. It included the aircraft carrier HMS *Eagle*, which would provide air defence after the Hunters left, the two commando carriers and the assault ship HMS *Fearless* from which the final withdrawal would be controlled and where I was allocated a position in its operations room. In the event, when the shooting stopped, we were able to carry out an orderly withdrawal by air from Khormaksar.

The first phase of the withdrawal, Operation RELATIVE, took place about six months before independence when the families were sent home. This meant that, at the same time, all the associated support, such as schools, hospital and so on, could be closed together with most of the married quarters. Many families, particularly those who lived in the Ma'alla Straight, had been through a very harrowing time – one of the Khormaksar aircrew had a rocket fired through his bedroom window when his wife and small baby were in the room. It was therefore somewhat of a relief to us when the families left. I accompanied my wife Kath on the military bus to the airfield, a journey of five or six miles. On the way, going through the built-up area of the Ma'alla Straight, we were stopped by an Army patrol when a young subaltern came on board and said, 'There is a little shooting going on so we will be held up for a few minutes, but don't worry everyone, we will look after you.' He had an air of confidence about him and we consequently felt very reassured. The flight home for the families was a bit tedious because it got held up in Teheran when the aircrew ran out of their crew duty time.

After the families had left there were several visits from well-known entertainers who gave performances in the open-air theatre. Two of the concerts stick in my memory because of their starkly contrasting characteristics. One well-known comedian gave a quite unnecessarily blue show which I personally found offensive, but this was followed a few weeks later by Harry Secombe. I was told that he asked what sort of programme he should give and that he was advised to "play it straight". He gave a stunning performance which included many operatic arias. The troops loved it – so did I – and it just goes to show that comedians don't need to get cheap laughs from blue jokes in order to please their audiences.

The High Commissioner, Sir Humphrey Trevelyan, left the day before independence and so did I, although I hasten to add that there was no connection. The final aircraft left on the last day with the few remaining personnel, the last two passengers to board being Air Commodore Freddie Sowrey (the Senior Air Staff Officer) and Brigadier Charles Dunbar (the Brigadier General Staff), with the airfield protected by a company of Royal Marines who were airlifted by helicopter to ships anchored out in the Gulf of Aden.

The morale of the Aden base was extremely high during our time there. Conditions were not ideal with a difficult security situation to deal with and a tiresome climate, but there was a strong feeling of everyone being in the same boat and co-operation between the three services could not have been better. I think it was a typically British approach – it seems that we are at our best when under pressure. It was certainly a memorable experience for me and my family and we are grateful for it.

Thus ended 128 years of British rule on 29 November 1967, a very interesting chapter in our colonial history. For the very small part I played during that time I was awarded the OBE.'

Nigel Walpole (Squadron Leader)

The author is indebted to Group Captain Nigel Walpole for allowing him to include extracts from his excellent book *Best of Breed*. Following on from tours flying Hunters and Swifts in Germany and an exchange posting to South Carolina where he flew the Voodoo, Nigel had an ideal background for a tour in Aden. In October 1963 he was appointed to the Air Offensive Staff in HQ MEC at Steamer Point, where the famous Second World War ace AVM "Johnnie" Johnson had just taken over as AOC.

Air Offensive Staff

'I would work in my office from 07:00 to 13:00 hours, normally the end of the working day, and then go to Khormaksar to talk to, or fly with, any of the four Hunter units, thereby acquainting myself with their operations and operating area. I recall only too well a flurry of activity in the HQ when a Russian-built Crate transport aircraft infringed WAP airspace and the pair of Hunters on patrol for just such an exigency requested authority to fire warning shots in an attempt to persuade the pilot to land. Unfortunately, the only officers able to give this permission were not immediately available before the intruder retreated across the border, followed by the Hunters – and an international incident was only narrowly averted. In a similar incident on 2 December 1963, a Crate landed on the Allied airstrip at Lawdar, perhaps in error, and was prevented from taking off again by a British officer who, with great presence of mind, parked his Land Rover immediately in front of the taxiing aircraft. The errant Crate was quickly flown back to Khormaksar by an RAF crew, escorted by 1417 Flight FR.10s.

Matters took a nasty turn on 10 December when a grenade was thrown at the High Commissioner as he and his entourage were walking across the pan on the civilian part of Khormaksar. His aide, George Henderson, promptly flung himself on to the grenade to take the full force of its detonation, a heroic act rewarded by a posthumous George Cross. This prompted increased vigilance and security measures; wire guards appeared on the windows of buses, military lorries and vulnerable buildings, the huge airbase thereafter patrolled by three RAF Regiment squadrons. The officers' mess was among the attractive targets, and indeed in the final years a bomb was hidden below the floorboards of the dining room, set to detonate at breakfast time; fortunately it exploded without causing injury during the night. With such threats, one officer slept with a sidearm under his pillow, firing it at a nocturnal intruder before recognising him as an RAF policeman searching for a villain. This excessive prudence earned him a court martial.

The tranquil days of relative calm in Aden may have been over but after acclimatising to the unfamiliar environment life was still good. With heat hovering consistently between 90-100 degrees F and humidity at 80 per cent by day and night for much of the summer season, air conditioning was highly desirable (but rarely provided) in working and living accommodation (I had only a fan in my bedroom). Much of the married accommodation was new, particularly the flats on the Ma'alla Strip, and officers' wives had the help of *ayahs*, often young Somali girls, who were given basic living quarters nearby. They would look after the domestic chores and any young children, allowing the British to take every advantage of the excellent sporting and social facilities in Aden. Many of the British servicemen (but not all) worked only in the mornings, spending the rest of the day on one of the beaches set aside for them, with every refreshment available and served at their whim. My log book shows that I flew on Christmas Day 1963 as No. 2 on the standby pair, with 43 Squadron flight commander Anthony Mumford in the lead. It was an uneventful trip but Anthony made sure that his wingman was properly debriefed on shortcomings in his performance before they joined the festivities – Aden fashion.

The Radfan Campaign

Then it began in earnest. A briefing on New Year's Day 1964, heralded a major offensive in the Radfan area, some thirty-five nautical miles north of Aden, an inhospitable, mountainous region, with peaks and plateaus towering to 7,000 feet traversed by deep wadis. It was home to a multitude of hostile tribes and ideal terrain for their hit-and-run tactics, the rebels hiding in numerous caves by day and striking by night over ground known well to them.

For some time Yemeni propaganda had been fermenting unrest among the local tribes and tension mounted when Egyptian-backed Yemeni intruders infiltrated across the nearby border. A counter-offensive was launched by the British-led but untried Federal Regular Army (FRA), the local Arab force which had replaced the Aden Protectorate Levies, but it had very limited success. The road from Aden to Dhala, close to Yemen, then became all but unusable through mining and ambushes and at this point it was decided to commit British forces. I went to the O Group to ensure that the potential of Aden's Hunter force in this context was fully understood, and that it would be employed productively. Events were to prove its contribution invaluable, a commitment shared between 8, 208 and 43 Squadrons and 1417 Flight, until 208 Squadron moved to Bahrain permanently, to bring to an end the turbulence of rotational detachments to the Gulf.

A brigade headquarters was set up at Thumier on the south-western edge of the Radfan to run Radforce (a combined FRA and British force), tasked with re-opening the Dhala Road and securing the Radfan (much easier said than done); a small BASOC was included in the HQ to co-ordinate all offensive and air transport support. The strike force consisted of the FGA.9s and FR.10s (which also fulfilled all their recce responsibilities), and Shackletons which maintained a continuous presence with flares to illuminate targets during the hours of darkness. HQ MEC issued pre-planned tasks but the BASOC could call for immediate assistance, moving their FACs forward to direct fire and safeguard their own troops from the air

FR.10 XE614 is dwarfed by the rocky landscape that typifies the terrain through which Middle East Command Hunters operated regularly during the last eight years of British rule in Aden (*Sandy Burns*).

strikes. The FACs were trained by British Army GLOs attached to Tactical Wing, and practised with the Hunter pilots they would control in earnest.

It was no surprise when Johnnie Johnson declared that he wanted to see action in the Radfan firsthand. I went too, sitting in the doorway of a Belvedere helicopter with an automatic rifle on my lap to witness the effect of the Hunter's 3-inch rockets and cannon against rebel positions and supply dumps discovered by FR.10s in well-concealed caves. As soon as the smoke had cleared, the FR.10s were there again to take post-strike photography. It was an awesome demonstration of the Hunters' capabilities and only the braver dissidents risked giving away their precise positions by retaliating with largely ineffective small-arms fire. That said, one bullet did find its mark in the backside of one of the helicopter pilots – without doing much harm.

Three particular actions in the Radfan illustrated the effectiveness of these joint operations involving the FR.10s. When an SAS patrol was ambushed and surrounded on 30 April 1964, Hunters carried out continuous recce and repeated attacks with rockets and cannon until nightfall, when the patrol was able to break out, albeit with the sad loss of two men. The Hunters were similarly helpful when a combined force of Royal Marine Commandos and Paras was tasked to seize "Cap Peak", a high point which dominated the Wadi Taym and Danaba Basin. During the action some of the Paras became separated but with immediate assistance from the Hunters they regrouped and the objective was taken. In a third emergency, soldiers sent to assist the crew of an Army Air Corps helicopter which had been shot down on the slopes of the Bakri Ridge, came under heavy fire and the Hunters again saved the day.

As in most of such actions in the region, operations were carried out in searing heat, immense convective clouds developing to cover high ground and blinding sandstorms sometimes reducing visibility to almost nothing. Aircraft canopies became sand-blasted, seriously affecting the pilot's vision and sand found its way into the Hunters' systems. All this made flying very difficult, added to the groundcrews' problems and made life on the ground generally most uncomfortable for all.

Coincidentally, trouble was brewing in East Africa. It was in the quiet hours of the New Year stand-down that the duty staff officer received a signal which he could not leave until morning, to the effect that British residents were being pulled from their houses in Nairobi and shot. This turned out to be a gross exaggeration, although one man did suffer a bullet wound in his foot. However, the signal was quite enough to galvanise the Paras in Aden,

!417 Flight FR.10 XF460-GT flies low over a typical up-country village in 1965 (*Ken Simpson*).

who were always spoiling for a fight; they were ready, willing and able to go to Kenya post-haste by Argosy and Beverley to deal with the problem, whatever it was, in their own inimitable way. As the confusion subsided and the situation was found to be less urgent they were stood down, but HMS *Centaur* embarked troops and Belvedere helicopters of No. 26 Squadron and sailed for Dar es Salaam on 20 January 1964. As back up, five FGA.9s and two FR.10s were brought to a high state of readiness to fly to Eastleigh in Kenya if required; they were not deployed but the crews were kept incommunicado on the airfield, much to the irritation of their wives.

With maps of the Radfan area so poor, 1417 Flight was often called on to find a target specified by soldiers in the field by name but without a precise grid reference, and then to produce nose oblique photographs of the attack direction to be used by the FGA.9 pilots. FR.10s were also on standby to update enemy movements and to give immediate support to ground forces in difficulty; this generated increasing confidence among Allied ground troops in the service provided by the flight and thus the number of demands made on it. Some of their requests were theoretically or practically beyond the FR.10's capability. Peter Lewis remembers that the army called on him for complete cover, with all three cameras, of a nine-nautical-mile wadi at 200 feet, which would have required more than the total film carried by the Hunters and involve some risky flying. Undaunted, Peter calculated that much of the cover could be obtained from the alternative of a very fast run using the nose facing camera with its 12-inch lens. He flew the sortie between 13:00-14:00 hours to keep the shadows to a minimum, coping with the severe turbulence along the valley bottom with its steep sides towering

1,000 feet above, his thoroughbred Hunter surviving the high G forces and a rifle shot through its fin. There were limits to what 1417 Flight could do, but they always did their utmost to satisfy.

On another exciting trip the fire warning light came on in Peter's Hunter after he had returned fire with all four guns at a group of tribesmen, leaving him with an agonising choice of ejecting over hostile territory or hoping that the warning was spurious. With no other signs of fire he chose the latter, only to find that the aircraft's desert survival pack had come loose and triggered the fire-warning-light test switch. It had indeed been a false alarm.

The Hunters were often involved in clandestine surveillance operations mounted by the SAS, and were once called to verify the position of a camel train thought to be resting on the border with the Yemen. Although certain that he was in the right place, Peter Lewis could not see his quarry, but then he heard an unannounced voice on a pre-arranged frequency say "They're there", and a closer look revealed telltale signs in the sand which led to the camels. These poor beasts of burden, with their cargoes of what turned out to be explosives, were then despatched to their maker with a two-second burst from the FR.10's cannon. Years later, in a most unexpected sequel to this story Peter was recognised by the local postman in The Sailor's Safety public house, West Wales, who told him that he was the man on the ground who had passed that curt message, "They're there".'

Nigel returned to the UK in February 1964 to take command of a squadron on the OCU at Chivenor, now better able to understand the requirements of the Hunter FGA and FR units in the Middle East.

Airman's farewell to Aden

Land of toil, sweat and strain
Land of sun and Marffish rain
Sweat rash, footrot, prickly heat
Aching hearts and blistering feet,
Swarms of flies that buzz and bite
Fans that hum throughout the night

Land of scorpions, camels and bugs
Hasheesh, henna and other drugs
Streets of sorrow, streets of shame
Streets that you could never name
Clouds of sand and dust that send
The sanest 'bod' clean round the bend.

Donkeys, goats and pyiad dogs
Cut-throat thieves and pestering clods
Land where children in their teens
Sell souvenirs outside canteens
Baksheesh! Baksheesh! Is their cry
For this alone they live and die.

Where tinea thrives and gypo gripes
Where clods smoke hubbly-bubbly pipes,
Where every native black and brown
Awaits for you to go downtown,
Obnoxious smells, eternal strife
O for blighty and a wife

TALES FROM THE FRONT LINE

Where tour-ex men just sit and gloat
While others dream about the boat,
Their only aim to dodge and skive
Until their clearance chit arrives,
Their chief delight to laugh and shout
At some poor 'erk' that's just come out.

Land of turbans, galabeah
Quais tamman, Quais quatir,
Land of Chi and mungaria
Moya chipatis and Alsopp's beer,
Where one can always hear men quake
About the thought of NAAFI break

Oh! For Britain's happy life
Where people never know such strife,
My final chit, I am going home
Away from there, I'll never roam,
I am going home and Oh! So grand
To see green fields instead of sand.

Land of sorrow, filth and shame
I've seen you once but never again,
I'll leave you now with no regret
The sights I've seen I'll not forget
Natives' heaven, white man's hell
This *******, ADEN, fare thee well!

Contributed by Bob Hambly.